T0293290

Get the eBook FREE!

(PDF, ePub, Kindle, and liveBook all included)

We believe that once you buy a book from us, you should be able to read it in any format we have available. To get electronic versions of this book at no additional cost to you, purchase and then register this book at the Manning website.

Go to https://www.manning.com/freebook and follow the instructions to complete your pBook registration.

That's it!
Thanks from Manning!

Automating API Delivery

Automating
API Delivery

IKENNA NWAIWU
FOREWORD BY MELISSA VAN DER HECHT

MANNING
SHELTER ISLAND

For online information and ordering of this and other Manning books, please visit
www.manning.com. The publisher offers discounts on this book when ordered in quantity.
For more information, please contact

Special Sales Department
Manning Publications Co.
20 Baldwin Road
PO Box 761
Shelter Island, NY 11964
Email: orders@manning.com

Manning Publications Co.
20 Baldwin Road
PO Box 761
Shelter Island, NY 11964

Development editors: Toni Arritola and Ian Hough
Technical editors: Daniel Kocot and Marjukka Niinioja
Review editors: Radmila Ercegovac
Production editor: Keri Hales
Copy editor: Julie McNamee
Proofreader: Melody Dolab
Technical proofreader: Marjukka Niinioja
Typesetter: Dennis Dalinnik
Cover designer: Marija Tudor

ISBN: 9781633438781
Printed in the United States of America

To my wife, Oluchi Ikodiya Nwaiwu

brief contents

contents

foreword

Over the past couple of decades, APIs have evolved from bits of code to business products, and I've been fortunate enough to spend my career working for API vendors that have helped to make this happen. We've established what have become the standard API best practices and operating models and built the tooling that's empowered companies to become API-led. In technical, customer-facing roles, I've helped hundreds of global organizations deliver APIs as part of their integration strategy, and I've celebrated the resulting impact from a people, process, and technology perspective. Seeing the API industry mature so much has been phenomenal.

But now we have a problem.

Great APIs accelerate project delivery, increase operational efficiency, and broaden market reach. APIs can be so transformative that they're now a business currency. They underpin every digital transformation. This is only possible when you treat your APIs as products, with a full life cycle: designing, building, and deploying them consistently and securely while thinking of your consumers as customers.

And wow, what a change we've seen since we've considered APIs in this way. Companies pivoted, and those that embraced the power of APIs flourished. New target architectures were defined based on modern APIs. APIs themselves became monetizable products. The more businesses started to really feel the value of this new way of approaching API development, the more they invested in it, the more they wanted it, and the faster they tried to achieve it.

The enthusiasm I saw from so many organizations to follow the API life cycle and treat APIs as products was palpable. The way in which millions of people worldwide have embraced the API economy has driven both technology and business forward. We're now in a digital world powered by APIs; we use them everywhere—millions of them.

But with this scale of API adoption, I've witnessed one common problem affecting companies of every size, industry, and maturity: it has become impossible for them to rapidly deliver APIs that are always high quality, secure, performant, and consistently representing their brand, and then to sustain and measure their impact long after they've been deployed.

How can we achieve all of this at the scale we're at today? How can we do it even faster tomorrow? How can we do it better and more securely? Most organizations don't yet know how to answer this. I've surveyed hundreds of companies on this topic, and 80% of them say they're currently forced to make a tradeoff between the delivery speed and quality of their APIs. Either you invest the time in properly following the API life cycle to ensure quality, adherence to standards, and security, which slows down delivery, or you ship quickly by shortcutting governance processes and consequently introduce risk.

We've not yet maximized the true value APIs can bring us because the processes we first put in place to manage the API life cycle haven't evolved at the same pace as API adoption. They're now holding us back.

The good news is we have a solution. We apply and tune the proven automation principles of DevOps and GitOps to the API life cycle in the form of APIOps. By combining the power of linting, declarative configuration, version control, and a CI/CD pipeline with your own API standards, you can ensure that every API is done your way, automatically, every time.

My evangelism in this area has inspired companies to adopt APIOps, and they now continually deliver high-quality, secure, measurable APIs at speed as a direct result. These benefits shouldn't be exclusive to them, however, and with this book, Ikenna brings the power and possibility of APIOps to every organization.

He masterfully navigates you through the journey of learning both the concept and reality of APIOps, until you find you've just built the end-to-end pipeline yourself and understood exactly why you're doing what you're doing. Through a powerful combination of stories, diagrams, and accessible language, Ikenna will walk you through the best practice, but he doesn't stop there. Step by step, he shows how to adopt it in real life, with examples, hands-on exercises, and frequent discussions on the nuances of applying the theory to your own company setup.

The hardest part of getting APIOps right isn't understanding the theory but executing the technical and cultural change, and the genius of this book is how clearly it lays out the path to achieve that. Whether it's a walk-through of the technical steps, examples of open source tooling to use, or tips for running an effective API design review meeting, Ikenna offers practical guidance, as well as advice from his lived experience on how to overcome the typical challenges that will present themselves along the way.

With the publication of this book, there's now nothing stopping any organization from harnessing APIOps to unleash the full power of APIs, and I can't wait to see this happen!

—MELISSA VAN DER HECHT, API startup advisor,
previously Office of the CTO at MuleSoft and Field CTO at Kong

preface

In October 2021, I joined 10x Banking as a product owner for the API platform team. At that time, the company was rapidly expanding the REST API for its core banking platform, which involved not only the development but also the governance and deployment of the API. Balancing the urgency of deploying APIs quickly with the need to adhere to our organization's API style guide amid collaboration with numerous feature teams presented a challenging yet exciting dilemma.

Despite our efforts to streamline processes, including improving our management of Jira tickets, I found myself constantly searching for more effective solutions. This search led me to Melissa van der Hecht's insightful presentation on "APIOps: Automating API Operations for Speed and Quality at Scale" at apidays London. Her emphasis on automating the entire API life cycle resonated with me, prompting weeks of research into how we could adopt these principles at 10x. By January 2022, I had devised an API Enablement plan, which was well received by our managers. I also shared it with colleagues in our internal API community of practice (which we called our API guild), and together we embarked on this journey of change.

Our initiative began with mapping out our API workflow to pinpoint manual intervention points and then exploring how we could make them more efficient or introduce automation to streamline them. This journey involved replacing outdated API tools and integrating our OpenAPI files into our Git repository, culminating in a significant enhancement of our continuous integration/continuous delivery (CI/CD) pipeline. This allowed for automated checks of OpenAPI files and deployment to our API gateway, transforming API reviews from a two-and-a-half-week ordeal to a single-day process. The resulting efficiency not only fostered consistency but also positively influenced our culture, encouraging a more thoughtful approach to API design and construction.

As organizations scale their API development efforts, automated controls and good API developer tools become paramount for ensuring reliable API governance, a stellar developer experience for API creators, and an optimal product experience for API consumers. Through this book, I aim to share techniques that can elevate your API workflow efficiency. Furthermore, I invite you to sign up for my ApiDelivery newsletter (https://ikenna.co.uk/newsletter) where I continue discussion on these topics. You can also join me on LinkedIn for ongoing discussions and insights into API workflow automation: www.linkedin.com/in/ikenna.

acknowledgments

I want to thank my development editors, Toni Arritola and Ian Hough, who patiently taught me Manning's writing style and guided me in completing this book. Big thanks also goes to my acquisitions editor at Manning, Brian Sawyer, for all his support. I also want to thank my technical editors, Daniel Kocot, head of API Experience and Operations at codecentric, and Marjukka Niinioja, API consultant and founding partner at Osaango, for their valuable suggestions that significantly improved the manuscript. Special thanks to Marjukka for meticulously working through all the examples on Windows and identifying many overlooked details. In addition, a huge thank-you goes out to the behind-the-scenes staff at Manning who helped shepherd this book into its final stage.

Thank you to my former employer, 10x Banking, for their support throughout this book project. 10x provided an environment conducive to discussion and refinement of the ideas presented in this book. I extend my gratitude to my former colleagues at 10x, including Graham Robinson, Joel Reich, Luke Andrews, Danilo Cugia, Joao Prado, and Stuart Coleman, for their executive and technical support in our APIOps transformation, which provided a great experience for this book.

My appreciation also goes to my former colleagues on the 10x FT4 API platform team. Thank you to Amuktha Akinpally, Suniti Dash, Hona Sankar, Haz Rahamathulah, Ola Afolabi, Dhananjay Shivagaje, Manav Pandey, and our excellent analyst, Yoneet Magarik, for implementing the APIOps ideas discussed in this book and providing invaluable insights and experience.

The 10x API review group, including Zoe Versey, Luke Andrews, Isabelle Choudhry, Ricardo Gonzalez, Akshay Negi, Yoneet Magarik, Thomas Crane, Ramzi De

Coster, Helena Gontsarik-Pichler, Cynthia Bethea, Ken Davies, Bailee Devey, and Valentin Nagacevschi, offered great ideas and suggestions on API reviews and delivery automation, many of which were incorporated into the book.

I'm also grateful to Richard Moore, Danilo Cugia, Akshay Negi, Abigail MacPherson, Simon Loftus, and Jakub Rożek for reviewing the manuscript and offering many valuable suggestions.

A heartfelt thank-you goes to Eric Wilde for his guidance. Thank you to Vaughan Sharman for sparking my interest in APIs during our time working at 11:FS. I would also like to thank José Haro Peralta for his support, as well as the awesome Mehdi Medjaoui for his help in promoting this book.

Thank you to the many reviewers whose helpful comments made this a better book: Michele Adduci, Laud Bentil, James Black, Sergio Britos, Gonzalo Huerta Cánepa, Ernesto Cárdenas Cangahuala, Prashant Dwivedi, Omar El Malak, Giacomo Gamba, Luke Greenleaf, Asif Iqbal, Satish Jupalli, Anant Kadiyala, Krzysztof Kamyczek, Oliver Korten, Vivek Krishnan, Vicker Leung, Alain Lompo, Sriram Macharla, Patrice Maldague, Nick McGinness, Richard Meinsen, Tede Morgado, Eder Andrés Ávila Niño, José Alberto Reyes Quevedo, Elias Rangel, Conor Redmond, Matteo Rossi, Andres Sacco, Satej Kumar Sahu, William Jamir Silva, Srihari Sridharan, Venkatesh Sundaramoorthy, Gilberto Taccari, Nolan To, Ferit Topcu, Antonios Tsaltas, Stefan Turalski, Naresh Waswani, Phil Wilkins, and Łukasz Witczak.

Finally, a profound thank-you to my wife, Oluchi Nwaiwu, for her incredible support and encouragement, without which this book would not have been possible. I also thank Prof. Kalu Uka and Sir & Lady C. O. Nwaiwu for their immense encouragement.

about this book

Automating API Delivery is a walkthrough of how to automate your end-to-end API workflow. It explores the concepts and implementation approaches you need to ensure faster lead times in your API development with less toil and a better experience for your API consumers. The examples in this book are based on REST APIs defined in OpenAPI. This book is less about API design and more about how to ensure your API designs are consistent, how to generate API artifacts reliably, and how to ensure you deploy APIs reliably.

Who should read this book

This book targets developers involved in API platform teams, API architects, API product owners, and API product managers. It addresses the challenges of scaling an organization's API offerings and delivering these APIs swiftly while adhering to governance standards. Because some chapters may apply more to some roles than others, I mention the particular roles it may apply most to in the introductory section of each chapter. In general, readers should have experience with the following:

- Designing RESTful APIs
- Participating in the software development life cycle, including design, implementation, testing, and deployment phases
- Writing basic service code and tests, preferably in Java (deep Java expertise isn't required)
- Using the Unix/Linux command line and managing version control with Git and GitHub

Although not mandatory, familiarity with microservices architecture, Docker, and Kubernetes will be beneficial. (The book does provide an introductory overview for those new to Docker and Kubernetes to ensure all readers can follow along comfortably.)

How this book is organized: A road map

This book is composed of 11 chapters, each dedicated to a specific aspect of APIOps. Here's what you can expect:

- Chapter 1 introduces APIOps, detailing the problems it addresses, its guiding principles, how it relates to DevOps, and its impact on the software development life cycle.
- Chapter 2 shifts focus from technology to strategy, discussing how to implement APIOps transformations using lean principles. It introduces process maps for API development workflows through value stream mapping and problem-solving with A3 diagrams, particularly in the context of organizational change.
- Chapter 3 lays the foundation for automating API delivery by exploring API linting. Readers will discover automated methods for ensuring API definitions adhere to organizational style guides.
- Chapter 4 covers managing API evolution and the use of automated tools to identify breaking changes and generate API change logs. It also offers insights into REST API versioning schemes and establishing an API-breaking change policy.
- Chapter 5 explains the necessity of API design reviews beyond what can be automated, including conducting reviews and measuring their effectiveness.
- Chapter 6 explores the concept of API conformances and teaches you how to generate API service code from the API definition. It also describes how to generate OpenAPI definitions from code and discusses creating API consumer SDKs.
- Chapter 7 advances API conformance by introducing API schema tests to validate that an API's behavior matches its published definition by using code-based tests and a validating proxy.
- Chapter 8 combines the discussed practices into a deployment pipeline framework using the GitHub Actions platform, focusing on managing OpenAPI definition source files as multifile definitions.
- Chapter 9 delves deeper into CI/CD pipelines for API artifacts, including transforming OpenAPI definitions, artifact storage, and API mocking, which culminates in deploying API gateway configurations via GitOps.
- Chapter 10 revisits API linting, teaching you how to write custom linting functions, how to use linting to detect OWASP API security vulnerabilities, and more.
- Chapter 11 addresses API monitoring and analytics, presenting metrics to measure the success of your API product and monitor its technical performance.

Designed to guide API architects and platform engineers through APIOps practices across the software development life cycle, this book is structured for sequential reading. API product owners and managers may find chapters 1, 2, 4, 5, 10, and 11 particularly relevant, offering insights into strategic planning, security, and performance monitoring.

About the code

This book contains many examples of source code both in numbered listings and in line with normal text. In both cases, source code is formatted in a `fixed-width font` `like this` to separate it from ordinary text. Sometimes, code also appears **in bold** to highlight code that has changed from previous steps in the chapter, such as when a new feature is added to an existing line of code.

In many cases, the original source code has been reformatted; we've added line breaks and reworked indentation to accommodate the available page space in the book. In rare cases when even this wasn't enough, listings include line-continuation markers (➡). Additionally, comments in the source code have often been removed from the listings when the code is described in the text. Code annotations accompany many of the listings, highlighting important concepts.

You can get executable snippets of code from the liveBook (online) version of this book at https://livebook.manning.com/book/automating-api-delivery. The complete code for the examples in the book is available for download from the Manning website at www.manning.com/books/automating-api-delivery. In addition, the source code for this book is available at https://github.com/apiopsbook/apiops. You can directly clone this repository to your GitHub account. The code repository includes OpenAPI files in YAML format, API configurations also in YAML, and some sample API services written in Java. Additionally, it contains Docker configuration files and Kubernetes manifest files. The CI/CD tool used for the pipeline examples is GitHub Actions, which is introduced in chapter 9. Comprehensive details about other necessary software tools and how to install them are provided in appendix B, appendix D, and appendix E.

liveBook discussion forum

Purchase of *Automating API Delivery* includes free access to liveBook, Manning's online reading platform. Using liveBook's exclusive discussion features, you can attach comments to the book globally or to specific sections or paragraphs. It's a snap to make notes for yourself, ask and answer technical questions, and receive help from the author and other users. To access the forum, go to https://livebook.manning.com/book/automating-api-delivery/discussion. You can also learn more about Manning's forums and the rules of conduct at https://livebook.manning.com/discussion.

Manning's commitment to our readers is to provide a venue where a meaningful dialogue between individual readers and between readers and the author can take place. It is not a commitment to any specific amount of participation on the part of the author, whose contribution to the forum remains voluntary (and unpaid). We suggest you try asking the author some challenging questions lest his interest stray! The forum and the archives of previous discussions will be accessible from the publisher's website as long as the book is in print.

about the author

IKENNA NWAIWU is the principal consultant at Ikenna Consulting, where he helps organizations improve their API experience and governance. He started his career as a software engineer at Thoughtworks and has worked at several companies, including UBS, Bank of America, and 10x Banking. He holds a BEng from the Federal University of Technology Owerri, an MSc in software systems technology from the University of Sheffield, and an MBA from the Warwick Business School.

about the cover illustration

The figure on the cover of Automating API Delivery is "Insulaires nord Est de l'Asie," or "Northeast Asian Islander," taken from a collection by Jacques Grasset de Saint-Sauveur, published in 1788. Each illustration is finely drawn and colored by hand.

In those days, it was easy to identify where people lived and what their trade or station in life was just by their dress. Manning celebrates the inventiveness and initiative of the computer business with book covers based on the rich diversity of regional culture centuries ago, brought back to life by pictures from collections such as this one.

What is APIOps?

Many organizations aim to build high-quality, well-documented, easy-to-use APIs, but they struggle with being able to implement this in practice. They may have API governance standards and functions and even adopt a design-first approach to API development. However, even with all of this, they still see a big gap between their governance standards and what they implement. This execution gap often leads to shipping out APIs that fail to meet their usability and security standards, lack proper documentation, and are neither discoverable nor accessible. Additionally, these APIs may suffer from problems related to performance, reliability, and scalability. The organization may also suffer from an expensive and inefficient API development process with a long lead time to getting their API products to market.

1

This gap is what APIOps aims to solve. You can think of APIOps as designing, building, testing, and deploying your API products more efficiently by automating your API delivery workflow. APIOps introduces automation into managing API definition and API configuration files in your continuous integration/continuous delivery (CI/CD) pipeline. APIOps is the end-to-end automation of the API life cycle using DevOps and GitOps principles to help API providers deliver more value to API consumers (I explain what DevOps and GitOps mean later). APIOps helps you automate API design governance by replacing manual API governance practices with automated checks such as API linting and breaking change checks. It also improves the reliability of your API releases through Git-controlled API configuration deployments. This improves auditability, compliance, and collaboration between developer and operations teams in your API deployments. In this way, APIOps helps organizations increase the speed of their API delivery and deployment, as well as increase the consistency of their APIs through automated standard governance and policy checks. Let me illustrate this with an example.

1.1 *Scaling API delivery: Problems arising*

Imagine a hypothetical e-commerce company—BookInc—that runs an online bookstore. Their flagship BookStore API product is a cloud-native platform that enables affiliates to market books on behalf of BookInc.

At the beginning of its API program, engineers at BookInc had free reign to design and deploy changes to the BookStore REST API. Without any API quality gates, they could make changes very quickly. However, as BookInc scaled its operations and the number of development teams making changes to the API grew, the BookStore API became inconsistent. Their API consumers complained that the same resource was given a different name in some sections of the API and that not all endpoints followed the same error message format. There were also complaints about missing API reference documentation, unsecured endpoints, and some endpoints that always failed.

In response, BookInc created a centralized API platform team to govern changes to the BookStore API. The team was responsible for creating API standards and ensuring API changes complied with them. In addition to this governance function, the team was also responsible for operating the API gateway and deploying APIs to it. They were responsible for writing functional tests to ensure the external API worked as documented in the published API reference.

As part of their API design-governance function, the API platform team manually reviewed any design changes to the BookStore API submitted by dev teams to ensure they were compliant. The platform team evangelized the best practice in their API standards document to the dev teams and made it clear that teams needed to read and closely follow it. To ensure the finished output delivered a great user experience, the API platform team also advocated a *design-first approach* to API development, requiring teams to complete their API designs in the OpenAPI Specification (OAS) first and get them reviewed and validated before starting any backend implementation on them.

This all sounded good. The quality gates the API platform team introduced were all well-intentioned. However, as BookInc scaled its operations and added more feature teams, a few problems came up:

- Feature teams had to raise a work ticket or schedule a meeting for the API platform team to review their API changes. A big backlog of API changes resulted, as multiple teams had to wait until their changes were scheduled, reviewed, and approved by the platform team. The net result is that it took longer (i.e., increased lead time) to get an API change deployed.
- The API platform team's manual compliance checks introduced increased consistency and standards compliance. But because they were manual checks, they were error-prone. They sometimes missed important problems that were only discovered later after the API change was deployed to production and in use by consumers.
- Faced with an increased number of API deployments and the large amount of time it took to create and maintain its automated tests, the centralized API platform came under pressure and had to limit its API review sessions to once a week to enable them to cope with other work they needed to do.
- Given the long time it took to get feedback on API designs under pressure to deliver features, some development teams abandoned the API-design-first approach advocated by the platform team and resorted to starting work on the backend microservices while they waited for the design review. This sometimes resulted in lots of rework (and the accompanying frustration) if the final approved design was very different.
- Feature teams now had the responsibility of internalizing and remembering all the standards and also keeping abreast of any changes. This increased their cognitive load.

In summary, BookInc transitioned from decentralized API management with a focus on speed to a centralized API management model with a focus on quality. In doing this, BookInc had to trade speed for API quality and reliability. In addition, BookInc now has a rather developer-unfriendly method of deploying API changes that involves handoffs (involving work tickets, emails, and meeting scheduling), long queue times, and long feedback cycles. The frustration and friction this causes affect the culture at BookInc.

1.2   Tackling the scaling problem

The problem here is that as BookInc scales, it's faced with having to make a tradeoff between API delivery speed and API quality. However, there is a well-established software delivery paradigm that addresses this challenge—DevOps. Anyone familiar with DevOps will see that this friction between the API development teams and the API platform or operations team is the kind of problem DevOps aims to solve. DevOps is about applying lean principles across the entire technology value stream, including development and operations, to deliver value to the customer quickly and reliably. One of the benefits of DevOps is decreased lead times (getting valuable work done quicker) coupled with a lower change failure rate (increasing quality). You can see how this would apply in the BookInc API development workflow.

As described by G. Kim in *The DevOps Handbook* (2nd ed., IT Revolution Press, 2021), DevOps is based on three principles:

1. Enabling the fast flow of valuable work from left to right in the value stream
2. Enabling the opposite flow of feedback to detect and fix problems quickly
3. Enabling a culture of continuous learning, sharing, and experimentation to build a high-trust work environment

DevOps practices are based on those principles. The DevOps practices include the following:

- *Version control*—Version control (also called source control) is the practice of tracking revisions and the change history of code and configuration files to make it easy to review and recover code or fix a mistake. Version control systems allow multiple developers to collaborate on authoring code and keep track of every code modification. An example of a popular version control system is Git.
- *Continuous integration and continuous delivery (CI/CD)*—In continuous integration, development teams integrate tested code into a shared branch multiple times a day. Continuous integration systems (also called build servers) build and package this code as deployable artifacts to drive frequent deployments. Continuous delivery is the next phase, where artifacts are deployed to one or more test and production environments in an automated way. CI/CD enables development teams to always have deployment-ready software artifacts that have gone through a standard test process.
- *Infrastructure as code (IaC)*—This practice is about defining and managing system resources and topologies (e.g., networks, virtual machines, and load balancers) using a descriptive model. This enables development teams to manage these resource definitions and store them in version control as they would code. Teams can avoid manual provisioning and environment drift by using IaC tools such as Terraform, Ansible, and AWS CloudFormation to automate the infrastructure provisioning. IaC helps teams re-create the same environment every time it's applied, making deployments reliable and repeatable.
- *Configuration as code (CaC)*—This practice is about managing application configuration using a descriptive model stored in version control. CaC is similar to IaC but is about deployed applications rather than infrastructure. Teams can templatize, roll out, and track application configuration changes to avoid drift.

- *Continuous monitoring and measurement*—This practice is about collecting, analyzing, and sharing metrics from the production system with the development team to foster a cycle of improvements. It involves implementing monitoring and observability. *Monitoring* involves setting up predefined metrics, dashboards, and alerting to enable teams to understand the internal state of their systems. Teams can set up alerts for predefined conditions in the system that require the team's attention. *Observability* is about querying and analyzing the behavior of instrumented systems and environments to determine the root cause of problems you can't anticipate beforehand. Monitoring and observability tools allow teams to get real-time visibility of their system's overall performance and health using telemetry—event data and logs collected from the running systems that can be analyzed and queried.
- *Learning from failure*—With complex software systems, failure is inevitable. But teams can learn from failure incidents by running blameless postmortems and experimenting with systems by injecting failure into them to understand how they perform under turbulent production conditions—a practice known as chaos engineering. They can run game days where they simulate system failure to test how their team and processes respond in an incident scenario. They can also run red team exercises to test the security of the organization's systems with a "red team" that plays the role of an adversary attempting to hack the system.

DevOps also includes other product, process, and cultural practices, such as gathering and implementing customer feedback, working in small batches, having a lightweight approval process, performing continuous testing, and supporting team experimentation and collaboration. Teams applying DevOps practices tend to measure their software delivery performance on four key metrics—deployment frequency, lead time for changes, change failure rate, and mean time to restore service. For an in-depth discussion of DevOps practices and metrics, see *Accelerate* (IT Revolution, 2018) by Nicole Forsgren, Jez Humble, and Gene Kim.

Coming back to the developer-unfriendly API design change approval practices at BookInc, we can refer to another well-known software delivery paradigm that addresses similar problems. GitOps is a developer-friendly way to manage application and infrastructure changes to cloud-native applications. In the GitOps model, engineers manage system configuration by using Git to store and update the desired state of the system. Delivery pipelines run automatically to apply the state specifications in Git to the required environments. Manual changes to configuration via a UI aren't permitted, and engineers can make changes only via Git pull requests (PRs).

One of the benefits of GitOps for application developers is that it promotes a self-service way of working. Traditionally, a dedicated operations team receives infrastructure-change work tickets from development teams. As development teams increase, this usually results in bottlenecks with the centralized operations team. With the GitOps model, developers can make the configuration changes themselves by raising a PR. The operation team can then review and approve the PR, which then triggers an automatic process that applies it to the required environment. This is a much more efficient and developer-centric way of working that uses Git, which is a tool most developers are familiar with. It provides the right balance between the developer speed and the control of infrastructure and configuration changes. Rolling back configuration changes can become as simple as running a `git revert` command.

Another benefit of the GitOps approach is that compliance and auditability are built into it. Because the configuration files are under version control, anyone can see who made a change, what change they made, and when. You can run automated checks on the files to verify and report on their compliance with the organization's standards.

As described by the GitOps Working Group (https://opengitops.dev), GitOps is based on four principles. The state of the system (i.e., all the configuration data required to re-create the system) must be the following:

- *Declarative*—The desired state of the whole software system (application configuration and infrastructure) is described with a declarative specification for each environment. A declarative description specifies the desired state of the system without specifying how the state will be achieved. The state is specified not as a set of implementation commands or instructions but rather as a configuration.
- *Versioned and immutable*—The state of the system is stored in a version control system, such as Git, that enforces immutability and retains a complete version history.
- *Pulled automatically*—Software agents can automatically pull the desired state of the system from the source. This enables them to compare it to the deployed configuration and alert on divergence. Software agents provide a feedback and control loop that ensures the system is self-healing.
- *Continuously reconciled*—Software agents automatically apply the desired state to the actual system state if any divergence occurs. Divergence can occur if the actual system state is changed directly or because the desired system state is intentionally changed. Regardless of how the divergence occurs, software agents detect the drift and change the actual state to match the desired state.

For a thorough treatment of GitOps for cloud-native environments, see *GitOps and Kubernetes* (Manning, 2021; https://mng.bz/Bdq0) by Billy Yuen, Alexander Matyushentsev, Todd Ekenstam, and Jesse Suen.

The combination of DevOps and GitOps principles outlined previously and applied to API design and delivery leads to the definition of APIOps as the end-to-end automation of the API life cycle. This is why I mentioned earlier that APIOps is about designing and delivering APIs more efficiently by automating your workflow. In this book, I discuss APIOps in the context of building RESTful API products for microservice architectures using OpenAPI as the language for defining APIs.

What about APIOps for other API specification formats?

The OpenAPI Specification (OAS; www.openapis.org), formerly known as the Swagger Specification, is an interface definition language (IDL) for describing and documenting HTTP APIs. However, OpenAPI isn't the only API specification format used to build APIs. Some others are listed here:

- *RAML* (RESTful API Modeling Language; https://raml.org) is also an IDL for HTTP APIs. RAML API definitions are defined in YAML.
- *API Blueprint* (https://apiblueprint.org) is an API description language based on the Markdown syntax.
- *AsyncAPI specification* (www.asyncapi.com) is inspired by OpenAPI. It's a protocol-agnostic interface definition format that describes and documents message-driven APIs. It can document messaging APIs for Advanced Message Queuing Protocol (AMQP), Message Queuing Telemetry Transport (MQTT), WebSockets, Kafka, Simple Text Oriented Messaging Protocol (STOMP), and other messaging protocols.
- *gRPC* (https://grpc.io/) is a high-performance remote procedure call framework for communicating between applications and services. gRPC is typically used along with Protocol Buffers (Protobuf)—a language-neutral data format used to serialize structured data.

Some APIOps principles I discuss in this book are certainly applicable to some of these API formats. For example, the API linting tool I discuss in chapter 2 can also be used to run automated style guide checks on AsyncAPI definition files. But even though some of the principles are applicable, a detailed discussion of how to apply them to other API formats is out of the scope of this book.

I look at how to apply APIOps principles across your entire API life cycle by automating the management of your API definition files, API conformance tests, and API gateway configuration to help you deliver APIs to the customer quicker (i.e., shorter lead times) while meeting governance and quality standards (see figure 1.1).

APIOps is about automating the API life cycle, but before we go any further, I want to explain what an API product is and how it differs from an API, which is just an integration service.

1.3 APIs and API products

An *application programming interface*, or *API*, defines the set of functions and protocols software systems use to communicate with each other. It's the shared boundary for information exchange between software systems. There are different kinds of API solutions, for example, REST APIs, SOAP APIs, RPC APIs, GraphQL APIs, and WebSocket APIs. On the other hand, an *API product* is a packaged API solution that exposes capabilities that solve a problem for the API consumer. It's secure and packaged with good documentation and support channels. A designated API team is responsible for overseeing its life cycle (from ideation to sunset) and for understanding the

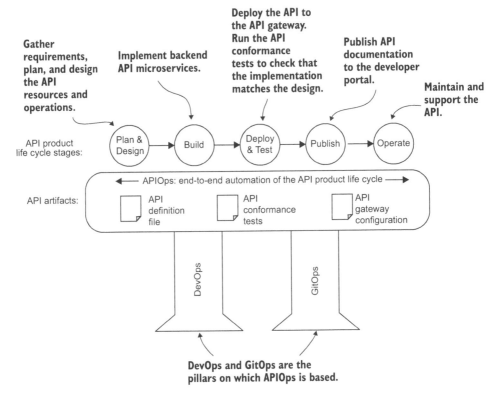

Figure 1.1   APIOps is about the end-to-end management of the API life cycle to achieve a fast flow of value while maintaining governance and quality standards.

needs of the API consumer, improving the user experience, and ensuring the API achieves key business metrics. If offered as a billed service, an API product specifies a pricing plan explaining how the API provider meters and charges for service consumption. The API product should have a service-level agreement that specifies its quality-of-service characteristics (e.g., uptime and rate limits). The nine components of an API product are illustrated in figure 1.2.

API products can be external-facing APIs that expose business capabilities or internal APIs that expose technical capabilities (e.g., an internal Permissions API). What makes it an API product is that it's managed as a product. That means the API team starts with identifying and understanding the problems API consumers face and the value the API should bring them. Then, the team designs the API to meet this need, validates the design, and implements, documents, and publishes the packaged API solution. They also continuously monitor and improve the API over its lifetime based on user and operational feedback of the API.

This product-led API differs from an API solution that is purely an enterprise integration interface lacking the same level of investment in documentation, support, or

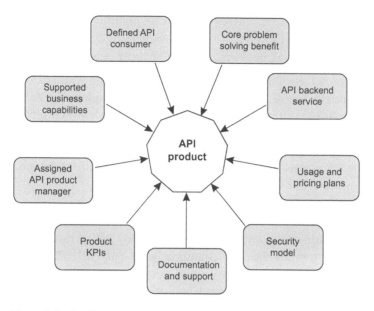

Figure 1.2   An API product is a packaged API solution that provides a core problem-solving benefit to an API consumer. It has nine components, including good documentation and support channels, and an API team that oversees its life cycle.

user experience. The principles and practices of APIOps discussed in this book are aimed at API products.

In product management, the model used to understand and manage products is the product life cycle. It's the succession of stages products go through during their existence, from development to growth, maturity, and decline. Understanding a product's life cycle stages helps product managers think about and communicate on product development, planning, and forecasting. Similarly, we can think of API products as having a life cycle from ideation to sunset. Having a shared vocabulary around an API product's life cycle helps API teams plan, build, and govern their API. But organizations define their API life cycle in different ways. For this book, I use the following simple life cycle:

1   *Plan and design*—New ideas for the API are generated and captured. Functional and nonfunctional requirements are identified and analyzed. A conceptual domain model is created. Requirements are translated into API definitions. API definitions are reviewed and validated with prospective users.

2   *Build*—The API is implemented in the backend microservices. This involves coding, unit testing, and packaging. The API design is also mocked out to enable parallel development of any upstream API consumers.

3   *Deploy and test*—The microservices are configured in an API gateway, and the API is deployed to a nonproduction environment for acceptance testing.

 4 *Publish*—API documentation and release notes are published to a developer portal.

 5 *Operate*—The API is deployed and run in production. The health of the API is monitored for functional, performance, and security problems.

Every conceptual model simplifies surrounding complexity to emphasize particular points, and this model is no different. I use this model to explain the APIOps practices and the governance controls API teams can apply at high-level stages in an API product's life. It's not meant to be exhaustive or to explain low-level process details of how APIs are actually designed and delivered (which usually occurs in a more iterative and agile workflow). For a more detailed discussion on the API life cycle, see *Enterprise API Management* by Luis Weir (Packt Publishing, 2019).

1.4   *Why should you care about APIOps?*

With APIOps, you automate how you govern and deploy API products. But before doing this, you need to start by understanding your current API product value stream—the key activities and stages involved in going from a customer request to a deployed API in production. Having a clear picture of your workflow shows you the priority areas that may benefit from automation. I talk more about mapping your API design and delivery value stream in chapter 2.

In this book, I discuss APIOps in the context of building RESTful API products for microservice architectures. Building and managing API products on a microservices project is a highly collaborative and iterative activity, requiring the input of multiple roles in an organization—developers, architects, product managers, security engineers, technical writers, operations teams, and more. Getting multiple teams and roles to collaborate on API design, development, and operation in an efficient way while introducing automation to reduce manual tasks, delays, and handoffs is the goal of APIOps.

To illustrate this, it's worth looking at the different components involved in a microservice architecture. A microservice architecture is composed of small, loosely coupled services, where each service implements a single business capability within a bounded context. Each microservice is managed by a small team, has its own codebase, is responsible for persisting its own data, and can be deployed independently. Microservices have well-defined APIs, which can be packaged into API products and exposed to the outside world via an API gateway.

> **NOTE** A bounded context is a concept from domain-driven design (DDD) and refers to a domain model that is a subdomain of a larger application. It's the boundary within which particular terms and rules in that domain apply consistently.

An API gateway is a reverse proxy that serves as an entry point to API products. Along with routing requests from the API products to the backend microservice APIs, API gateways can also offer security, traffic management, analytics, message transformation, and orchestration capabilities. The API gateway exposes the API product interface to API consumers. API consumers are the developers creating software applications that integrate with the API. A developer portal is used to publish documentation about the API—usually an API reference, API user guides, and API product tutorials (see figure 1.3).

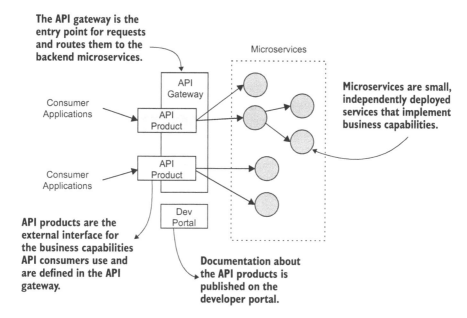

Figure 1.3 In a microservices architecture, API gateways define API products and route requests to backend microservices that implement the business capabilities.

Each API product has an API definition that describes the operations and resources that the API product provides to API consumers. The API gateway also has an API configuration that describes how external requests are routed to internal microservices, along with other constraints on the interface, such as rate limiting and applied security mechanisms.

API specifications, API definitions, and Swagger

In this book, when I use the term *API Specification*, I'm referring to the OpenAPI Specification (OAS), which is an industry-standard way of describing REST APIs in a way humans and machines can understand. You can find the latest version of the specification at https://spec.openapis.org/oas/latest.html. At the time of writing, this is version 3.1.0. The standard is maintained by a consortium of industry experts called the OpenAPI Initiative (OAI), which sits under the Linux Foundation.

(continued)

When I use the term *API definition* or *OpenAPI definition*, I'm referring to a file that contains the description of a particular API using the OAS format. API definition files are usually YAML or JSON files. In other words, when you use the OAS to describe your API, you create an API definition file. An API definition file is a contract that details the operations your API supports, the security mechanisms it employs, and the details of the expected request and possible responses for each operation.

Due to the wide adoption of the OpenAPI standard, many tools can read OpenAPI definition files. This includes GUI and text editors, SDK generators, mock servers, and documentation tools. You can find a good list of these at http://OpenAPI.tools.

As I previously mentioned, OAS used to be known as the Swagger Specification. In November 2015, SmartBear Software donated the Swagger Specification to the OAI and renamed it to the OpenAPI Specification. OpenAPI 3.0 was the first release of a new version of the specification after the name change. Now the name Swagger officially refers to SmartBear's suite of open source, free and commercial tools for working with the specification. These include Swagger Editor, Swagger UI, Swagger Codegen, and SwaggerHub.

These two files—the API definition file and the API gateway configuration file—are at the heart of the APIOps discussions in this book. Different roles are involved in creating, updating, reviewing, deploying, and publishing these files throughout the life cycle of the API product, and APIOps helps make this efficient while complying with quality and compliance standards.

1.5   Key principles of APIOps with OpenAPI

The focus of this book is on implementing the APIOps goal of end-to-end automation of API product development using OpenAPI as the API definition language. Based on that, the following are six principles of APIOps with OpenAPI:

- Use a design-first approach to API development.
- Store API definitions in version control.
- Automate API standards compliance.
- Run API conformance checks to validate that the implementation matches the design.
- Store declarative API configurations in version control.
- Continuously reconcile the desired state of your API gateway configuration with the actual state.

1.5.1   Use a design-first approach to API development

The product-led approach to building APIs described in section 1.3 is about designing APIs and getting feedback from prospective API consumers and colleagues to validate the design before writing any code to implement the API. This is akin to the product management technique of building a prototype and validating that it meets the customer's needs before building the real product. With this analogy, you can consider your OpenAPI definition file to be a high-fidelity prototype that you can render as documentation. You can also mock it to simulate a real API. Creating the API definition file first helps you get it in front of prospective API consumers to validate that it provides the core problem-solving benefit for them. This is the design-first approach to API development.

Note that at this stage of defining your API product, the API team needs to think not just about the functional aspects of API design but the nonfunctional aspects and business metrics as well. They need to ensure that the security mechanisms to protect the API are defined, that the breaking change and API deprecation policies are stated, and that the relevant API rate limit and API usage plans are defined.

Creating and agreeing on your API definition first means that you can parallelize your work. The backend team can start implementing the API backend service, the test teams can start creating functional tests for the API, and the client systems can start building integrations against a mock of the agreed-on API definition. This parallel flow helps reduce development lead time.

The design-first approach and API-first

The design-first (also called specification-first or contract-first) approach to API development is the practice of iteratively creating an API definition before writing the code to implement it. The design-first approach is an important part of managing an API as a product. It means thinking about who the consumer of the API is, the core problem-solving benefit the API provides for that consumer, and prototyping and validating the design that addresses these before building the API product.

There are several advantages to the design-first API approach:

- *Strong value and usability proposition*—This approach enables you to focus on designing an API that fits the job the user is trying to fulfill. This means you begin with understanding the user's goal and then work backward with stakeholders such as product managers and business analysts to define an API that fulfills this goal. This helps you build APIs that satisfy the consumer and have a great user experience, as opposed to building an API driven by technology and implementation concerns.
- *Get early feedback*—Managing your API as a product means you can apply the product management practice of prototyping. Using the API definition, you can create documentation and mock the API early to get early feedback from API consumers. This feedback enables you to discover design problems with the API early, thus reducing the time and cost involved in having to fix these problems later on.
- *Parallel development*—Given that the API definition specifies the expected interface, your downstream teams can start building, integrating with, and writing tests for the APIs based on the validated API definition. This reduces the lead time of the API.

(continued)

- *Reuse*—It's easier for you to discover and reuse API components and API design patterns within your organization when you start with the design first. You can reuse components such as schemas and resource models. This saves time and implementation costs.
- *DDD*—Many tools exist to generate server and client stubs, test code, security policies, and API configuration from API definition files. All the tools can work from the same definition file, and the design-first approach helps you save time by automating these tasks.

The design-first approach is in contrast to the *code-first approach*. The code-first approach is about going from the business requirements to implementing the API in code and then generating an API definition file from the code afterward. It has the advantage of being a quick process to follow, especially for simple API changes. It's more familiar to developers who are used to going straight from requirements to code and are unfamiliar with API design tools and designing APIs in API definition files. However, the disadvantage of this approach is that while it may deliver the functional aspects of the API, it doesn't prioritize the usability and consistency of the API from the user's perspective.

The design-first approach is sometimes confused with *API-first*, but they are different. API-first is the business strategy of investing in and managing your APIs using product principles, thus making them first-class citizens of your system and critical business assets. It's about the organization treating APIs as the most important UI of their application or platform.

You don't need to handwrite your OpenAPI definitions in YAML or JSON. OpenAPI editors such as Stoplight (https://stoplight.io), Apicurio Studio (www.apicur.io/studio), Postman (www.postman.com), and others can provide you with an easy-to-use GUI to help you create your API definition files.

1.5.2 *Store API definitions in version control*

Your OpenAPI definition files should be stored in a version control system such as Git to enforce immutability and retain a complete version history of your file. This gives you auditability and enables you to use Git-based processes to drive automation via your CI/CD pipeline. Team members can also collaborate on changing API definition files through the normal Git workflows of raising PRs.

I recommend you have a dedicated Git repository for storing your API definitions. This enables team members to discover the API definitions, follow common patterns, and reuse shared API components. Git gives you an excellent audit history, but it also enables a vast amount of integration options, allowing you to integrate your OpenAPI definition files into your CI/CD pipeline.

TIP Some vendor API design collaboration tools allow you to store your API definition files within their platforms. My recommendation is that you make your API definition Git repository the primary storage for your API definitions and allow vendor tools to retrieve or update them there. Along with all the CI/CD automation options you get with using a Git repository, this approach allows you to avoid vendor lock-in and gives you the option to use other tools to edit your API definition files if you want.

Storing your API definitions in Git and using PRs to make changes means you can get colleagues to review them (just as they do a PR for any other code change), and you can also run automated checks on your PRs for compliance. This leads to the next principle.

Note that an alternative way to store API definition files is to use an API registry. An API registry is a server that allows users to store browse, search, view, update, or remove API definition files. But I recommend using a version control system such as Git instead because the PR workflow is developer-friendly, and version control hosting platforms such as GitHub and Bitbucket open up many integration options. Some of them have plugins to allow users to view rendered OpenAPI definitions directly in the repository. I talk more about this in chapter 9.

1.5.3 *Automate API standards compliance*

You can convert your API style guide into a set of executable rules that can be run on your API definition files to check that your API definitions comply with them. In addition, you can implement checks for some of the rules in your style guide with an API linter—a tool that interprets your rulesets and reports areas where your static API definitions don't follow the rules. For others, you may require special scripts. For example, if your API guideline stipulates that you should not introduce breaking changes, you may need a script or tool that compares the before and after versions of your API definition file to check for breaking API design changes.

This guidance on creating executable rules for your API style guide assumes that your organization has an API style guide. If you don't already have one, creating an API style guide from scratch for your organization is a major task, but there are open source examples you can use as a foundation.

The route to getting your APIs to follow your standards is to have automated ways of checking for compliance; for example, encode your API standards so an API linter or script can validate your API definitions against those rules to check that your API design is compliant with them. Building this automated check into your CI/CD pipeline for fast developer feedback is one of the important practices of DevOps, which is a foundational pillar of APIOps.

When your API definitions successfully pass your automated API standards and you've validated the design with your stakeholders, you're ready to build. This doesn't mean the API definitions can't change afterward (remember that API designs are iterative), but if the definitions do change, you have a quick automated process of rechecking them for compliance.

1.5.4   *Run API conformance checks*

After you've implemented your API, you need to validate that the implemented API matches the agreed-upon design in the OpenAPI definition. You can run API conformance tests—tests automatically generated from the OpenAPI definition file—to validate the API. These tests check that your API definition is correct by exercising the operations defined on it and checking that the responses received match what is specified in the definition. This includes checking response object schemas for correctness and checking for unimplemented operations. API conformance tests can also include fuzzy testing—sending random, unexpected data to your API to see if it responds in a way that isn't documented in the API definition file. If your API conformance tests pass, you should be confident that the API definition file you tested is an accurate description of your API implementation.

1.5.5   *Store declarative API gateway configurations in version control*

With your backend API services implemented, you need to deploy them as API products to your API gateway to make them available to API consumers. To do this, create or update your API gateway deployment configuration. This configuration should be in a declarative format and stored in an environment Git repository. All updates to your API configuration should be done via Git and not by clicking an API gateway UI. Your API gateway configuration holds information such as the backend services to route each API product to, how to identify and authenticate API clients, what usage plans should be applied to each API client, what rate limits to apply for each client, how to log and monitor API requests, and more. Your API configurations should be defined in a declarative way and should specify the desired state for each environment.

> **NOTE**   A *declarative* approach to configuration describes the expected state of a system, such as settings and properties, in a file. When writing a declarative configuration file, you only need to write the property's value. A software tool or agent is responsible for reading the declarative file and running commands that set up the system to match your desired state. When the agent runs, you may not know exactly what commands it runs or in what order it runs them, but you can be sure the final result is what you specified. This declarative approach differs from an *imperative* approach, which specifies the nature and order of commands to be run to achieve the desired state in a script. When the script is run, the commands you specified are executed to set the desired state.

With your API configuration stored in a version control system (e.g., Git) as immutable, versioned files, your team can collaborate on them using Git workflows. This approach of managing configuration in version control is an application of the configuration as code and the GitOps approach mentioned in section 1.2.

Different API gateways have different options for specifying API deployment configurations. Some gateways (e.g., Amazon API Gateway and Kusk API Gateway) allow you to specify the declarative configuration in your API definitions as OpenAPI vendor extensions. Some gateways have separate declarative configuration files (e.g., Apigee Edge). Other gateways that can be deployed as Kubernetes ingress controllers have their configurations as Kubernetes Custom Resource Definitions (CRDs) in Kubernetes manifest files (e.g., Kong gateway's Kubernetes Ingress Controller and Tyk gateway's Tyk Operator Ingress Controller). Regardless of how the declarative configuration is specified, it should still be stored in version control to enable an APIOps workflow.

1.5.6   *Continuously reconcile the desired and actual state*

You should have software agents that continuously compare the desired state of your API gateway configuration as stored in your environment repository with the actual state of the configuration in each environment. Drift can occur if the actual system state is changed directly (e.g., through the API gateway admin UI) or because the desired system state in the environment repository is intentionally changed. Regardless of how the drift occurs, software agents detect the drift and change the actual state to match the desired state. This continuous reconciliation of the desired and actual state is an important principle of GitOps.

Software agents (e.g., Kubernetes controllers) automate the creation, configuration, and management of the deployed applications. Software agents are responsible for detecting any drift between the system's desired configuration state in the environment repository and the deployed state in a runtime environment. They can raise an alert when a divergence occurs and automatically deploy the desired state so the actual state matches. In this way, software agents provide a feedback and control loop that ensures the system is self-healing.

Manual changes to API gateway configuration via a UI aren't permitted, and engineers must make all changes via Git PRs. Because the configuration files are under version control in the Git repository environment, auditability is built in. Anyone can see who made a change, what change they made, and when. Combined with the automatic deployment provided by the software agents, rolling back a configuration change can be done with a `git revert` command. Figure 1.4 illustrates this GitOps approach.

In regard to adopting the six APIOps principles discussed earlier, the first step is the first principle—organizations need to adopt the product mindset in creating and updating the API definition files for their API products. From there, the next step is the next principle of ensuring that the API definition files are versioned in Git to support CI/CD automation. The principles layer on one another up to the last—reconciliation-based software agent deployment of API configuration. Building the organizational

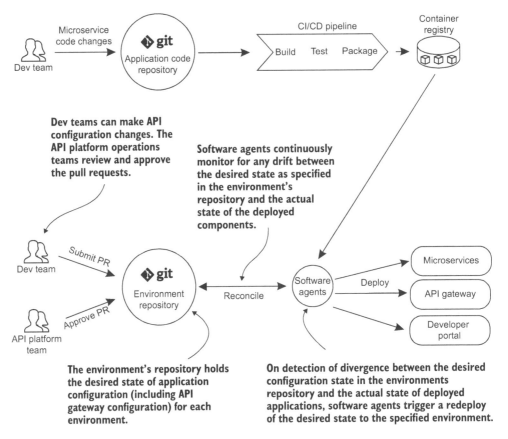

Figure 1.4 APIOps is based on the GitOps approach of having the desired configuration state of the API gateway, and services are defined declaratively in an environment repository in Git. Dev teams make all changes to the desired system state via Git, and operations teams can review and approve. Software agents automatically detect any difference between the deployed state and the desired state (as defined in the environment repository). If the agent detects a drift, it automatically deploys the desired state to the specified environment so the actual state matches.

capabilities that each of these principles entails can be represented as an APIOps maturity pyramid, as shown in figure 1.5.

   These principles affect the different roles that work on API products. Later, in section 1.7, I discuss how these principles affect three of those roles—developers, operations managers, and API product managers.

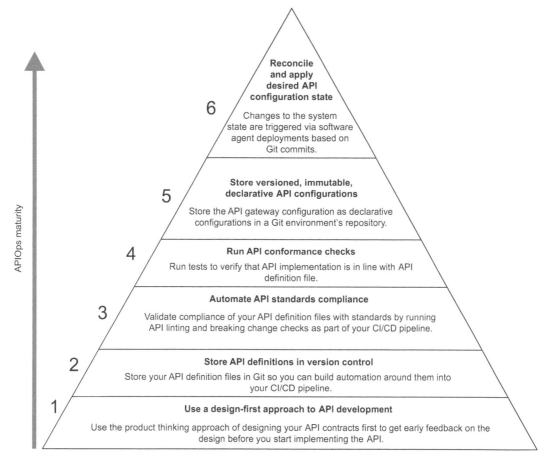

APIOps maturity

6   **Reconcile and apply desired API configuration state**
Changes to the system state are triggered via software agent deployments based on Git commits.

5   **Store versioned, immutable, declarative API configurations**
Store the API gateway configuration as declarative configurations in a Git environment's repository.

4   **Run API conformance checks**
Run tests to verify that API implementation is in line with API definition file.

3   **Automate API standards compliance**
Validate compliance of your API definition files with standards by running API linting and breaking change checks as part of your CI/CD pipeline.

2   **Store API definitions in version control**
Store your API definition files in Git so you can build automation around them into your CI/CD pipeline.

1   **Use a design-first approach to API development**
Use the product thinking approach of designing your API contracts first to get early feedback on the design before you start implementing the API.

Figure 1.5   The APIOps maturity pyramid illustrates the six APIOps principles. Organizations can use this to assess their APIOps adoption.

1.6   APIOps practices you'll learn in this book

In this book, I walk you through several practices on applying the six principles of API-Ops at the various API life cycle stages shown earlier in figure 1.1. These practices are as follows:

- Run API linting checks.
- Run automated breaking change checks.
- Create and execute API conformance tests.
- Generate server and client code from API definition files.
- Mock your API definition files to enable parallel development.
- Create and deploy declarative API gateway configuration.
- Automatically publish the API reference to the developer portal.

- Generate API release metadata from API configuration and definition files.
- Set up monitoring and analytics for your API.

At the design stage of the API product, you'll learn how to create and execute linting rules to enforce governance standards on your API designs in your API definition files. With this automation, you'll learn where to focus on applying a human review of the API product design with your colleagues. You'll understand how to automatically detect breaking changes between different versions of your API definition files. You'll also learn how to create API conformance tests for verifying that the implementation matches the design. Finally, you'll see how to run your API linting and breaking change checks in your CI/CD pipeline.

At the build stage of the API product, I'll show you how to generate server stubs and client code from the API definition files. In addition, you'll learn how to easily mock your OpenAPI definition file to enable parallel development of acceptance tests and integration code.

At the deploy and test stage, I'll show you how to create and deploy your API gateway configuration using the Git-based configuration reconciliation approach of GitOps. You'll also learn how to execute the API conformance tests you created in the design stage.

At the publish stage, I'll show you how to publish your API definition files as API reference documentation to your developer portal. You'll also learn how to generate release note data from the metadata specified in your API definition and API configuration files.

Finally, at the production stage, I'll introduce you to setting up runtime monitoring and analytics. Additionally, you'll learn how to use product analytics to enhance the experience and value of your API.

Figure 1.6 illustrates these practices in the API life cycle model discussed earlier. The API team gets feedback from the APIOps activities they carry out at each stage. Remember that this simplified model only shows the high-level stages and feedback loops. It's not a process flow diagram and isn't a recommendation for the process to follow in building APIs. In practice, teams get fast feedback as they carry out activities in the stages of the delivery workflow. But it should give you a picture of how APIOps practices can fit into your organization's distinctive API life cycle.

Apart from the activities in the product life cycle stages, you'll also learn tips on how to iteratively evolve your current API delivery workflow to introduce APIOps practices.

1.7   *How APIOps affects API governance*

I've discussed how APIOps is important for organizations that need to enhance their API design governance and increase the tempo of their API design and delivery while maintaining the consistency, quality, reliability, and security of their APIs. In adopting APIOps, organizations go through three broad phases in how they approach API governance.

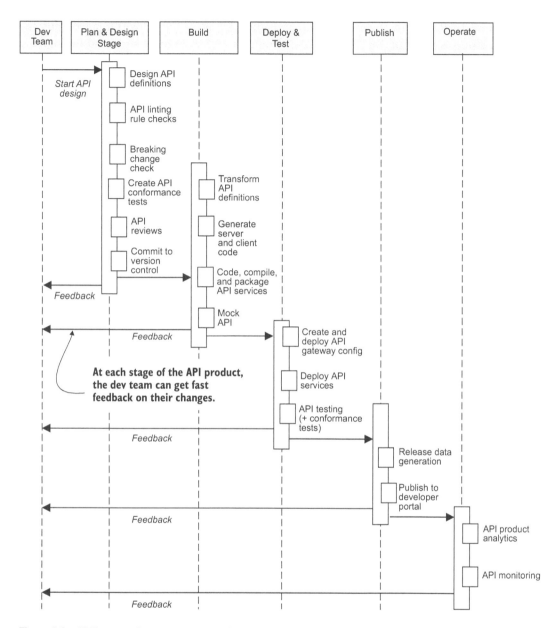

Figure 1.6 **APIOps practices and how they fit alongside other activities at each stage of the API life cycle**

The first approach is to have no centralized API standards. Without centralized API guidelines, development teams are left to define and enforce their own API standards. This results in faster API delivery but poor consistency across APIs as they follow different standards. It also causes a greater cognitive load for the API consumers who have to deal with the inconsistency. Figure 1.7 illustrates this. Organizations that adopt this start out working quickly, but as they scale, the inconsistent API design and API quality tend to cause poor API adoption and high maintenance costs.

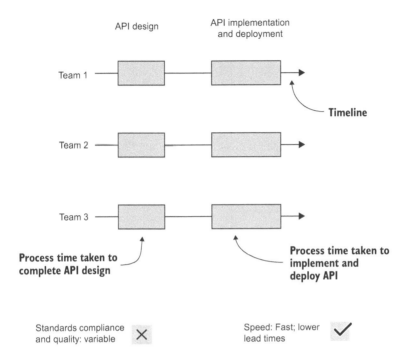

Figure 1.7   With no centralized API standards and no centralized compliance checks, teams can deliver APIs quickly. But the organization can end up with little consistency across its APIs and poor reuse of API components and patterns.

To address these problems, organizations may adopt a second approach—defining API standards as API style guides that all teams must follow. This is combined with a manual review of API designs by a central API governance team to ensure that the API style is followed. This results in more consistent, better-designed, and standards-compliant APIs.

But manual centralized design governance can become a bottleneck. It leads to slower API delivery, as teams may have to wait a long time to get reviews or may go through repeated manual reviews based on the review feedback. This back and forth can lead to further delays. And manual reviews, by their nature, can miss things. The time delay resulting from this approach is illustrated in figure 1.8.

APIOps advocates a third approach—automating API governance checks. This makes it possible to achieve fast API delivery flow while maintaining high compliance and API quality standards. Note that automating API governance doesn't eliminate the need for colleagues to review APIs to check for things that can't be automated or that haven't been automated yet. For example, colleagues or teams responsible for

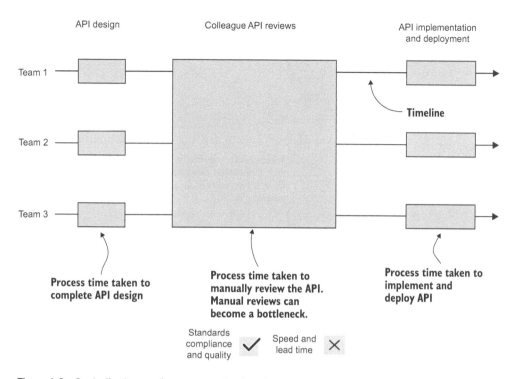

Figure 1.8 Centralized manual governance leads to better standards compliance but is slower.

API governance may want to review the API resource model to validate that there is a shared understanding within the team on the naming of web resources and attributes. This is a balance between the centralized and decentralized models. Automated API standards checks help deal with the standards checks to give the governance team more time to focus on more important problems around resource models and API operation design. This is illustrated in figure 1.9.

When teams adopt the APIOps way of API governance and deployment, the key benefits for developers are as follows:

- *Simpler API development workflow*—APIOps recommends you store your API definition files and API configuration in Git, and most teams are already familiar with working with Git. Using Git to version control your API definition files and API configuration enables you to build API-related automation into your pipeline and simplifies your development process.
- *Faster feedback and reduced frustration*—Your developers can get early and fast API standards checks on their API design from automated API linting in their API design editor and in the CI/CD pipeline. APIOps reduces the cognitive load on developers, as they aren't required to read and remember all the organization's API standards. It eliminates the time-consuming, error-prone back-and-forth from manual API reviews, which can be frustrating.

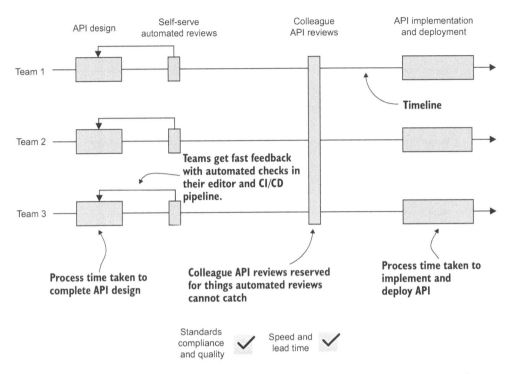

Figure 1.9   In APIOps, you automate API governance as much as possible to deliver better compliance and reduced lead times.

- *Improved API discovery and reuse*—Storing API description files and API configuration in a shared version control system makes it easier for developers to search for, discover, and reuse API components and design patterns.

The key benefits for API operations (platform) teams are as follows:

- *Faster, smoother API deployments*—APIOps eliminates manual deployments. All API deployments go through approval via a Git repository PR and through the API CI/CD pipeline.
- *More consistent and compliant APIs*—With APIOps, companies no longer have to choose between the consistency of having centralized but entirely manual API compliance checks (phase 2 described earlier) and the speed of having no API standards (phase 1 described earlier). The automated compliance checks and the Git-based deployment workflow implemented in the API CI/CD pipeline ensure that the API definitions are compliant with governance standards.
- *Improvements in the mean time to restore (MTTR) service*—When a failure does occur relating to your API configuration, the continuous reconciliation of API configuration by software deployment agents makes it easy to roll back and revert to a previously working version of the API configuration with just a `git revert` command.

NOTE   Some companies have API gateway teams responsible for maintaining their API gateway, governing APIs, and creating the API gateway configuration to route microservices to API products. That last part means the API gateway team is directly involved in product delivery and is effectively a technology component team. Technology component teams can become a bottleneck, and you may want to avoid this. With the APIOps workflow, the role of such a team is different. The team's responsibility shifts to allowing other development teams to self-serve on creating and updating API product configuration in the API gateway. They review API configuration change PRs and can consult on API design and governance (as well as still being responsible for maintaining the API gateway). Their role changes from a component delivery team to an API platform and enablement.

The key benefits for API product managers are as follows:

- *Reduced lead times*—APIOps reduces the time it takes from when an API has been designed and committed to the Git repository to when it's deployed. It reduces the handoffs and toil involved, resulting in a faster time to market. Importantly, APIOps also allows teams to take advantage of the parallel development workflow that designing the API definition file first makes possible. Test scripts can be written and integration with a mocked version of the agreed design can begin while implementation is ongoing.
- *Product-led APIs*—API product managers not only lead in the definition of API products but can also review and understand the changes being made to API definitions.

1.8   *Challenges with adopting APIOps with OpenAPI*

OpenAPI is the most popular standard for defining RESTful APIs. However, creating an OpenAPI definition file before the API service is built poses a challenge: How exactly do you go about creating the OpenAPI definition? Writing API definitions in YAML by hand can be unpleasant and time-consuming, so good tooling is required. Tools such as Stoplight and Apicurio that provide a GUI for creating OpenAPI definition files help make this much easier.

Whichever tools you choose, they should have good integration with Git, which will hold the master record of the API files. While most development teams are familiar with working with Git, it's worth mentioning that the APIOps approach means that anyone who wants to update the API definition files has to be familiar with working with Git and the team's Git workflows.

As I also mentioned, APIOps requires an investment in automating the API value stream as well as a proper API platform team to support it. An API platform team focuses on building infrastructure, libraries, and tools to support and enable API development teams to do their work in a self-service manner. This requires a shift in mindset for traditional API gateway component teams.

Summary

- An API product is a packaged API solution, overseen by an API team, that provides a core problem-solving benefit for a customer.
- APIOps is the end-to-end automation of the API life cycle based on DevOps and GitOps practices. It enables organizations to achieve shorter lead times, as well as higher API standards compliance, quality, and reliability.
- APIOps with OpenAPI is based on storing your API definitions and API configuration in a version control system such as Git and building automation to validate and deploy those artifacts using Git workflows.

Leaning into APIOps: Problem-solving and leading improvements

This chapter covers

- Using A3 problem-solving for your APIOps improvements
- Mapping your API delivery process and identifying waste
- Leading your APIOps transformation

In chapter 1, I introduced APIOps and discussed its principles and benefits. In later chapters of this book, I dive into the details of specific software tools and practices you can use to improve your API development workflow. But before getting knee-deep in API workflow automation tools, there are a few big questions to answer: Although the API tools I talk about in this book may advertise many benefits, how can you be sure they will improve your API delivery workflow? Introducing automation is one thing, but how can you check that the automation actually improves your end-to-end API delivery performance? The key outcome you want for your customers is that any API workflow automation you introduce with APIOps helps you quickly deliver more valuable, high-quality APIs they can easily integrate with and use. It's important for your company to see the automation reduce costs and, where possible, increase revenue. Along with these outcomes, you must consider the cultural aspect of embarking on a process improvement drive. How will it be received by your colleagues and other teams you work with?

To answer these questions, I show you how to use some ideas from *lean thinking*. Lean is a way of continuously improving the value a business delivers to its customers using fewer resources and reducing any waste created in the production process. In this chapter, I show you how to apply lean thinking in improving your API delivery workflow using *A3 problem-solving sheet*s. An A3 problem-solving sheet, originally developed at Toyota, is a structured and iterative way to approach problem-solving and process improvements, develop alignment with colleagues, and efficiently capture learning from improvement efforts. It's named after the A3-size paper (297 × 420 mm) Toyota employees used to document and present their problem-solving reports. As part of creating the A3 sheet, I also show you how to create process maps for your API delivery process using techniques and notation from *Value stream mapping* (VSM), a technique for visualizing the flow of work and the time taken in the production process. This technique originated from the Material and Information Flow maps at Toyota.

In the concluding parts of the chapter, I discuss different kinds of waste that can occur in your API delivery process and provide suggestions for how you can introduce and sustain the change in your organization for your APIOps transformation effort. The focus of this chapter is on conceptual tools to help you analyze what automation makes sense for you, get alignment and buy-in for the changes across your organization, and systematically introduce the APIOps changes. This chapter involves no coding. Rather than an IDE or text editor, you need a sharp pencil, an eraser, and several sheets of plain paper. This chapter is particularly relevant to API product managers, product owners, and those in similar roles who want to drive an APIOps improvement in their organization.

2.1   Your company's API quality and lead-time problem

Imagine that your company, Acme Pet Supplies Inc., has a crisis. Acme has quickly built several RESTful APIs for its platform but is now receiving a constant stream of API documentation defects raised by its customers. Customers complain about the poor quality of its API reference documentation (which is generated from Acme's OpenAPI definition files) and the confusing and inconsistent design of some of its RESTful APIs. To combat this problem, Acme has set up an API gateway team to review API changes and to be responsible for exposing APIs via the API gateway. It's clear to the API gateway team that many of the APIs being produced by Acme teams don't follow Acme's API style guide. So to carry out this task, the gateway team has mandated that all teams follow an API design-first approach and submit their design changes for manual review against the style guide. This has improved the quality, but now internal teams complain that it takes too long to design and review APIs, slowing down the tempo of their API delivery.

To resolve this dilemma, the Acme leadership set up a corporate objective to not only improve its APIs but also reduce the time it takes for design reviews. Your manager has chosen you to lead this initiative. How do you go about this? A company objective resulting from a crisis like this presents an excellent opportunity to adopt APIOps.

The goal of solving both the API documentation problem and the design problem as a company or departmental initiative is a good context in which to start APIOps, as it aims to resolve the tension between having good quality APIs and delivering them quickly. To trigger a discussion around APIOps and kick-start an improvement initiative, you can use an A3 sheet to make the problem visible, think through the problem, and develop countermeasures.

2.2 The A3 approach to APIOps improvements

An A3 report is a visual and iterative problem-solving method incorporating a continuous dialogue with colleagues. It's a one-page report based on the plan-do-study-act (PDSA) cycle, which I discuss later in this chapter. It's a succinct way to tell a story of how a problem is being solved on one page instead of a wordy, written report spanning several pages or many PowerPoint slides. There is no standard A3 format, as the report can vary based on its goal and audience, but the one I use in this book has the following sections:

- *Theme*—Provides the title of the improvement you want to make.
- *Background section*—Provides the business context of the problem and the organizational goals that highlight the importance of the problem.
- *Current Conditions and Problem Statement*—Describes the problem and how it manifests.
- *Goal Statement*—Specifies the desired outcome.
- *Root-Cause Analysis section*—Illustrates how underlying causes were identified.
- *Countermeasures and Target Conditions section*—Presents proposals for corrective actions.
- *Effect Confirmation section*—Presents data to confirm that the applied countermeasures had the desired effect.
- *Follow-Up Actions*—Describes a plan for standardizing the successful countermeasures and rolling them out widely. It also includes actions to share lessons learned with other organizational units.

These sections are illustrated in the A3 template in figure 2.1, with arrows showing the order in which the A3 should be completed.

Let's revisit the scenario in section 1.1. Imagine your manager has asked you to prepare an A3 report on improving Acme's API consistency and reducing design review time. Where do you begin? In the following sections, I walk you through completing this A3 report. So gather the tools you need to create your A3 report—just a pencil, sharpener, eraser, and an A3-size sheet of paper. With the prevalence of digital diagramming tools such as Lucidchart, Miro, diagrams.net, and so on, you may be tempted to reach for these first, but the risk with these tools is that you may spend too much time trying to create the perfect diagram. Creating an A3 is an iterative process

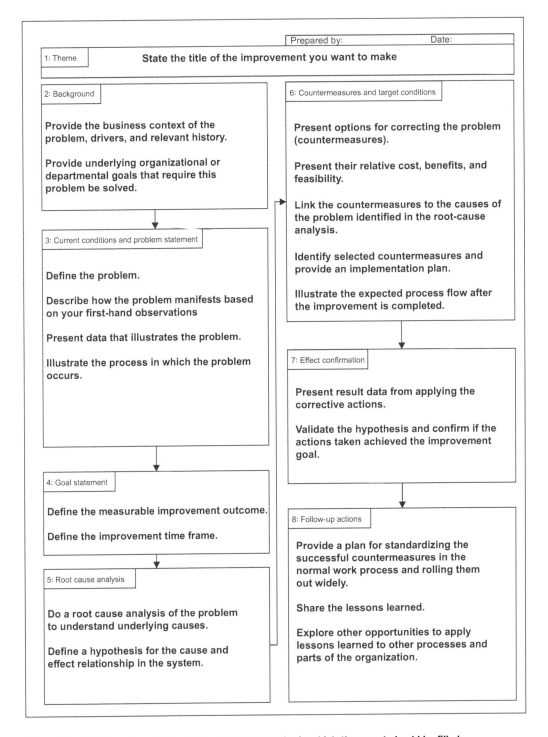

Figure 2.1   Sections of an A3 template showing the order in which the report should be filled

requiring cycles of thinking, discussion, and sketching, and you'll make many changes to your sketches. Using a pencil and paper for your first draft rather than graphics software helps you get going quickly and focuses you on the important problem-solving that the A3 embodies, rather than spending time preparing a picture-perfect digital diagram. After you have a first draft and are ready to share your A3 for wider discussion and collaboration with your colleagues and your manager, you can create a digital version.

Different kinds of A3 reports

As I mentioned, most A3 problem-solving reports are similar in form and style, but there is no standard A3 format. What matters is that the A3 report helps you structure your thinking with a plan-do-check-act (PDCA) cycle and present your ideas to the target audience efficiently. For an in-depth treatment of A3 reports and how they are applied in a lean manufacturing setting, see *Managing to Learn: Using the A3 Management Process to Solve Problems, Gain Agreement, Mentor, and Lead* by John Shook (Lean Enterprise Institute, 2008).

It's also important to note that there are different kinds of A3 reports. The example I show in figure 2.1 is geared toward problem-solving, but A3 reports can also be used for making proposals and providing status updates. When used in these ways, their structure may be different. For more on different kinds of A3 reports, see *Understanding A3 Thinking: A Critical Component of Toyota's PDCA Management System* by Durward Sobek and Art Smalley (CRC Press, 2008).

2.3 Theme and background

The theme of an A3 provides the title of the improvement you want to make. It should give the reader an overall idea of the change you discuss in the report and describe the problem that the improvement effort addresses. Start your A3 report by writing the report's theme at the top. In this example, state it as "Increasing API consistency and reducing API design review lead time." Along with the theme, your reader needs to know who owns the resolution of the problem. The problem owner is accountable for both the results and the process for achieving the results. As your manager has asked you to own the resolution of this problem, put your name on the report. One more thing you need to provide in the top section is the date. You'll revise your A3 frequently as you get new information and go through the problem-solving process. Updating the date on the latest draft copy helps your reader differentiate the new version from any older copies of the draft. Fill in the theme, your name, and the date, as shown in figure 2.2.

Figure 2.2 The theme of an A3 report shows the title of the improvement you want to make.

Be careful your theme doesn't ascribe a cause to the problem or prescribe a predetermined solution. One of the goals of the A3 is to help you investigate and uncover the underlying problem. At this stage, use the theme to tell the reader the nature of the change or improvement you want to make. For a problem-solving A3, a rule of thumb I use is to start the theme with words like *improve, increase, reduce, streamline,* and so on.

Next comes the Background section of the A3 report. When your busy manager reads the A3, how do you remind your manager of why it's important to solve this problem? Use the Background section to provide the business context and relate the problem to the company or departmental goals. (To do this, you need to find out the quarterly or annual objectives of your organization.) In addition, provide any relevant history related to the problem. Where possible, provide the information with illustrations, tables, or bullet points. An example Background section for the Acme scenario is shown in figure 2.3.

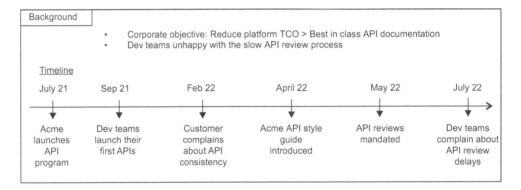

Figure 2.3   The Background section of the A3 report provides the context of the problem for the reader.

The Background section should be tailored to the audience. Give reasons why the improvement should be made and include a sense of urgency. Using bullet points and diagrams provides the information succinctly and captures the attention of the reader. Pictures often convey much more than words can in these scenarios. Consider using bar charts, pie charts, histograms, trend lines, timelines, and Pareto charts to illustrate your points.

2.4   *Current conditions and problem statement*

You've provided your manager with the background of the problem. Now look at the problem itself. Imagine that in the Acme scenario, when a customer requests an enhancement to the API, the request is captured by an API product owner. An engineer designs the API and sends it to the API gateway team for review and approval. The gateway team meets twice a week to review APIs from all the dev teams. If any amendments are required, they ask the engineer to make them. After that, the design is approved. This whole process is too slow for the developer teams and results in delays in meeting customer commitments. OK, so that is what happens at a high level. But how do you use data and verified facts to help your manager and any reader of your A3 thoroughly understand the details of the problem and how it's being manifested?

Use the Current Conditions and Problem Statement section of the A3 report to define the problem in one or two sentences and illustrate the current process in which it manifests. Present verified facts and data about the problem. Describe how long it lasts and how frequently it occurs. The best way to get information and a deep understanding of a problem and how it manifests is to observe the problem firsthand. This is a very important point. Observing the problem and process closely for yourself is a crucial part of the problem-solving process. This is referred to by lean professionals as "Going to the *gemba*" or doing a "gemba walk," where *gemba* is the Japanese word for the "actual place" where work happens. For example, in the Acme scenario, here are things you can do to observe the process:

- Interview colleagues to understand the problems they experience with the process. Ask about any problems they encounter and any roadblocks they face.

- Ask colleagues for permission to observe them as they work so you can see how the problem manifests. For example, if they work on a computer to complete a task, sit with them and observe their screens as they do it. Or, if they work remotely, ask them to share screens or make a screen recording.

- Note what tools they use and how they do the task. In addition, watch out for what they don't use. For example, if you have a company API style guide or a recommended API design tool, note whether your colleagues actually use them.

- If there are meetings in the process where important tasks are done or problems are surfaced and discussed, attend and observe. For example, in the Acme scenario, attend API review meetings.

- If there are defect tickets, incident tickets, or other documents that capture manifestations of the problem, study them.

- During your observation, it's important you don't make any suggestions or improvement recommendations. Just focus on understanding the process by asking why, when, who, what, and how. Make notes of the information you get during the session.

TIP Ideally, you should gather data from three or four observations of your process and get an average value for the metrics at each step.

A work process is made up of several process steps. When improving a process (in the Acme scenario, the API design and review process), there are two important axes of improvement. The first is how long the process takes overall, which depends on how long each step in the process takes (if we ignore steps that occur in parallel). The other is the quality of the process output, which will be the cumulative result of the quality of the output at each step of the process. Here are some important metrics you should capture during your observation of the process:

- *Task time (TT)*—This is the time it takes to actively work on a task, assuming all information and dependencies needed are available and colleagues involved can work on it without interruption. It includes the time required to think, read, and discuss to understand what needs to be done. TT doesn't include time spent waiting in a backlog or any delays that interrupt colleagues after they have started their tasks. TT is also referred to as process time or touch time.

- *Lead time (LT)*—The duration from when work is made available to a step in the process to when it's completed and made available to the next step in the process. This includes all the time spent waiting to get information or any other dependencies required before the task can begin and time spent on interruptions. That is, LT includes time spent on delays and work queues (backlogs). The difference between TT and LT is illustrated in figure 2.4. LT is also referred to as throughput time.

- *Percentage complete and accurate (%CA)*—The percentage of time that tasks sent from upstream processes are ready for the colleague to work on because they have no defects, require no further information, and have no dependencies. In other words, this is the percentage of incoming work that is usable as it is, without the need to do any corrections, additions, or clarifications. It's a measure of the quality of output from a process. You can get the %CA value by asking the colleagues at that stage of the process how often they receive incoming work items (from upstream processes) that are completely ready for them to work on. For example, API reviewers may report that they are only given all the information they need for the review 80% of the time.

- *Work-in-process (WIP) inventory*—The number of ready work items or tickets waiting to be processed. In the Acme scenario, an example of WIP inventory is the backlog of developer-ready API review tickets awaiting review. Note areas where work is being batched up either by performing work at a given frequency (reviews occur twice a week for Acme) or by work being held until the number of work tickets reaches a particular number before processing.

Apart from these metrics, also consider getting any other data points you think are important. For example, the number of defect tickets caused by the problem, the frequency of occurrence of the problem (in the Acme case, are there times in the year when the review delays are particularly high?), the number of colleagues involved at different stages of the process, and so on.

You've now had discussions with colleagues involved in the process, verified the facts of the problem, and gathered important data to show how the problem manifests. But how do you present this in your A3 report in an efficient way so that your manager can quickly grasp the problem without having to read through paragraph after paragraph of your findings?

With the insights and data you've gathered from going to the gemba, describe the problem visually. You can illustrate the problem using the diagrams I mentioned earlier: bar charts, pie charts, Pareto charts, and so on.

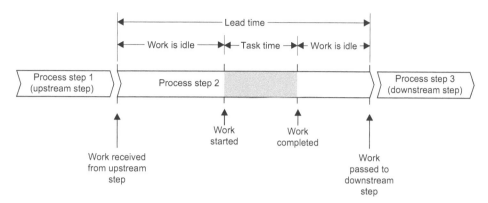

Figure 2.4   TT and LT for a step in the process

> **TIP**   Pareto charts are a good way to visualize data about how frequently the problems occur. This bar chart helps focus attention on the vital few causes or problems that have the most effect. Discussion on this is out of the scope of this book, but you can find more at https://asq.org/quality-resources/pareto.

Map out the process, and present the metrics you gathered for each step. You can use various business process modeling techniques, but I recommend the techniques and notation of value stream mapping (VSM) applied at a process level. As mentioned previously, VSM is a technique for visualizing and analyzing the sequence of activities involved in fulfilling a customer's request, including the flow of work and information. VSM is usually done at the macro level, showing how value is added to a product or family of products across multiple high-level processes in the organization. However, you can create a low-level process map by adapting and using the techniques and notation from VSM, which you'll see how to do next.

2.4.1   Create the work process steps

Start by showing the customer who has made a request and the main process steps in the map. In the Acme example, the customer is internal—a product manager who has requested an API design change. Create the customer at the top of the sheet using the customer icon. (You can see the definition of the VSM icons I use in appendix A.) Next, draw the main steps of the process using the process step icon. (If there is a variability in the process steps, draw the process steps that are carried out, say, 80% of the time. You want to focus your improvements on these so you don't get distracted by details.) In the top part of the process step icon, add the process name (preferably in verb and noun format, e.g., Design API Operation). Add the team or role that performs the activity in the bottom part. Connect the process steps with the push arrow, showing work being passed from one step to the next. Figure 2.5 shows how this looks for the Acme example.

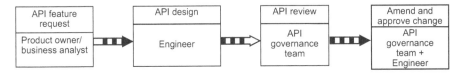

Figure 2.5   Draw the customer, and outline the main process steps.

2.4.2   Draw the information flow

Identify the main information systems that each process step in the value stream uses to store and transmit data. Understanding the flow of information in the process is important to discover some kinds of waste in the production process, but I discuss this more in a later section. Use information flow arrows to connect the process blocks with the information systems. An arrow pointing to an information system means that data is entered into the system, and an arrow pointing away from the system means that data is retrieved from the system.

In the Acme example, the product owner or the team's business analyst discusses the requirements with the engineers and creates a work ticket in the Jira ticketing system to capture them. The engineers design the API, creating or updating the OpenAPI definition file, and they may consult the Jira ticket while doing this. They also consult Acme's API style guide in Confluence. The engineers use a cloud-based API design tool that also stores their OpenAPI definition files. When they finish, they raise a ticket for the API gateway team to review their API. When the gateway team picks up the review task, they open up the cloud-based API design tool to review the API definition files and add review comments. The lines showing these information flows are shown in figure 2.6.

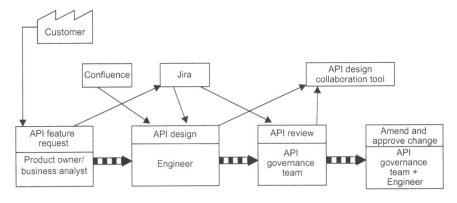

Figure 2.6   Add information flows.

2.4.3 Add performance metrics

Using the data you gathered from your observation of the value stream, add performance metrics to each process step, including your LT, TT, and %CA metrics. The metrics should go in the *data box* icon, which is a box used to record important data for each process step. It's also important to know the number of work items awaiting processing at each process step. Visualizing this queue or work backlog can help analyze the waste areas in the process. Use the inventory triangle icon to add the tasks awaiting processing between steps where applicable. In the Acme example, this is the number of Jira tickets.

Now show the time metrics at each step. A *time ladder* summarizes each block's LT and TT and shows the total LT and TT. Draw out a time ladder for your process, showing the TT at the top and the LT at the bottom. For Acme, the completed process map in the Current Conditions and Problem Statement section is shown in figure 2.7.

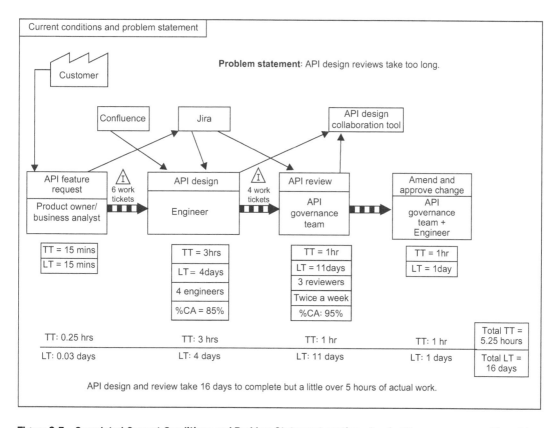

Figure 2.7 Completed Current Conditions and Problem Statement section, showing the process map with metrics

NOTE In this book, I focus on process mapping to drive APIOps improvements using VSM techniques. For a wider discussion of VSM and how it can be applied to different processes, refer to *Learning to See* by Mike Rother and John Shook (Lean Enterprise Institute, 2009). Also see the book *Value Stream Mapping* by Karen Martin and Mike Osterling (McGraw-Hill, 2013). Another useful mapping technique to consider is *Metric-Based Process Mapping* (MBPM), which is a low-level process mapping technique used to capture process metrics, usually done collaboratively using whiteboards, paper, and sticky notes. For more on MBPM, see https://mng.bz/y8NG and Karen Martin's MBPM slides at https://mng.bz/OZWR.

2.4.4 Review your map

Let's see what the process map shows about the problems with the current state. You can see from figure 2.7 that Acme's product owner or business analyst takes 0.25 hours (15 minutes) to create a work ticket for the API design change. The TT equals the LT, so there are no delays here. Then, the engineers take 3 hours to update the API design (the API definition file). The team has four engineers, but they have a backlog of six work tickets to complete before they get to this design change ticket, so the ticket spends a few days in the backlog before they can get to it. The LT for this step of the process is four days. Based on discussions with the engineers and your observations, you find that on average, the engineers have all the information they need (in the Jira work ticket and in the API style guide in Confluence) 85% of the time. For the rest of the time, some important information may be missing that they then need to ask around and wait for. So their %CA value is 85%.

After they complete their API design, the engineers raise a ticket in Jira for the API gateway team to review their design update. The gateway team is the central group that reviews design changes from all teams in the organization and is the custodian of the organization's API style guide. However, they serve Acme's 16 development teams. They have a backlog of four design change tickets awaiting review, apart from many other API gateway routing and testing tickets they have to work on. To balance the competing demands on their team, the team meets twice a week (Tuesdays and Thursdays) to review and approve designs, and the review sessions last about an hour for a ticket. Given the four-ticket backlog, it will take the team 11 working days to get to this ticket. When the ticket is up for review, the gateway team invites the engineers to the review meeting to explain their design changes. Part of the reason they do this is that the API design collaboration tool Acme uses doesn't support running a diff (i.e., showing the difference) between different versions of a file, so it's difficult for the gateway team to see exactly what has changed in the submitted API definition file.

During the API review meeting, the gateway team finds three problems the engineers should fix. They ask the engineers to make amendments to the design, and the gateway team approves the design after the changes are made. The amendment and final approval take an hour of TT, but there is some time spent waiting for the engineers to make the recommended changes because they are busy working on other tasks. So the LT for this ends up being a day (8 hours in a standard working day).

The time ladder shows that the value stream's LT is 16 working days (128 hours for an 8-hour working day). That's a long time to wait to approve adding one new API operation, but the actual TT is 5.25 hours. Therefore, the *activity ratio*, which is the total TT divided by the total LT, is 4.1%. This means that 95.9% of the time, work is sitting idle in the value stream, waiting to be worked on. That's not very efficient! The process map has helped us see the waste in the process.

2.5 Goal statement

You've done a great job of illustrating the metrics of the process, and your manager can see how the problem manifests, but before exploring how you can improve the process, there is something your manager would like to know: What standard or basis will you use to measure the success of your improvement effort? What will success look like? The Goal Statement section of your A3 helps you answer this and think ahead regarding the metrics you intend to use to confirm the effectiveness of your improvement efforts.

Based on your study of the current conditions, identify one or two performance metrics you want to improve. In the Acme scenario, the goal can be to reduce the total LT for the API design review process by 20%. This would mean decreasing the total LT for the process from 16 days to 12.8 days. You can also specify the time frame in which you would like to achieve this goal. This can range from a few weeks to a few quarters. Following the preference to show information in A3 charts using charts, diagrams, and tables, you can represent this with a simple table, as shown in figure 2.8.

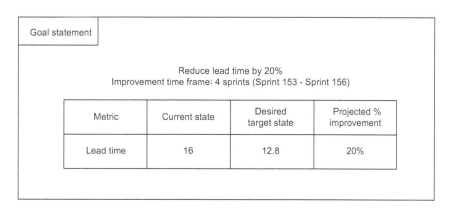

Figure 2.8   Example goal statement showing improvement target table

You can specify the time frame up front or come back and add it after you've filled in the Countermeasures section. Because I work with Agile teams that usually plan work based on sprints, I like to specify a time frame in terms of the number of sprints I expect it will take to accomplish.

Don't use the Goal Statement section to discuss solutions to the problem. The Goal Statement provides a measurable objective—the performance metric that is the clear standard for comparison and judging success. After your improvement efforts, you'll revisit the values in this section to check if the improvement achieved the intended goal.

2.6   *Root-cause analysis*

You've defined the problem and how it manifests and set a goal for improvement. But why did the problem occur in the first place? You need to perform a root-cause analysis to discover the underlying reason the problem occurred so you can prevent it from reoccurring. One common way to do this is the Five Whys approach. This involves asking "Why?" or "What caused this problem?" about five times. Note that it doesn't have to be exactly five times, and some causes may have more than one reason. The goal is to figure out the underlying process problem so that similar problems don't arise in the future. In Acme's case, figure 2.9 shows an example root-cause analysis tree.

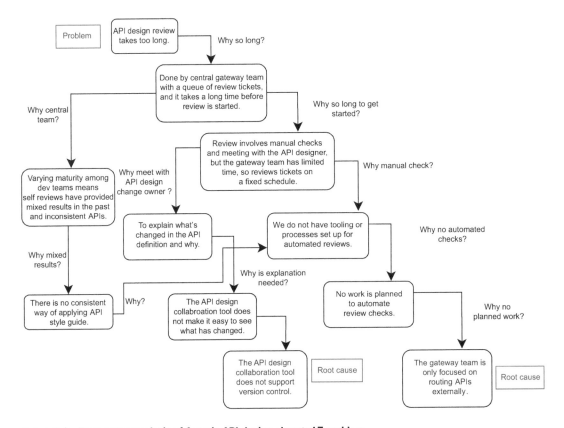

Figure 2.9   Root-cause analysis of Acme's API design change LT problem

The analysis identifies two root causes. The first is that the API design collaboration tool the team uses doesn't support version control. The second is that the central API gateway team is a component team that focuses only on routing APIs and doesn't do any work on automating review checks and other aspects of the end-to-end API design and delivery process.

Root-cause analysis aims to find and address the deeply rooted or underlying causal factor so that the problem doesn't reoccur. It uses deductive reasoning to establish cause-and-effect relationships and so requires critical thinking. The analysis helps you avoid jumping to conclusions and applying Band-Aid fixes. By digging deeper than just opinions and surface symptoms, you can uncover underlying problems. In the Root-Cause Analysis section of your A3, you're coming up with a predictive theory of how your system works. Your theory will generally be that if the root causes are addressed, then the overall system can be improved. When you do a root-cause analysis, review your thinking with your colleagues and other stakeholders in the affected process. It's useful to get others to validate your thinking and explore alternative causes you may not have thought of.

> **TIP**   Apart from the Five Whys approach, another thinking tool you can use here is the Ishikawa diagram (also known as the fishbone diagram). Discussion of this is out of the scope of this chapter, but you can find more at https:// asq.org/quality-resources/fishbone.

2.7 *Countermeasures and target conditions*

So far, you've focused on the problem—providing the background, defining the problem, presenting data on the problem, and analyzing its root cause. Now it's time to propose how you intend to tackle it. In lean terminology, the actions you take to reduce or eliminate the root causes of problems are called *countermeasures*. In the API-Ops context, your countermeasures include actions and APIOps practices you think should improve your API delivery process.

In the Countermeasures and Target Conditions section of the A3 report, brainstorm and note down what countermeasures you can use to address the cause(s) you identified in your analysis. Specify your countermeasures in a table, listing the cause they address. To help you be innovative in your problem-solving, consider as many options as you can, and consult with colleagues involved in the process. Cross-functional involvement and consensus help you get better countermeasures. As you refine these ideas, you can narrow down the list, combine similar countermeasures, and pick the ones you think are feasible.

Prepare a plan for implementing the chosen countermeasures. Do this by specifying in the table who would be responsible for implementing each countermeasure and the date by which it should be done. To help you prioritize your countermeasures, you can have a benefit/effort column that specifies the anticipated benefit (high/medium/low) and anticipated effort (easy/medium/difficult). Countermeasures that are high benefit and easy to implement should be the highest priority, while those that are low benefit and difficult should be the least priority or even eliminated.

As you implement your countermeasures, you update the Status column. You can see an example of this in figure 2.10.

Cause	Countermeasures	Responsible owner	Anticipated benefit/effort	Due date	Status
Gateway team is only focused on routing APIs externally.	Gateway team should plan for review automation work.	Gateway team	High/low	2023/01/06	Done
Gateway team is only focused on routing APIs externally.	Create automated linting and breaking change checks.	Gateway team	High/medium	2023/02/24	Done
API design collaboration tool does not support version control.	Migrate API definitions to Git.	Gateway team	High/medium	2023/01/20	Done
API design collaboration tool does not support version control.	Do API reviews as pull requests with links to the user story.	Gateway team	High/low	2023/01/23	Done

Figure 2.10   Countermeasures are the actions taken to address the root cause of the problem. A countermeasures table shows the plan for who will do what and when.

TIP   When implementing your countermeasures, narrow your focus to a small subset of the problem instance. At this stage, you're in "experimental" mode, and you want to keep the surface area of the application of your countermeasures small while you verify what works and what doesn't. For example, in the Acme scenario, you can focus the improvement on the API changes related to one API or the design changes submitted by one dev team. If the countermeasures are successful, in a later section of the A3, you can explore how to roll them out widely.

In the lean method, the word *countermeasure* is used instead of *solution* because countermeasures imply that the action fixes the problem in the current situation but may not be the final solution to the problem. You could discover a better remedial action in the future, or the problem itself could evolve, requiring a new or updated countermeasure. Because a fundamental principle of lean is the pursuit of perfection, that is, continuous improvement, the aim is to review the current state of problems and improve on countermeasures. What these countermeasures do is improve *flow*. Flow occurs when work proceeds from one process step to another without delay, interruption, idle time, or rework. The APIOps improvements should reduce time spent waiting and so improve the flow of work inside a process.

You've defined your countermeasures, but it still may not be very clear to your manager and readers of your A3 how the improved process will look after your proposed countermeasures have been implemented. How can you illustrate the expected future process?

Describe the *target condition* by creating a future state process map. This target condition helps your manager see at a glance how the improved process will work, along with the expected performance metrics for each step of the process. Figure 2.11 shows

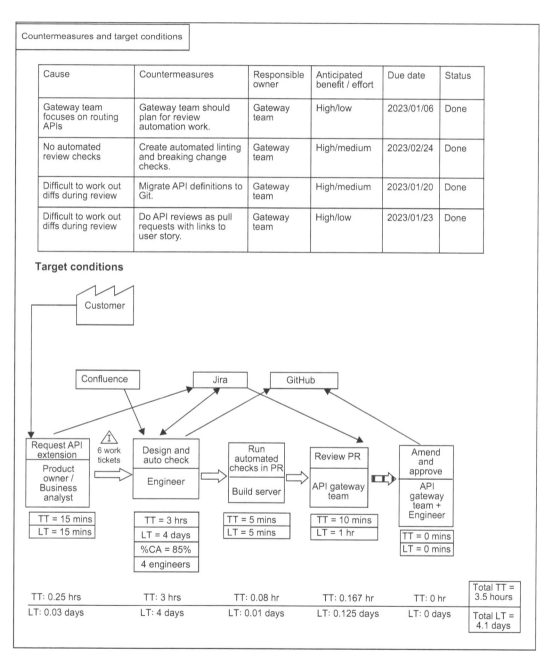

Figure 2.11   Future state value stream map

the completed Countermeasures and Target Conditions section for Acme with a future state map. You can see that engineers can now run automated design checks earlier at the Design & Auto Check stage. Because they can run automated checks locally, the time to detect a problem with the API design is reduced. Note also that there is an additional process to run automated checks in the pull request. The inventory of review tickets has disappeared, and the LT has decreased from 16 days to 4.1 days.

To summarize, in your Countermeasures and Target Conditions section, you should accomplish the following:

- Brainstorm, come up with countermeasures, and refine these with colleagues.
- Come up with a plan of implementation—that is, who will do what and when.
- Draw your target conditions showing how the improved process should look.

2.8   *Effect confirmation*

After the countermeasures have been implemented, how do you verify that they reduced or eliminated the problem? In the Effect Confirmation section of the A3, you need to gather data to verify that the applied countermeasures had the expected effect as defined in the Goal Statement section. Capture and summarize your new key learnings based on your improvements. You should also establish a cause-and-effect relationship between the countermeasures you applied and the observed effect. For the Acme scenario, you can plot a simple graph showing LT and style-guide compliance problem metrics observed over a few weeks as you apply the countermeasures. Mark the points on the graph when the countermeasure was applied. If your theory on cause and effect is correct, your target goal metrics should show improvement after that point. Figure 2.12 shows an example Effect Confirmation section for the Acme value stream.

The goal of the Effect Confirmation section is to show whether your theory on the cause-and-effect relationship from your Root-Cause Analysis section is correct. This demonstrates your understanding of your process or system. This is powerful because if

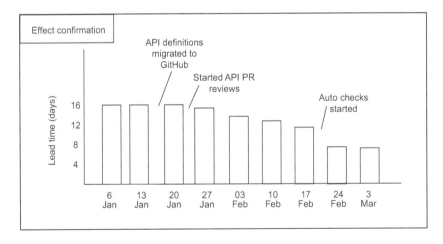

Figure 2.12 An example Effect Confirmation section

you have a proven theory of how your process works, then you have validated new knowledge that is potentially applicable to other processes or other areas of your organization.

2.9   *Follow-up actions*

Imagine that the results from the Effect Confirmation section of the A3 report show your countermeasures were successful when you applied the process to one dev team that volunteered to take part in the process improvement exercise. Now how can you roll out the countermeasures more widely? In the Acme case, this can be done by other dev teams and APIs in the organization. At this point, you can start creating stories and epics to expand the application of your validated countermeasures. In addition, look for other teams and parts of the organization you can share the new learnings with. Figure 2.13 shows an example Follow-Up Actions table for Acme.

Follow-up actions			
Task	Owner	Due	Status
Apply auto checks to all types of web API design changes.	Gateway team	2023/04/07	In progress
Federate API PR reviews to engineering teams.	Dev teams	2023/04/21	Planned
Apply auto checks to Async API definitions.	Dev teams	2023/05/01	Planned

Figure 2.13   Example A3 follow-up actions for Acme

One advantage of the A3 size and presentation format is that it can easily be used to share what has been learned. Sending a reader with sufficient background an A3 should allow them to quickly get the gist of what you've done and what you've learned.

2.10   *Reviewing your A3*

Get your manager or a superior to review your A3 periodically and check your thinking. It's an opportunity to get someone with a wider organizational context to check how objective and rigorous you've been in solving the problem based on underlying PDSA principles. You also have the chance to communicate with your manager on the problem, show how much problem-solving work you've done, and ensure you and your manager are aligned on the problem you're solving.

Apart from the manager's review, you can also review the A3 periodically with your team or other important stakeholders. I like using the organization's API community of practice meetings (also called an API guild in some companies) to review the A3. It's a good opportunity to get input from others interested in API process improvements. Such a community of reviewers can suggest useful countermeasures and follow-up actions you may have missed. Both formal and informal reviews should occur throughout the preparation of the A3 as you engage and consult with different parties to contribute to and validate the A3. It's important to integrate feedback from various parties into the report.

2.11 *Identifying waste in your value stream*

One important principle of the lean method is to identify the value created in a product. When reviewing your current condition process map, you should identify activities that add value and those that don't.

Lean thinking

The term *lean* was coined by John Krafcik in his 1988 *Sloan Management Review* article "Triumph of the Lean Production System" to describe the superior productivity and quality levels exhibited by Toyota's way of producing vehicles compared to competing vehicle manufacturers. Krafcik noted that Toyota's production philosophy is characterized by a corporate-led drive to continuously improve efficiency and quality while reducing production costs. Lean was further popularized by James Womack, Daniel Jones, and Daniel Roos in *The Machine That Changed the World* (Free Press, 2007), which expanded on lean practices. Womack and Jones also wrote *Lean Thinking* (Free Press, 2010), in which they identify the following five principles of lean thinking drawn from companies that have successfully implemented lean ideas:

1 Specify the value created by individual products.
2 Identify the value stream for each product.
3 Make value-creating steps flow; eliminate large batches of work and queues, which are by nature inefficient.
4 Let the customer pull value from the producer.
5 Pursue perfection.

Lean is a framework for clearly specifying the value of a product or service, sequencing the value-creating tasks efficiently, performing them with minimum waste when the customer demands, and continuously improving how the tasks are done. Lean thinking teaches how to identify and eliminate different kinds of waste involved in the production process. Lean principles help a company waste the least amount of effort and capital but produce more value for the customer. One of the goals of this book is to help you apply lean principles to how you design, govern, build, deploy, and publish APIs so that you produce valuable APIs as efficiently as possible.

When some development teams hear of lean, they may quickly think of the particular Agile framework they use, such as the Scaled Agile Framework (SAFe) or Large Scale Scrum (LeSS). It's true that these frameworks build on some lean principles, pillars, and practices in applying Agile to organizations building software, but it's important to understand the distinction between Agile frameworks and underlying lean thinking principles.

There are three kinds of activities in a production process. The first is value-adding (VA) work. Value is what the customer says is useful and important. For external customers, value is what they are willing to pay for. An activity is value-adding if it involves transforming some inputs into some outputs that are valuable for the customer. For example, analysis, design, coding, and creating API documentation are VA activities.

The second type of activity is value-enabling (VE) work, which doesn't contribute to transforming inputs into a finished product or service the customer wants, but is still required in the current conditions for other VA activities to be carried out. For example, acceptance and security tests on software deployed in a test environment are activities that don't add value to the software directly but are VE activities because they spot problems that need to be fixed before the software product is delivered to the customer. In the Acme example, API reviews don't add value by themselves but are VE activities. In addition, creating a work ticket by the ACME business analyst or product owner doesn't add value. Still, it enables the engineers to get the requirements they need to carry out their VA work of API design.

The third type of activity is waste or nonvalue-adding (non-VA) work, which consumes resources but doesn't contribute anything the customer is willing to pay for. Waiting for a colleague to finish their work so you can begin yours is an example of wasteful activity. Are there any unnecessary handoffs you can eliminate or processes you can combine in your value stream? In the Acme example, waiting 11 days for an API review is wasteful!

Improvements aim to increase VA activities to provide more value to the customer, minimize VE activities where possible, and eliminate non-VA activities.

Seven wastes of lean

In *Toyota Production System* (Productivity Press, 1988), Taiichi Ohno identified seven kinds of waste during the production process. According to Ohno, "All we are doing is looking at the time line from the moment the customer gives us an order to the point when we collect the cash. And we are reducing that time line by removing the nonvalue-added wastes." While he identified these kinds of wastes in the Toyota vehicle-manufacturing process, the same concepts apply to software development, like building APIs. The wastes identified by Ohno are as follows:

- *The waste of making defective products*—For API products, API defects, such as incorrect API reference documentation or wrong API configurations, result in waste from the effect of the defect itself, the effort taken to detect it, and the rework required to fix it. QA testing activities are VE rather than VA activities.
- *Overproduction of unwanted goods*—For APIs, this can translate to designing and building an API or API features that API consumers don't need or aren't going to use (i.e., there is no economic need for them). Remember that API features take time, introduce complexity, and include the opportunity cost of time that could have been used in working on something else.

(continued)

- *WIP inventories*—This can translate to partially completed API design and delivery work awaiting further processing. This is a manifestation of batching. Large WIP batches consume resources and capital.
- *Unnecessary processing*—An example of unnecessary processing at the API design stage is redesigning an OpenAPI component every time instead of reusing a shared component (e.g., a shared OpenAPI schema component), or, at the API service build stage, reimplementing some frequently used code. For example, this could be rewriting code for idempotency checking instead of using a shared idempotency library.
- *Unnecessary movement of people*—An example of this in manufacturing is when an assembly worker has to walk around to fetch parts from another location to carry out their assembly task. Assembling parts is a VA task in transforming materials into a finished product, but if workers spend a lot of their time walking around to fetch the parts to carry out the assembly task, that unnecessary movement detracts from time better spent doing the task itself. In this case, the movement is a VE activity but doesn't directly add value and should be minimized. In the same way, in API development, if an engineer has to spend time chasing people to get permission to access some necessary API definition file or to clarify some API requirements, they are engaging in what may be a VE activity but also a non-VA activity.
- *Unnecessary transport of materials or finished goods*—In API product development, this can translate to unnecessary movement of information from one place to another, for example, in handoffs, sending information or email to people who don't need it, or creating internal reports and documentation no one uses.
- *Waiting by employees for machines to finish work they depend on or for an upstream activity to complete*—In software development, examples include waiting for information or approvals (e.g., manual API reviews), testing results, and so on.

For other examples of how the seven wastes show up in software development, see *Implementing Lean Software: From Concept to Cash* by Mary and Tom Poppendieck (Addison-Wesley, 2007) and *Lean for Systems Engineering with Lean Enablers for Systems Engineering* by Bohdan Oppenheim (Wiley, 2011). *The 8 Wastes of Lean in API Development* e-book by Marjukka Niinioja (Osaango Ltd; https://mng.bz/MZw7) also provides another view on how the wastes apply to API design and delivery.

This book is about automating your API delivery process, but it's important to note that automation by itself may provide little or no improvement to the performance of your process if some wasteful activities are in the way. In the Acme example, introducing the linting step has improved process performance, but as you can see from the target state process map, the Design & Auto-Check step is an area that requires further attention due to the high LT (4 days) compared to the low TT (3 hours). At this step, work remains idle a majority of the time. To optimize this, you need to observe this step closely (i.e., go to the gemba) to understand why this is happening, if there are any wasteful activities at this step, and what the root causes are. This can be a new A3 improvement iteration. Based on your observations, some of the countermeasures you may propose may not involve automation. For example, it can involve changing some other aspect of how the team works or the structure of the team. So you should consider as many options as possible. Your goal isn't automation in itself but continuously improving the process performance metrics (e.g., LT and %CA) to provide as much value as possible to your customer. This is what it means to follow the lean principle of pursuing perfection.

2.12 Benefits of using the A3

In APIOps, you aim for end-to-end automation of your API design and delivery value stream. However, automation makes sense only if it leads to reduced costs or helps the organization provide more value for its customers, for example, by freeing up resources that can be focused on more VA activities. Approaching your APIOps improvement using the A3 helps you think carefully about how the automation changes you introduce benefit the organization. The following describes some advantages of using the A3 approach for your APIOps improvement.

2.12.1 Think logically and objectively

The underlying philosophy of the A3 is the plan-do-study-act cycle (PDSA cycle, also called the Deming cycle), mentioned earlier, which was proposed by W. Edwards Deming, and the closely related plan-do-check-act (PDCA). These iterative methods are used for carrying out change and continually improving processes.

In the Plan phase of the PDSA cycle, you observe a problem or opportunity and gather data to help you assess it quantitatively. You analyze it to understand the root causes and formulate a theory to explain the relationship between the observed effect and its root cause. Then, you plan a test or change to fix the problem or exploit the opportunity. These are the steps you took in the A3 when you identified a problem in your theme, researched it in your Background section, and observed and gathered data that you presented in the Current Conditions section. The Plan phase also includes your Root-Cause Analysis section, where you came up with a hypothesis for the cause-and-effect relationship, and the Countermeasures section, which is the experiment you designed to test the hypothesis. In the Do phase of the cycle, you carry out the change or test on a small scale to test your hypothesis. This corresponds to executing your countermeasures. In the Study phase, you collect the results and evaluate them to see if they match expectations and your theory. You also capture any new knowledge gained on how your system works. The cycle, therefore, promotes continuous learning. This is the Effect Confirmation section of your A3.

> **NOTE** The difference between the PDSA cycle and the PDCA cycle is about revising the theory of how a system works, as opposed to just checking and revising an implementation plan. In the PDCA cycle, the Check phase focuses

on the success or failure of the implementation of the Plan. In the event of failure, corrections to the Plan are generated. But in the PDSA cycle, Dr. Deming stressed the importance of having not just an implementation plan but also a theory of how the system works. He focused on predicting the results of an improvement effort (to come up with a theory), studying the actual results, and then comparing the results to the original theory to revise the theory if necessary. He stressed that new knowledge of how a system works is only created when there is an existing theory, which can be invalidated and revised based on results and learning from the Do phase. In other words, to generate new knowledge about a system, your improvements should be based on a *falsifiable* theory of the system. For more on Dr. Deming's PDSA cycle, see *The New Economics for Industry, Government, Education* by W. Edwards Deming (3rd ed., MIT Press, 2018).

And, finally, in the Act phase, you adopt the change more widely and share learnings. If the change isn't successful, you can abandon it or rerun the cycle. This is the Follow-Up Action section of your A3. The PDSA cycle is shown in figure 2.14.

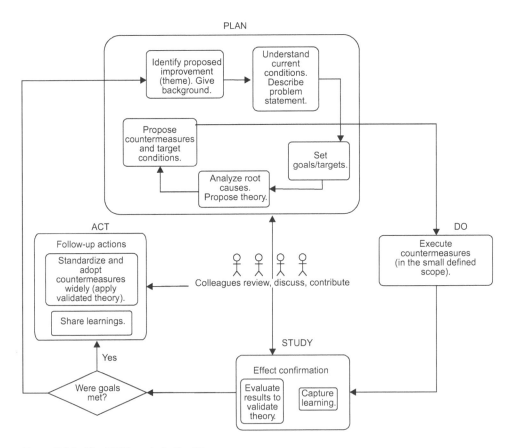

Figure 2.14   The PDSA cycle in the A3

You can see that the PDSA aligns with the scientific method—identify a problem, research and gather data on it, develop a hypothesis, test the hypothesis, interpret the results to see whether they match your theory, and report your conclusions.

Apart from the logical approach, the observation and data-driven nature of the A3 helps you focus on facts, not opinions. The focus on capturing quantitative data about your process in your VSM (e.g., LT, TT, and %CA) helps you remove any assumptions and misconceptions and be objective in your analysis.

2.12.2 Gain alignment, and increase collaboration

Reviewing your A3 with your colleagues involved with the value stream helps build consensus and alignment on the improvement efforts. Colleagues can join in observing the value stream, see the process and data presented in the A3, and contribute to and review the report. The objective and logical nature helps you gain the alignment you need from all the interested parties to implement the change.

2.12.3 Apply a systems thinking approach

A3 forces you to take a holistic—systems-thinking—view of the problem and take countermeasures to address it. Systems thinking is a way of analyzing the system as a connected whole, including the relationships between different parts, rather than analyzing the individual parts in isolation. It's about taking a big-picture view of a workflow problem, which can lead to a very different conclusion than analyzing separated parts of the workflow. In your A3, you're taking into account not just the problem but any historical background, your organization's objectives and priorities, feedback from colleagues, and the countermeasures themselves. The root-cause analysis helps you understand the behavior of your system.

> **Other problem-solving approaches**
> In this book, I recommend the A3 approach for your APIOps improvement effort, as it's a popular problem-solving method used by lean professionals. But it's important to know that A3 isn't the only process improvement methodology available. Others include the Define, Measure, Analyze, Improve, and Control (DMAIC) method from Six Sigma, and the Eight Disciplines (8D) method developed at the Ford Motor Company. At their core, these methods follow the logic of the PDSA cycle, but discussion of these methods is outside the scope of this book. For more on DMAIC, see https://mng.bz/eoBz, and for more on 8D, see https://quality-one.com/8d.

2.13 Leading your APIOps transformation

Before ending this chapter, let me provide you with some general suggestions on introducing change. Introducing APIOps in your organization is introducing change, and change in a large organization is never easy. In *Leading Change* (Harvard Business Review Press, 2012), John P. Kotter provides an eight-stage process for leading change efforts. Here is how you can apply them to your APIOps transformation:

1   *Create a sense of urgency.* Examine the market and the organization's competitors to understand the threats, crises, potential crises, and opportunities facing the organization. For example, how quickly are your competitors shipping code and APIs to production? How do the consistency, design quality, and documentation of your APIs compare with your competitors? Use this to establish a sense of urgency with managers and colleagues on the need for change. Develop scenarios of what could happen in the future if change doesn't occur. Convince managers that maintaining the status quo is dangerous. Remember that convincing people to move away from their comfort zones takes effort.

2   *Form a powerful coalition to guide the transformation.* Assemble a group of influential change leaders (a guiding coalition) with a shared commitment and enough power to lead the APIOps change effort. This coalition should work as a team outside the normal company hierarchy. Where possible, the coalition should include an executive sponsor (e.g., a departmental head or director overseeing your API program) who can aid the initiative with support and resources, senior API product managers, and API architects.

3   *Create a vision for the transformation.* Define a clear vision for your APIOps transformation, and capture it in a few sentences to help people see the envisioned future. Decide the values that guide the change. Develop strategies to achieve the vision. Be careful not to present a vision that is too complicated or vague. Your guiding coalition should be able to describe the vision in 5 minutes or less.

4   *Communicate the vision.* Communicate the new vision and strategy using every opportunity. Be careful not to under-communicate the vision—talk about it often. Your guiding coalition should model the vision and lead by example. Internal communities of practice and company briefings are good opportunities to continually communicate your APIOps vision.

5   *Empower others by removing barriers.* Remove obstacles, systems, and structures that slow down progress in achieving the vision. Review the need for existing tools that are obstacles to an APIOps way of working, and consider migrating away from them. Enable colleagues with APIOps-friendly tools and processes to innovate and work across silos to achieve the APIOps vision.

6   *Create short-term wins.* To energize the transformation, plan and create visible performance improvements. Ensure you show success in the first few weeks of the change effort. Depending on the problems your organization faces, finding a way to show quick results with API linting (chapter 3), breaking change checks (chapter 4), or a minimal API definition pipeline (chapter 8) can be a good place to start. Recognize and celebrate colleagues involved with leading and delivering the improvements.

7   *Consolidate improvements.* After a few quick wins, be careful not to declare victory prematurely. Consolidate the gains and the credibility achieved from them to implement larger change in the organization, changing systems, and structures. How can you apply APIOps practices to other web API development workflows

in your organization or even your messaging APIs? Hire, promote, and develop employees and change agents who can implement and reinforce the vision.

8 *Institutionalize the change.* Where possible, show the connection between the new APIOps principles and practices and the resulting corporate success. Ensure prospective new hires are aware of your DevOps and APIOps way of working. Create or update your internal API development training programs to include APIOps practices so that new and existing colleagues can apply them.

Summary

- As organizations adopt DevOps and build many API products, they encounter the problem of scaling their API design, documentation, and deployment processes to match their increased tempo of software delivery.

- These problems are exhibited in long API design LT, API documentation problems, and API consistency problems. A good time to introduce APIOps improvements is when organizations make it an objective to fix these problems.

- A3 problem-solving is a thinking and reporting tool you can use to apply a scientific approach to your APIOps improvements. You can use it to think through the improvement effort, get alignment with your colleagues, validate that your improvements will achieve the expected outcomes, and communicate your progress.

- Process mapping using VSM techniques is a useful way to visualize the process you want to improve with APIOps automation. It helps you identify wasteful activities that can be eliminated and VA activities that can be improved.

- Start your APIOps transformation by creating a sense of urgency, forming a guiding coalition of people who can effect change, and creating and communicating your APIOps vision.

API linting: Automating API consistency

This chapter covers

- Using linting to ensure your API is consistent with your style guide
- Writing custom API linting rules
- Creating AI-assisted linting rules

In chapter 1, I introduced APIOps and its benefits, and chapter 2 gave you some conceptual tools to approach your APIOps transformation. In this chapter, you'll take a more hands-on first step of applying APIOps. This chapter introduces you to running API linting rules to check that your API is consistent with your API style guides. This chapter is relevant to developers designing and implementing APIs, but API product owners and product managers will also benefit from getting an overview of how API linting works. I'll show you how to run API linting in your API design editor and on your command line, as well as how to create a simple API linting rule. I'll also show you how AI can support you when creating linting rules.

Follow the instructions in appendix B to install the tools you require for this chapter, that is, Spectral CLI, Visual Studio Code (VS Code), OpenAPI (Swagger) Editor VS Code plugin, yq, jpp, and GitHub Copilot. To work along with the exercises in this chapter, clone the book's code repository at https://github.com/apiopsbook/apiops, and navigate to the chapter3 directory. However, if you just want to see the files with the completed exercises, navigate to the chapter3-completed folder.

3.1 API linting in APIOps

At the design stage of an API product, you need to ensure the API design is in line with your API style guide. An API style guide is a reference document containing accepted API naming conventions, pagination patterns, error formats, path patterns, and other API design conventions to enable organizations to standardize their APIs. API standardization is important because consistency helps improve API usability, adoption, and security. API style guides are also called API standards or API design guides and are an important part of API governance. API style guides usually describe the rules an API design must follow. For example, a style guide may specify that URI paths must be in CamelCase, OAUth2 must be used for authentication, and error responses should have a message and an identifier code. Organizations with established API programs usually have an API style guide, but those just starting out on their API journey can use publicly available style guides and adapt them to create their own.

> **Examples of API style guides**
> Here are some popular public REST API style guides:
>
> - Zalando RESTful API and Event Guidelines: https://mng.bz/aE9z
> - Microsoft REST API Guidelines: https://mng.bz/d6KN
> - Haufe-Lexware API Style Guide: https://mng.bz/rV4B
> - Belgian Interoperability Framework REST Guidelines: https://mng.bz/Vx4P
> - Curated list of publicly available API style guides categorized by design topics (maintained by Arnaud Lauret): http://apistylebook.com

API linting is the automated analysis of your API definition files to check for compliance with your API style guide. It's similar to the idea of static code analysis, but for API definition files. API linting tools help you get quick automated feedback on the level of compliance of your API design with the rules specified in your API style guide document. This is a more effective way for developers to check that their designs follow their organization's API standards than having to read and remember several pages of API standards documentation. At the design stage of your API product life cycle, API designers run API linting locally via their IDE or command line, as well as in the continuous integration build for their committed API definitions. This is shown in figure 3.1.

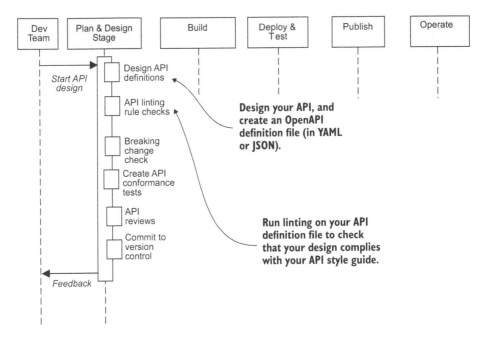

Figure 3.1   **At the design stage of your API, run API linting to get feedback on how closely your design is following your API style guide.**

3.2   *An API design compliance problem*

Let's say a development team has been asked to design an API following the JSON:API (https://jsonapi.org) standard. The JSON:API specification is for building REST APIs; it specifies how a client should request resources to be fetched or modified, as well as how a server should respond to those requests. JSON:API is a detailed specification and has precise rules on how REST API JSON responses should be formatted, how to specify error messages, what media types to use for requests and responses, and much more.

REST, JSON:API, and OAS

REST (Representational State Transfer) is an architectural style for web services invented by Roy Fielding. Fielding specified that APIs following this style should be stateless, decouple client-server relationships, have a uniform interface, provide for cacheability, and also provide code on demand. A RESTful API allows a user to provide a uniform resource locator (URL) and an operation to perform actions on a resource on a server. The operation is an HTTP verb, for example, GET, POST, or PATCH.

When describing REST APIs in this book, I use the following terms:

- *Resource*—An object with a type, associated data (also called attributes), and relationships with other resources. An example of a request to a resource is

> GET /users/1234. This fetches the user resource identified with the unique reference 1234.
> - *Collections*—A homogenous group of resources. Collections are also resources themselves. An example of a request for a collection is GET /users.
> - *Subresource*—A resource that is below a parent resource in hierarchical order. A subresource has a parent-child relationship with its parent. For example, a request to GET /users/1234/article/9876 fetches the subresource, article 9876, which is nested under the parent resource, user 1234.
>
> The OpenAPI Specification (OAS) is a description format for any HTTP web API—whether RESTful or not. It specifies how to describe an HTTP API in a YAML or JSON definition document. JSON:API, on the other hand, is an opinionated specification of how to design a REST API. You can represent an API that follows the JSON:API guidelines in an OAS definition document.

The team has studied the JSON:API specification and has designed the API based on its guidelines. They think their API design is compliant, but they aren't sure. You've been requested to validate that their API design follows the JSON:API guidelines. How can you use an API linter to check that they have followed the standard?

> **NOTE** The focus of APIOps is to ensure that whatever design API designers produce is consistent with the API style guide. While I mention aspects of API design in different sections, a detailed discussion of API design is out of the scope of this book. For more on API design, I recommend *Principles of Web API Design* (Addison-Wesley Professional, 2021) by James Higginbotham and *The Design of Web APIs* (Manning, 2019) by Arnaud Lauret, both of which provide excellent treatment of API design techniques.

Of course, you don't have to use an API linter. You can read the full JSON:API specification and manually review every request and response in the team's API definition file to see that it follows the standard. However, there are many rules to remember in the JSON:API specification, and you could miss something. So instead of a manual review, let's see how you can use an API linter in this scenario.

3.3   *Introducing API linters*

API linting tools take two inputs: the API definition file to check and a collection of rules (usually called a ruleset) on which to base the linting checks. When an API linter runs, its output is a set of identified problems with the API definition file, detailing the line in the API definition file the problem was found in and the rule that was violated. API linters can be integrated into API design editors or can run as standalone command-line tools.

The most popular open source OpenAPI linter is Stoplight's Spectral (https://github.com/stoplightio/spectral), which supports linting JSON and YAML files. It has been integrated into API design and collaboration tools such as Stoplight Studio,

Postman, Insomnia, and more. Spectral also has extensions or plugins for many IDEs and text editors, including IntelliJ IDEA and VS Code. Besides Spectral, the Redocly CLI (https://github.com/Redocly/redocly-cli) has an API linter well known for its easy-to-use OpenAPI file management features. Vacuum (https://github.com/daveshanley/vacuum) is a very fast OpenAPI linter that works with Spectral rulesets. One final tool worth mentioning is Kevin Swiber's Spego (https://github.com/kevinswiber/spego), which uses the Open Policy Agent (OPA) to validate OpenAPI definitions. In Spego, linting rules are defined in Rego, which is a declarative policy language used by OPA.

In this chapter, I use the Spectral CLI to illustrate how to run API linting on the command line. I also show you how to use the Spectral plugin to get linting reports in VS Code, which is a popular text editor used by developers for editing API definition files.

> ### API style guides for smaller organizations?
> Small organizations just starting out on their API program may not yet have an API style guide prepared. Without an API style guide, is it worth bothering about API linting because there is nothing to check consistency against?
>
> It takes a while to prepare an API style guide (there are many great examples online, but you may have to adapt them for your uses), but there are things in your OpenAPI definition file that an API linter can help you check for, even before you define your own custom API linting rules. First, you can check that your OpenAPI definition file is valid, which is important if you're generating API reference documentation from your definition file, sharing your definition file with your API consumers, or feeding it as input into some other tool. Second, linters such as Spectral and the Redocly CLI come with a default set of linting rules for basic consistency checks that apply to most API definitions. For example, they have rules checking that the example objects in the definition files match the declared schema. For small organizations with one or just a few development teams, I recommend putting in API linting early on and enabling the out-of-the-box rules that come with the linter. These organizations can later enhance these standard rules with custom rules when their API style guide takes shape.

3.4   *Running Spectral to check for compliance*

In the scenario I presented in section 3.2, you can run the Spectral CLI against the team's API definition file and a JSON:API ruleset. A ruleset is a collection of rules written in JSON, YAML, or JavaScript based on your API style guide. In the chapter3 directory of the sample project you cloned, you find a json-api.ruleset.yaml file that contains rules for the JSON:API standard. You also find the product-catalog.oas.yaml file that contains the API definition file created by the team in our hypothetical scenario. Run the Spectral lint command with the verbose option:

```
$ spectral lint product-catalog.oas.yaml
  --ruleset json-api.ruleset.yaml --verbose
```

You should see something like the following output:

```
Found 23 rules (23 enabled)
Linting /Users/ikenna/chapter2/product-catalog.oas.yaml
No results with a severity of 'error' found!
```

Spectral has successfully linted your API definition against the ruleset and found no problems with it. That's great! The team's API definition follows all the rules specified in the ruleset, and you didn't even need to read and understand the JSON:API specification to check that.

But what happens if the API design did violate a rule? A different file in the directory, product-catalog-v2.oas.yaml, does this, and you can run the Spectral `lint` command against it to see what happens:

```
$ spectral lint product-catalog-v2.oas.yaml
➥ --ruleset json-api.ruleset.yaml
➥ --verbose
```

You should see output similar to the following:

```
Found 23 rules (23 enabled)
Linting /Users/ikenna/chapter3/product-catalog-v2.oas.yaml
/Users/ikenna/chapter3/product-catalog-v2.oas.yaml
 41:30  error  response-content-type  All JSON:API response bodies MUST
➥ be returned with the header Content-Type: application/vnd.api+json
➥ paths./v1/catalog/categories.get.responses[200].content.
➥ application/json
```

Spectral has reported a problem with line 41 of the API definition file. The JSON:API specification requires that all responses must be returned with Content-Type header `application/vnd.api+json`, but the definition of the response of the `GET /v1/catalog/categories` operation doesn't do this.

Here is a snippet of lines 40 to 43 of the file:

```
content:
  application/json:          ⟵  | Line 40 defines application/json
    schema:                       | instead of application/vnd.api+json.
      $ref: '#/components/schemas/CategoriesResponse'
```

Now go back to the problem report from Spectral. You can see that the problem output starts with a line and column number (`41:30`), a problem severity (`error`), the name of the rule in the ruleset file that was violated (`response-content-type`), the output message associated with the rule (`All JSON:API response bodies MUST be returned...`), and finally the location in the API definition file that has the problem (`paths./v1/catalog/categories.get.responses[200].content.application/json`).

3.5   *Running Spectral linting in VS Code*

If you followed the instructions in appendix B, you should have VS Code installed on your computer and the Spectral extension installed and enabled. You can configure the Spectral extension so that it uses your ruleset file to validate your API definition file. To do this, go to your VS Code settings, and search for the Spectral extension. In the `Spectral:Ruleset` configuration, specify `json-api.ruleset.yaml`. Go back to your product-catalog-v2.oas.yaml API definition file. Beginning from line 41, VS Code highlights the lines with the problem. Hovering over the problem line gives you full details of the problem message. You can also see the message in the Problem tab at the bottom of the editor, as shown in figure 3.2.

You can see that with the Spectral integration into your API design editor, you get rapid feedback on API compliance as you edit your API definition files at design time. In this book, I use VS Code as the editor for OpenAPI files along with the 42Crunch OpenAPI (Swagger) plugin for VS Code, but there are other popular OpenAPI editors available. Many of these are API design and collaboration tools that are well suited to team workflows and API reviews: Stoplight, Postman, Apicurio, SwaggerHub, and Insomnia. Some of them support visual GUIs for editing OpenAPI definitions, comments, API linting, and mocking.

3.6   *Creating a Spectral rule for info.description*

So far, you've run Spectral rules from an existing ruleset. What if you wanted to write your own Spectral rule for a guideline in your organization's style guide? Let's say you're asked to write a Spectral rule specifying that OpenAPI definitions must have a description field in their info object. For example, the rule should report a violation in the following minimal OpenAPI definition snippet with a missing `$.info.description` field:

```
openapi: 3.0.3
info:
  title: Acme Product Catalog API
  version: 0.0.1
paths: {}
```

How will you go about this? To begin, you need to understand the basic structure of a Spectral rule. A Spectral ruleset file can be specified as a JSON, YAML, or JavaScript file, but for this chapter, you'll be defining rulesets in YAML. A Spectral ruleset file has a top-level `rules` field that holds an array of Spectral rules. A rule has a name and several properties. For the simple rule you want to create, you can start with four elements: `message`, `given`, `then`, and `severity`.

The value of the `message` property is displayed in the output when a linting rule is violated. It should give the reader a helpful explanation of the problem. For your scenario, it can be "API definition files must have a description field."

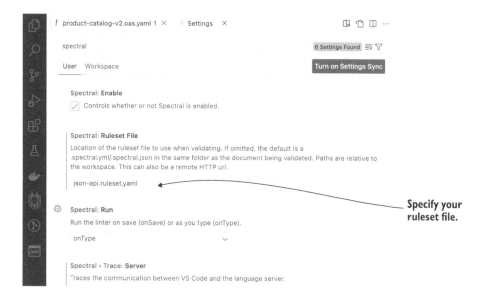

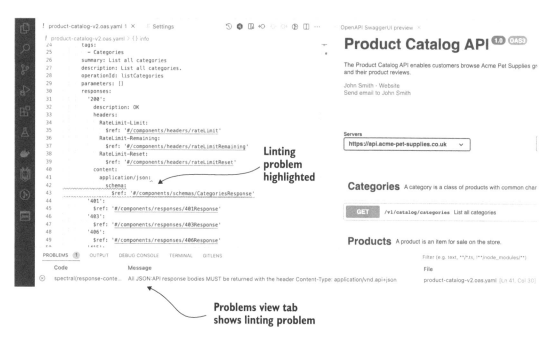

Figure 3.2   Viewing linting errors from a custom ruleset in VS Code

The `given` property is a JSONPath expression or collection of expressions that specify the parts of the document where the rule should be applied. The JSONPath expression can return zero or more elements, but if it returns no elements, the rule won't be evaluated. For your scenario, the given property can be the JSONPath expression `$.info`, which returns the entire info object. This allows you to use the `then` property to specify a function to check if the object contains the description element.

> **NOTE** JSONPath is a query language for JSON, similar to XPath for XML. With a JSONPath expression, you can select and extract data from a JSON document. A JSONPath expression starts with a $ character, which refers to the document's root element. This is followed by a series of child elements separated with a period (when using the *dot notation*) or with square brackets (when using the *bracket notation*). For example, when the OpenAPI snippet shown earlier is translated to JSON, the JSONPath expression `$.info.version` returns the value `0.0.1`. For more on JSONPath expressions, see https://github .com/json-path/JsonPath.

The `then` property is where the rule evaluation on the object returned by JSONPath expression takes place. The `then` property has two main keywords: `function` and `field`.

The `field` keyword is optional and is used to specify the specific property or field in the object to apply the function to. In your scenario, the `field` keyword should have the value `description` because that is the field that you want to make sure exists in the info object.

The `function` keyword is used to specify the name of the Spectral function to execute on the input object. The function reports a violation only if it finds a problem with the input. Spectral comes with some predefined core functions, but it also allows you to write custom functions of your own in JavaScript or TypeScript. In your scenario, the function keyword should have the value `truthy`. This is the name of the Spectral core function that checks to ensure a value isn't `false`, an empty string, `0`, `null`, or `undefined`. In a case where `info.description` returns `null`, this function will be triggered and report a rule violation.

Finally, the rule's `severity` property specifies the severity level associated with the rule to enable you to group and filter rule violations by importance. When you run the Spectral CLI, you can also use the `--fail-severity` flag to specify that the failure of a rule with the given severity level (or higher) will trigger a failure exit code. In order of highest to lowest, Spectral has five severity levels for error results: `error`, `warn`, `info`, `hint`, and `off`. The structure of these rule properties in a ruleset file is illustrated in figure 3.3.

A simplified railroad diagram that shows the four rule elements (`message`, `given`, `then`, `severity`) is shown in figure 3.4.

Now that you understand the basics of a Spectral rule, you can create the rule that checks whether `$.info.description` has been defined. Locate the simple.ruleset.yaml file in the project, and open it in VS Code or your favorite text editor. Enter the code from listing 3.1, and save the file.

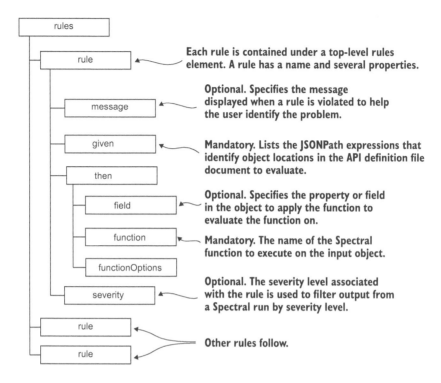

Each rule is contained under a top-level rules element. A rule has a name and several properties.

Optional. Specifies the message displayed when a rule is violated to help the user identify the problem.

Mandatory. Lists the JSONPath expressions that identify object locations in the API definition file document to evaluate.

Optional. Specifies the property or field in the object to apply the function to evaluate the function on.

Mandatory. The name of the Spectral function to execute on the input object.

Optional. The severity level associated with the rule is used to filter output from a Spectral run by severity level.

Other rules follow.

Figure 3.3 Structure of a simple rule in a Spectral ruleset. The given property specifies the location in the API definition file to apply the rule, and then the property specifies the rule to apply.

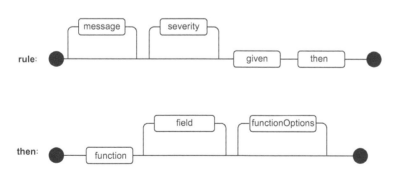

Figure 3.4 Simplified railroad diagram for a Spectral rule. Although this isn't a comprehensive syntax diagram for Spectral rules, as rules have more elements and loops than shown here, it's sufficient to explain the example in this section.

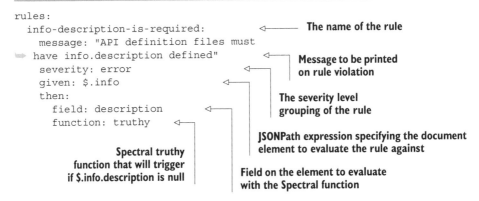

Listing 3.1 A Spectral rule to check that `info.description` is present

```
rules:
  info-description-is-required:        ◁——— The name of the rule
    message: "API definition files must
➡ have info.description defined"       ◁——— Message to be printed
    severity: error                    ◁———     on rule violation
    given: $.info                      ◁———
    then:
      field: description               ◁———  The severity level
      function: truthy   ◁———               grouping of the rule
```

JSONPath expression specifying the document
element to evaluate the rule against

Spectral truthy
function that will trigger
if $.info.description is null

Field on the element to evaluate
with the Spectral function

Try out your new rule on an API definition file with no `info.description` element.
Run the following on your command line:

```
$ spectral lint minimal.oas.yaml --ruleset simple.ruleset.yaml
```

You should see the following output:

```
2:6  error  info-description-is-required  API definition files must have
➡ info.description defined  info
✗ 1 problem (1 error, 0 warnings, 0 infos, 0 hints)
```

You've now created and executed your first Spectral rule. You used the Spectral
`truthy` function, which evaluated the value returned by the JSONPath expression.
Spectral comes with other core functions such as `length` (for counting the length of a
string, array, and object properties, and checking that they meet maximum or minimum values), `casing` (for checking that text matches a casing pattern, e.g., CamelCase
or kebab-case), and `pattern` (for matching regular expressions). You can find the list
of Spectral core functions at https://mng.bz/gvml.

In the scenario you just ran, the `truthy` function took no extra inputs or `function-`
`Options`. The values provided via `functionOptions` are simply extra input values that
a Spectral function requires. In the next section, you'll look at a scenario that requires
`functionOptions`.

3.7   Creating a Spectral rule for path versioning

Imagine that you've been asked to implement an API style guide rule that requires all
URI paths to start with a version number. In this case, you need to select all URI paths
in the API definition file and check that they start with the pattern /v{digit}/ where
{digit} is a number. Let's imagine that when you write your new rule, you want to run
your new rule on the product-catalog-v3.oas.yaml definition file.

To create your new Spectral rule, the `given` property should be a JSONPath
expression that selects all the URI paths in the API definition, but this isn't possible

with basic JSONPath expressions. To overcome this, Spectral supports an extended set of JSONPath expressions called JSONPath Plus. The JSONPath Plus expression you need to retrieve all the paths in your document is `$.paths[*]~`. You can find out more about JSONPath Plus expressions at https://github.com/JSONPath-Plus/JSONPath.

Testing JSONPath Plus expressions

Suppose you want to test the preceding JSONPath Plus expression against the product-catalog-v3.oas.yaml API definition file to see if it retrieves the four URI paths in the file. You can do this by first converting the product-catalog-v3.oas.yaml file to JSON and then evaluating the JSONPath Plus expression against it. There are online tools to convert YAML to JSON, but you can also use the yq command-line tool you installed in appendix B to convert product-catalog-v3.oas.yaml to product-catalog-v3.oas.json by running the following:

```
$ yq eval -o=json product-catalog-v3.oas.yaml >
   product-catalog-v3.oas.json
```

To test the JSONPath Plus expression against product-catalog-v3.oas.json, you can proceed in two ways. First, you can use an online JSONPath Plus testing tool such as JSON Query (www.jsonquerytool.com). Copy the contents of the product-catalog-v3.oas.json file into the page, select JSON Path Plus as the transform, and enter `$.paths[*]~` as the query.

The second way you can test this is to run the jpp command-line tool, which is a tool for evaluating JSON Path Plus expressions. (Installation instructions are also in appendix B.) You just provide the expression and JSON file as inputs, and jpp will print out an array of paths that match the expression:

```
$ jpp "$.paths[*]~" product-catalog-v3.oas.json
```

Next, you need to specify the `then` property as Spectral's `pattern` function. `pattern` is a Spectral core function for performing regular expression matches, but you need to pass the required regular expression to the `pattern` function. You can do this with the `functionOptions` keyword:

```
then:
  function: pattern
  functionOptions:
    match: '^/v\d+/.*$'
```

The `functionOptions` for `pattern` has two keywords—`match` and `notMatch`. If provided, the value of `match` is the regular expression the function will match the located element against. `notMatch` is the converse—the located element should not match the provided regular expression.

One other property you can specify in your rule is the `description` property. The description is just that—a short description of the rule that helps give you more context on what the rule does as you read through your ruleset file.

Also note that your `message` property can take optional placeholder values that are evaluated at runtime. Some of these placeholders include `{{description}}` for the rule description, `{{property}}` for the name of the API definition element that triggered the violation, and `{{path}}` for the full path to the element.

Now create the rule you need by entering the `uri-path-must-include-version` rule shown in the next listing into the simple.ruleset.yaml file.

Listing 3.2   Adding a rule to check for path version numbers

```
rules:
  info-description-is-required:
    message: "API definition files must have info.description defined"
    severity: error
    given: $.info
    then:
      field: description
      function: truthy
  uri-path-must-include-version:               ◄─── The name of the new
    description: The URI path must include the version   ◄───┐ rule you're adding
    message: `{{description}}; {{property}}                    │ A short
⇒   should start with /v{digit}/'   ◄─────────┐               │ description
    severity: error                           │               │ of the rule
    given: '$.paths[*]~'   ◄──────────┐        │
    then:                             │        │
      function: pattern               │        │
      functionOptions:   ◄─────────┐  │        │
        match: '^/v\d+/.*$'         │  │        │
```

The message property can take placeholders evaluated at runtime.

The regular expression required by the Spectral pattern function is provided with the functionOptions keyword.

JSONPath Plus expression to fetch the array of URI paths in the API definition

Now execute your rule by running the following on your command line:

```
$ spectral lint product-catalog-v3.oas.yaml
⇒   --ruleset simple.ruleset.yaml
```

You should see Spectral report a problem with the output message `The URI path must include the version: /catalog/categories should start with /v{digit}/`.

And there you have it—you've created your second linting rule in your simple.ruleset.yaml file. You have two rules in this ruleset now, and you could add more. But you could also import rules defined in different rulesets into this one. Next, we'll look at how to import or extend rulesets in Spectral.

3.8   *Extending rulesets*

Spectral allows you to import rulesets defined elsewhere into your ruleset file using the `extends` property. These imported rulesets can be on a built-in Spectral ruleset, a ruleset on your local filesystem, a ruleset on an HTTP server, or a ruleset defined in a node package manager (NPM) module. To import a ruleset, use the `extends` property. You can try this by locating the .spectral.yaml file (which is empty) and entering the next listing, which imports Spectral's built-in OAS (`oas`) ruleset. Spectral's `oas` ruleset contains general rules that should apply to OpenAPI 2.x and 3.x definitions. It's a useful ruleset for checking whether an OpenAPI definition file is valid.

Listing 3.3   Basic ruleset that extends the Spectral `oas` ruleset

```
extends: ["spectral:oas"]
```
◁— **The extends property takes an array of rulesets to import. Here, you're specifying just one—Spectral's oas ruleset.**

Test the ruleset on the minimal.oas.yaml API definition file, which is an API definition containing the bare minimum elements required to comply with `oas`:

```
$ spectral lint minimal.oas.yaml
```

Note that in this case, where you haven't specified what ruleset file to use, Spectral looks for a file named .spectral.yaml, .spectral.yml, or .spectral.json in the current working directory and uses that file. It should find your .spectral.yaml ruleset and report an output like the following:

```
1:1  warning  oas3-api-servers  OpenAPI "servers" must be present
⇒ and non-empty array.
 2:6  warning  info-contact      Info object must have "contact"
⇒ object.                 info
 2:6  warning  info-description  Info "description" must be present and
⇒ non-empty string.  Info
```

Spectral reports three warning-level problems, but no error-level ones. This shows that you have a valid API definition file. To see the full set of rules in the Spectral `oas` ruleset used to validate your document, see the Spectral documentation at https://mng .bz/ppZG.

When you import a ruleset, you can modify its severity level. For example, let's say you want to turn off the `info-description` rule from the imported `oas` ruleset. You can do this by updating your .spectral.yaml file to reflect the next listing.

Listing 3.4 Switching off the imported `info-description` rule

```
extends: ["spectral:oas"]
rules:
  info-description: off
```
→ Sets the severity level of the imported rule to off

Rerun the Spectral `lint` command on the minimal.oas.yaml file. Now you should get only two problems reported in the output, and the `info-description` warning shouldn't show up.

Public Spectral linting rules

You may be wondering if there are public Spectral rulesets you can reuse in your project. Here are three for your reference:

- *Postman Governance Rules*—This is a Postman workspace that has Spectral linting rules as Postman collections, which makes it easy for you to fork and test them (https://mng.bz/OZwn).
- *APIs You Won't Hate API style guide*—Phil Sturgeon maintains a collection of rulesets that implement the API recommendations he provides in his *Build APIs You Won't Hate* books (https://github.com/apisyouwonthate/style-guide).
- *Azure API style guide*—This Microsoft Azure GitHub repository has rulesets used to validate OpenAPI definitions for Azure services (https://github.com/Azure/azure-api-style-guide).

Finally, suppose you want to extend a ruleset defined on an HTTP server. You can do this by adding the URI of the ruleset to your `extends` property, as shown in the following listing. Note that the ruleset you extend can be in any valid Spectral ruleset format—YAML, JSON, JavaScript, or TypeScript.

Listing 3.5 Extending remote rulesets

```
extends:
  - spectral:oas
  - https://unpkg.com/@apisyouwonthate/style-guide@1.3.2
➡ /dist/ruleset.js
rules:
  info-description: off
```
← Adds the URI to the remote ruleset as an added ruleset to import

Again, run the Spectral `lint` command on the minimal.oas.yaml file, and you should see two more problem reports (`api-health` and `api-home`) from the imported ruleset.

3.9 Overriding API linting rules

It's great when you have a comprehensive linting ruleset you can apply to a brand-new API project. These rules help guide your API design, and because you're still in the design stage and haven't written any code yet, you can modify your API design if it violates any of the rules. However, what if you have an existing API project with production code that doesn't fully comply with your linting ruleset? Imagine you've been asked to apply it to this API that doesn't fully comply with your latest API style guide. How can you ensure automated consistency with the style guide?

There are three ways you can approach this. The first is to add the ruleset to the project and update the project's API design and code to match. This can involve significant changes to the project's OpenAPI file and the project code and may even involve breaking changes (breaking changes are covered further in chapter 4) to make the API comply with the ruleset. This *big bang consistency* approach not only involves a lot of work but can also lead to a disruptive experience for API users.

The second is to have a different ruleset for each project—the *multi-ruleset consistency* approach. You can create a different ruleset for the existing project that contains only passing linting rules. This ensures that new extensions to the API at least meet the minimal rules enabled for the API. However, you don't get a chance to enforce automated compliance for the rules that aren't present on new API design extensions that could probably be updated to meet those rules. You also end up with multiple copies of the rulesets.

A third approach is to use the same ruleset across all projects but introduce the changes gradually by configuring the rules to selectively apply them. You can enable just the rules in the ruleset that currently pass and disable (or modify the severity of) the ones that are failing for specific OpenAPI objects. With this *gradual consistency* approach, you can automatically ensure that any new changes or extensions to the API comply with the current standards. Then, when you have time and resources, you can look at the disabled rules to see if it's possible to change the API in a nondisruptive way to comply with the rules. You may not be able to change them all, and some rules may remain permanently disabled for some live endpoints, but where you can, you can improve consistency.

As mentioned, this gradual consistency technique depends on the ability to disable or modify the severity of specific linting rules for particular objects in the OpenAPI document. To do this, you need a way to tell your API linting tool exactly which rules to disable for a given OpenAPI document and object. The way Spectral does this is called *overrides*. Spectral overrides allow you to customize the same ruleset for different projects or OpenAPI documents. Overrides specify the OpenAPI documents and object to be overridden (using an override reference made up of a file path glob and a JSON pointer) and the rule name to switch whose severity should be modified, as illustrated in figure 3.5. A JSON pointer identifies a specific value in a JSON document (an introduction to the JSON pointer syntax is provided in appendix C).

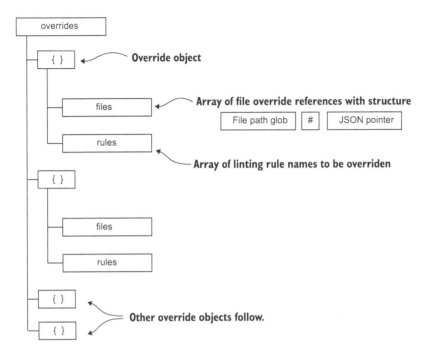

Figure 3.5   Structure of Spectral overrides

Let's see this in action. Consider the chapter3/overrides/openapi.yaml file, which is shown in part here. Notice that the GET /users/{id} has an operationId defined, but the PUT /users/{id} and DELETE /users/{id} operations do not:

```
openapi: 3.0.0
info:
  title: User API
  version: 1.0.0
servers:
  - url: http://localhost:8080
paths:
  /users/{id}:
    get:
      summary: Get a user by id
      operationId: getUserById          ⟵┐ OperationId
      parameters:                            defined
        - name: id
          in: path
          required: true
          schema:
            type: integer
      responses:
        '200':
          description: OK
```

```
put:
  summary: Update a user by id        ◁──────┐
  parameters:                                 │
    - name: id                                │
      in: path                                │
      required: true                          │
      schema:                        No OperationId
        type: integer                defined
  responses:                                  │
    '200':                                    │
      description: OK                         │
delete:                                       │
  summary: Delete a user by id        ◁───────┘
  parameters:
    - name: id
      in: path
      required: true
      schema:
        type: integer
  responses:
    '204':
      description: No Content
```

Suppose you had an `operation-must-have-operationId` rule but wanted to disable all the rules in the file. Your ruleset file could look like the chapter3/overrides/ruleset1.yaml file:

```
overrides:                    │ Disables the
  - files:                    │ rule for the
    - openapi.yaml    ◁───┘   entire file                     Changes the severity
    rules:                                                    of the rule to off,
      operation-must-have-operationId: off       ◁──          which disables it
rules:
  operation-must-have-operationId:
    message: 'Each operation must have an operationId'
    severity: error
    given: '$.paths[*][get,put,post,delete,options,head,patch,trace]'
    then:
      field: operationId
      function: truthy
```

Test this against the openapi.yaml file by navigating into the chapter3/overrides directory and running the command `spectral lint openapi.yaml --ruleset ruleset1 .yaml`. You get no results linting violations as shown here:

```
No results with a severity of 'error' found!
```

Now turn off the linting rule for the PUT /users/{id} operation, but set the severity of the operation to `warn`, as shown in the chapter3/overrides/ruleset2.yaml file here. Note that the JSON pointer to the API operation has to be percent-encoded (so it's /paths/~1users~1%7Bid%7D/put, not /paths/~1users~1{id}/put):

```
overrides:
  - files:
      - openapi.yaml#/paths/~1users~1%7Bid%7D/put          ◁──   Percent-encoded
    rules:                                                        JSON pointer
      operation-must-have-operationId: off
  - files:
      - openapi.yaml#/paths/~1users~1%7Bid%7D/delete             Linting rule severity
    rules:                                                        overridden from
      operation-must-have-operationId: warn              ◁──   error to warning
rules:
  operation-must-have-operationId:
    message: 'Each operation must have an operationId'
    severity: error
    given: '$.paths[*][get,put,post,delete,options,head,patch,trace]'
    then:
      field: operationId
      function: truthy
```

Running linting on this file returns only a warning-level linting violation for the `delete` operation, even though the `PUT` operation has the same problem, as shown here:

```
$ spectral lint openapi.yaml --ruleset ruleset2.yaml
36:12  warning  operation-must-have-operationId  Each operation must have an
operationId  paths./users/{id}.delete
```

You've now seen how to override API linting rules in Spectral. Consider using the gradual consistency approach when introducing API linting to an existing production API by using overrides. However, use this feature carefully because where possible, you want to make your API design comply with your style guide without exception.

As you've seen, when writing a linting rule, you have to be careful to follow the linting rule syntax correctly. For Spectral, you need to specify a JSONPath expression, and this can involve playing with a JSONPath expression evaluator so you get the expression just right. What if you wanted an artificial intelligence (AI) assistant to help you create linting rules so you could create them quickly? And what if the AI assistant could help you generate tests for the rule so you could quickly validate that it works? I'll show you how to do this, but first, let me introduce you to AI assistants.

3.10   *Introducing AI coding assistants*

An AI assistant is a type of software agent that uses AI to execute tasks based on the commands or queries it receives from its user. AI assistants are capable of understanding human language, thanks to natural language processing (NLP), which allows users to interact with them using text prompts. One specific type of AI assistant is the AI coding assistant, which is designed to assist software developers. These assistants provide suggestions and completions for whole lines of code and entire functions. Some examples of AI coding assistants are GitHub CoPilot, Tabnine, Amazon Code-Whisperer, Sourcegraph Cody, and JetBrains AI.

A coding assistant helps developers analyze code, generate code, and provide personalized and relevant code improvement suggestions, including bug fixes. They do this by sending instructions and the code context to a large language model (LLM), which is an AI model trained on massive datasets to enable it to generate human-like responses. LLMs use deep learning techniques such as transformers (a type of neural network designed for understanding the contextual relationships within language and other complex language tasks) to understand the context, syntax, and semantics of language. This enables LLMs to perform content generation, translation, and conversation tasks. LLMs continuously learn and improve as they are exposed to new data and feedback.

GitHub Copilot is an AI assistant designed by GitHub and powered by LLMs developed by OpenAI. This AI assistant provides suggestions for a wide range of programming languages and software frameworks and is especially adept at Python, JavaScript, TypeScript, Go, Ruby, C++, and C#. By automating routine coding tasks, Copilot acts as a junior pair programmer and raises the level of abstraction so that developers focus on higher-level problems and less on things such as boilerplate code and code syntax. In essence, Copilot helps developers be more productive.

Coding assistants are designed to help developers work more efficiently, but they aren't a replacement for understanding the fundamental concepts of the programming language and tools being used. Developers still need to test and review the generated code. One of the reasons for this is that LLMs can hallucinate; that is, they can generate incorrect, nonsensical, or misleading information and present it as accurate. And because LLMs aren't search engines, they don't usually cite what their response is based on.

There are also legal and ethical considerations around data privacy, licensing, and copyright when using LLMs. The LLM's training data is drawn from code repositories that may have biases. As I've mentioned regarding hallucinations, there is also a risk that the code generated may not be semantically or syntactically correct or may have security vulnerabilities.

> **TIP** For a general (and fun) introduction to LLMs, see *The Complete Obsolete Guide to Generative AI* by David Clinton (Manning, 2023; https://mng.bz/5l2D).

In the following sections, I describe how to use a Copilot as a coding assistant to generate API linting rules. To do this, you need to provide Copilot with prompts, as discussed next.

3.10.1 Prompting Copilot to create linting rules

Prompt engineering is about carefully crafting good prompts—instructions, context, and examples for LLMs—so that the LLMs can generate more useful responses. The GitHub Copilot extension helps you with prompt engineering by analyzing the context of your code, but you can help it by providing hints and examples as guidance.

Copilot provides inline suggestions as you type, and you can press the Tab key to accept them. The Copilot chat extension provides an inline chat interface that helps you talk with Copilot while writing code. Here is how you can use this to create a linting rule.

In section 3.6, you wrote a linting rule that verifies the `$.info.description` field is present in an OpenAPI file. Now let GitHub Copilot help you create this rule. First, create a chapter3/copilot/rules.yaml file. With the file open, press ⌘–I on Mac or Ctrl–I on Windows to bring up the Copilot inline chat. In the inline chat, enter the following prompt:

```
Write a Spectral linting rule for an OpenAPI file that
  checks that the info.description field is present
```

LLMs are nondeterministic, so the code they generate may differ between runs. For me, this generated the following:

```
rules:
  openapi-info-description-present:
    description: "Check if the info.description field is present"
    message: "The info.description field is missing"
    given: "$.info"
    then:
      field: "description"
      function: "truthy"
```

Click the button to accept this suggestion. Now how about writing a test to verify that this works? Create a chapter3/copilot/openapi.yaml file. With it open, again press ⌘–I on Mac or Ctrl–I on Windows to bring up the Copilot inline chat, and provide the following prompt:

```
Create an OpenAPI document to test the rule. The document
  should make the rule fail.
```

For me, Copilot generated the following:

```
openapi: 3.0.0
info:
  title: My API                    ◁──┤  No info.description
  version: 1.0.0                        property present
paths:
  /path/to/endpoint:
    get:
      summary: Endpoint Summary
      description: Endpoint Description
      responses:
        '200':
          description: Successful response
          content:
            application/json:
              schema:
                type: object
```

Switch to the chapter3/copilot directory, and then run the linting rule against the test OpenAPI document to check that the rule works:

```
spectral lint openapi.yaml --ruleset rules.yaml
```

You should get a linting rule violation validating that the rule is correct.

Here are some things you can do to provide Copilot with good prompts when working with VS Code:

- Copilot looks at the file you're working in and other open files in your editor. Leaving open files related to the problem you're solving, such as related OpenAPI documents and Spectral rulesets, gives Copilot more context to generate appropriate suggestions.
- Providing a top-level comment with a high-level introduction to the file's contents gives Copilot some overall context.
- Providing some sample code that is close to what you're working on can also help Copilot. For example, you can paste a related linting rule in your ruleset file so that Copilot can use that as a sample. You can delete this sample code later if you wish.
- When working in code (in chapter 9, I discuss writing Spectral rules in JavaScript files and writing JavaScript unit tests for them), provide relevant import or include statements at the top of the file to let Copilot know what dependencies, libraries, and frameworks you're using. Using meaningful function names and function comments also helps in providing details to Copilot on how to generate code for a specific function. In the comments, you can provide the expected inputs and outputs of the function as well.
- Thinking about what order you create your code in is important. I like creating the linting rule and then asking Copilot to create OpenAPI documents to test it with.
- One aspect of Spectral linting rules that can be a challenge is writing JSON-Path, JSON pointer, and regular expressions. The good news is that Copilot can help you with these. You can prompt Copilot to create the expression. You can also ask Copilot to create sample code to test the expression by logging the result to standard output (e.g., `console.log()` with JavaScript).

TIP For an example of using Copilot for regular expressions, watch the video at www.youtube.com/watch?v=dTAZui3k4LU. For a general introduction to Copilot, see the video at www.youtube.com/watch?v=Fi3AJZZregI.

I've demonstrated how a coding assistant can assist you in creating, writing, and testing Spectral linting rules using YAML. If you're wondering if you can have linting rules in natural language but without any code, the answer is yes—and I'll explain how in the next section.

3.11   *Using LLMs for automated linting*

Imagine you want to create a linting rule stating that all request and response object property names implying they are monetary amounts must have values in a number format; that is, you don't want monetary amounts as strings. For example, this rule should ensure that the value of a property named `cost_price` is a number. Sure, you can add a Spectral linting rule that checks the value of any property named `cost_price` in number format, but what about `selling_price` or just `price`? And what about `amount` and `vat_amount`? There are so many property names that may imply monetary amounts that defining them all in a Spectral rule would be impractical.

In addition, consider the case where you want to automatically check that the description provided for a property is meaningful. For example, rather than a description that just says "The vat_amount," you want the property `vat_amount` to have a meaningful description such as this: "Amount of value added tax (VAT) added to an item's price. This depends on the configured VAT rate." So how would you write a Spectral rule that checks to ensure every property description is meaningful? This isn't just about checking the length of the description or using a regular expression. Again, there is no easy way to do this using just Spectral.

Here are two more examples of generic linting rules you may want to enforce:

- URI paths must use nouns to represent resources.
- If a GET operation has query parameters that appear sensitive or have personally identifiable information (e.g., `date_of_birth` or `first_name`), require the operation to use the `POST` method instead.

There are many cases like these where it may not be possible or practical to write a Spectral rule. Usually, teams reserve detecting things like this for the API review (API design reviews are discussed in chapter 5). However, there is an automated method—using an LLM. LLMs can run linting on code with the rules you provide and give you violation reports in the format you specify. There is a cost-benefit to this method—it's much cheaper to have the LLM do automated linting on changed files than the time cost of a senior engineer being involved in API reviews. There is also a time-saving benefit to using natural language to specify linting rules. Team members who may not be versed in Spectral rule syntax or the syntax of any other linting tool can still write linting rules.

3.11.1   *Linting with Anthropic Claude*

Let's look at an example of OpenAPI linting with an LLM. Suppose that, using the first scenario I proposed in this section, you want a linting rule stating that all property names that imply monetary amounts must have values in a number format. You want to lint the chapter3/llm-linting/openapi.yaml OpenAPI document, which has only one operation: `GET /v1/products`. The operation returns a response with four properties: `id`, `cost_price`, `selling_price`, and `vat_amount`. Now try this with Anthropic Claude. (If you've followed the instructions in appendix B, you've set up an Anthropic Claude account.)

Log in to Anthropic Claude (https://claude.ai). Using the chat interface, upload the chapter3/llm-linting/openapi.yaml file. Now give it the following prompt:

```
I have attached an OpenAPI document. List all response properties
⟹ whose names imply that they are a monetary amount.
```

In my run, Claude gave me the following result:

```
Based on the OpenAPI document you provided, the response properties
⟹ whose names imply they are monetary amounts are:
- cost_price
- selling_price
- vat_amount
The reasons are:
- cost_price - The "cost" in the name implies this is the
⟹ cost price of the product, which is a monetary amount.
- selling_price - The "price" in the name clearly indicates
⟹ this is the selling price of the product, which is a monetary value.
- vat_amount - "VAT" stands for Value Added Tax, which is a
⟹ monetary amount charged on products.
So in summary, these 3 property names directly indicate
⟹ they store monetary/currency values.
```

Now provide it with the following prompt to lint the OpenAPI document:

```
Lint the OpenAPI document based on the following rule:
- If a property's name implies it is a monetary amount,
⟹ it must use number format. Show me the linting rule violations.
⟹ An example of a violation can be: "The property 'cost_price'
⟹ implies a monetary amount but is defined with 'type: string'.
⟹ It should be defined with 'type: number' to accurately
⟹ represent a monetary value."
```

In my run, Claude provided the following response:

```
Based on the linting rule to check that properties implying monetary
⟹ amounts use number format, here are the violations in the OpenAPI
⟹ document:
1. The property 'cost_price' implies a monetary amount but is defined with
⟹ 'type: string'. It should be defined with 'type: number' to accurately
⟹ represent a monetary value.
2. The property 'selling_price' implies a monetary amount but is defined
⟹ with 'type: string'. It should be defined with 'type: number' to
⟹ accurately represent a monetary value.
3. The property 'vat_amount' implies a monetary amount but is defined with
⟹ 'type: string'. It should be defined with 'type: number' to accurately
⟹ represent a monetary value.
In summary, the properties cost_price, selling_price, and vat_amount
⟹ violate the linting rule that monetary amount properties should use
⟹ type number instead of type string. Defining them as numbers will make
⟹ the API more accurate.
```

You didn't tell Claude the exact name of the properties to check for, but it successfully found the four properties you expected and gave you the violation message using the format you specified.

But doing this via a chat interface isn't ideal for developers who spend most of the time working in their text editor or IDE. Instead, you can integrate an LLM like this into a linting tool that runs in your CI/CD pipeline by using the Optic API tool (www.useoptic.com).

3.11.2 *Linting with Optic's LintGPT*

Optic is an automated API governance tool that does API discovery, breaking change checks, and OpenAPI diff generation. Optic supports natural language AI linting rules, which it calls LintGPT. Optic is a proprietary tool, but it does have a free tier. Although at the time of writing, you need to be on the paid enterprise tier to use the LintGPT rules, I'll provide a brief introduction to how it works here.

First, you specify LintGPT rules in its configuration file, optic.yaml, at the root of the project directory. The following shows an example of two LintGPT rules:

```
ruleset:
  - lintgpt:
      v3_standards:
        rules:
          - "If a property's name implies it is a monetary amount,
 it must use number format."
          - "GET responses with a top level data property of type
 array should have some form of pagination."
```

Using "must" specifies an error-level severity.

Using "should" specifies a warning-level severity.

When Optic runs the LintGPT rules, you get the following errors:

```
[Warn] The response for the GET request contains a top-level 'data'
 property of type array but does not include any form of pagination.
 Pagination is important for performance and usability when dealing with
 potentially large datasets.

[Error] The properties 'cost_price', 'selling_price', and 'vat_amount'
 imply monetary amounts but are defined with 'type: string'. They should
 be defined with 'type: number' to accurately represent monetary values.
```

Optic provides a UI that makes it easy to see which areas of the API definition file the linting violation applies to, as shown in figure 3.6.

Let's recap. You've seen that LLMs can be used to define linting rules that you can easily create in traditional linting tools such as Spectral. LLMs make it possible to define linting rules in natural language, thus making the writing of linting rules accessible to more people on the team (not just those who know the syntax of a particular linting tool). However, when using LLMs, you need to test the output and make sure it's finding the right problems before rolling it out.

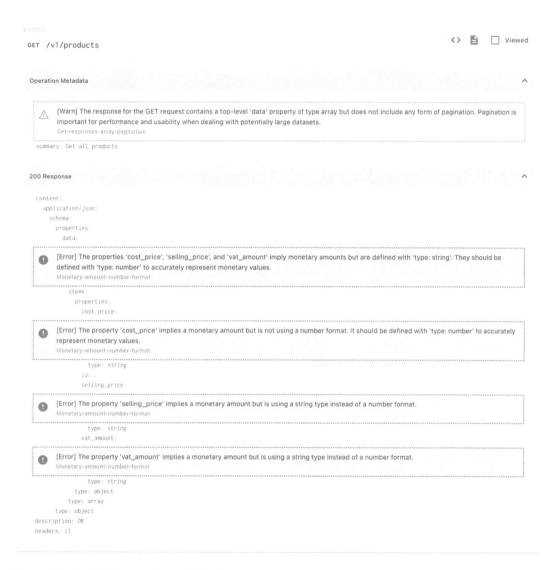

Figure 3.6   LintGPT linting violations in Optic

Summary

- An API style guide is a reference document containing an organization's API design conventions and guidelines.
- API linting is an automated way of checking that an API definition complies with the style guide, and it's an important part of the design stage of your API-Ops workflow.

- You can use Spectral as an API linting tool to execute rulesets containing executable rules based on your API style guide. Spectral can be run on the command line but also has integrations, plugins, and extensions with many editors and API design tools.

- You write Spectral rules by defining the JSONPath expression that locates the elements in the API definition document to check and specifying a Spectral function to do the required check.

- Using the `extends` property, you can import one or more Spectral rulesets defined locally or remotely.

- When adding new rulesets to an existing OpenAPI document, you can adopt a gradual consistency approach and disable rules for specific parts of the document.

- AI coding assistants can help you create API linting rules. You can also ask an LLM to lint an OpenAPI document with the rules you provide.

Breaking change checks: Managing API evolution

This chapter covers

- Running breaking change checks
- Using API versioning schemes
- Defining a breaking change policy

At the design stage of your API product, your API team iterates on your API design and updates your OpenAPI definition files. It's useful to know whether any change your team introduces isn't backward compatible. In this chapter, I show how to use API diff tools to understand API definition file changes and how to detect which of them are breaking changes. One way to avoid introducing breaking changes to existing API consumers is API versioning, and I discuss different API versioning schemes and scopes used by different organizations. I also explain the costs of introducing new API versions and how you can communicate your API change management approach to consumers using a breaking change policy document. I end the chapter by providing some tips on managing breaking changes in your workflow. The topics covered in this chapter will be of importance to both API developers and API product managers and owners.

If you've followed the instructions in section B.8 of appendix B to set up the API tools, then you have the Tufin/oasdiff tool installed for the exercises in this chapter.

To work on the exercises in this chapter, navigate to the chapter4 directory in this book's code repository at https://github.com/apiopsbook/apiops.

4.1   API definition changes in your APIOps workflow

At the publish stage of your API product life cycle, when you publish a new version of an API definition file, your API consumers will likely want to know what has changed between the old and new API versions. But even earlier than that, if you're asked to review an API definition file change at the design stage, before diving into the detail of inspecting the file, you would probably first want to understand what changed at a structural level (not just a simple text file diff). For example, was a new path added? Was a new response attribute added? Was an endpoint removed? Sometimes this is easy to spot if the change is small or if it's a brand-new API definition file (so everything is new), but if you have several changes to a large existing API definition file, it may not be so easy to work out. And lastly, it's important to know if any existing consumers that integrate with the API will keep working when the change is released; that is, if the change is backward compatible. Figure 4.1 illustrates the points in your API-Ops workflow where it's helpful to answer the question of what changed.

4.2   The problem of understanding what changed

Suppose you're asked to review a change to an API definition file. Let's say the old version of the API definition is in file api.yaml, and the new version of the API definition is in apiv2.yaml. In the new version, an endpoint GET /v1/catalog/categories was removed (including any reference objects linked only to it). In addition, the description and headers of endpoint GET /v1/catalog/products were updated. Two new header values—x-rate-limit and x-rate-limit-remaining—were also added. This is illustrated in figure 4.2.

But imagine that you haven't been told what changed. Yes, you can do a simple text diff to see which lines have changed across the two files, but how do you quickly work out what API operations the changed lines relate to? You can render the API definition file and see what operations the changed lines belong to, but that takes some working out. Is there a simple way to quickly get a high-level view of what changed? Ideally, this high-level view should show the changes to the OpenAPI document structure.

Before you proceed with solving this problem, take a step back and review the structure of an OpenAPI definition file. An OpenAPI definition document can be in JSON or YAML format, and the root object in the document is the OpenAPI object. As in OpenAPI version 3.0, this has fields, as shown in figure 4.3.

The OpenAPI paths object can have several path item objects, and each path item object can have several child operation objects, as shown in figure 4.4.

Representing changes to API definition files as changes to the OpenAPI document structure can give you the high-level view you need. OpenAPI diff tools that present changes to you using the OpenAPI document structure can help you do this.

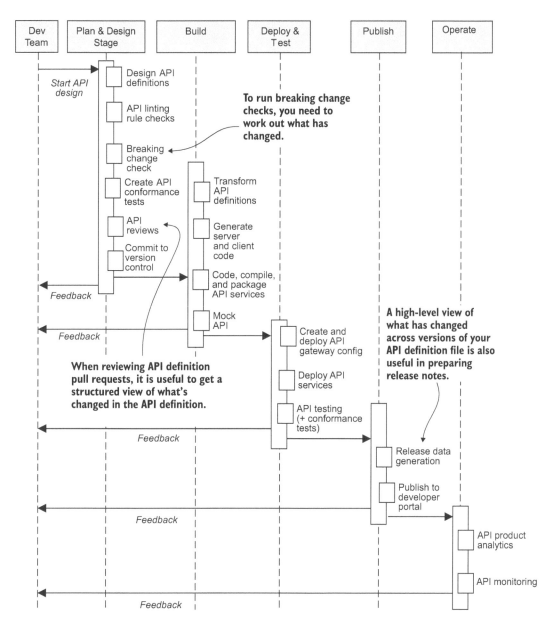

Figure 4.1   Points in your APIOps workflow where it's useful to get a structured view of what has changed in your API definition files

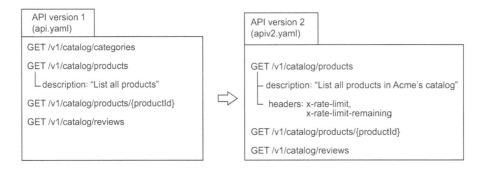

Figure 4.2   Two versions of an API definition file showing one endpoint and another updated

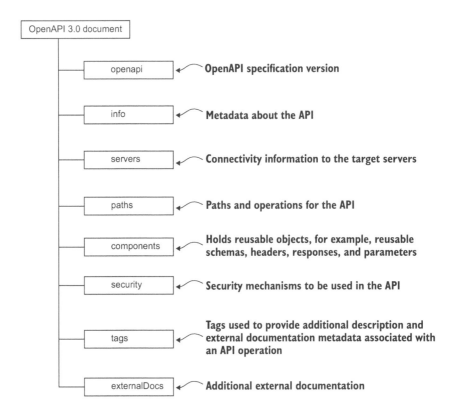

Figure 4.3   Top-level structure of an OpenAPI document structure

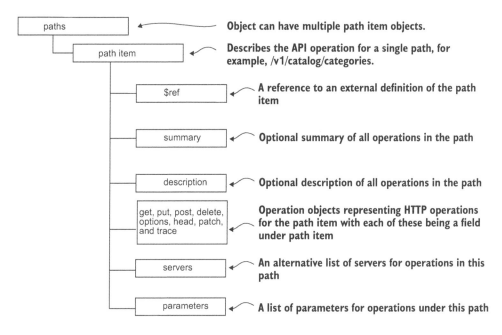

Figure 4.4   The OpenAPI object hierarchy showing paths, path item, and operation objects

4.3   *API diffs*

An OpenAPI diff tool takes the before and after versions of an OpenAPI definition file as inputs and outputs information about the OpenAPI objects that have changed across the versions. In this scenario, a diff between the two versions of the API definition files—api.yaml and apiv2.yaml—should show that one endpoint was removed and another updated, as illustrated in figure 4.5.

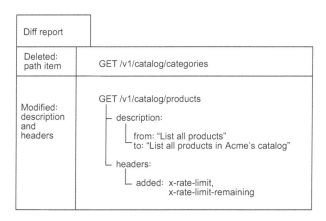

Figure 4.5   A conceptual diff report shows what has changed between two versions of an API definition file.

One such diff tool is Tufin/oasdiff (https://github.com/Tufin/oasdiff), which I describe in this chapter. But it's not the only open source API diff tool. Others include openapi-diff (https://github.com/OpenAPITools/openapi-diff) and optic (https://github.com/opticdev/optic).

> **TIP** Some other interesting commercial API tools have been designed to check for breaking changes. Bump.sh (https://bump.sh) offers an API definition change management solution that includes checks for breaking changes and features a very neat, automatically generated API changelog. Unlike many other tools I've encountered, Relio (www.getrelio.com) detects breaking changes by performing code analysis on the application code. It then compares the results against the OpenAPI definitions to ensure the API documentation is comprehensive and accurate.

OpenAPI diff tools allow you to report the diff in different formats (e.g., YAML, JSON, Markdown, or HTML). As command-line tools, they are well suited to running in your continuous integration/continuous delivery (CI/CD) pipeline. With Tufin/oasdiff, its default diff output is in YAML format. I've chosen Tufin/oasdiff for this chapter because its default YAML diff output follows the OpenAPI specification's (OAS) hierarchical object model. Note that at the time of writing, it supports OpenAPI 3.0, but support for 3.1 is planned.

In your chapter project, you can run the following to see the difference between the two versions of the API definition:

```
$ oasdiff diff api.yaml apiv2.yaml
```

This gives the following output:

```
paths:
    deleted:
        - /v1/catalog/categories
    modified:
        /v1/catalog/products:
            operations:
                modified:
                    GET:
                        description:
                            from: List all products.
                            to: List all products in Acme's catalog.
                        responses:
                            modified:
                                "200":
                                    headers:
                                        added:
                                            - x-rate-limit-hour
                                            - x-rate-limit-remaining
    ...
    components:
        schemas:
            deleted:
                - CategoriesResponse
```

The description of GET /v1/catalog/products was updated with "in Acme's catalog".

Path /v1/catalog/categories was deleted (including the referenced CategoriesResponse component).

Two new headers were added to the 200 response for GET /v1/catalog/products.

The diff report has a top-level `paths` node whose value is a mapping that can have three possible keys: `added`, `deleted`, or `modified`. The value of each of these keys lists all the `paths` whose changes fall under these headings. When a path appears in the modified category, it goes further to list the operation objects that were modified and what the modifications are—again, using the `added`, `deleted`, or `modified` headings.

Tufin/oasdiff has an alternative and simpler model of presenting the diff. This model groups changes by `endpoints` rather than `paths`. An endpoint is the combination of a path and an operation, for example, `GET /v1/catalog/products`. This model renders a top-level `endpoints` node whose value can also have three possible keys: `added`, `deleted`, or `modified`. The value of each of these keys lists all the `endpoints` whose changes fall under these headings. Again, when an endpoint appears in the modified category, it goes further to list the operation objects that were modified and what the modifications are—again using the `added`, `deleted`, or `modified` headings. You can see this in the following part of the output:

```
...
endpoints:                          The GET /v1/catalog/categories endpoint was deleted
    deleted:                ◁───┘   (including the referenced CategoriesResponse component).
        - method: GET
          path: /v1/catalog/categories
    modified:                       ◁
        ?   method: GET             The description of GET
            path: /v1/catalog/products   /v1/catalog/products was updated
        :   description:        ◁   with "in Acme's catalog".
                from: List all products.
                to: List all products in Acme's catalog.
            responses:
                modified:           Two new headers were added
                    "200":          to the 200 response for GET
                        headers:    ◁── /v1/catalog/products.
                            added:
                                - x-rate-limit-hour
                                - x-rate-limit-remaining
components:
    schemas:
        deleted:
            - CategoriesResponse
```

The only difference between the paths and endpoints model is that in the paths model, a change is represented as a node whose key is a YAML scalar—a path string—while in the endpoint model, a change is represented as a node with a YAML mapping object—the path and the HTTP operation.

Can a YAML entry have two elements as a key?

The native data structure in YAML is the node. There are three kinds of nodes: scalar nodes (e.g., strings or digits), sequence nodes (an ordered series of nodes), and mapping nodes (an unordered set of key/value node pairs). This is shown in the following figure.

(continued)

Sequence nodes begin with a leading hyphen (-), and mapping nodes have a colon (:) between the key and value elements.

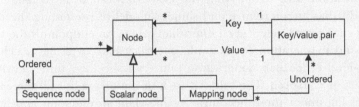

Unified Modeling Language diagram of YAML node model

Most YAML files you've encountered probably use only scalar nodes as mapping node keys. Here is an example of a YAML mapping node with a scalar node key `deleted` and a sequence node value:

```
deleted:
    - method: GET
      path: /v1/catalog/categories
```

However, you can also use a sequence node or another mapping node as a mapping node key. This is called a complex mapping key. Here is an example of a YAML mapping node with a mapping node as a key—indicated by the ? character—and another mapping node as the value:

```
?    method: GET
     path: /v1/catalog/products
:    description:
         from: List all products.
         to: List all products in Acme's catalog.
```

Tufin/oasdiff uses complex mapping keys for an endpoint diff model, as shown in this example:

```
endpoints:
    deleted:
        - method: GET
          path: /v1/catalog/categories          Complex mapping
    modified:                                    key starts with ?.
        ?    method: GET
             path: /v1/catalog/products          The value of the complex
        :    description:                        mapping key starts with :.
                 from: List all products.
                 to: List all products in Acme's catalog.
             responses:
                 modified:
                     "200":
                         headers:
```

```
                        added:
                            - x-rate-limit-remaining
                            - x-rate-limit-hour
```

To find out more about the YAML specification, see https://yaml.org/spec.

With the full diff report from oasdiff, you now know where to focus when reviewing apiv2.yaml. If you want a summary of the changes and not the full diff, you can get one by running the following command:

```
oasdiff summary api.yaml apiv2.yaml
```

This should give you the following output:

```
diff: true
details:
    endpoints:
        deleted: 1
        modified: 1
    paths:
        deleted: 1
        modified: 1
    schemas:
        deleted: 1
```

4.4   Detecting breaking changes

A *breaking change* is a change that forces an API consumer to change their code to ensure their application keeps working. In other words, it's a non–backward-compatible API change that causes client applications that integrate with the API to stop working or suffer degraded service. For example, removing an API path (e.g., /v1/catalog/categories in the previous scenario) means that existing consumers who make a call to that endpoint now receive a 404 Not Found error. On the other hand, a nonbreaking or backward-compatible change causes no disruption to API consumers, and they can extend their code to use it at their own time and convenience.

Imagine you want to find out if any of the changes in apiv2.yaml in your chapter project are breaking changes. Using Tufin/oasdiff, you can compare it with the original version to work this out by running the following on your command line:

```
oasdiff breaking api.yaml apiv2.yaml
```

This gives you the following output:

```
1 breaking changes: 1 error, 0 warning
error    [api-path-removed-without-deprecation] at
⇨ original_source=api.yaml
    in API GET /v1/catalog/categories
        api path removed without deprecation
```

This shows you that removing the /v1/catalog/categories path is a breaking change. But the output doesn't have to be text; you can get it in JSON format too by running the following:

```
oasdiff breaking api.yaml apiv2.yaml --format json
```

You should see the following output:

```
[
  {
    "id": "api-path-removed-without-deprecation",
    "text": "api path removed without deprecation",
    "level": 3,
    "operation": "GET",
    "operationId": "listCategories",
    "path": "/v1/catalog/categories",
    "source": "api.yaml",
    "section":"paths"
  }
]
```

Great! You can now run an automated check to see if a change introduced to your API definition file is a breaking change. However, there is a special case of a breaking change you may want to treat differently—sunsetting an API—discussed next.

Deprecation is about notifying API consumers that an API or an API endpoint will be removed in the future, and *sunsetting* is about making the API unavailable in production after the deprecation window has closed. I discuss more on deprecation and sunsetting later.

Now imagine that you have an API endpoint deprecated in an API definition file, and the time has come to sunset it. Let's say that in your chapter4 directory, apiv1-dep.yaml is the API definition file with the deprecated GET /v1/catalog/categories endpoint, and apiv2.yaml is the API definition where you have sunset (i.e., removed) the endpoint. Sunsetting an endpoint is a special kind of breaking change—one you've notified your users about beforehand—so you may not want your automated breaking change check to fail in that case. How can you run a breaking change check that ignores the endpoint you've sunset?

Tufin/oasdiff allows you to do this using the x-sunset OpenAPI extension. When checking for breaking changes, oasdiff ignores any endpoints with an x-sunset date in the past.

> ### OpenAPI Specification extensions
> OAS extensions allow the OAS to be extended to support specific use cases by allowing additional data to be added to your API definition files. You can use this custom data to provide data that is there for documentation purposes or to enable some third-party tool to operate on the API definition file.

> To specify an extension property, you specify fields following the pattern "x-". An example is using the `x-sunset` field to specify the sunset date of an API. Note that field names beginning with `x-oai` and `x-oas-` are reserved by the specification.

You can check this out by running a breaking change diff between apiv1-dep.yaml and apiv2.yaml. In apiv1-dep.yaml, you can see from the following snippet that the deprecated `GET /v1/catalog/categories` endpoint has the `deprecated:true` property and also has the sunset date specified with the `x-sunset` property:

```
paths:
  /v1/catalog/categories:
    get:
      deprecated: true
      x-sunset: "2022-08-30"
      tags:
        - Categories
      summary: List all categories
```

Run the following command to check for breaking changes:

```
oasdiff breaking apiv1-dep.yaml apiv2.yaml
```

You get no breaking change message output because 2022-08-30 is a date in the past. Remove or comment out the `x-sunset` line, and rerun the check. This time, you should get a breaking change message.

TIP To see the changes Tufin/oasdiff considers as breaking, see https://mng.bz/aEAB.

One more interesting feature about Tufin/oasdiff is that it allows you to modify the prefix of the endpoints in the API definition before comparison. For example, suppose that in moving from api.yaml to new version apiv3.yaml, the prefix of all the URI paths was changed from `/v1/` to `/v2/`. `GET /v1/catalog/products` is the same as `GET /v2/catalog/products` apart from the changed path prefix, that is, `/v1/` to `/v2/`. Ignoring the changed path prefix, you may want to know what other breaking changes have been introduced. You can do this by making the URI prefixes the same before comparison. oasdiff allows you to do this by specifying an alternative prefix either for the base version or for the revised version.

To see this, run the following diff command, which changes the prefix of the base version to `/v2/` before comparison:

```
oasdiff diff api.yaml apiv3.yaml --strip-prefix-base /v1/
➥  --prefix-base /v2/
```

The `strip-prefix-base` flag removes the `/v1/` prefix from api.yaml paths, and the `-prefix-base` gives them a new `/v2/` prefix. This occurs only in memory and doesn't affect the file. You can do something similar to the revised version by using the `-strip-prefix-revision` and `-prefix-revision` flags.

You've seen how to run the API diff tool locally to check for breaking changes. In chapter 8, I revisit this when I discuss how to run your breaking change checks in a CI pipeline. Before I finish discussing API diff tools, I want to mention a use case in which they come in handy—generating the basis for an API changelog entry—in the following section.

4.5   *Generating API changelogs*

An API changelog is a historical record of all changes made to an API over time. It serves as a detailed logbook of additions, modifications, and removals of different elements within the API, such as changes to the following:

- *Endpoints*—A list of new endpoints that have been added to offer new functionalities and any old ones that have been deprecated or removed
- *Parameters*—A list of parameters within existing endpoints that have changed their data types, become optional/mandatory, or disappeared altogether
- *Response formats*—A list of changes to the structure of data returned from the API, for example, where new fields have been added, unnecessary ones removed, or the message format changed entirely
- *Authentication and authorization*—A description of changes to the API's security mechanisms

By keeping track of the changelog, developers can stay informed about any updates to the API that might affect their applications and proactively adjust their code to maintain compatibility and functionality. Thus, it acts as a communication channel to help developers anticipate changes and address any compatibility or stability problems beforehand.

Across different API providers, the level of detail and format of the changelog varies. Some changelogs are simple lists of changes, while others might include more details, such as these:

- Versioning information and date
- Descriptions of new features, enhancements, and bug fixes
- A list of breaking changes
- Deprecation timelines
- Support information and links to related documentation

Here is an example of an entry to an API changelog:

```
API Changelog
Version 2.1.1
Date: 2023-09-08
New features and enhancements:
• Optimized /search endpoint performance by 20% using caching mechanisms.
Added support for pagination to /products endpoint with limit and offset
```

```
    parameters.
Breaking changes:
• Removed legacy_mode parameter from /users endpoint. Use the new version
  header instead.
• Data type of price field in /products response changed from string to
  float.
Bug fixes:
• Resolved issue with authentication failing for certain user roles in
  /admin endpoints.
• Fixed incorrect error message returned for invalid requests in /payments
endpoint.
Deprecations:
• Use of old_format flag in /reports endpoint is deprecated. It will be
removed in version 3.0.
Additional notes:
• Please contact support for any migration assistance related to breaking
changes.
```

> **TIP** For other examples of API changelogs, see Intercom's API changelog https://mng.bz/gv8E and Stripe's API changelog https://stripe.com/docs/changelog.

OpenAPI diff tools can help you work out the changes between two different versions of an API definition file to enable you to create an API changelog entry. For example, to generate a changelog entry showing the summary of changes between api.yaml and api2.yaml using Tufin/oasdiff, run the following:

```
oasdiff changelog api.yaml apiv2.yaml
```

This gives you the following output:

```
2 changes: 1 error, 0 warning, 1 info
error   [api-path-removed-without-deprecation] at api.yaml
        in API GET /v1/catalog/categories
                api path removed without deprecation

info    [api-schema-removed]
        in components/schemas
                removed the schema 'CategoriesResponse'
```

Here, `error` indicates it's a breaking change. You can use this output as the basis (editing and formatting as required, and adding any supplementary information) for creating an API changelog entry, which you can publish to your developer portal.

I've discussed how to detect breaking changes and how you can mention breaking changes in your API changelog. Next, I'll cover how breaking changes fit into the evolution of your API.

4.6 Breaking changes and API evolution

As mentioned, a breaking change is a non–backward-compatible change that forces an API consumer to change their code. For REST APIs, compatibility means that the

API client application and the API server can communicate successfully. When a new change is released by the server that isn't compatible with the client application, it means the client application is forced to update, or else it can no longer communicate with the server. This has time and cost implications for the client. On the other hand, a nonbreaking or backward-compatible change doesn't disrupt the API client, and API consumers can extend their client code to use it at their own time and convenience.

An API version is a group of compatible API operations that promises compatibility with client applications over time. Changes to an API version are expected to be stable or nonbreaking. Introducing a breaking change usually means introducing a new API version. Without doing this, the change will need to be coordinated with all API consumers, which can be difficult to do with a widely used API.

But why would a provider introduce breaking changes? APIs evolve as new features get added, existing features get enhanced, and bugs are fixed. Some of those new changes may not be backward compatible. However, once an API has been published, API consumers depend on its behavior. So evolving the API has to be handled with care, or a change in the API can lead to a break in the client code. API evolution is a balancing act between adding new features to improve the API consumer experience and the cost to the API provider of maintaining old API versions. The ideal situation is to evolve the API while reducing the cost of maintaining old API versions.

> **TIP** For smaller organizations just starting out as API providers, setting some basic expectations with external API consumers on how the provider intends to evolve their API is quite important. As part of launching the first public version of the API, I would recommend defining a basic breaking change policy and enforcing that with automated breaking change checks in the API definition pipeline (discussed in chapter 8).

We've looked at what an API version is. Now let's look at how that version can be specified.

4.7   API versioning schemes

Versioning scheme refers to how the API consumer specifies the version of the provider's API they want. There are eight schemes for specifying REST API versions.

4.7.1   Path-based versioning scheme

This versioning scheme is based on the URI. The version identifier is included in the URI path of the API request. A common pattern for this is `https://{domain}/{api-name}/{version-identifier}/{operation-id}`. Here are a few examples:

- Slack's Status API describes the health of the Slack platform and reports on incidents, outages, and maintenance. It uses path parameters with a semantic versioning identifier:
  - The request `curl https://status.slack.com/api/v2.0.0/current` checks for active incidents.

- The request `curl https://status.slack.com/api/v2.0.0/history` provides information on past incidents.
- Twilio's Short Message Service (SMS) API is used for programmable SMS messaging. It uses path-based versioning with a Calendar Versioning identifier (CalVer, which will be discussed later):
  - The request `curl -X GET https://api.twilio.com/2010-04-01/Accounts/{TwilioAccountIdentifier}/Messages/{MessageIdentifier}.json -u {TwilioAccountIdentifier}:{TwilioAuthToken}` fetches a single message from the Twilio servers.
- OpenAI's REST API allows you to run tasks that involve generating natural language or code. It uses path parameters for versioning, with the main version from the semantic version in the path using the `/v{majorVersion}/` pattern:
  - Request `curl https://api.openai.com/v1/models -H 'Authorization: Bearer {api-key}` lists the available language models.

Path-based versioning is the most common versioning scheme in use. This scheme makes it very clear which version is being requested and is simple to understand and implement. In addition, API consumers can explore the API using their browser. However, it can lead to a large number of APIs for the provider, as a new version of an API requires a new path. Technically, it violates the REST guideline that a URI should be a unique identifier for a resource because the URI can change for a new API version even though the underlying resource entity hasn't changed.

4.7.2 Hostname-based versioning scheme

This is also called domain versioning. It's similar to path-based versioning, but the version identifier is specified as part of the hostname instead of the URI path. A common pattern for this is `https://{apiversion}.{domain}.com/uri-path`. For example, Tik-Tok used hostname-based versioning in its v1 API. To fetch information on a TikTok user, an API consumer made a request to `POST https://open-api.tiktok.com/user/info`. TikTok's v2 API is served from a different hostname, and making the same request using the v2 API is `POST https://open.tiktokapis.com/v2/user/info`. Hostname-based versioning allows routing to a different server, but API consumers may need to change their security settings to communicate with the new host.

4.7.3 Query string-based versioning scheme

This versioning scheme provides the version identifier in the API request query string parameter. A common pattern for this is `https://{domain}/{api-name}/{operation-id}?{query-string-parameter-versoin-name}={version-identifier}`. This is simple to understand and use for clients. In some implementations, the server defaults to the newest version if the client doesn't specify a query-string version, but other implementations make the version parameter mandatory.

The Snyk REST API (https://mng.bz/eo8v) uses URI query parameter versioning with a mandatory CalVer identifier. You can make a request as follows:

```
curl -X GET "https://api.snyk.io/rest/groups/?version= 2023-03-08~beta
  --header "Accept: application/vnd.api+json"
```

4.7.4   *Custom-header versioning scheme*

With this scheme, users specify a dedicated header in the request containing the version information. This allows the URI of your resource to remain the same across different versions of the API, unlike the path-based versioning scheme. An example of an API that uses custom version headers is the GitHub REST API. You can make a request as follows:

```
curl --header "X-GitHub-Api-Version:2022-11-28" https://api.github.com/zen
```

If the version header isn't specified in the request, at the time of writing, the GitHub API defaults to the 2022-11-28 version.

4.7.5   *Accept header versioning scheme*

This is also known as content-negotiation versioning or media-type versioning. In this scheme, the version of the API requested is specified in the `Accept` header, along with the media type. Example patterns for this are `Accept: application/vnd.example+ json;version=1.0` and `Accept: application/vnd.example.v1+json`.

GitHub's old REST V3 API (now sunset) used this pattern, with the header `Accept: application/vnd.github.v3+json`. Another example of Accept header versioning is the new Tableau REST API. I discuss this further in section 4.8.2.

4.7.6   *Pinned versioning scheme*

This is also known as point-in-time versioning or dynamic-date versioning. The first time an API consumer makes a request to an API, the current API version is pinned to their account profile and used to process the request. All further API requests from that consumer default to that pinned version. When the API consumer is ready to upgrade to a new API version, they can log in to their account profile and update their default version setting.

An example of this is the Stripe API. Imagine that the current Stripe API version is 2022-11-15, and the first request a new API consumer makes is the following, which fetches the list of charge objects: `curl https://api.stripe.com/v1/charges -u {api-key}`. From then on, all API requests implicitly default to the 2022-11-15 version. To change to a different version of the API, an API consumer can sign into their account on https://dashboard.stripe.com and change the default version for all requests. Note that although the Stripe path does have a `/v1/` path version parameter, it's not actively used.

Plaid also uses the pinned versioning approach. The following Plaid request fetches the bank account, identification numbers, and account balance data associated with a login at a financial institution:

```
curl --request POST https://sandbox.plaid.com/auth/get
➡ --header 'Content-Type: application/json' --data '{"client_id": {Plaid-
    client-id},
  "secret": {Plaid-API-secret},
  "access_token": {access-token}
}'
```

The request will use the API version (e.g., 2020-09-14) defined on the API consumer's account on https://dashboard.plaid.com/team/api.

Square (https://mng.bz/ppo8) is another financial API provider that uses the pinned versioning approach. Stripe, Plaid, and Square combine this pinned versioning approach with other versioning schemes to allow users to override the API version setting at the per-request level. This is explained in section 4.7.8.

The pinned versioning scheme allows API providers to evolve the API without changing the endpoint. The API provider also can see what versions customers use via their account profile information; however, it's complex to implement.

4.7.7 *No versioning scheme*

With this scheme, the API may have a version, but the API consumer can't specify the version of the API they want in the request. For example, AWS S3 API has version 2006-03-01, but an API consumer can't specify an alternative version of the API in the request. To fetch an image resource from an S3 bucket, an API consumer can make the following request:

```
curl https://{bucket-name}.s3.amazonaws.com/my-image.jpg
➡ --header " Authorization: {authorization-string}"
```

As you can see, the API consumer has no option to request a different version of the API. Another example of this is the Slack Web API (https://api.slack.com/web). It's not strictly a REST API, as it provides remote procedure call (RPC) style operations over HTTP, in the format `https://slack.com/api/{method-family}.{method-name}`. Still, anyone familiar with a REST API will be comfortable using it. A consumer can search for messages matching a query by making the following request:

```
curl https://slack.com/api/search.messages?query=test
➡ —header "Authorization: {authorization-string}"
```

API providers who provide no versioning scheme in the request try to provide a stable API with no breaking API changes. But if they have to introduce a breaking change, they must coordinate it with all their consumers, which can be costly.

4.7.8 *Combination of various schemes*

Some APIs allow consumers to specify the version of the API they require in multiple ways. Previously, we looked at how the Stripe API uses a pinned versioning scheme. It also combines this with a custom header versioning scheme to allow users to override the API version on a per-request basis. For example, consider the following request:

```
curl https://api.stripe.com/v1/charges  -u {api-key}:
    -H "Stripe-Version: 2022-11-15"
```

The custom header `Stripe-Version` allows the user to specify the calendar-based version identifier that overrides the default API version setting on their Stripe account. Plaid also follows a similar approach with its `Plaid-Version` header, and Square with its `Square-Version` header.

Note that Stripe also combines these schemes with path parameter versioning (i.e., /v1/) in its path. While Stripe reserves the right to use this approach, it's unlikely to because that would have a huge effect on many users. So as previously mentioned, it's not actively used.

The Foursquare REST API combines query parameter versioning using a mandatory *Calendar Versioning* (*CalVer*) version identifier and path-based versioning. The CalVer version identifier is specified with the 'v' query parameter (CalVer is an API version identifier format based on calendar dates, as discussed in section 4.9.2). For example, to use the Foursquare API to return a list of sushi venues at a given location, a consumer can make the following request:

```
curl --request GET
    https://api.foursquare.com/v2/venues/search?client_id={client-id}
    &client_secret={client-secret}
    &ll={latitude,longitued}
    &query=sushi&v={YYYYMMDD}
```

Even though the API does specify a path-based versioning identifier parameter, /v2/, it's only there for legacy reasons and is unlikely to change.

4.8   API versioning scope

We've looked at API versioning schemes that describe how an API consumer can request a particular version of the API. Another thing to consider is the level or scope at which a provider wants to evolve an API. For example, the provider may want to introduce a change to a small part of the API, say, just one endpoint; the provider may want to evolve a resource used by multiple endpoints; or the provider may want to make a large change, say, change the authentication system used by the whole API, which affects all API operations. The different granularities at which a provider can evolve the API are referred to as the *versioning scope*. This section covers three versioning scopes: global versioning, per-resource versioning, and per-endpoint versioning.

4.8.1   *Global versioning scope*

With global versioning, all API operations have the same version. When a new version is added, all API operations must be updated to match that version. An example is Zoom's API, which uses a path-based versioning scheme with a global versioning scope. The v1 version of the API had operations beginning with the base path `https://api.zoom.us/v1/` as in the following:

- Create a user on Zoom:

```
curl --request POST  https://api.zoom.us/v1/user/create
  -d api_key={api-key} -d api_secret={api-secret}
  -d email={email-address} -d type={user-type}
```

- List scheduled meetings for a user:

```
curl --request POST  https://api.zoom.us/v1/meeting/list
  -d api_key={api-key} -d api_secret={api-secret}
  -d host_id={user_id}
```

- Get information about a Zoom webinar:

```
curl --request POST   https://api.zoom.us/v1/webinar/get
  -d api_key={api-key} -d api_secret={api-secret}
  -d host_id={user_id} -d id={webinar-id}
```

When Zoom upgraded to version 2 of the API, it used OAuth 2.0 for authorization. All the operations were updated to use the `https://api.zoom.us/v2` base path as shown here:

- List scheduled meetings for a user:

```
curl --request GET https://api.zoom.us/v2/users/{userId}/meetings
  --header "Authorization: {access-token}"
```

- Create a user on Zoom:

```
curl --request POST https://api.zoom.us/v2/users
  --header "Authorization: {access-token}"
  -d { "action": "create",  "user_info": {"email":
  "jchill@example.com",  "type": 1 } }
```

- Get information about a Zoom webinar:

```
curl --request GET https://api.zoom.us/v2/webinars/{webinar-id}
  --header "Authorization: {access-token}"
```

Global versioning is commonly used and popular with implementors who use a path-based versioning scheme. It's simple to understand and promises that all operations provided in the API are consistent. However, when using a purely global versioning scope, the cost of updating the version can be high for both the provider and the consumer, especially if the API has many endpoints. API consumers have to reintegrate everything from scratch.

Some API providers who use global versioning rarely update their major versions. For example, Amazon's S3 API uses global versioning but has been very stable over the years. The current version is 2006-03-01.

4.8.2   *Per-resource versioning scope*

With this versioning scope, single resources are versioned instead of versioning the entire API. That is, rather than create a new version of the API, the API provider introduces a new version of a specific resource (or specific resources). Per-resource versioning is commonly used with Accept header and custom header versioning schemes. An example of per-resource versioning is the Tableau API. Tableau's new RESTful endpoints start with the /api/- base path and provide new versions of resources only when the new resource introduces a breaking change. For instance, to list the Tableau dashboard extension settings for a site, the API consumers make the following request:

```
curl --request GET https://us-west-2b.online.tableau.com
  /api/-/settings/site/extensions/dasboard
  --header "Accept: application
  /vnd.tableau.extensions.dashboard.v1.SiteSettings+json"
  --header "X-Tableau-Auth: {authentication-token}"
```

The response has the content-type header set with the resource version as follows:

```
Content-Type:
  application/vnd.tableau.extensions.dashboard.v1.SiteSettings+json
{
  "extensions_enabled": true,
  "allow_sandboxed": true,
  ....
}
```

If the Accept header isn't specified in the request, Tableau serves the latest version of the resource.

> **TIP**   To learn more about Tableau's approach to per-resource versioning, see https://mng.bz/OZXR.

In general, with per-resource versioning, the new version of the resource introduced may not be compatible with the old version. Per-resource versioning gives more granular control of the versioning scope. Introducing a new version can touch a smaller surface area of the codebase. All operations that use a resource should support the new version added, but other API consumers may have to determine if other types of resources work well with the new version of the resource added.

4.8.3 *Per-endpoint versioning scope*

API endpoints (operations) have their own release and support life cycle independent of other endpoints. They have API version numbers that may not apply to other endpoints in the API. This is also called operation or method versioning. An example of this is the Snyk REST API, which uses a query string-based scheme with per-endpoint versioning scope, for example:

```
GET https://api.snyk.io/rest/groups/{group-id}?version=2023-01-30~beta
GET https://api.snyk.io/rest/groups/{group-id}/settings
➥ /iac?version=2021-12-09
```

One advantage of this approach is that it gives granular version controls that enable the provider to grow and evolve the API at an endpoint level while supporting other endpoints. Because each endpoint has its own life cycle, it goes through its own live, deprecation, and sunset phases separate from other endpoints.

> ### Version requested and version served
>
> Some APIs provide the user with information on the version of the API or API resource served to them in their response. The Snyk REST API uses the custom response header `snyk-version-requested` to show the version of the endpoint requested by the caller and another header `snyk-version-served` to show the version of the resource the server returns. The Shopify API uses the customer `X-Shopify-API-Version` response header to show the version of the API used to execute the request, and this can be different from the version specified by the caller in their request. When there is a difference, it indicates that the caller is still using an out-of-date and unsupported version of the API and needs to update their client code to use a supported version.

One challenge with per-endpoint versioning is providing an OpenAPI definition file that the API consumer can use as a consistent whole because each endpoint has its independent version identifier and life cycle and may not interoperate with endpoints of different versions. Snyk solves this problem by allowing users to download the OpenAPI definition file at a given version identifier from their developer portal, for example, https://api.snyk.io/rest/openapi/2023-03-03 or https://api.snyk.io/rest/openapi/2023-02-15~beta. In addition, in the API definition file, each API operation has a specification extension `x-snyk-api-version`, which shows each endpoint's API version, and `x-snyk-api-releases`, which shows all the API versions an endpoint has been released under.

4.9 *API versioning identifiers*

With the different versioning schemes and scopes, API providers can also decide how they want their version identifiers to look. There are three different main options: SemVer, CalVer, and Stability.

4.9.1   *SemVer*

The Semantic Versioning specification (SemVer) https://semver.org recommends a version identifier in the format MAJOR.MINOR.PATCH. The MAJOR version number is incremented for breaking changes, the MINOR version for nonbreaking changes for new functionality, and the PATCH version for nonbreaking bug fixes.

When REST APIs use semantic versioning, they typically only specify the major version in the request. For example, with path-based versioning, the major version is used in the path, such as /v1/ or /v2/. Any breaking changes (i.e., backward-incompatible changes) require the major version number to change. The minor version isn't specified. This allows for a stable API, so new versions are added to the same major API version number.

Some companies put the full SemVer in the `$.info.version` field of the OpenAPI definition. For example, at the time of writing, Pinterest v5 API has an `$.info.version` field value of `5.8.0` in its API definition file but only the major version number in the URI path, for example, `https://api.pinterest.com/v5/user_account`.

> **TIP** You can find the Pinterest OpenAPI definition at https://mng.bz/Y7zB.

eBay also follows the same pattern, for example, with their Inventory API (https://mng.bz/GZBv), but they also return an `X-EBAY-C-VERSION` header in the response with the value of the SemVer.

4.9.2   *CalVer*

The Calendar Versioning (CalVer) convention (https://calver.org), mentioned earlier, is based on a project's release calendar. Software projects use different CalVer formats, but for REST APIs, a commonly used pattern is to make the API version identifier the date the API was released. The Stripe API uses CalVer in the format YYYY-MM-DD (e.g., 2022-11-15), while Shopify's Admin API uses a CalVer identifier in the YYYY-MM format. People are calendar oriented and may find this easier to remember. As described in section 4.7.6 on the pinned versioning scheme, the Stripe API also uses CalVer.

4.9.3   *Stability version*

This is a special version name that indicates the stability level of the API. The API can specify named versions such as stable, unstable, beta, and alpha to indicate the stability level of the API. Shopify's REST Admin API uses path-based versioning with CalVer version identifiers, for example, GET `https://{shop}.myshpoify/admin/api/2023-01/products.json`. But it also supports using a version identifier, `unstable`, to allow API consumers to preview features and changes that are still being designed and built, as in this example: GET `https://{shop}.myshpoify/admin/api/unstable/products.json`. The unstable version can contain breaking changes, and there is no guarantee any changes in that version will be released.

Some organizations use version identifiers that combine stability versions with SemVer or CalVer identifiers. Snyk's REST API has version identifiers that follow the pattern {calver}~{stability-version}. For example, `2023-03-03~experimental` is for the experimental version, which has unstable features still being built and which may not be released; `2023-03-03~beta` is for the beta version, which is a release candidate preview; and `2023-03-03` is for the generally available version recommended for use in production.

API versioning from a product perspective

In "API Evolution without Versioning" (https://mng.bz/z8eB), Brandon Byars suggests that versioning shouldn't be viewed from an architectural perspective only. With your API product lens on, you should also look at API versioning as part of the product interface you expose to users. Providers sometimes version an API to minimize implementation complexity and eliminate old code, but this can introduce high migration costs for the API consumer. Byars suggests the following three criteria to evaluate the versioning system you adopt for your APIs:

- *Viability*—Does the versioning system solve problems your API consumers have? Does it reduce cognitive load for them and hide underlying complexity?
- *Usability*—Does the versioning system make it easy for API consumers to use your API? *Easy* here means it should be obvious and elegant and make a clear stability promise. The system should follow the principle of least surprise, be intuitive to the user, and be simple to use and learn.
- *Feasibility*—Is the versioning system done in an architecturally sound way? Does it make your system more understandable and intellectually manageable? Does it protect your downstream systems?

Apart from these, there are other things to consider when versioning an API from a product perspective. In her talk "The Right Way to Version Your API: The API Consumer's Perspective" (www.youtube.com/watch?v=5M8g-4CsOsI&t=1398s), Marjukka Niinioja discusses the following four organizational and product management-related factors that affect versioning:

- *Pace of the business and industry*—Some businesses may have API consumers demanding rapid evolution of the API, while others may have API consumers who generally push back on changes because of the difficulty of migration. For instance, regulated industries and industries that use lots of embedded devices may have a lot of difficulty migrating to a new API version due to the high cost involved. Examples of this include the automotive and healthcare industries.
- *Relationships and power structures between the API provider and the API consumer*—API providers who are more powerful may be able to force API consumers to migrate to a new version. But in situations where the API consumers are more powerful or influential, they may be able to decide the pace of evolution instead. Industries in which the relationship between the provider and consumer is highly regulated may experience a slower pace of API evolution.

(continued)
> In addition, changes are only considered breaking if a feature is being used; that is, changing a feature no consumer is using should cause no disruption to consumers.
> - *Tooling support for API versioning schemes*—Some older API management tools and API documentation portals may not support some versioning schemes. You may also need to check whether the tools your API consumers are using support your proposed versioning scheme.
> - *Product management strategy of the API provider*—Niinioja explains that the API versioning strategy an API provider finally arrives at may have evolved out of getting a better understanding of their value proposition to the market. They may evolve their API boundaries, versioning scheme, and scope over time to arrive at a suitable API product market fit. This is why it's important to start with tools such as the API value proposition canvas (discussed in chapter 5, section 5.2.3), as that can help the API design process arrive more quickly at a versioning scheme that addresses the pains and expected gains of the API consumer.

We've talked about different versioning schemes, scopes, and identifiers. You can use a combination of these to manage your API versioning. Next, we'll consider what costs you need to consider when introducing a new API version.

4.10 *Costs involved with version migration*

Defining an API versioning scheme and the scope at which you want to evolve your API is important. However, you must also consider how you communicate these to API consumers and migrate them to new API versions when you release them. Switching to a new API version can involve significant costs.

When introducing a new API version due to a breaking change, there are several costs to consider. The first is the cost to the provider to build, test, deploy, and support the new API version. The new version must also be communicated to users, along with migration advice. If the API provider makes SDKs available to consumers, these must be updated, republished, and documented. In addition, old versions of the API need to be supported. There is an opportunity cost involved because the cost spent on supporting old versions could have been spent on adding new features and improving the developing experience in new versions. This is why providers aim to reduce the number of older versions they support and encourage consumers to migrate to new API versions.

The second category of costs relates to the API consumer. The consumer has to migrate to the new API. They have to update, test, and release their client code. But this is only the direct cost. There are other indirect costs to the API consumers. Updating and releasing new client code involves some risk to the consumer. There is also the opportunity cost of working on this migration rather than some other pressing business problem. Even if the cost of the migration is perceived as small by the provider, it must still be within the consumer's budget. Consumers may hesitate to migrate to a new API version that provides little business benefit to them.

Jean-Jacques (JJ) Dubray describes three patterns for migrating API consumers to new versions of an API, which are all shown in figure 4.6. The first is the Knot migration pattern. In this case, all API consumers (and the ecosystem around them) are tied to a version of the provider API and forced to migrate together in a coordinated migration to a new version of the provider's API. JJ argues that over the lifetime of the API service, this is the most expensive kind of migration as the number of versions increases. The cost involved may become so high that every change in services becomes tactical.

> **TIP** For more of Jean-Jacques Dubray's mathematical estimations for API migration costs, see https://mng.bz/0GON.

The second is the Point-to-Point migration pattern, in which different versions of the API services exposing the different API versions are left running in production. Not all API consumers can afford the time and cost involved with migrating immediately, so API consumers are allowed to migrate at their convenience. Some consumers may never migrate if they are satisfied with the existing version. Unlike the Knot pattern, this involves the provider absorbing the cost of maintaining several versions of the API service in production. It's less expensive than the Knot pattern.

The third pattern is the Compatible pattern. All API consumers communicate with the same API service, which offers compatible API versions. Even though consumers still depend on different API versions, the same API service can handle their requests.

JJ argues that the total cost of the Compatible pattern is the lowest. The cost of the three different patterns as the number of API versions grows is also illustrated.

An example of a company that uses the Compatible migration pattern is Stripe. Stripe uses a version change module to ensure that the latest version of the API service can still handle backward-incompatible requests from API consumers. This is done using a version change module. This is a bit of declarative code that, based on the requested API version, applies a transformation on the API resource returned by the operation so that it matches the expected API version. The collection of version change modules is kept separate from the API service code itself, which is on the latest version. On receiving a proposed API response from the latest version of the code, the version change modules are applied backward, starting from the current API version and applying the transformation functions in order until the desired API version is reached.

This is a separation of concerns and means that developers can focus on adding new features to the core code, knowing that support for older API versions is abstracted away in separate version change modules responsible for transforming the resource to match old API versions. The version change modules contain documentation describing what transformations they apply, and along with the declarative nature of the functions,

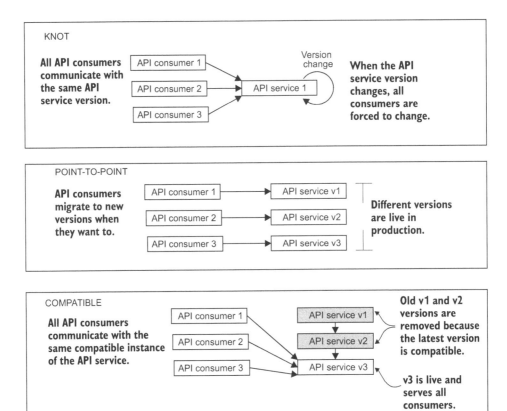

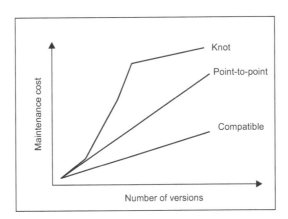

Figure 4.6   Jean-Jacques Dubray's three models of API version migration. The cost of version migration for each model is illustrated in the chart. (Source: This is adapted from JJ's original diagram available at https://mng.bz/0GON, along with the accompanying equations.)

they can be used to programmatically generate notifications on the API changelog to inform users of what has changed in the API. For more on Stripe's approach to the Compatible migration pattern, see https://stripe.com/blog/api-versioning. Another company that follows this pattern is Intercom, as explained at www.intercom.com/blog/api-versioning.

Version change modules help reduce the cost of introducing a new version for the provider. They help API consumers migrate to the new version of the code, even though it's still exposed via the old API. But they aren't free because they involve code that has to be written, tested, and maintained. Most of Stripe's version change modules are pure functions that transform the response, but not all are. Some have side effects, for example, making changes to data in the database. These are less encapsulated and more complex to maintain.

4.11 Breaking change policy

According to Hyrum's law, "With a sufficient number of users of an API, it does not matter what you promise in the contract: all observable behaviors of your system will be depended on by somebody" (www.hyrumslaw.com). This means that whatever you define in your API definition as your contract, at a large enough scale, some consumers may ignore it and depend on your implementation as the de facto interface, so any deviation from your current implementation can break their expectations. This is why it's important for API providers to publish an explicit breaking change policy. This is a document in which the API providers explain what they consider to be breaking changes, how they define a stable API, and how they expect API consumers to evolve along with the API. You can think of your breaking change policy as communicating your API change management approach.

You should share your breaking change policy with your API consumers by publishing it on your developer portal. Some organizations call it an API versioning policy rather than a breaking change policy page. Whatever way you present it, your breaking change or API versioning policy should cover the following:

- Your API versioning scheme, scope, and version identifiers
- The list of API changes you consider breaking and nonbreaking
- Your API stability levels
- Your API version schedule

Examples of REST API breaking change policies include the following:

- Microsoft's "Versioning, Support, and Breaking Change Policies for Microsoft Graph" (https://mng.bz/KZnj)
- LinkedIn's "LinkedIn API Breaking Change Policy" (https://mng.bz/5lza)
- HubSpot's "Breaking Changes on the HubSpot Platform" (https://mng.bz/9d87)
- Onfido's "API versioning policy" (https://mng.bz/67By)

I've already discussed API versioning schemes, scopes, and identifiers in sections 4.7 to 4.9. In the following sections, I'll explain the other three points: breaking changes, API stability levels, and the API version schedule.

4.11.1 Defining your breaking and nonbreaking changes

Defining and publishing the list of what you consider breaking and nonbreaking changes is important so that your API consumers can consider this information when building their client integrations. Based on your list, you can create automated checks for breaking changes using OpenAPI diff tools or other scripts. Table 4.1 lists examples of breaking changes, but note that organizations may differ on what changes they consider breaking. For example, I list adding a new enum (also called enumeration or enumerated) value to a response as a breaking change, but some organizations (e.g., Onfido and GitHub) list this as a nonbreaking change. (Problems with enum extensibility are covered in section 4.12.) In addition, some API diff tools differ in what they consider breaking and nonbreaking.

Both of these reasons are why it's important to publish your own list so that you can set expectations with your API consumers and also check that the OpenAPI diff tool to use works in line with your definition. Otherwise, you may need to supplement it with additional scripts.

Table 4.1 Examples of breaking changes to an OpenAPI definition file

API object	Category of change made	Change details
Path	Deleting	Deleting an endpoint
	Adding	Adding a new required path parameter
Request	Adding/increasing	Adding a new required property in the request body Adding a new, validated pattern to a request schema Adding a new required header parameter Increasing the minimum number of items in an array in the request
	Changing	Changing a request header parameter from optional to mandatory Changing an optional property in a request body to mandatory Changing a validated pattern in a request parameter
	Deleting/reducing	Deleting an enum value Reducing the max number of items in an array in the request Reducing the max length of a string
Response	Adding/Increasing	Increasing the max length of an array in a response Adding a new enum value (potentially breaking depending on client code implementation)
	Changing	Changing a required property in the response body to optional Changing an existing response header from required to optional

Table 4.1 Examples of breaking changes to an OpenAPI definition file *(continued)*

API object	Category of change made	Change details
	Deleting/reducing	Deleting a required property Deleting a media-type from a response Deleting an enum value. Deleting a required response header Reducing the min number of items in an array in a response Reducing the min length of a string in a response

I haven't provided a list of nonbreaking changes here, but you can also prepare a similar list. Generally, nonbreaking changes involve an additive operation, for example, adding new endpoints, adding optional request parameters and request headers, and adding new response fields and response headers.

4.11.2 API version stability

API stability refers to the guarantees an API provider gives on how a version of the API will change in the future. The goal of specifying the level of API stability is so that API consumers know how often they expect to update their code after they integrate with your API. It also helps you communicate and get feedback from API consumers on your upcoming API changes as you evolve your API.

APIs should define their stability guarantees. Google offers the following guidance (defined in AIP-181 https://google.aip.dev/181) to its API designers on defining the stability levels of its APIs:

- *Alpha*—The API is under rapid iteration, and breaking changes are allowed. It's used by a known set of users who are tolerant of the rapid level of change.
- *Beta*—The API is feature complete and ready to be declared stable after public testing. The API can be exposed to an unknown and large set of users, which can mean exposing it publicly. Beta APIs should be as stable as possible but may still allow breaking changes. However, they must provide a reasonable deprecation period to allow users to migrate their code.
- *Stable*—A stable API must be fully supported and must not introduce any breaking changes except for cases due to security or regulatory requirements.

The Ghost REST API (https://ghost.org/docs/content-api) defines only three stability levels:

- *Experimental*—For API versions that are being actively worked on and can receive breaking changes
- *Stable*—For API versions that can have only nonbreaking (forward compatible) changes
- *Deprecated*—For API versions that are scheduled for removal

However you define your API's stability levels, it should be documented clearly on your developer portal so that API consumers can understand it.

4.11.3 API version scheduling

You should also document how long you intend to support the stable API so that API consumers can plan for upgrades. Shopify releases a new, stable API version every 3 months and supports them for at least 12 months. This gives API consumers at least 9 months between consecutive stable versions to test and migrate their apps to the next stable version. API consumers can plan around this release schedule.

> **TIP** You can find out more about Shopify's release schedule at https://mng .bz/oe6M.

Communicating your API stability levels should also include discussing your approach to deprecating and sunsetting your API, which is part of your API life cycle. *Deprecation* is a formal notice that continued dependence on an HTTP resource is at risk. When you deprecate an API, you discourage API consumers from using it. From the deprecation date, API consumers should be aware that the API will no longer be supported or available at some point in the future, and they should start planning to migrate away from it. They probably shouldn't be building any new applications that depend on that API. Deprecating an API is supported by the OAS with the Deprecated field, which takes a Boolean value. You can set the field on an OpenAPI operation, parameter, and schema object.

On the other hand, *sunsetting* is what happens when the deprecation window has expired. On the sunset date, the API is removed from the server and is no longer available for consumption; consumers get a 404 Not Found error if they access the endpoint. Figure 4.7 illustrates the difference between the deprecation and sunset dates.

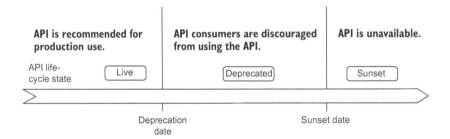

Figure 4.7   API deprecation and sunset dates. After the deprecation date, an API isn't recommended for use. But after the sunset date, the API is unavailable.

Sunsetting an API is a breaking change, as consumers can't continue using the API. But if you've issued a deprecation notice to your consumers and given them enough time to migrate, you may not want to treat sunsetting as a breaking change in your automated checks. If you've automated your breaking change check in your CI/CD pipeline, you may not want it to fail for a planned sunset.

4.12 Managing breaking changes

As you've seen, API versioning involves several considerations around version schemes, scope, stability, consumer communication, and scheduling. And according to Hyrum's law, breaking changes may involve not just the API design as stated in your API definition contract but also any observable behavior of your API that consumers depend on. An API diff tool such as Tufin/oasdiff is useful for detecting design-level breaking changes, but depending on your codebase and workflow, you may also need to adopt other controls too. Here are a couple of other things you can consider to help you manage breaking changes in your workflow.

MAKE API VERSIONING A FIRST-CLASS CONCEPT IN YOUR API

With a new API, consider using a versioning scheme, even if you don't get to use it. This gives you the option to use the scheme if you have to. Ensure the scheme or combination of schemes helps you evolve your API at the scope you want to. In addition, pick a version identifier that makes sense for your project and is easy for your API consumers to understand. Making versioning a first-class concept in your API also helps you explain API changes in your changelog and API documentation.

DESIGN YOUR API FOR EXTENSIBILITY

Bertrand Meyer's open-closed principle states that software should be open for extension but closed for modification. Applying this to APIs means you should design your resources so you can extend them by adding properties but you can't modify existing properties that consumers depend on.

Consider using an open-ended list of values instead of enums when the final list of values is unknown or when there is a likelihood that the list of values will change. Enums are properties that have a fixed set of values. Client integration code (created by developers or generated with automation tools from the OpenAPI definition) may not robustly handle new and unknown enum values. This can potentially lead to a breaking change and the client integration code throwing an error if the API designer extends the enumeration in the future. Enums are best used when the list of values is never expected to change. Given the way APIs evolve, this can be hard to guarantee at the early stages of an API when some requirements may still be unclear. So where there is a likelihood that the list will be extended in the future, use an open-ended list of values instead. For example, instead of using an enum like

```
properties:
  role:
    type: string
    enum:
    - all
    - admin
    - member
```

just keep the list open as follows:

```
properties:
  role:
    type: string
```

Zalando recommends using the `x-extensible-enum` extension to give API consumers a hint on the current list of supported values. An example of using the `x-extensible-enum` element is shown here:

```
properties:
  role:
    type: string
    x-extensible-enum:
    - all
    - admin
    - member
```

But with this approach, API consumers must be prepared for extensions of the enums and implement fallback logic to properly handle unknown enums (https://mng.bz/ng5K). API providers must also be careful in extending enums. They should do so in a way that doesn't change the semantics of existing enum values.

When you've determined that the list of values won't change, you can easily turn the list of strings in the API definition into an enum, as this isn't a breaking change. This gives new client integrations the better type-safety that the enum provides.

Another instance of designing APIs for extension is to avoid returning JSON arrays as top-level data structures. A top-level JSON array is a JSON document where the root element is a JSON array, not a JSON object, for example:

```
[
  {
    "name": "Acme Rope Toy",
    "description": "Acme Rope Toy provides hours of fun for your dog",
    "price": 100
  },
  {
    "name": "Acme Dog Food",
    "description": "Healthy food for your dog",
    "price": 50
  }
]
```

With a JSON document like this, you can't add a new top-level attribute that provides extra information (e.g., a "meta" object or "pagination" object that provides pagination information) without introducing a breaking change. But you can do this if you wrap the array in a top-level JSON object as follows:

```
{
  "data": [
```

```
  {
    "name": "Acme Rope Toy",
    "description": "Acme Rope Toy provides hours of fun for your dog",
    "price": 100
  },
  {
    "name": "Acme Dog Food",
    "description": "Healthy food for your dog",
    "price": 50
  }
],
"pagination": {
  "self": "https://api.acme-pet-supplies.com/v1/catalog/products?
cursor=bccf5512",
  "prev": "https://api.acme-pet-supplies.com/v1/catalog/products?
cursor=0242ac120",
  "next": "https://api.acme-pet-supplies.com/v1/catalog/products?
cursor=651b1f06"
  }
}
```

For this reason, always use JSON object's rather than JSON arrays as top-level data structures in your API request and response messages.

Using an open-ended list (e.g., the `x-extensible-enum` extension) and avoiding top-level JSON arrays are ways to design APIs for extensibility and minimize the risk of introducing breaking changes later. Your API review process can help with this too. Lightweight peer reviews should check for opportunities to make the design extensible. API reviews are discussed later in chapter 5.

Summary

- A structured diff of the changes between API definition file versions helps you work out what has changed as you iterate on the OpenAPI design.
- A breaking change forces an API consumer to update their client application. OpenAPI diff tools help you automate detecting breaking changes across API definition versions.
- API versioning is a way to evolve your API while maintaining your integration with existing clients. There are several options for API versioning schemes, scopes, and identifiers to allow you to evolve your API along the axes that best fit your system. Still, consider API versioning as part of your API product interface, and keep usability in mind.
- Your breaking change policy should include the list of what you consider breaking and nonbreaking changes, your API version stability levels, and your API version schedule. You should publish your breaking change policy so your API consumers can use it to plan their integration work.

API design review: Checking for what you cannot automate

Imagine you've created a new API, and your API definition file has passed all the automated commit stage checks in your continuous integration/continuous delivery (CI/CD) pipeline. You raise a pull request (PR) to get your change merged to the main branch of your API definition project. Is there still a need to get your colleagues to review the API definition change in your PR? Yes, there is. Reviewing an API change proposal with colleagues and even prospective users enables you to get feedback that the automation can't provide. It's also an opportunity to review the reports from the automated checks. In this chapter, I discuss how to conduct API reviews in your APIOps workflow to get colleague feedback. People in different roles involved in designing APIs will be interested in this chapter, but API product owners or similar roles accountable for API consistency will particularly benefit from learning how to set up an effective API review process.

5.1 What is an API design review?

An *API review* is about getting feedback from colleagues and internal API consumers on an API design to improve it and check its compliance with the organization's API usability and consistency standards. In the context of APIOps, you initiate an API review at the design stage when you raise a PR for a change to an API definition file (figure 5.1). The review should occur after you've run automated linting and breaking change checks, so it's different from a traditional API review that depends purely on error-prone manual checks against an organization's API style guide. An API review in APIOps supplements the automated governance checks with a human review to check for things that can't be automated. For example, have all the relevant API operations been included in the design? Does the team agree on the naming of resources and resource attributes? In your review, you may discover new consistency problems that can be prevented with automation, and you can make a note to create automated checks for them.

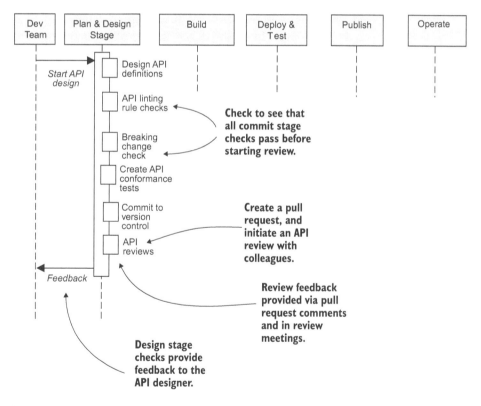

Figure 5.1 API reviews happen at the design stage of your APIOps workflow. API reviews start after the automated checks all pass. The API review is completed when all review comments have been resolved and the PR is merged.

You can do API reviews asynchronously or face-to-face. In an asynchronous API review, an API designer requests an API review from colleagues by posting a PR containing the API definition change. Reviewers can go through the PR, which includes the API definition change and associated metadata, render the API definition to see what the API reference looks like, and make trial requests against an autogenerated mock of the API to see how it behaves. In their own time, they can post their review comments in the version control system using a Git collaboration tool such as GitHub, GitLab, or Bitbucket. The API designer can read and address these comments later and make any required changes. Where the API design change is small or closely follows the organization's style guide, this lightweight review and approval process is preferred.

But other API design change PRs require a face-to-face review (i.e., an in-person API design review meeting). This can be because the PR touches a large API surface area or requires the API designer to explain a lot of background context for the reviewers to understand. The design may also be proposed by a less mature team that needs help with getting started with the organization's API design-first approach, API product thinking (outside-in, user-centric), or help with applying domain modeling to the API (i.e., API modeling). In a face-to-face review, API reviewers meet with API designers to discuss the PR, understand the drivers for the change, understand the reason for design decisions, check the API for consistency, and provide detailed advice and support on improving the API design. You can also have a combination of these; some organizations start with an asynchronous review and have an in-person review meeting if needed (usually for a major API change or a change requiring detailed discussion). In smaller organizations, the review process can be informal and involve one other colleague, but larger organizations may have a dedicated API governance team for API reviews. Again, I emphasize that regardless of whether the review is face-to-face or asynchronous, the review should happen after the automated checks have run.

Reviewers approve the PR if they are satisfied with it. This indicates an agreed API contract that server-side teams and client-side teams can build against. This enables the parallelization of work to improve delivery speed.

However, reviewers not only need to provide their feedback when the proposed API definition change is submitted in a PR but also during the early stages of API design. Depending on the complexity of the domain, API designers can create a model of the business operations and data models for the API based on the user stories or job stories (job stories are discussed later), the user journey, and the domain model. API reviewers can help API designers review this API model to ensure the designers align with the correct bounded context and follow principles of single responsibility, encapsulation, and so on.

Domain-driven design

A domain model is a structured representation of business concepts, relationships, and workflows as interconnected software objects that have behavior and data. Domain-driven design (DDD), made popular by Eric Evans's book *Domain-Driven Design: Tackling Complexity in the Heart of Software* (Addison-Wesley, 2003), is an approach to software design that focuses on creating a domain model based on a rich understanding of the business domain. DDD helps software teams develop a ubiquitous language—a shared, pervasive, and rigorous language that teams can use to identify and communicate domain concepts with domain experts and users in an unambiguous and consistent way. That ubiquitous language should be used to embed domain terminology into the software system being created.

One pattern in DDD is the idea of establishing bounded contexts. This is a way of dealing with modeling a large business domain by splitting the domain model into groups, called *bounded contexts*, and explicitly defining the relationships between them. Inside a bounded context, the definitions of domain terms and concepts apply consistently.

After the API model and API operations are conceptually defined, API designers can translate this design into OpenAPI definition file changes. They use the organization's API style guide to help them in creating or updating the API definition files in a manner consistent with the organization's guidelines. They also reference and include any shared reusable OpenAPI component libraries they require. This saves them from rewriting everything from scratch and also makes the API review process easier because the definition reuses approved components. The designer submits their changes as PRs, and automated checks run on the PR. If the linting and breaking change checks raise errors, the API designer should check and fix the problem before the API review. When the PR is ready for review, API reviewers review, approve, decline, or schedule it for further discussion in a face-to-face review. This process is shown in figure 5.2.

When reviewing a PR, who decides if the PR requires a design review meeting? API reviewers should use their judgment. Generally, API reviewers can invite the API designers to an API review meeting if there are significant departures from the API style guide that require more in-depth discussions than would be suitable over PR comments or that introduce new API patterns.

Along with the main benefit of having colleagues review APIs for consistency and usability improvements, reviews also have other benefits. API reviews have a synchronization and coordination aspect for internal teams, as API reviews involve stakeholders, including any teams interested in or affected by the API change. For example, this can be internal teams who need to consume the API, colleagues who need to test the API, product teams, and technical writers. It's a good opportunity for the teams to understand what the change is, provide feedback, and understand the effect of the change on the applications or parts of the platform they manage. API reviews also have an educational aspect. Team members who want to improve their API design skills can join API review meetings to learn how to design and review APIs.

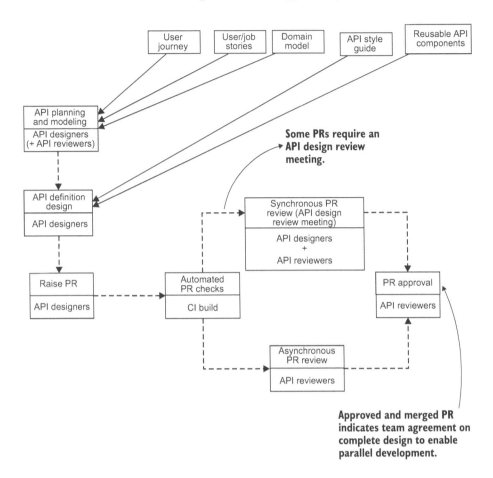

Figure 5.2   A sample process map for API design reviews. API reviewers can review the PR, leave review comments, approve the PR, or decide if the PR requires an in-person API review meeting for wider review discussion.

TIP   Small organizations with a few development teams and a relatively small external API surface area will likely not have a separate API governance or review group, so they won't need an elaborate API review process. Pairing or chatting over API design may be enough. And for APIs with a small number of operations in a simple business domain, the recommendations in later parts of this chapter about creating and reviewing an API resource model may be overkill. For such teams, setting up basic automated linting may be sufficient to reach an acceptable level of API consistency.

Note that while an API review PR helps API designers get peer feedback on their API design, designers need to publish the change externally to get wider feedback from external API consumers. Depending on your API stability levels (as discussed in section 4.10.2), publishing an alpha or beta API can help API consumers preview, experiment with, and provide further feedback on your API design.

5.2 Running an API review meeting

Imagine you work as an API reviewer in the API governance team. An API design PR has been raised, and a couple of your API review colleagues have reviewed it and decided they need to meet with the API designers to discuss some of their design decisions. You've been asked to facilitate an API design review meeting to review an API design PR. How would you begin?

The following is a suggested format for how you can run an API review meeting, which you can customize to meet your needs as well:

1 Set up the review meeting, and invite participants.
2 At the meeting, present the review agenda.
3 Provide the business context for the review.
4 Review the API resource model.
5 Review the API definition, and capture review feedback.
6 Note new API patterns or discovered style guide gaps.
7 At the end of the meeting, ask participants to fill out a short survey.

Let's look at these points in detail, starting with why you need to do the reviews.

5.2.1 Set up the meeting, and invite participants

Given the API to review, the review meeting facilitator should invite all the right stakeholders from the teams who build and consume the API. This can involve people from different roles, including engineers, product owners, product managers, business analysts, technical writers, and more. When running an API reviewing session, it's useful to think of participants as falling into three main roles:

- *API designers*—Typically, these individuals are developers who create or update an API definition file. Designing an API can involve more than one person and also involve collaboration from different roles—product owners, product managers, architects, and so on. In this book, when I refer to *API designers*, I mean the team of people who contribute to proposing an API design change.
- *API reviewers*—These individuals review the API design change and must include engineers who are highly experienced with API design. For larger organizations, this can be members of a dedicated API governance team. It can also be API platform teams responsible for the organization's API gateway, security champions, and technical writers and teams responsible for the developer portal or developer experience.
- *Facilitator*—This individual organizes and moderates API review sessions. A facilitator is responsible for scheduling the review, taking notes, and moderating the meeting when reviews require them.

It's important to identify important stakeholders and involve them in the API review. Asking the following questions can help facilitators identify these stakeholders:

- Who will be integrating with and consuming this API? Apart from external API consumers, one or more internal teams may be involved and may want to help share the design of the API they will be consuming.
- Who will be creating guide documentation and tutorials for this API? Technical writers who will be involved in documenting the API may want to be part of the API review to understand the context of the API and suggest editorial changes to API description fields.
- Are there security champions, security engineers, or security testing teams interested in securing the API or testing the security of the API?
- Are there API platform teams who will be involved in exposing the API via an API gateway?
- Who are the solution architects and engineers interested in the API?
- Who are the product owners or product managers interested in the API?

This isn't an exhaustive list, but it should be a helpful guide. In addition, I find it useful to open up API review meetings to anyone who wants to take part by publishing API meeting invitations in internal communication channels and publishing open-invite reminders. As I mentioned, API review meetings have both an educational and informational aspect to them, and one way to train up prospective API reviewers is to open up API review meetings for those interested to join, learn, and contribute.

5.2.2 *Present the review agenda*

For formal API review meetings, I recommend that the API review facilitator start the meeting by presenting the meeting agenda to participants. This helps set expectations with participants on how the meeting is structured and the scope of issues to be discussed in the allotted time. An agenda keeps participants on track and avoids going down a design debate rabbit hole. It's also an opportunity to introduce any new participants to how your API reviews generally work.

The following is an example API design review agenda, but you should tailor your meeting agendas to your organizational context:

1. Check that the right stakeholders are present.
2. Introduce the theme of the API review.
3. Review the API resource model.
4. Review REST API elements:
   - Summary and description
   - Idempotency requirements
   - API paths
   - Happy path request and response payloads
   - Error messages
   - Security scheme

5 Note new API patterns or style guide gaps discovered.

6 Perform end-of-meeting survey.

Having a standard agenda for API review meetings helps different people facilitate reviews more consistently and minimizes dependency on particular individuals.

5.2.3 Provide the business context for the review

After checking that you have the right participants in the meeting (which should include engineering, product, and other roles as necessary), present the topic of the review. To help participants in the meeting understand the change to be reviewed, introduce the business context, explain the goal the API user is trying to fulfill, and—where possible—show the user journey (user journeys are discussed further in section 5.3.1). When facilitating API reviews, I usually ask API designers to introduce the business context of their API change in 3 to 5 minutes, and I ask for questions from participants to ensure everyone understands it.

Another way to give participants a high-level view of what an API should do is to present an API profile that explains the job of the API. Table 5.1 provides an example.

Table 5.1 Example of an API profile

Item	Description
API name	Product Catalog API
API value proposition	An API to discover Acme's great range of products so users can find products to care for their pets
API consumer	The end user is a customer browsing Acme Pet Supplies products to make a purchase. Client API developers will use this API to build three end-user channels: the Acme mobile app, the Acme web store, and an affiliate's store.
Job stories	Story 1: When exploring what products Acme has available, I want to browse the Acme catalog by category so I can find new and exciting pet products that interest me. Story 2: When exploring what products Acme has available, I want to search for particular pet products in the Acme catalog so I can view details of the product and decide if I want to buy. Note: Search catalog capability will be in phase 2.
Access level	Public API, made available for use by both Acme-owned digital channels and registered affiliates
Usage plans	Acme mobile app: 10 requests a minute Acme web store: 10 requests a minute Affiliate stores: 8 requests a minute
Security model	API requests should be authorized using OAuth2. We'll start with the read permission scope for the MVP but will add more scopes as the API functionality is expanded.

Job stories and digital capabilities

A job story is an enhanced version of a user story motivated by applying *Jobs to Be Done (JTBD)* thinking. It focuses on the triggering situation, the motivation or goal the user is trying to fulfill, and the expected outcome. In the Product Catalog API profile example in table 5.2, the job story is "When I need a product to care for my pet, I want to discover a great range of products in that category with quality reviews so I can choose which one I like."

JTBD is a framework for finding the goal or "job" a customer "hires" a product or service to fulfill. It helps product managers discover the underlying needs and motivations that drive customers to buy a product or service. An API consumer will use an API to fulfill a particular task, and expressing that job clearly helps the product manager design a better API product. From a job story, the API team can work out the high-level tasks or *digital capabilities* the API needs to have to support the job. For more on using job stories and digital capabilities to identify the requirements, scope, and boundaries of an API, see *Principles of Web API Design* by James Higginbotham (Addison-Wesley, 2021).

Another technique for providing the business context to reviewers is to present the *API value proposition canvas* for an API (also called a value proposition interface canvas). An API value proposition canvas is a template for defining the value an API provides by making explicit how the API features address the pains API consumers experience and the gains they seek in fulfilling their goals or jobs. It's a tool that should be used in the early stage of the API design to facilitate discussions with engineers, architects, product managers, business sponsors, and other stakeholders to define and get alignment on what the API should do.

The API value proposition canvas is made of two broad sections. On the left is the consumer (or customer) profile section that describes the jobs the API consumer needs to get done, as well as the pains they experience and the potential gains they want to achieve. On the right is the value map section that presents the internal data sources, internal APIs, applications, and processes that can be combined to provide an API that relieves the API consumer's pain or creates gains for them. The left and right sections meet in an interface—a box containing a statement that defines the value the API provides to the consumer—as shown in figure 5.3.

By filling in the API value proposition map at the API design stage, you can follow the numbered sequence shown in figure 5.3. Figure 5.4 shows a partially filled-in API value proposition map for the Product Catalog API. In the next section, the operations and resources in the API box will be filled in.

The API value proposition canvas is described in Andrea Zulian and Amancio Bouza's book, *API Product Management* (Leanpub, 2017) where they call it the *value proposition interface canvas*. The API value proposition canvas is an adaptation of Alexander Osterwalder's Value Proposition Canvas (www.strategyzer.com/canvas/value -proposition-canvas). The canvas is also discussed as one of the first steps of Marjukka Niinioja's APIOps Cycles method.

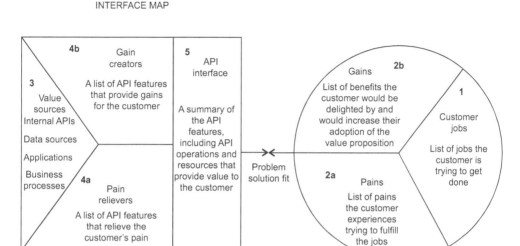

Figure 5.3   The main sections of an API value proposition map (Source: Adapted from the value proposition interface canvas by Andrea Zulian and Amancio Bouza in *API Product Management*, Leanpub, 2017)

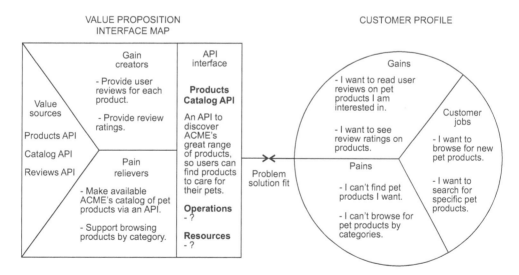

Figure 5.4   An API value proposition canvas for the Products Catalog API. The Product Catalog API fetches the data it needs from the internal APIs of the Products, Catalog, and Reviews microservices.

Introduction to the APIOps Cycles method

The APIOps Cycles method (www.apiopscycles.com/the-method), developed by Mar-jukka Niinioja of Osaango, is a collaborative and lean method for creating API solu-tions and developing API strategies. It starts off the API design process by focusing on the business needs and the business model the API should support. It helps orga-nizations define the following:

- What APIs they should have
- How to design new APIs
- How to improve their current APIs

The APIOps Cycles method consists of eight phases:

- *Phase 1: Business first with API canvas*—Start with the API value proposition canvas, the API business model canvas, and customer journey maps to help stakeholders (architects, solution owners, product managers, and business analysts) answer questions on what APIs they should build and why. Stake-holders can provide details and get alignment on which APIs will provide the most value for the business, the target API consumers, the required benefits of an API, the cost of developing the API, and how the API affects the busi-ness's revenue stream. These questions relate to the value proposition of the API and its effect on the business model.
- *Phase 2: Mind the developer experience*—Stakeholders define how to ensure that an API can be discovered and used by the intended API consumers. This also includes defining how the organization intends to support and build a developer community.
- *Phase 3: Minimum viable API architecture*—Define the minimum architecture the business needs to cater to the nonfunctional requirements for each API. This helps optimize the work schedule of the API.
- *Phase 4: Build the API*—Design the data and interaction models, prototype the API, and implement the API following the organization's API style guides. It takes into account data requirements such as international and industry data standards, common identifiers, and the data freshness.
- *Phase 5: API Audit*—This involves using checklists to audit an API prototype, an API design, or a production API to confirm that it complies with the organi-zation's API guidelines.
- *Phase 6: Publish API*—Stakeholders define what API assets, including product and technical documentation and specifications, will be published and how to help API consumers discover and use the API.
- *Phase 7: Monitor, measure, and analyze*—Define and monitor business and technical metrics to measure the API performance and success of the API.
- *Phase 8: Learn and improve*—Improve the API development process by review-ing the qualitative and quantitative data on API behavior and using that to improve the API.

Apart from the methods website, more information on its different phases can be found in *API Economy 101* by Jarkko Moilanen, Marjukka Niinioja, and Marko Seppänen (Books on Demand, 2019).

5.2.4 *Review the API resource model*

Where possible, it's useful to review the list of expected API operations and the data model that the API seeks to expose. Getting alignment with API designers and stakeholders on an unambiguous API model helps resolve some questions that may arise when creating API definitions. But capturing that model as part of the API design process is an important step. For example, in *Principles of Web API Design* (Addison-Wesley Professional, 2021), James Higginbotham presents the Align-Define-Design-Refine (ADDR) process for designing APIs. It's an API design-first process involving seven steps:

1 Identify digital capabilities that deliver customer outcomes.
2 Capture activity steps and tasks the user should perform to achieve the outcomes.
3 Identify API boundaries as groupings of digital capabilities.
4 Model API profiles by defining the resources and operations the API should provide.
5 Do a high-level API design of the API for the given architectural style (e.g., REST, GraphQL, gRPC).
6 Refine the API design, incorporating design feedback to improve the user experience.
7 Document the API by providing reference documentation and getting-started guides.

Getting different roles and teams involved with the API design to review and get consensus on the output of the fourth step—model API profiles (the conceptual data model and operations on which the API is based)—gives those involved a shared understanding of the data model and the terminology used to describe it. This model and the functions that operate on it can be captured with entity-relationship diagrams, tables, and so on.

As an example, consider a simple Product Catalog API where the data model that the API exposes consists of products, reviews, and categories. This data model constitutes the core resources the RESTful API exposes. A product resource has zero or more reviews, and a review is associated with one and only one product. A product can belong to one or more categories, and a category can contain zero or more products. Figure 5.5 shows the relationship between the resources using crow's foot notation.

TIP Crow's foot notation is a way of representing entity relationship diagrams using a three-pronged "many" symbol to indicate the many side of the relationship. For more on crow's foot notation, see https://vertabelo.com/blog/crow-s-foot-notation/.

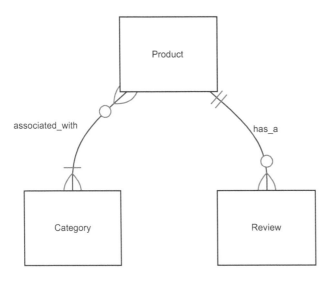

Figure 5.5   The relationships between the web resources that support the API operations for the Product Catalog API

Imagine that this API also supports the following operations on these objects: `list-Categories`, `listProducts`, `viewProduct`, `listProductReviews`, and `viewReview`, as shown in table 5.2. With this API model defined, the team can have a reference for judging how these functions and data are translated to a RESTful API design in OpenAPI.

Table 5.2   An API operations table for the Product Catalog API

Operation name	Operation Description	Participant	Web resource	Request	Response
listCategories	List all categories	Customer	Category	Filter by field, sort by field, order direction, page size, page cursor	Category
listProducts	List all products	Customer	Product	Filter by field, sort by field, order direction, page size, page cursor	Product
viewProduct	View a product's details	Customer	Product	Product ID	Product
listProductReviews	List all reviews for a product	Customer	Review	Filter by field, sort by field, order direction, page size, page cursor	Reviews
viewReview	View a product review	Customer	Review	Product ID, Review ID	Reviews

These API operations and resources also fit into the API box in the value proposition map to complete the API value proposition canvas, as shown in figure 5.6.

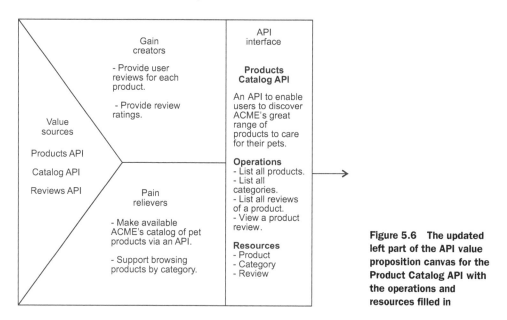

Value proposition
interface map

Figure 5.6   The updated
left part of the API value
proposition canvas for the
Product Catalog API with
the operations and
resources filled in

You've seen the high-level requirements and the desired API model. But how will this new API fit into Acme's microservice architecture? Acme's API gateway is responsible for authentication and proxies all authenticated requests to the Product Catalog API service. The Product Catalog API service implements the API product interface and orchestrates requests to the backend microservices: products service, category service, and reviews service. These services provide the data the Products Catalog API can use to compose and serve responses, as shown in figure 5.7.

With the context of the required API operations and resource model, reviewers now have a good understanding of the domain of the API and are ready to review the API definition files. This is a simplified scenario, but in practice, it's useful to have similar contextual information to give reviewers an overview of the problem domain and enable them to see how these should translate to REST API operations.

5.2.5   *Review the API definition*

This is the time to do an in-depth review of the design-change PR. If the team has a comprehensive suite of automated linting and breaking checks that have run on the PR and passed, then API reviewers don't need to check for those items. Remember that one of the goals of introducing automation is to reduce the lead time for doing reviews. Rather, reviewers should focus on elements of the API style guide and general design problems not covered by the automated checks. Reviewers should check the report from the automated checks to see if there are any INFO or WARN level problems that require

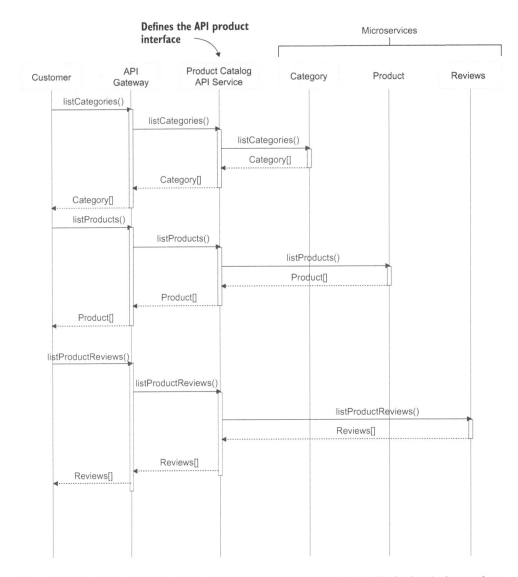

Figure 5.7   The Products Catalog API service orchestrates requests back to the backend microservices.

attention. In addition, if there are any comments noted by reviewers when they initially looked at the PR, the review should focus on these.

When doing a review, I find it useful to use a checklist. Assuming that most of the recommendations of the organization's API style guide have been implemented as automated checks, the checklist shows problems reviewers can check for. If the organization doesn't yet have a comprehensive suite of automated checks for API definitions, then API reviewers will also need to consider more detailed style guide consistency checks. Of course, doing this work isn't a good use of reviewers' time (hence the need for linting and automation!), so the API governance function should look to auto-mate these checks as much as possible. Following is the example checklist:

- *Review the reports from the automated checks.* Check that your automated checks (linting and breaking change checks) have been completed successfully and that the reports from these checks have no warnings that require attention.

- *What is the user journey, and how does the design change help fulfill the job the user is try-ing to perform?* Look through the rendered API reference documentation. Does the API documentation clearly describe the goal of the API and what job it helps the user fulfill?

- *Is the web resource model consistent with the accepted domain model?* Check if the API design has the right operations and resources as contained in the requirements. Are there any missing operations? Are the API operations within the right API boundary? Take note of any inconsistencies and unclear attribute or resource names, and add comments to the PR to point this out. On a real project, this would be the time to discuss any differences in terminology on resources and attributes with colleagues. The DDD idea of having a ubiquitous language used by the team to describe the domain also applies to APIs.

- *Is the API design extensible?* Think about how the API can be extended in the future, either by extending existing operations or by adding new operations.

- *Are the API description, summary fields, and examples clear and understandable?* Read the API description in the info object, the description of each endpoint opera-tion, and the description of message attributes. Check that the API descriptions are correct and will make sense to the developers integrating with the API. Check that any example values in the API definition are as useful and realistic as possible.

- *Are all the important error responses returned along with the right error codes?* Check that the HTTP error response codes are appropriate for the operation and that no important response scenarios are missing. In addition, check that any cus-tom error fields in the failure response body make sense.

- *Are the idempotency requirements for API operations satisfied?* When an endpoint is idempotent, the same request can be run multiple times, but the resulting state change on the server will occur only once. Check if the API operations are nat-urally idempotent or have an idempotency key if they require one.

NOTE According to the HTTP specification, GET, PUT, and DELETE are natu-rally idempotent; POST and PATCH aren't naturally idempotent. If you use these HTTP verbs in an operation that needs to be idempotent (e.g., an end-point that makes a payment), you must add an *idempotency key* to enable you to detect and handle duplicate requests.

- *Consider the nonfunctional aspect of the API design.* Think about security, pagina-tion, and any aspects of the design that can affect application performance. Apart from security considerations around authentication and authorization, other security guidelines around the structure and validation of request and response messages need to be considered. I discuss running linting security checks in chapter 9.

In API review sessions, I usually ask reviewers to provide feedback as PR comments, and we discuss the most important comments raised. Capturing review feedback in this way helps the facilitator track the resolution state of the problem.

5.2.6   *Note new API patterns or style guide gaps*

API review meetings are a good opportunity to discover new API patterns that may need to be captured in the organization's style guide. They can also reveal ambiguity and gaps in the style guide that leave API designers with a lack of clarity on how to handle particular elements of the design. An API review facilitator should capture these for further discussion with the relevant function (e.g., API governance teams or internal API communities of practice), possibly leading to the update of the API style guide and linting rules. API review facilitators should listen to spot gaps and see how the style guide can be improved to cover any such scenarios that arise.

5.2.7   *Present an end-of-meeting survey*

To help improve future review meetings, the facilitator can close the review meeting by asking meeting participants to fill out a short one- or two-question feedback survey. I discuss this further in section 5.5.

You've seen the basic structure of running an API design review. Now let's look at some challenges teams typically face with API reviews.

5.3   *Challenges with API reviews*

Here are some challenges I see teams encounter with API design reviews. The first is the continual effort required to get less mature API designers and reviewers to adopt an outside-in, user-centric view of their APIs. The second is the extra review effort required where APIs have been modeled poorly. API reviews occurring too late in the API design process are a problem, and deciding the level of review to apply can be a challenge as well.

5.3.1   *Adopting a user-centric approach*

It's sometimes difficult for less experienced API designers to adopt a user-perspective approach to API design. This is exhibited by API designs that make it easy for the back-end implementation at the expense of usability for the API consumer or poor documentation. A lot of API review effort is spent on getting teams to adopt a user perspective, starting with the end user journey map and working backward (figure 5.8).

One thing that can help with this is getting the API design team to submit not just the OpenAPI definition file but also an early draft and guide documentation around the API. Writing the guide documentation for the APIs first helps the API designers look at the API from the user's view.

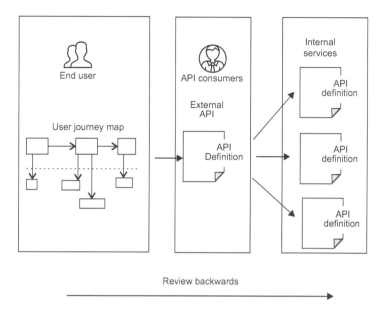

Review backwards

Figure 5.8 **When reviewing an external API, where possible, work backward by reviewing the user journey map before reviewing the external API. This presumes that you have a user journey map prepared. Review the external API before reviewing any internal service APIs they depend on.**

Another useful tool that can help reviewers develop a user-centric view is a user journey map. A *user journey map* (also called a customer journey map) is a way of visualizing the process a user goes through when interacting with a product or service to fulfill a goal or job. A user journey is drawn from the point of view of the actor or persona who performs the actions. It describes the scenario, the goal the actor aims to achieve, the different phases or high-level stages in the user's journey, and the actions the user performs at these stages. A service blueprint takes the user journey map further and describes the different service components (e.g., the provider's APIs) the user interacts with on their journey. Service blueprints help shift the perspective of reviewers from an inside-out view (where internal processes and systems drive user experience decisions) to an outside-in view that focuses on the actions and thoughts of users.

TIP For more on service blueprints, see the Nielsen Norman Group web page at https://mng.bz/aEeB.

A service blueprint can help designers and reviewers focus on user actions and opportunities at the different stages in the user journey and produce APIs that are more extensible to fit opportunities that may come up in the future.

But a user journey map will only be available at the API review stage if the API designers created one beforehand to facilitate the API design process. This is where a method such as the APIOps Cycles method comes in handy because the first phase of the method—Business first with API canvas—guides designers to create user journeys. More information on this is available at www.apiopscycles.com/method/api-canvas.

5.3.2   Poor modeling before reviews

RESTful API design is based on understanding API resources, relationships between resources, and operations on API resources. Where the less experienced API designers haven't done proper modeling of the API, API reviews will likely discover problems with the API conforming to RESTful conventions. This may lead to long, drawn-out review discussions. Helping teams model their API can help resolve these problems, but this would be better done much earlier, which leads us to the next point.

5.3.3   Reviews occur late in the process

API review meetings and automated checks do a good job of catching API consistency and usability problems after the API design has been proposed, but this may already be too late. API reviewers can provide more value for teams by engaging them at the early stage of the design to provide them with the tools and guidance on how to design the API. This can involve ensuring teams can find the API style guide, use API linters, and engage in proper API modeling and service design. API reviews and automated checks aren't a substitute for early engagement with design teams.

5.3.4   Deciding the level of review to apply

Sometimes teams aren't sure if they should apply the same level of governance to all categories of APIs, that is, internal, partner, and public APIs. Once automated checks are set up in a pipeline, they are usually cheaper to extend to more API definition files, so it makes sense to apply these to as many APIs as possible. API reviews, on the other hand, require coordination and scheduling of people and teams and are more expensive to execute because of the time demand they place on reviewers and designers. A good rule of thumb is to reserve API design review meetings only for external-facing APIs (public and partner) or APIs that have the potential to become external-facing. Internal APIs that will never be exposed should not be mandated to go through the same rigor (although API designers can opt into them if they desire).

Hierarchy of API design principles

In *API Product Management*, Andrea Zulian and Amancio Bouza present the Hierarchy of API Design Principles. They state that the foundation principle of a valuable API is to provide a clear value proposition to the API customer (i.e., the end user who uses the features of the API to fulfill their job) and that the job of the API product manager is to help define and validate this value proposition. On top of this foundation principle comes the next level, which is creating a great developer experience for the API developers integrating with the API. This is about providing developers with great API documentation; a frictionless onboarding process, including the provision of API keys or any other authentication mechanisms they require; sandbox environments to test the

API; API SDKs; and so on. An API management platform and developer portals help make this possible.

The third level principle in the hierarchy is defining the API philosophy. This is about defining the API based on the constraints of the value proposition and the developer experience, and applying API governance, API style guides, and API engineering knowledge, as shown in the following figure.

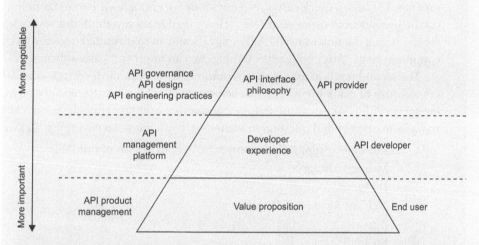

Hierarchy of API Design Principles (Source: *API Product Management* by Andrea Zulian and Amancio Bouza)

Andrea and Amancio advocate that the value proposition of the API is the most critical, followed by the developer experience. Where tradeoffs need to be made on API design principles, they suggest that adjustments should be made at the API philosophy level so that the value proposition and developer experience don't suffer. This is useful guidance to keep in mind when reviewing APIs.

5.4   *Measuring review effectiveness*

Imagine that you've implemented automated checks on API design PRs and have implemented a process for doing API design review meetings where required. How do you measure the effectiveness of these processes?

5.4.1   *Automated checks*

For your automated checks, you can keep an API design quality score of APIs by tracking the number of linting problems, breaking change defects, and API conformance problems (API conformance in discussed in chapters 6 and 7) that arise from your automated checks. For small teams, it's sufficient to store these as build artifacts in the CI server. However, larger teams may need an API scoreboard that collects and displays these API-consistency and API-design quality metrics.

5.4.2   *Design review meetings*

Getting feedback from API designers on how useful they find the API review meetings is worthwhile, as you can use this feedback to improve and fine-tune your reviews. There are two ways I recommend getting review meeting feedback—session-based feedback and periodic feedback. In *session-based feedback*, the facilitator ends the review session meeting by asking the API design team to fill in a quick, anonymous survey, perhaps providing them with a survey link. The survey is to provide feedback on how useful the design review session was. For such a quick survey, two questions are enough—a 1- to 5-star rating question on the usefulness of the session (e.g., "How valuable do you think this review session was for improving the quality of the API design?") and an open-ended question to gather any comments (e.g., "Any comments on things we can improve?") are sufficient.

The second way is to ask for more comprehensive periodic feedback from API designers, say once or twice a year. This can be presented as Likert-style questions on overall API design, usability, API documentation, consistency, and breaking changes. It should also include an open-ended question to gather any comments. An example is shown here:

1   API design reviews help improve the overall design of our APIs.
    – Strongly Disagree
    – Disagree
    – Neither Agree nor Disagree
    – Agree
    – Strongly Agree
2   API design reviews help improve the usability of our APIs.
    – Strongly Disagree
    – Disagree
    – Neither Agree nor Disagree
    – Agree
    – Strongly Agree
3   API design reviews help improve our API documentation.
    – Strongly Disagree
    – Disagree
    – Neither Agree nor Disagree
    – Agree
    – Strongly Agree
4   API design reviews help improve the consistency of our APIs with our organization's API style guide.
    – Strongly Disagree
    – Disagree
    – Neither Agree nor Disagree
    – Agree
    – Strongly Agree

5   API design reviews help teams avoid making breaking changes.
    – Strongly Disagree
    – Disagree
    – Neither Agree nor Disagree
    – Agree
    – Strongly Agree
6   Any comments on things we can improve?

Comparing these results over time should show the effect of improvement efforts in your design review process.

Besides getting feedback from API designers, the API reviewers or the API governance team (if your organization has one) can also meet and run Agile retrospectives to see how they can improve their API design review process. In addition, depending on the size of your API governance function and the number of teams it serves, one key performance indicator (KPI) API reviewers can track is the number of outstanding API design PRs. Hosted version control services such as GitHub and Bitbucket provide reports on PR statistics. Your review team should aim to respond to API design PRs quickly and keep the average time of open PRs awaiting review low.

5.5 Defining your API design review process

To facilitate an efficient API design review at scale, it's important to document your process to help reduce ambiguity and confusion and improve the consistency of design reviews. Documenting it also helps simplify the training and onboarding of new joiners to the organization. The documentation helps you analyze and improve the review process itself.

For larger organizations that build APIs at scale, there is usually a central API governance team responsible for maintaining design quality and consistency standards on external APIs and defining the design review process that teams need to go through to expose APIs.

Software teams vary significantly in terms of the nature and scope of the API project they work on, their existing practices, organizational culture, and so on, so there are no general API design review process rules that may apply to all teams. Instead, each team must consider what guidance solves the problems they face in their context. However, the following subsections provide a few suggestions for teams to consider when creating their API design review process document.

5.5.1 Make it easily discoverable

Place your API design review process document where teams can easily find it. This can be an internal wiki page or shared document. For my organization, an internal survey showed that most stakeholders preferred to have the document (along with our API style guide) in the same repository as our API definitions. Wherever the document is, it should be easy to find and link to because teams will reference it regularly.

5.5.2   *Define principles and goals*

Outline the values and principles that guide the design of your API review process. For example, you may decide that you value APIs that are easy and obvious for consumers to use over APIs that reflect your organization's internal technology systems and organizational structure. And (borrowing from the agile manifesto), you value responding quickly to a business need for an API design change over following an agreed design or plan. You can include that external APIs should be designed and reviewed first before development (API design-first) because designing first and reviewing that design with colleagues before implementing leads to better API design and usability for the API consumer and a more efficient and cheaper design process for the API provider. Another principle you may consider is that API reviewers and, ultimately, API consumers should be able to understand what an API does by reading its API reference and guide documentation. This means that the provided documentation has to be sufficiently explanatory and easy to understand. These are just examples—consider what values and principles make sense in your context and include them. Based on the general principles, your API design review process should aim for the following process goals, which you can have metrics to measure:

- *Quality*—Improve API design quality and consistency with standards.
- *Speed*—Reduce the time required to review and approve a design change.
- *Dependability*—Set expectations, and schedule and complete API reviews promptly to enable project managers, product managers, and sales teams to plan and meet customer commitments and delivery deadlines on time. This involves making sufficient provision for API reviewer capacity, which is the primary resource of the process.
- *Flexibility*—Flexibility should be optimized for different kinds of reviews. The review process should handle small reviews (e.g., extending an existing API endpoint by adding one new property to an existing resource) or large reviews (e.g., a whole new API consisting of many API endpoints and many new resources). It should also handle changes in API review priority based on changing delivery priorities.
- *Cost*—The process should aim to lower the cost of conducting reviews. API reviews take the time of key engineers, architects, product managers, security professionals, and so on. It's expensive to synchronize and keep stakeholders in a review in a face-to-face meeting for a long time, so the review should justify the cost. The process should minimize waste from API design errors, delays, miscommunication, preparing information that isn't needed, and unneeded meetings.

5.5.3   *Describe review process metrics*

In section 5.4, I described some KPIs for measuring the effectiveness of your API review. The design review process document should describe these so API stakeholders can understand and view performance data.

5.5.4 *Define roles and responsibilities in the process*

When doing design reviews at scale, you should explicitly define who does what in the design review. As I mentioned in section 5.2.1, the three main roles in the API design review process are API designers, API reviewers, and review facilitators.

> **TIP** One way to define roles and responsibilities is to use a responsibility assignment matrix (also called a RACI chart). It's a table that outlines the tasks to be performed and defines the roles that are *responsible, accountable, consulted,* and *informed* (hence, RACI) about them. For more on the RACI chart, see www.mindtools.com/agn584l/the-raci-matrix.

For example, you can make an API review facilitator accountable and responsible for handling the administrative work involved with design reviews. This involves scheduling review meetings and ensuring that review PRs, tickets, and review status boards are up to date. It also involves assigning reviewers, ensuring PRs are reviewed on time, and ensuring stakeholders can find any required information about the review process. For smaller organizations, a dedicated facilitator may not be necessary.

API reviewers can be accountable for providing review feedback, preferably captured as PR comments for reference. Large organizations may have a few dedicated reviewers, but smaller ones may have volunteers or ad hoc reviewers. Reviewers should carve out time to conduct reviews and also have PR approval permissions on the API repository.

API designers can be accountable for proposing API design changes for review. They should be responsible for discussing and implementing any recommended changes made by API reviewers.

5.5.5 *Face-to-face reviews on request*

Suppose you have a CI/CD pipeline that runs automated checks on your API design change PRs, and API designers also provide supporting early drafts of API guide documentation (that will be published on the developer portal) along with the PR. In that case, you can consider making face-to-face review meetings only necessary if API reviewers or designers ask for them. This can be because a problem can't be resolved over a PR discussion thread. Ideally, API reviewers should be able to understand and review an API design-change PR based on the provided API definition file and any other supporting API documentation. Remember that API consumers will mostly be relying on the API documentation to work out what the API does, so API reviewers should do the same without having to rely on someone in a review meeting to explain it. As previously mentioned, depending on the number of people at a review meeting and how long it takes, review meetings can be expensive to run, considering the time value of those involved, so they should only be reserved when needed.

5.5.6   *Categorize APIs by review level required*

In your process, it may be useful to make clear what level of governance is required for the different categories of APIs in your organization. This helps teams know if they should engage the API governance team for a review or not. You can describe the level of review required for each category of API in a table. Table 5.3 is an example of this.

Table 5.3   An example of defining the review required for different categories of APIs

API category	API exposed externally by the organization	Automated API CI/CD checks	PR review by the internal dev team	PR review by the governance team
Internal API	No	Yes	Yes	No
Internal API (Externalizable)	Yes	Yes	Yes	Optional, but recommended
Private API	Yes	Yes	Yes	Yes
External API	Yes	Yes	Yes	Yes

5.5.7   *Have an explicit approval step*

Following the API design-first principle, your review process documentation should make clear to all stakeholders the action that marks a design change as having been accepted, thus transitioning the API from the design to the implementation stage. For example, this can be approving and merging a PR or transitioning a related review ticket status. This is important for enabling parallel development workstreams, as development teams don't want to start implementing if the design is still in flux.

5.5.8   *Changes after approval*

Having an approval step doesn't mean you can no longer accept changes if a need to review the design arises during implementation. The API designer can simply raise a new design-change PR and notify the API reviewers and all other stakeholders of the change (e.g., frontend integration teams). The PR can be reviewed and merged as usual. This should happen relatively quickly if it's a minor modification of the existing design. Unlike in Waterfall, an Agile process embraces change. As a principle in the Agile manifesto states, "Welcome changing requirements, even late in development. Agile processes harness change for the customer's competitive advantage" (see https://agilemanifesto.org/principles.html).

5.5.9   *Define a way of signifying exceptions*

Sometimes, there may be a good reason to depart from an organization's API style guide for a particular design change proposal. For example, there may be a need to extend legacy APIs that existed before the API style guide was written. To provide this flexibility, your process should state clearly how API designers can signify that they have chosen to depart from the style guide and their reasons for doing so. One option is to tag the affected API components using a custom OpenAPI extension. API designers should also document why this should be an exceptional case. API review facilitators should consider if an update to the API linting rules is required to add an ignore for this exceptional case.

5.5.10 *Describe how reviews will be prioritized*

This may not apply to smaller teams, but for organizations with many APIs, it may be necessary for the API review facilitators to prioritize API design change proposals. The API design review process document should make clear the prioritization criteria; for example, this may be based on a delivery or release target date. This helps meet the goal of dependability. For hosted code collaboration systems that support them, a PR label can be one way of assigning priorities. Or, if the PR is associated with an issue ticket, the priority label on the ticket can be used.

5.5.11 *Provide expected review timelines*

To meet the goal of dependability, it's useful to describe how long API designers should expect to wait for their PRs to be reviewed by the central governance team. This helps product and project managers plan and set expectations with customers and other stakeholders. The timelines can be categorized by the nature of the review. Table 5.4 shows an example.

Table 5.4 An example of defining the review required for different categories of APIs

Type of change	Review time (business days)
Extending existing resources on existing endpoints	Up to one day
Adding a new endpoint for existing resources	Up to two days
Adding new resources and new endpoints	Up to five days

5.5.12 *Make review work visible*

Some larger teams associate a review PR with an issue ticket, and the governance team has a status board that shows the status of these tickets. Other teams apply priority labels on PRs. This provides good visibility to API designers and other process stakeholders. But the API review facilitators have to ensure that the ticket status or PR labels are up to date. Here is an example of possible state transitions for a status board:

- *Backlog*—PR is created, awaiting assignment and prioritization.
- *Assigned* or *Scheduled*—PRs have been allotted to named reviewers or scheduled for an API review session.
- *In Review*—API reviewers are currently reviewing the PR.
- *Changes Requested*—API review completed, and the reviewers have left recommendations for the API designers to reply to or action.
- *Approved*—API design change has been accepted, and the contract agreed on. Stakeholders can now work based on the agreed contract.
- *Rejected*—Design-change PR declined with the reason provided.

5.5.13 *Describe how to become an API reviewer*

Organizations with many development teams building APIs usually have a central API governance team with a few dedicated team members, including reviewers with extensive API design and review experience. However, it's useful to supplement this with volunteer reviewers from other teams to improve the breadth of the feedback on the API design review. Some of these reviewers, such as security professionals or technical writers, can contribute their specialized knowledge to reviewing API design and documentation. Having a large pool of API reviewers improves the quality, speed, and dependability of API reviews. It's important to publicize the need for people to join as API reviewers and make the joining process clear in your API review process documentation.

5.6   *API review examples*

So far, I've described a simple way to do API reviews. But it's also worth looking at how API reviews are done in organizations that build APIs at scale. Let's look at two—Microsoft Azure and Google.

5.6.1 *API stewardship at Microsoft Azure*

The Microsoft Azure developer division follows the idea of API stewardship. They describe API stewardship as working with their internal developer teams as early as possible to help them adopt good API design practices into their development process. The goal is to create a culture that helps internal developer Azure teams design and build APIs that are easy to use, consistent across Azure products, aligned with industry conventions, and scalable. The API Stewardship Team is run by a board of experienced practitioners, which includes members of the customer success field teams, Azure services engineers, SDK architects, members of the CTO office, and more. But anyone in the organization who is interested in APIs is also welcome to participate. It's an open, broad interest group that also includes passionate volunteers.

The API Stewardship team applies a three-pronged approach to the task of API stewardship. First, they engage teams early at the API design stage, educate them on the API design process, and help them define their API style guides, API documentation, and breaking change policies. They also provide other supporting content that teams need on general API and service design.

Second, they enable teams with infrastructure and tools for automatic API design checks on PRs (including linting and breaking change checks) and generating API artifacts such as client libraries, mobile SDKs, mock servers, REST API docs, and so on. Two-thirds of their API guidelines are covered by the automated checks they have in their pipeline; the other third is covered in their API design reviews.

Third, they empower teams with API design reviews and API previews. In the API design review at Microsoft Azure, the API Stewardship team starts review meetings by asking teams to explain the domain and goal of the API. Then they look at sample request/response messages in OpenAPI definition files using the Swagger editor. They look for common API design pitfalls (e.g., idempotency and pagination for collections). They then discuss other important design decisions around the code flow, the future evolution of the API, polymorphism, batch operations that were present, and so on. The API Stewardship team includes product managers in their design reviews, as some design decisions may affect product decisions. Apart from API design reviews, they also empower teams by helping them structure how they provide API previews (i.e., experimental, early-sight versions of the API that customers can integrate with) to get feedback from partners and early adopters. They help teams define clear objectives for the preview stage so the team is clear on what they expect to learn from early adopters who use the API.

> **TIP** For more on Microsoft Azure's Stewardship model, see "Building APIs at Scale: Moving from API governance to API stewardship" by Mike Kistler and Mark Weitzel (www.youtube.com/watch?v=sboH7zyfEnA) and "Lessons Learned on the Azure API Stewardship Journey" by Adrian Hal (https://mng .bz/gv0E).

At Azure, API stewardship required an investment in dedicated staff, including a product manager and an architect, and the creation of content and tools to support the mission. The emphasis in API stewardship is on enabling teams to do good API design early at the design stage, instead of applying governance and oversight at the general-availability stage of the API when it's too late to make many changes.

5.6.2 *The API Improvement Proposal process at Google*

The goal of API design reviews at Google is to ensure that Google APIs are simple, intuitive, and consistent with Google's existing APIs. The Google API style guide is a high-level, concise document called the API Improvement Proposal (AIP; available at https://aip.dev). Google also provides a linter (available at https://linter.aip.dev), for checking APIs for compliance against the AIPs. Not every aspect of AIP guidance can be expressed as lint rules, so API designers still need to read and understand the AIP.

API design review approval is required for launching an API that Google's users can write code to interact with at the beta (complete and ready to be declared as stable subject to public testing) or general availability (open to all customers, ready for production use) quality levels. Google API design reviews aren't required for APIs that will only ever be used by Googlers or Google's internal tools.

Google has a small number of full-time reviewers on its API governance team, but it also has a large number of engineers who have gained experience in API best practices and volunteer as API reviewers. API reviewers at Google approach a review by thinking through the actions, resources, and user-facing documentation that the API provides from the perspective of naive users. They also look to see that the API is consistent with Google's AIPs and is extensible. API design review is done asynchronously using Google's internal code review tool to review PRs (also called change lists). But for complicated problems that can't be resolved through PR thread discussion, API designers can reach out to reviewers and schedule a half-hour meeting.

TIP   To get an early view of how API design reviews were introduced at Google to address API quality and consistency problems, see the 2016 Google paper, "API Design Reviews at Scale" (CHI'16 Extended Abstracts, 2016; https://research.google/pubs/pub45294) by Macvean, Maly, and Daughtry.

Google's API design review process gives API designers an idea of how long it will take to review their design proposals. Incremental changes to an existing API take a few days, and new, small APIs take around a week. Larger APIs can take more time.

5.6.3   *The API design review process at Slack*

At Slack, the API design process starts with the development team defining the use cases for the API and the goal of the API design change. They create an API definition file that contains their design and share this on an internal #api-decisions Slack channel for review. The channel comprises a cross-functional group of reviewers and stakeholders from different organizational functions, including engineering, product management, developer relations, and security. For some changes, this asynchronous review is enough to get approval on the design. For others, a deeper discussion is required, and the API designers schedule a slot for a face-to-face review session with reviewers in the regularly scheduled API office hours.

After the internal review, the API definition file is subject to one more level of review before the build stage. The API definition file is made available to a select group of partners who provide further feedback on the API design. When all the feedback has been processed, the API is implemented and made available for preview and beta testing with a few select partners, and any feedback they provide is used to further enhance the API. This allows Slack to further improve on any problems identified before public release. You can read more about the Slack API review process in the "How We Design Our APIs at Slack" post (https://mng.bz/eoGv).

5.6.4   *The Kubernetes API review process*

Kubernetes (https://kubernetes.io/) is an open source platform for managing containerized applications. It's used for running and managing large cloud-native workloads and provides mechanisms to deploy and scale applications based on CPU, memory, and other metrics. The Kubernetes control plane has an API server that provides a REST API for managing the state of Kubernetes objects, allowing clients to configure workloads and containers in Kubernetes. The API is large and has hundreds of endpoints. To aid the extensibility of the API, resources are grouped into *API groups*, and these API groups are versioned. The *core* (also called *legacy*) group resources use the path prefix /api/v1/ (e.g., GET /api/v1/namespaces/test/pods). Other groups use the path prefix /apis/ $GROUP_NAME/$VERSION (e.g., /apis/batch/v1/).

The Kubernetes API design review process (https://mng.bz/ppX8) describes how the Kubernetes project uses API reviews to maintain API consistency and usability. It defines which API changes require a mandatory API review (e.g., changes to core

APIs) and which are voluntary. The Kubernetes project has an API style guide, called the *API conventions*, that Kubernetes API designers must follow when updating the API. An API designer is required to have read and followed the Kubernetes API conventions before submitting an API change PR. The PR should also specify the goal of the proposed change and reference a completed Kubernetes enhancement proposal (similar to a feature or requirements document).

API reviewers and facilitators regularly triage API review requests. If they meet the project prerequisites, they are added to the API review board—a status board used to provide visibility of the outstanding API review PR status and reviewer load. API review facilitators (called moderators on the Kubernetes project) adjust the prioritization of reviews in the backlog. The prioritization is based on which release milestone the change is targeting, feedback from the project leads on relative priorities and the size and complexity of the change, and the stability level of the change (general availability takes precedence over beta, which takes precedence over alpha changes). Moderators prioritize the review backlog, so some high-priority API changes take review precedence when required. The moderator assigns the API reviewer to the PR based on the reviewer's capacity and domain knowledge. Moderators remove the burden of administrative trivia from API reviewers so they can spend the majority of their time performing reviews, and they help schedule face-to-face API review meeting sessions when necessary.

On the API review board, the API review requests a transition through the following states: Backlog > Assigned > In Progress > Changes Requested > API Review Completed. The approved PR is linked to when requesting a review of the implementation PR so code reviewers can check for conformance. On rare occasions, an API review PR may be declined, for example, for a change that should be done outside the Kubernetes project.

The Kubernetes API design review process document gives designers an idea of how long the process takes. It specifies that reviews can take up to a week to prioritize and schedule and up to three weeks for the first review to be complete.

To become an API reviewer on the Kubernetes project, aspiring reviewers must gain a high level of proficiency in the Kubernetes API style guide. They also need to have a good understanding of the project structure and the system architecture. They are required to have participated in preliminary API reviews where mentors coach them. Mentors help train them and facilitate their inclusion as formal reviewers.

Summary

- In an APIOps API review, you review your API design PR after the automated checks have run. Your review is aimed at finding problems the automated checks can't find.

- An API review can be asynchronous or face-to-face, and API reviewers can leave their review comments on the PR.

- Use a consumer-centric approach in your API review by starting from the API definition the API consumer will use and then working backward to the internal interfaces. Ensure you understand the problem context before starting your review.

- API reviews in larger organizations typically involve an API designer, API reviewers, and an API review facilitator. Reviews should also include any colleagues interested in reviewing APIs.
- User surveys are a good way to measure the effectiveness of API design review meetings. Reports from automatic checks can be collected to keep an API design quality score.

API conformance: Generating code and API definitions

This chapter covers

- Handling the API server, client, and documentation conformance problem
- Generating server code for conformance
- Generating OpenAPI definitions for conformance
- Generating SDKs for conformance

Imagine you're building a public REST API. You've designed your OpenAPI definition and passed it through your linting and breaking change checks as described in chapters 3 and 4. You've built and deployed your API to your API gateway and made it live. You've also generated your API reference documentation from your API definition and published it to your API developer portal. Things are going well.

But now your API consumers are complaining that some details of your published API reference don't match your live API's behavior. For example, your API reference documentation specifies that one of the API endpoints always returns a certain field in the 200 OK response. But when consumers get a response from your API, the field is absent. There is a discrepancy between the API reference documentation and the deployed API. How do you ensure that your API server and client SDK implementation all conform to your OpenAPI definition?

Your API reference documentation is human-readable content on your developer portal that describes the API operations you provide. Typically, you generate the API reference documentation from your OpenAPI definition. You may do this using some tool or by uploading your OpenAPI definition to a developer portal that renders the API reference for you. API consumers depend on your API reference documentation to learn what they can do with your API. So it can be confusing and a poor end-developer experience for them if they find aspects of it don't match the actual behavior of your API. They can raise defect tickets about this, increasing your support costs. And as you scale, these reference documentation problems can hamper the wide adoption of your API.

There are two main approaches to ensuring your API server, API client SDKs, and API reference conform to your OpenAPI definition. The first, generated consistency, involves generating either the API server stub code from the OpenAPI definition or generating the OpenAPI definition from the API server code. Either way, you generate the client SDKs and the API reference from the created OpenAPI definition. *Stub code* here refers to generated software objects representing the request and response messages in the API call, as well as controller and routing logic. The second approach, API conformance testing, involves running tests (including runtime checks in the API gateway) to check that the responses from the API server conform to the OpenAPI definition.

This chapter focuses on the first approach, and you'll learn how to use the generated consistency techniques in your APIOps workflow. Typically, you would apply this at the build stage of the APIOps workflow, as shown in figure 6.1.

This chapter covers how to generate server stub code, OpenAPI definitions, and SDK clients to ensure they are all consistent. In addition, I discuss several points to consider in keeping your generated artifacts in sync. Appendix D has information on how to set up the tools and code you need for this chapter, including information on how to install, start, and stop the Kong API gateway. Make sure you have all the tools set up before continuing with this section. To work on the exercises in this chapter, navigate to the chapter6 directory in this book's code repository at https://github.com/apiopsbook/apiops. This chapter is more relevant to developers, but API product owners will benefit from getting an overview of the API conformance problem.

6.1 The API conformance problem

Consider the following scenario. Your users are noticing discrepancies between the published API reference for an endpoint—let's say GET /v1/catalog/products/{id}—and the behavior of the endpoint on the live server. They aren't seeing a particular field—keywords—which your API reference documentation stated was mandatory in

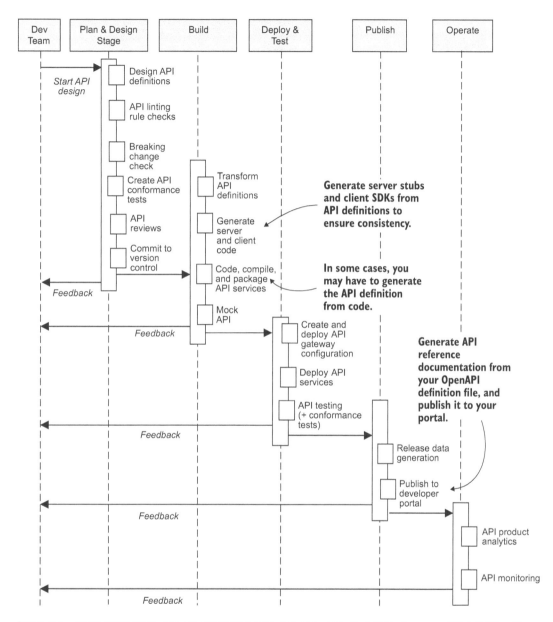

Figure 6.1   At the build stage, you can generate server stub code and client SDKs from your API definition. You transform your OpenAPI definitions into API reference documentation and publish it to your developer portal.

the response. Figure 6.2 illustrates this drift between the API reference and API behavior. In this illustration, the API service receives a request from the API gateway and orchestrates it to various upstream microservices to process.

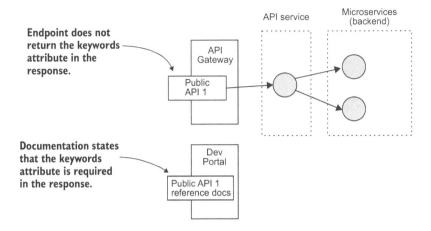

Figure 6.2   The response from the public API is missing a field marked as mandatory in the API reference. There is a drift between the API reference and the live API.

How did this happen? Well, there are multiple ways. Perhaps the developer who built the API service created the controller logic by hand, using the OpenAPI definition from the design stage as a guide. During this manual process, the developer may have missed the fact that the keywords attribute should be in the response. The OpenAPI definition from the design stage is the source of truth (SOT) on what the API should do, but the developer created the API service controller code manually, leading to human errors in the translation of the OpenAPI definition to code. Perhaps there was a change in requirements during the development process and the keywords attribute is no longer required. The developer updated the code but didn't update the OpenAPI definition file. In this case, the development team didn't treat the OpenAPI definition as the SOT for updating the code.

Whichever way, the net result is that the developer deploys the API service to the API gateway but publishes the API reference based on the original API definition. Now there is a drift between the API implementation and the published OpenAPI definition (see figure 6.3).

There needs to be a way to ensure that both the controller code and the OpenAPI definition are in sync. One option is for the developer to always remember to update the original API definition when a new requirement comes in. The downside is that it depends on human memory, and updates must happen in two places—the code and the API definition. If the developer forgets to update the API definition (from which the API reference is published), there is no way of knowing there is a problem unless someone manually checks the API reference for consistency or an API consumer raises a defect ticket to complain.

Another option is to make the update in just one place—the OpenAPI definition— and generate the API service controller code, the API client SDK, and the API reference

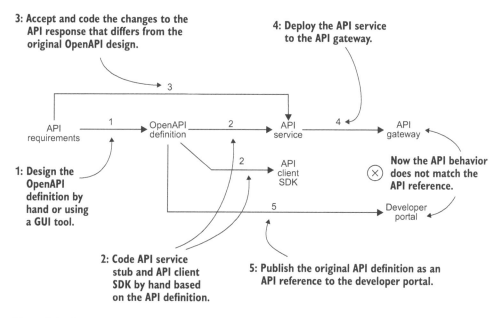

Figure 6.3   Changes to the API design during the development phase may lead to a drift between the deployed API behavior and the original API design.

documentation from that. That is, treat the OpenAPI definition from the design phase not just as the SOT, but minimize the chance of human translation errors by generating the API service stub code, API client SDK, and reference documents from it. This approach requires using a tool to generate API service stub code for the given programming language and application framework from the OpenAPI definitions. Every time the developer receives a requirement to change the API request or response, the developer updates the OpenAPI definition first and then regenerates the API service controller stub from it. Figure 6.4 illustrates this.

Let's look at how you can apply this to an example Java project using the OpenAPI Generator library as the server stub code generation tool.

6.2   *Generating code from OpenAPI*

You can ensure your API behavior conforms to your OpenAPI definition by treating it as the authoritative specification of your API and generating the API service controller, request, and response objects from it using a code generation tool. In this section, I walk you through an example of doing this with a Java Spring Boot application. Don't worry if you're not familiar with Java and Spring Boot—I've completed examples that you can just run. And if you're familiar with Spring Boot, there are sections about the project structure you may skip over. While I go into detail on the files created by the code generation library, the goal of this section isn't to teach you Java or Spring Boot or to show the recommended way of structuring a Spring Boot application;

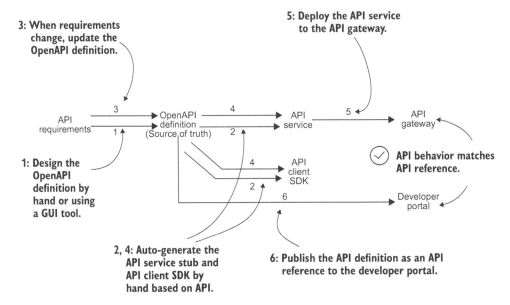

Figure 6.4   Update the OpenAPI definition every time the API requirements change, and then generate the API service controller stub from the OpenAPI definition. This ensures the implementation and published API reference conform.

the goal is to show you an example of how to generate controller, model, and routing code for a service using an OpenAPI definition as the SOT.

6.2.1   *Spring Boot from OpenAPI*

Suppose your team lead asks you to apply the code generation approach in building an API. The technical requirement is that the API service should be a Java Spring Boot application, and you should generate the controller, routing logic, request, and response objects from an OpenAPI definition file, which serves as the SOT, using OpenAPI Generator.

> **NOTE**   If you're familiar with Java and Spring Boot, you can code through this example in the chapter6 directory using either Visual Studio Code (VS Code) or your favorite Java IDE. But if not, you can look in the chapter6-completed directory to see the completed example.

OpenAPI Generator (https://github.com/OpenAPITools/openapi-generator) is a popular open source tool for generating API client code, server code, and documentation from OpenAPI documents for many different programming languages, frameworks, and documentation formats. If you followed appendix D, then you have the openapi-generator-cli installed (https://github.com/OpenAPITools/openapi-generator-cli). The openapi-generator-cli is a command-line Node application that downloads and runs the OpenAPI Generator Java executable. Navigate to the chapter6 directory. Make a directory called product-catalog-service. Now run the `openapi-generator-cli` command in the next listing to create your application with the model objects in the com.acmepetsupplies.model package and the stub controller in the com.acmepetsupplies.api package.

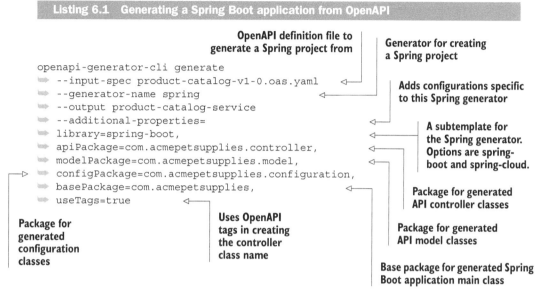

Listing 6.1 Generating a Spring Boot application from OpenAPI

OpenAPI definition file to generate a Spring project from

Generator for creating a Spring project

```
openapi-generator-cli generate
    --input-spec product-catalog-v1-0.oas.yaml
    --generator-name spring
    --output product-catalog-service
    --additional-properties=
    library=spring-boot,
    apiPackage=com.acmepetsupplies.controller,
    modelPackage=com.acmepetsupplies.model,
    configPackage=com.acmepetsupplies.configuration,
    basePackage=com.acmepetsupplies,
    useTags=true
```

Adds configurations specific to this Spring generator

A subtemplate for the Spring generator. Options are spring-boot and spring-cloud.

Package for generated API controller classes

Package for generated API model classes

Package for generated configuration classes

Uses OpenAPI tags in creating the controller class name

Base package for generated Spring Boot application main class

TIP After the `--additional-properties` element in the command, ensure there are no spaces between subsequent elements. In addition, if you don't want to type out the full command, you can run the helper script in the chapter6 folder, listing-6-1-generate-spring-boot-app.sh (or for Windows, listing-6-1-generate-spring-boot-app.bat).

Take a look at the files created in the folder. The README.md file has information telling you the project was created by OpenAPI Generator. The openapitools.json file contains information on the version of the OpenAPI Generator package it downloaded and executed by the openapi-generator-cli to generate your project. You can also use this file to specify configuration option shortcuts for the command-line interface (CLI), but that is out of the scope of this chapter (you can find out more about this at https://github.com/OpenAPITools/openapi-generator-cli). The .openapi-generator/FILES file lists all the generated files in this run. The pom.xml file (POM stands for project object model) contains information needed by the project build tool to build and configure your project. OpenAPI Generator has created your project as a Maven project (i.e., the project is configured to be built by the Maven build tool), and Maven looks in the pom.xml file for project build information. The .openapi-generator-ignore file is used to specify the file names and patterns to exclude from being overwritten whenever the generator is rerun. Finally, the src directory is the folder containing your Java source and test code. The following snippet shows the directory structure of the files created:

```
.
├── .openapi-generator
│   ├── FILES
│   └── VERSION
├── .openapi-generator-ignore
├── README.md
├── openapitools.json
├── pom.xml
└── src
    ├── main
    │   ├── java
    │   │   └── com
    │   │       └── acmepetsupplies
    │   │           ├── OpenApiGeneratorApplication.java
    │   │           ├── RFC3339DateFormat.java
    │   │           ├── configuration
    │   │           │   ├── HomeController.java
    │   │           │   └── SpringDocConfiguration.java
    │   │           ├── controller
    │   │           │   ├── ApiUtil.java
    │   │           │   ├── ProductsApi.java
    │   │           │   └── ProductsApiController.java
    │   │           └── model
    │   │               ├── Error.java
    │   │               └── Product.java
    │   └── resources
    │       ├── application.properties
    │       └── openapi.yaml
    └── test
        └── java
            └── com
                └── acmepetsupplies
                    └── OpenApiGeneratorApplicationTests.java
```

You've seen the directory structure of the files generated for your project. Now take a look at the source code in the src folder. In the application directory, navigate to the src/main/java/com/acmepetsupplies folder. The controller/ProductsApi.java file is a stub controller interface that contains routing information as a Java `@RequestMapping` annotation. This annotation tells the Spring Boot framework to route requests for GET `/v1/catalog/products/{id}` to this controller and that the controller returns a response with content-type `application/json`. It has a `viewProduct(id)` method, and the name of the method is based on the `operationId` of the endpoint in the API definition file. The `viewProduct(id)` method has a default implementation that returns a response based on the example in the chapter6/product-catalog-v1-0.oas.yaml OpenAPI file. The `@Tag`, `@Operation`, and `@ApiResponse` annotations contain the document metadata from the OpenAPI definition. This metadata can be used to regenerate the OpenAPI definition from the code. The `ProductsApi` interface is shown in the following snippet:

```
@Generated(value = "org.openapitools.codegen.languages.SpringCodegen",
    date = "2022-12-31T13:20:55.039973Z[Europe/London]")
```

```
@Validated
@Tag(name = "Products", description = "A product is an item for
  sale on the store.")
public interface ProductsApi {

    default Optional<NativeWebRequest> getRequest() {
        return Optional.empty();
    }

    @Operation(
        operationId = "viewProduct",
        summary = "View a product's details",
        tags = { "Products" },
        responses = {
            @ApiResponse(responseCode = "200", description = "OK",
  content = {
                @Content(mediaType = "application/json",
  schema = @Schema(implementation =
  Product.class))
            }),
            …
        security = {
            @SecurityRequirement(name = "ApiKeyAuth")
        }
    )
    @RequestMapping(
        method = RequestMethod.GET,
        value = "/v1/catalog/products/{id}",
        produces = { "application/json" }
    )
    default ResponseEntity<Product> viewProduct(
        @Parameter(name = "id", description = "Product identifier",
  required = true) @PathVariable("id") UUID id
    ) {
        getRequest().ifPresent(request -> {
            for (MediaType mediaType:
  MediaType.parseMediaTypes(request.getHeader("Accept"))) {
                if (mediaType.isCompatibleWith(
  MediaType.valueOf("application/json"))) {
                    String exampleString = "{ \"keywords\" :
  [ \"keywords\", \"keywords\", \"keywords\", \"keywords\",
  \"keywords\" ], \"price\" : 100, \"name\" :
  \"Acme Uber Dog Rope Toy\", \"description\" :
  \"Acme Uber Dog Rope Toy provides hours of fun for your dog.
   Great for bouncing, throwing and catching.\",
  \"id\" : \"dcd53ddb-8104-4e48-8cc0-5df1088c6113\" }";
                    ApiUtil.setExampleResponse(request,
  "application/json", exampleString);
                    break;
                }
            }
        });
        return new ResponseEntity<>(
  HttpStatus.NOT_IMPLEMENTED);
```

Metadata on
OpenAPI document
API operations

Metadata on
OpenAPI document
API responses

Routes requests to GET
/v1/catalog/products/{id}
endpoint to the viewProduct
method

Default
implementation
returns an example
response if the
Accept header is
application/json

Returns a 501 Not
Implemented error if an
Accept header isn't present

```
        }
    }
```

The controller/ProductsApiController.java file implements the `ProductsApi` interface. In the real world, your controller will contain some logic or call a service object that contains business logic and may retrieve data from a database. For this example, I want you to override the `viewProduct(id)` method and return a dummy object to show that you can return a custom response.

To do this, first add the following imports to the top of the ProductsApiController .java file, just after the package declaration:

```
import io.swagger.v3.oas.annotations.Parameter;
import java.math.BigDecimal;
import java.util.Set;
import java.util.HashSet;
import java.util.Arrays;
```

Now write the code in the next listing inside the ProductsApiController.java file to add a new `viewProduct` method that returns a hard-coded `Product` object in the response.

> **Listing 6.2 Adding a `viewProduct` method to ProductApiController**

Parameter Swagger annotation describes the ID method parameter with information that can be used to generate an OpenAPI definition from the code.

Overrides the viewProduct defined in the ProductsApi interface

```
    @Override
    public ResponseEntity<Product> viewProduct(    ⟵
        @Parameter(name = "id", description = "Product identifier",
    required = true)
    @PathVariable("id") UUID id){
        Product product = new Product();           ⟵
        product.setId(id);
        product.setName("Acme Uber Dog Rope Toy");
        product.setDescription
    ("Acme Uber Dog Rope Toy provides hours of fun for your dog.");
        product.setPrice(new BigDecimal(50));
        Set<String> keywords = new HashSet<>(Arrays.asList("rope", "toy",
    "dog"));
        product.setKeywords(keywords);
        return new ResponseEntity<Product>(product, HttpStatus.OK);
    }
}
```

Creates a hard-coded product object the method returns

The Spring Framework PathVariable annotation indicates the ID method parameter should be bound to a Spring URI template variable.

OpenAPI Generator created two files in the model package—model/Product.java and model/Error.java. The `Product.java` class is returned by the controller for successful (2xx) responses, and Error.java should be returned by the application error handler code. When serialized as a JSON message, the `Error` class matches the error response

schema defined in your OpenAPI document. At the moment, however, there is no error
handling code set up to use the `Error.java` class. Fix this by creating an error handler
that intercepts any exceptions thrown by the controller and returns an instance of
object type `Error`. Do this by creating an ApplicationExceptionHandler.java file in the
src/main/java/com/acmesupplies/controller directory, as shown in the next listing.

Listing 6.3   Common error handling

```
package com.acmepetsupplies.controller;

import com.acmepetsupplies.model.Error;
import org.springframework.http.HttpHeaders;
import org.springframework.http.HttpStatus;
import org.springframework.http.ResponseEntity;
import org.springframework.lang.Nullable;
import org.springframework.web.bind.annotation.RestControllerAdvice;
import org.springframework.web.context.request.WebRequest;
import org.springframework.web.servlet.mvc.method.annotation.
    ResponseEntityExceptionHandler;

import java.util.UUID;

@RestControllerAdvice
public class ApplicationExceptionHandler extends
ResponseEntityExceptionHandler {

    @Override
    protected ResponseEntity<Object> handleExceptionInternal(
            Exception ex, @Nullable Object body, HttpHeaders headers,
    HttpStatus status, WebRequest request) {
        Error apiError = new Error();
        apiError.setId(UUID.randomUUID());
        apiError.setStatus(status.value());
        switch (status.series().value()) {
            case 4: apiError.setCode("validation." +
    status.series().name().toLowerCase());
                    break;
            case 5: apiError.setCode("error." +
    status.series().name().toLowerCase());
                    break;
            default:
    apiError.setCode(status.series().name().toLowerCase());
                    break;
        }
        apiError.setTitle(status.getReasonPhrase());
        switch (status.value()) {
            case 400: apiError.setDetail("Bad request. Please check
    the request is valid.");
                    break;
            case 404:
                    apiError.setDetail("Resource not found. Please check
    the path and resource identifier in your request");
                    break;
```

Intercept exceptions from
the controller, and apply
error handling logic.

A method for
customizing the
response body of all
exception types

Depending on the
HTTP status, set
the detail on the
error object.

```
            case 429: apiError.setDetail("Too many requests. Request
➡ quota exceeded in time window. Try again soon");
                    break;
            default: apiError.setDetail(status.getReasonPhrase());
                    break;
        }
        return new ResponseEntity<>(apiError, headers, status);
    }
}
```

You've generated your Spring Boot project, created a controller, and created some common error-handling code. Now you need to tell Spring Boot how to auto-configure and start your project. Run your application from the command line by running the `mvn spring-boot:run` command. This starts up your Spring Boot application and makes it available on localhost:8080. Using your favorite HTTP client, make a request to your application using any Universally Unique Identifier (UUID) of your choice as the product identifier, and you'll see the product returned in the response. In the following example, I use curl and format the response with jq:

```
curl --silent --request GET
➡ http://localhost:8080/v1/catalog/products
➡ /612b4280-b5c0-4ad5-bce7-ede7ab2b80fc | jq .
```

> **TIP** For Windows users, the preceding command works in the Cmd.exe command prompt. But in PowerShell, curl is a built-in alias to the `Invoke-WebRequest` cmdlet. So to run this command in PowerShell, you need to replace curl with curl.exe.

This gives the following response:

```
{
  "id": "612b4280-b5c0-4ad5-bce7-ede7ab2b80fc",
  "name": "Acme Uber Dog Rope Toy",
  "description": "Acme Uber Dog Rope Toy provides hours
➡ of fun for your dog.",
  "price": 50,
  "keywords": [
    "rope",
    "dog",
    "toy"
  ]
}
```

You get a successful response, and that's great. But what if you send a request with a product ID that isn't a UUID? Will the application validate the input parameter? Remember that you didn't write any validation logic. Check out what happens by making a request with a simple non-UUID string:

```
curl --silent --request GET
➡ http://localhost:8080/v1/catalog/products/not-a-uuid | jq
```

```
{
  "id": "d207deea-cef0-4598-ae86-ebb56340b4ac",
  "status": 400,
  "code": "validation.client_error",
  "title": "Bad Request",
  "detail": "Bad request. Please check the request is valid."
}
```

The application correctly validates your input and returns a response matching your OpenAPI definition error schema. The Spring Boot application framework uses the validation annotations on the controller and model objects to validate user input.

Congratulations! You've successfully generated your API service by generating it from your OpenAPI definition SOT. You can stop the running service by typing Ctrl–C, but for now, keep it running. In the next section, I show you how to deploy your API service to your API gateway.

6.2.2 Deploying to the gateway

Suppose that as a next step, your team lead asks you to deploy your API service to an API gateway (step 3 in figure 6.5). An API gateway is a reverse proxy and central ingress point that channels external requests to your backend API services. Apart from routing, an API gateway can also fulfill other cross-cutting concerns such as authentication, protocol translation, rate limiting, and monitoring. API gateways allow you to decouple the external client interface from the internal backend service.

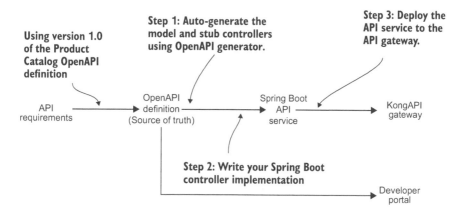

Figure 6.5 **Your next step is to deploy your API service to the API gateway.**

In this section, I walk you through deploying your API to Kong, a popular open source API gateway. While I use the Kong gateway for this example, again, the point of this section isn't to teach you how to use a particular API gateway technology. The goal is to show that for the public API you're building here, the API reference documentation has to reflect the behavior of all the components that contribute to the externally observed behavior of the API. This includes both the API service and the API gateway. As you'll see, the API gateway can return a response the API service doesn't know about, but this still needs to be captured in the API reference.

When you deploy an API service to a gateway, you're creating a route between the external request and the API service. By default, Kong listens for public HTTP traffic on port 8000. Set up Kong to match and forward any requests to `GET /v1/catalog/products/(id)` and host header `api.acme-pet-supplies.com` to your product catalog API service running on port 8080 by updating the chapter6/kong/kong.yaml, as shown in the following listing.

Listing 6.4   Kong API gateway declarative configuration

```
_format_version: "1.1"
services:
  - name: Product_Catalog_API
    protocol: http
    host: localhost
    port: 8080
    path:  /
    routes:
      - tags:
          - Product Catalog
        name: viewProduct
        methods:
          - GET
        hosts:
          - api.acme-pet-supplies.com
        paths:
          - /v1/catalog/products/(.+)$
        strip_path: false
    plugins:
      - name: key-auth
        config:
          key_names:
            - x-api-key
consumers:
- username: my_api_consumer
  keyauth_credentials:
  - key: my_secret_api_key
```

> Route requests to GET /v1/catalog/products/{id} requests with host headers set as api.acme-pet-supplies.com to backend API service on localhost:8080.

> The key-auth plugin sets up API key authentication.

NOTE Users running Kong in Docker (e.g., Windows users) should set the `host` value in listing 6.4 to `host.docker.internal`. This is a special domain name system (DNS) name that resolves to the internal IP address used by the host Windows computer. This enables the Kong instance running in Docker to route the request to the backend Product Catalog API service running on the Windows host.

The kong.yaml file contains declarative configuration for routing requests to the Kong gateway. With this configuration, all requests to your API gateway must provide the `Host` header `api.acme-pet-supplies.com` to be routed to the backend API service.

The `securityScheme` section of the OpenAPI definition SOT specifies that the API is protected with an API key. An API gateway is a usual place to implement API key authentication. An API key is used to identify the application (i.e., the API consumer) calling an API. The configuration in listing 6.4 sets up Kong to require API consumers to send an API key by enabling Kong's key-auth plugin. In this case, an API consumer needs to send an `x-api-key` header with the value `my_secret_api` to make a successful request to the server.

Navigate to chapter6/kong, and start Kong by running `kong start -c kong.conf`. (For Windows users, use the run_kong_docker.bat script in the chapter6/kong folder to start Kong. If you're using a Unix-like operating system, you can also use the start_kong.sh and stop_kong.sh helper scripts to start and stop Kong.) Then, using your favorite API client, make a request to the API gateway providing the API key in the request providing the `Host` and `x-api-key` headers. Here is how you can make the request with curl:

```
curl --silent --header "Host: api.acme-pet-supplies.com"
  --header "x-api-key: my_secret_api_key"
  --request GET http://localhost:8000/v1/catalog/products
  /612b4280-b5c0-4ad5-bce7-ede7ab2b80fc | jq .
```

You should see a product response printed on your console. Congratulations! You've successfully deployed your API to the gateway and made a request to your secured public API.

6.2.3 Publishing to the developer portal

Let's say that now your team lead asks you to publish the API definition SOT to the developer portal as an API reference (figure 6.6).

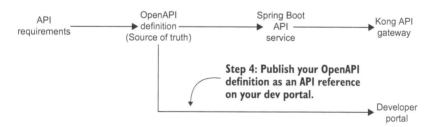

Figure 6.6   Publish your OpenAPI definition as an API reference on your developer portal.

A developer portal is the authoritative documentation that API consumers go to when they want to understand how to use a public API. Developer portals have API user guides and tutorials to help developers get started quickly on using an API. They also have an API reference that shows the API operations supported by the API. In the real world, you could upload your API reference to a developer portal service, use the developer portal that comes with your API gateway platform, or even build your own developer portal. For this example scenario, create a folder in the chapter6 directory called dev-portal. Use this as the folder for holding and serving the API reference you create.

Generate an API reference from your API definition SOT using the Redocly CLI. The Redocly CLI generates an API reference in a three-panel responsive layout with the left panel containing a search bar and navigation menu. If you followed the instructions in appendix D, then you have the Redocly CLI installed. In the chapter6 directory, run the following command to generate a static zero-dependency HTML file of your API reference:

```
redocly build-docs product-catalog-v1-0.oas.yaml
➡ --output dev-portal/reference.html
```

Inside the dev-portal folder, start an HTTP server to serve up the HTML file by running `http-server --port 9000`. In your browser, go to `http://localhost:9000/reference.html` to see your API reference rendered.

Congratulations, you've successfully published your API reference. As it stands, your API reference accurately documents the 200 success response of the GET /v1/catalog/products/{id} endpoint on your API. But what if the behavior of the API definition SOT changes and that is no longer correct? Remember that this scenario can lead to the API reference or code being out of sync. Next, let's look at how to sync the changes to the code and API reference when the SOT is updated.

6.2.4   *An update to the SOT*

Suppose you receive a change in requirements leading to a change in the API definition SOT. The business analyst on your team informs you that there is a requirement to return two new mandatory fields, reviewRating and numberofReviews, both of which are integers. The following snippet from the Products schema in the updated API definition SOT in the product-catalog-v1-1.oas.yaml file shows the new mandatory attributes in the endpoint response:

```
reviewRating:
  maximum: 5
  minimum: 1
  type: integer
  description: Average product review rating.
  format: int32
  example: 5
numberOfReviews:
  type: integer
  description: Number of product reviews.
  format: int32
  example: 10
```

Because the OpenAPI definition is the SOT on the API operations, it has been updated as product-catalog-v1-1.oas.yaml to reflect the new requirements. Now you have to regenerate the response model objects in the API service to support these two new fields and populate them. To keep your API reference consistent with the behavior of the API service, you need to update it based on the SOT.

You can regenerate the API service code from the updated product-catalog-v1-1.oas.yaml file. But you don't want to overwrite the custom changes you added to the ProductsApiController.java file. To prevent this, add **ProductsApiController.java to the product-catalog-service/.openapi-generator-ignore file. Then, navigate to the chapter6 folder, and run the command shown in the next listing to generate the code using the product-catalog-v1-1.oas.yaml file.

Listing 6.5 Regenerating the Spring Boot service

```
openapi-generator-cli generate
    --input-spec product-catalog-v1-1.oas.yaml        ⟵─┤ Uses updated
    --generator-name spring                                 SOT definition
    --ignore-file-override                            ⟵─── Specifies the location of
    product-catalog-service/.openapi-generator-ignore      ignore file to prevent
    --additional-properties=                               ProductsApiController.java
    library=spring-boot,                                   from being overwritten
    apiPackage=com.acmepetsupplies.controller,
    modelPackage=com.acmepetsupplies.model,
    configPackage=com.acmepetsupplies.configuration,
    basePackage=com.acmepetsupplies,
    useTags=true
```

TIP Alternatively, you can also run the `listing-6-5-generate-spring-boot-app.sh` or `listing-6-5-generate-spring-boot-app.bat` helper scripts, depending on your operating system.

Notice that the ProductsApiController.java file isn't updated, but the regenerated Product.java file now has getter and setter methods for `reviewRating` and `numberOf-Reviews`.

Using the OpenAPI Generator Maven plugin

As an alternative to using the openapi-generator-cli, Java developers may prefer to have a Maven goal (i.e., an executable plugin task) to regenerate the project. The openapi-generator-maven-plugin enables you to generate your server stub code from inside your Maven project. This is useful, as you can use Maven commands to generate your code. Add the following snippet to the plugins section of your pom.xml file to generate the server stub code to the target/directory:

```
<plugins>
    <plugin>
        <groupId>org.openapitools</groupId>
        <artifactId>openapi-generator-maven-plugin</artifactId>
        <version>6.2.1</version>
        <executions>
            <execution>
```

(continued)

```
            <goals>
                <goal>generate</goal>
            </goals>
            <id>buildApi</id>
            <configuration>
                <inputSpec>
${project.basedir}/../product-catalog-v1-1.oas.yaml
</inputSpec>
                <generatorName>spring</generatorName>
                <library>spring-boot</library>
                <ignoreFileOverride>
${project.basedir}/.openapi-generator-ignore
</ignoreFileOverride>

        <modelPackage>com.acmepetsupplies.model</modelPackage>

        <apiPackage>com.acmepetsupplies.controller</apiPackage>
                <invokerPackage>com.acmepetsupplies</invokerPackage>
                <configOptions>
                    <useTags>true</useTags>
<configPackage>com.acmepetsupplies.configuration</configPackage>
                </configOptions>
            </configuration>
        </execution>
    </executions>
</plugin>
...
```

> References the location of your API definition file

> Specifies the generator ignore file

Next, create a Maven plugin goal to copy over the generated files to your src/ folder.
You can do this with the Maven AntRun plugin as shown here:

```
<plugin>
    <artifactId>maven-antrun-plugin</artifactId>
    <version>3.0.0</version>
    <executions>
        <execution>
            <phase>generate-sources</phase>
            <configuration>
                <target>
                    <move todir="src/main">
                        <fileset dir=
"target/generated-sources/openapi/src/main"/>
                    </move>
                </target>
            </configuration>
            <goals>
                <goal>run</goal>
            </goals>
        </execution>
    </executions>
</plugin>
...
```

> Maven AntRun plugin to copy the generated source files from the target directory to src/main/

Now run `mvn clean compile` to clean the target directory and generate and copy over the files as part of the compile phase. Note that unlike other Maven plugins, running the plugin goal directly with `mvn openapi-generator:generate` won't work, as it throws an error.

Update your ProductApiController.java class to set the `reviewRating` and `numberOf-Reviews` fields on the returned product to any integer value. The next listing shows how your `ProductApiController` `viewProduct` method should look.

Listing 6.6 Updating `viewProduct` in `ProductApiController`

```
@Override
public ResponseEntity<Product> viewProduct(
        @Parameter(name = "id", description = "Product identifier",
        required = true) @PathVariable("id") UUID id) {
    Product product = new Product();
    product.setId(id);
    product.setName("Acme Uber Dog Rope Toy");
    product.setDescription(
    "Acme Uber Dog Rope Toy provides hours of fun for your dog.");
    product.setPrice(new BigDecimal(50));
    Set<String> keywords =
    new HashSet<>(Arrays.asList("rope", "toy", "dog"));
    product.setKeywords(keywords);
    product.setNumberOfReviews(11);          Sets the number of reviews
    product.setReviewRating(3);              and the review rating
    return new ResponseEntity<Product>(product, HttpStatus.OK);
}
```

Stop your application (press Ctrl–C to stop the running server instance), and restart your application with `mvn spring-boot:run` to pick up your latest changes. Because your application is already routed through your API gateway, you can make a request to the gateway using your API client and see the updated response by running the following command:

```
curl --silent --header "Host: api.acme-pet-supplies.com"
  --header "x-api-key: my_secret_api_key"  --request GET
  http://localhost:8000/v1/catalog/products
  /612b4280-b5c0-4ad5-bce7-ede7ab2b80fc | jq .
```

You should see the following response with the two new fields:

```
{
    "id": "612b4280-b5c0-4ad5-bce7-ede7ab2b80fc",
    "name": "Acme Uber Dog Rope Toy",
    "description": "Acme Uber Dog Rope Toy provides hours
  of fun for your dog.",
    "price": 50,
    "keywords": [
        "rope",
```

```
        "dog",
        "toy"
    ],
    "reviewRating": 3,          Note the new fields
    "numberOfReviews": 11       in the response.
}
```

Your API now functions in accordance with the new requirements, and the updated endpoint can be reached from your API gateway. However, your API reference in your dev portal is now out of sync and has to be updated.

6.2.5   Republishing your SOT to the portal

Your next task is to regenerate your API reference from the SOT API definition so that it matches the behavior of your API. First, kill the running instance of the HTTP server with Ctrl–C. Then, run the following commands in your chapter6 directory to delete the old API reference, and generate a new one from the updated version of the updated API definition:

```
rm  dev-portal/reference.html
redocly build-docs product-catalog-v1-1.oas.yaml
➥ --output dev-portal/reference.html
```

Go into the dev-portal folder, and start the HTTP server by running `http-server -port 9000`. Navigate to `http://localhost:9000/reference.html` to see your updated API reference. It has the two new attributes (`reviewRating` and `numberOfReviews`) in the 200 response of the `viewProduct` endpoint, which is consistent with the behavior of the API.

6.2.6   Generating client SDKs

One thing you didn't do in the example you worked through was generate a client SDK. Let's say you're asked to generate a Java SDK for the Product Catalog API from the SOT. An API client SDK provides a programming language library for API consumers to use in making requests to the API as an alternative to making direct HTTP requests themselves using their code. The SDK wraps an underlying HTTP client to make HTTP requests to your API server, as illustrated in figure 6.7.

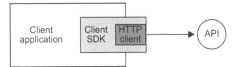

Figure 6.7   An API client SDK is a library that wraps an HTTP client that makes calls to an API.

OpenAPI Generator allows you generate a client library just the same way you generated the server code—by specifying the name of the generator to use and the options that apply to that generator. Depending on the client generator you specify, you may have the option of also specifying the underlying HTTP client to be used in making the HTTP requests.

> **TIP** To see the list of generators available in OpenAPI Generator, run `openapi-generator-cli list` on the command line, or see https://openapi-generator.tech/docs/generators.

To see this in action, create a java-client directory folder in your chapter6 directory, and run the code in the next listing to generate the Java API client SDK project.

Listing 6.7   Generating the Java API client SDK

```
openapi-generator-cli generate
    --input-spec ../product-catalog-v1-1.oas.yaml          Name of the client
    --generator-name java                                  SDK generator
    --output java-client
    --additional-properties=                               Library template to use: okhttp HTTP
    library=okhttp-gson,                                   client with a gson JSON processor
    invokerPackage=com.acmepetsupplies.client,
    apiPackage=com.acmepetsupplies.api,
    modelPackage=com.acmepetsupplies.model,                Maven groupId used to
    groupId=com.acmepetsupplies,                           identify the project
    artifactId=acmepetsupplies-java-client
                                                           Maven artifactId used to
                                                           name the created JAR file
```

> **TIP** You can also use the helper scripts `listing-6-7-generate-java-client.sh` or `listing-6-7-generate-java-client.bat` in the chapter6 directory, depending on your operating system.

OpenAPI Generator has created a chapter6/java-client/src/main/java/com/acmepetsupplies/api/ProductsApi.java class that exposes a `viewProduct(id)` method that uses an underlying OkHttp client to make calls to your API. You can see this snippet starting from line 70 in the file:

```
public Product viewProduct(UUID id) throws ApiException {
    ApiResponse<Product> localVarResp = viewProductWithHttpInfo(id);
    return localVarResp.getData();
}
```

To try out this library, write a test class in the project that makes a request and prints out the response without making any assertions. Open the java-client directory with either Visual Studio Code (VS Code) or your favorite Java editor to see the generated files. Open the src/test/java/com/acmepetsupplies/api/ProductsApiTest.java file, and update as shown in the following listing. (Be sure to remove the `@Disabled` annotation on the `ProductsApiTest` class.)

Listing 6.8   Using the SDK

```
public class ProductsApiTest {
    @Test
```

```
    public void viewProductTest() throws ApiException {
        ProductsApi api = new ProductsApi();
        api.getApiClient().setBasePath(
  "http://localhost:8000");
        api.getApiClient().addDefaultHeader(
  "Host", "api.acme-pet-supplies.com");
        api.getApiClient().setApiKey(
  "my_secret_api_key");

        UUID id = UUID.randomUUID();
        Product response = api.viewProduct(id);
        System.out.println(response);
    }
}
```

Initializes the ProductsApi class that wraps the API client

Uses the underlying API client to set header and API key values

Calls the API operation to send an HTTP request

Now run the test. You can do this from the command line by running `mvn test`. You should see the printout of the product API response to the console.

To package the library as a JAR file so API consumers can add it as a dependency to their Java projects, run `mvn install`. This creates the reusable library target/acmepet-supplies-java-client-1.0.jar. A copy is also added to the local Maven repository on your computer so it's available to other Maven projects you create. You can also publish the library to an external Maven repository, but that is outside the scope of this book.

Just like generating server code, generating an API client SDK is quick, and you can regenerate SDKs every time your API definition SOT is updated. Along with the OkHttp client, this generator supports other Java HTTP clients, including Open-Feign, Spring RestTemplate, Jersey, and more.

If you build a public API and make your OpenAPI definition available to your API consumers but don't offer programming language SDKs, some of your API consumers may generate SDKs themselves. So it can be a good idea to generate SDKs from your OpenAPI internally in a few programming languages to verify that the classes and methods produced are what you expect. For example, it's valid to start an OpenAPI `operationId` name with a digit, but Java method names can't start with a digit. Therefore, when generating a Java client, OpenAPI Generator will need to rewrite the method name with a prefix to make it valid.

6.2.7   *Advantages of generating from the SOT*

In the example you worked through, you see that changes to API requirements are reflected first in the SOT, and then generated artifacts—server code, client SDKs, and reference documentation—are generated from the SOT. In the next chapter, you'll see that tests can also be generated from the SOT. Depending on the number of teams involved, using the SOT this way lends itself well to parallelization. Once the SOT has been agreed upon, potentially different teams working on the server side, client side, tests, or documentation team can go away and generate the artifacts they need from the agreed API definition (figure 6.8).

In regard to code and API documentation conformance, another advantage of generating code from the SOT is speed. Code generation happens quickly with relatively

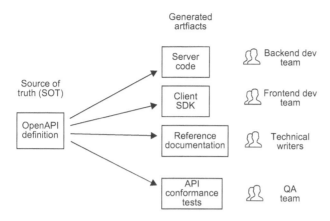

Figure 6.8 Using the OpenAPI definition as the SOT for generating artifacts

low-maintenance overhead compared to having to create or maintain schema tests to check for code and documentation conformance. There are no tests to write or maintain. The developer can quickly regenerate the API service stub code from the command line. This speed ties in well with the flexibility required for iterative API design. In practice, API design is usually not a linear process with clear-cut design and build phases. Even during the build phase, some aspects of the API design may still be updated as the team gains new knowledge of the requirements, the system under development, and technical constraints. Whenever this happens, with the generation approach, you can easily re-create all the generated artifacts from the updated SOT and carry on with development.

With the SOT approach, I find it useful to have two views of an API definition—a *to-be* view and an *as is* view. The to-be view is the forward-looking design view of the API definition that contains changes that reflect what the API should do but which may not yet be generated in code. The as is view is the API definition that accurately reflects what is implemented in the API right now. For instance, in the example you just worked through, a change in requirements to add two new fields to the API response was first applied to the product-catalog-v1-1.oas.yaml API definition file (the to-be view). At that point, because the change had not been implemented in the API service yet, the to-be view differed by two fields from product-catalog-v1-0.oas.yaml file (the as is view), which correctly reflects what is implemented. Of course, after the API service code is regenerated from product-catalog-v1-1.oas.yaml, product-catalog-v1-1.oas.yaml becomes the as is view.

In a design-first (or contract-first or specification-first approach—people call this by different names) approach of creating an API definition SOT before API development begins, it's important to note that different team members need these different views (to-be and as is) at the different phases of the API product life cycle. At the design phase, API designers and API governance teams are interested in the to-be view. But as API development moves from the build to the publish phase, there will be interest in the as is view because that is what gets published to the developer portal for

API consumers. Some teams find it useful to generate the as is view from the code, as this most accurately reflects what has been implemented.

6.2.8   *Dealing with responses from the gateway*

There are challenges with generating API server code from the API definition. One is that API responses may not come from your API service, but from a component that sits in front of your service. So you need to configure the relevant components to generate responses in the required format. For example, the API gateway can have the responsibility of authenticating the consumer's API key and can send a response for key authentication failures (a 401 error). Test this in your example application by sending a request without an API key. Run the following command:

```
Curl --include --header "Host: api.acme-pet-supplies.com"
  --request GET http://localhost:8000/v1/catalog/products
  /612b4280-b5c0-4ad5-bce7-ede7ab2b80fc
```

This gives a response from the gateway similar to the following:

```
HTTP/1.1 401 Unauthorized
Date: Thu, 15 Dec 2022 06:57:52 GMT
Content-Type: application/json; charset=utf-8
Connection: keep-alive
WWW-Authenticate: Key realm="kong"
Content-Length: 45
X-Kong-Response-Latency: 0
Server: kong/3.0.0

{
  "message":"No API key found in request"
}
```

You have two options here: (1) you can update the 401 response of your API definition SOT to reflect this response message structure; or (2) you can configure Kong to return an output that matches your error response object structure (with fields ID, status, code, title, and detail). At the time of writing, this requires writing a custom Kong plugin.

Ensuring consistency by generating the API service from the external SOT API definition works best when the API gateway is doing as little transformation as possible to the request and response from the API service. Consider the scenario where for some reason (perhaps to support some legacy functionality), the API gateway is required to transform the request it receives before forwarding it to the API service. This could be transforming the path or query string, removing or adding headers, or removing or replacing attributes in the request body. In the Kong API gateway, you can achieve this with the Request Transformer plugin. The SOT API definition used to generate the API reference has to accurately represent the external API behavior, but due to the significant transformation logic in the gateway, it's not useful in generating the API service code. In a microservice architecture, you can also have other components handling requests before they hit your API service. For example, a policy engine component such as the Open Policy Agent (OPA) can intercept requests and return authorization error responses. Because components outside your API service may introduce some logic in the request flow, it's a good idea to complement your API conformance generation approach with API conformance testing (discussed in the next chapter) to ensure consistency in your API reference.

6.2.9 Customizing code generation

OpenAPI Generator supports more than 40 different programming languages. In the example, you ran OpenAPI Generator from the command line using the openapi-generator-cli. But OpenAPI Generator has plugins for integrating with build automation tools such as Maven, Gradle (Java build tools), SBT (a Scala build tool), Cake (a C# build tool), Bazel (a multilanguage build tool), and more.

> **NOTE** I've looked at OpenAPI Generator in this section, but there are other open source OpenAPI code generators. For example, NSwag (https://github .com/RicoSuter/NSwag) allows you to generate C# controller stubs from an OpenAPI specification. OpenAPI Client and Server Code Generator (https:// github.com/deepmap/oapi-codegen) allows you to generate code for Go applications.

If none of the bundled generators that come with OpenAPI Generator serve your needs, you can extend it to define your own custom code generation logic. You can do this in three ways. First, if you need to only slightly modify the template used by a built-in generator, you can extract and modify the template for the generator. For example, suppose you wanted to modify the template for the Spring Boot generator to remove the `@Generated(value = "org.openapitools.codegen.languages.SpringCodegen"`, `date ..)` annotation that shows up on generated controllers. To do this, in your chapter6 directory, run the command shown in the next listing to extract the templates for the Spring Boot generator spring-boot library you want to modify. The templates are extracted to the out directory.

Listing 6.9 Generating templates for the Spring Boot generator

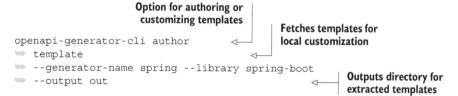

> **TIP** You can also use the helper scripts `listing-6-9-generate-templates`
> `.sh` or `listing-6-9-generate-templates.bat`, depending on your operating system.

OpenAPI Generator uses the Mustache templating language (http://mustache.github .io, as implemented by JMustache https://github.com/samskivert/jmustache) for the templates used to generate code. Edit the template-test/out/apiController.mustache template, and remove the `{{>generatedAnnotation}}` line.

Now generate your project by running OpenAPI generator with a reference to the modified template directory, as shown in the following listing. This generates new project files in the myapp directory.

Listing 6.10   New project using the modified Spring Boot templates

```
openapi-generator-cli generate
--generator-name spring --library spring-boot
--template-dir out                              ◄──── Directory containing
--output myapp                                  ◄──── modified templates
--input-spec product-catalog-v1-1.oas.yaml      ◄──── Directory for generated
                                                      application code
                                                      API spec to generate code for
```

> **TIP**   You can also use the helper scripts `listing-6-10-generate-from-custom-template.sh` or `listing-6-10-generate-from-custom-template.bat` in the chapter6 directory, depending on your operating system.

Look in the generated myapp/src/main/java/org/openapitools/api/V1ApiController.java file. Notice that the `@Generated` annotation isn't present.

Apart from the built-in templates that come with the generators, the other two ways you can customize the code generation are to create user-defined templates and define new generators. These detailed customizations are outside the scope of this book, but you can find out more at https://openapi-generator.tech/docs/customization.

6.3   *Generating OpenAPI from code*

Rather than generating code from the OpenAPI definition, you could go the other way. To ensure reference documentation and code conformance, you can generate your OpenAPI definition from the code and then create artifacts (e.g., client SDKs and the API reference documentation) from the generated definition. In this code-first approach, you first make any changes that should be reflected in the API reference in the application code, and then you generate the OpenAPI definition from the application code.

6.3.1   *Generating OpenAPI with springdoc*

Consider this scenario in the context of the following problem: users have reported that the `numberOfReviews` and `reviewRating` fields are being returned by your live API but aren't in the reference documentation. (This is the opposite of the case you looked at in the generation scenario.) Your OpenAPI definition file uses the `additionalProperties:false` entry to specify that there should be no additional properties in the response except those specified in the definition. So your documentation is inconsistent with the API behavior, as the live API is returning additional fields. Your team asks you to solve this problem by generating the API reference from your application code.

To do this for Spring Boot, you can drop in Java libraries that automatically generate an OpenAPI definition from your project by inferring it from the application configuration, classes, and annotations. Two examples of such libraries for Spring Boot include springdoc-openapi Java library (https://springdoc.org) and the SpringFox library (https://springfox.github.io/springfox). In this example, I'll illustrate how to do this with springdoc-openapi.

The generated product-catalog-service already has a springdoc-openapi library as a dependency. By default, the library makes the OpenAPI definition available at `http://server:port/context-path/v3/api-docs` in JSON format, and a YAML version is available at `http://server:port/context-path/v3/api-docs.yaml`. (Note that the context-path here is the name with which the web application is accessed.) The library also enables you to visualize and interact with the API using the Swagger UI at `http://server:port/context-path/swagger-ui.html`. To add extra information to the generated API definitions, you can add Swagger annotations to the Java classes, as shown in figure 6.9.

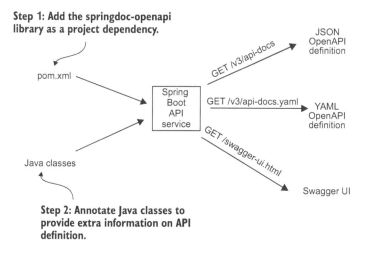

Figure 6.9   Generating OpenAPI definitions from a Spring Boot application

Try this out in your example project. In the chapter6/product-catalog-service folder, if it's not already running, start your application by running `mvn spring-boot:run` on the command line. Navigate to the following URLs to see the output:

- `http://localhost:8080/v3/api-docs`
- `http://localhost:8080/v3/api-docs.yaml`
- `http://localhost:8080/swagger-ui.html`

Great, you've automatically generated your OpenAPI definition from the code!

6.3.2 *Things to consider with generated definitions*

Using the springdoc-openapi library, you added API description information to your Spring Boot API service code and generated an API definition from it. Code libraries exist for doing this with other static and dynamic languages; for example, the Django REST Framework (www.django-rest-framework.org/api-guide/schemas) and flask-smorest (https://flask-smorest.readthedocs.io) for Python applications.

> **TIP** OpenAPI.tools (https://openapi.tools) is a good place to find out about other OpenAPI generation libraries and many other OpenAPI tools.

As with the generated code approach, you need to take note of any API responses that may be coming from the API gateway (or any other component that sits before the API service in the stack). Again, if the API gateway is heavily transforming the API request and response messages, then the API definition generated from the API service won't accurately reflect the external API behavior exposed by the API gateway.

You also need to add enough descriptive API information in the code, including example values. I find that for some teams, it's easy to miss adding examples and other schema constraints (`maxLength`, `minLength`, string pattern expressions, etc.). You can work iteratively, reviewing the generated API definition to ensure it contains a good schema description and examples that a reader of the documentation finds useful.

Rather than generate code from the API definition, some teams take the approach of writing the code for the API service, generating an OpenAPI definition from it, comparing the generated definition to the SOT definition from the design phase, and fixing any differences. Some other teams take the approach of building a prototype of the API in code first to help them gain more information (on technology constraints, requirements, etc.), generating an API definition from the prototype, and then using that generated definition to iterate and refine the API design. While this can be seen as code-first, you can also view this as exploratory work in the context of large unknowns to get more information to support the design. Being able to generate a definition from code in this scenario is very useful, and there is a blurring here between what is traditionally considered to be code-first and design-first in creating the API definitions.

Summary

- API conformance is about ensuring that the published API reference documentation is consistent with the API server behavior and the API client SDK.
- One way to help ensure API conformance is by generating artifacts such as API service code, API client SDKs, and API reference documentation from the OpenAPI definition. In this approach, the API definition is the SOT on the expected or to-be behavior.

- Generating artifacts from OpenAPI has the advantage of being quick (compared to writing schema tests) and allows teams to work in parallel from an agreed API definition SOT.
- Generating an API definition from API service code (and then using the definition to create reference documentation and client SDKs) is another approach for ensuring that the API behavior matches the API reference.
- The published API reference has to take into account API responses that come from components outside the API service, such as the API gateway.
- OpenAPI generator is a popular library for generating server code, client SDKs, and reference documentation from OpenAPI definitions. It has various options for customizing the generated code.

API conformance:
Schema testing

This chapter covers

- Writing code-based schema tests
- Auto-generating API schema tests
- Using a validation proxy for schema tests

In the previous chapter, I explored how generating the OpenAPI definition from the API service helps ensure that the OpenAPI definition conforms to the behavior of the service. But in some cases, it may not always be possible to generate the OpenAPI definition from a service. This can be due to technical limitations in legacy API services or organizational constraints. And even if you can generate the OpenAPI definition from the API service, the behavior of the service under exploratory testing may reveal surprising behavior from the application, which may not be captured by the OpenAPI definition. For example, a bad request with illegal characters can cause the backend application server to return an error before the request is processed by your controller's error-handling logic. An OpenAPI definition generated based on the controller code may not cover this case.

So it's still valuable to have an additional layer of verification to check that the published API reference matches the API behavior. One way to do this is with schema testing using the OpenAPI definition as the definition of the API schema.

In this chapter, I discuss three techniques for writing OpenAPI schema tests: code-based schema tests, generated schema tests, and a validation proxy.

This chapter is aimed at developers who need to create schema tests, but API product owners can gain from getting an overview of the different schema testing approaches. I start by giving an introduction to schema testing. Then, I show you an example of writing code-based schema tests with Atlassian's Swagger Request Validator library. To demonstrate the technique of generating schema tests from an OpenAPI definition file, I show you examples with two tools—Schemathesis and Portman. Finally, to demonstrate the last technique, I show you how to plug in the Prism validation proxy into an existing suite of end-to-end tests. I end the chapter by discussing how schema tests are different from contract tests.

For this chapter, make sure you've installed all the tools in appendix D. The code for this chapter is in the chapter7 folder in the sample project. Writing the tests requires a knowledge of Java. However, if you don't have a background in Java, you can find the completed examples in the chapter7-completed folder.

7.1 Schema tests

Before talking about schema testing, let's start by looking at what an OpenAPI schema is. The OpenAPI specification uses a schema object to describe the data type of a parameter, a request, or a response message in a human-readable and machine-readable form. The data type can be a primitive (e.g., an integer or string), an array, or an object. Following is an example schema object in an API response object from an OpenAPI definition file. It's for a simple `Product` schema object with only two possible fields—`id` and `name`:

```
responses:
  "200":
    description: OK                      Response
    content:                             description
      application/json:                              Response
        schema:                                      media type
          title: Product                    Response
          required:                          schema object
          - id
          type: object
          additionalProperties: false           Response has only
          properties:                            the properties
            id:                                  specified here.
              type: string
              format: uuid
              description: Identifier for the product.
              example: dcd53ddb-8104-4e48-8cc0-5df1088c6113
            name:
              maxLength: 50
              minLength: 1
              type: string
              description: Name of the product.
              example: "Acme Uber Dog Rope Toy"
```

This response message definition specifies that a 200 successful response returns content of type JSON. The required field on the schema shows that the `id` field is mandatory, but `name` is optional. A schema object specifies the data type with the `type` field whose possible values are `boolean`, `number`, `string`, `array`, or `object`. The `id` and `name` properties are the only two properties that messages following this schema can have because the schema uses the `additionalProperties: false` attribute to specify that messages should have no other properties than the ones defined. The `id` property is of type string and follows the universally unique identifier (UUID) format. The `name` property is also of type string and can be between 1 and 50 characters long.

As of version 3.0, OpenAPI schema objects are based on the JSON Schema specification. Because schema objects describe the structure of the message, they are useful for automated testing and validating client-submitted data.

A schema test for the preceding message checks that the actual message returned from the API operation conforms to the schema. This is an automated test that compares the response of the API with the schema in the API definition and fails if they don't match. For example, for the preceding schema, a schema test checks that the `name` property is of type string and has a length not less than 1 or greater than 50. In a schema test, you can also check that the content type returned by an API call matches what is defined in the API definition file and that the headers returned by an API call match what is defined in the API definition file.

An OpenAPI definition includes the schema for request and response messages. When discussing schema tests in the context of APIs documented in OpenAPI, I use the term *consumer* to mean the client application or service that makes a request to an API. And I use the term *provider* to mean the service that provides an API response. This service supports API operations that provide data or some functionality to API consumers. Using these definitions, a schema test is about ensuring that a provider abides by its published provider contract, as shown in figure 7.1.

Unlike functional tests, schema tests don't check for side effects (e.g., that an object is persisted in the database) or check for the correctness of the values in the response message (e.g., that the value of an integer property is 5 or 10). Schema tests aren't performance tests, so they don't make any checks on speed, stability, or responsiveness. Schema tests are also different from consumer-driven contract tests. Contract testing is a more comprehensive technique for testing an integration point between two software services because it uses concrete examples to check that the consumer and provider services have a shared understanding of the messages they exchange in given scenarios. Schema tests only check that the data type of the message communication to an API matches the published documentation at a point in time, but contract tests (using tools such as Pact and Spring Contracts) go much further and enable close team collaboration and the evolution of communicating services over time. I discuss more on the differences between schema tests and contract tests in a later section.

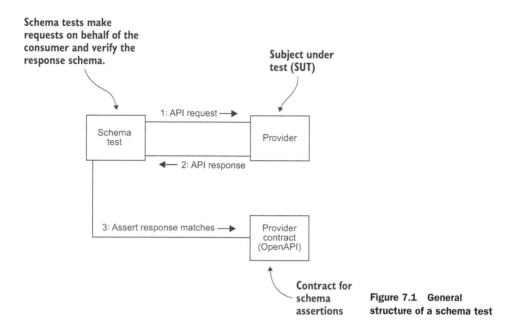

Schema tests make requests on behalf of the consumer and verify the response schema.

Subject under test (SUT)

1: API request →

Schema test

Provider

← 2: API response

3: Assert response matches →

Provider contract (OpenAPI)

Contract for schema assertions

Figure 7.1 General structure of a schema test

NOTE An OpenAPI definition can be thought of as a contract, and some online references use the term *contract test* to refer to schema tests. This can be confusing, but in this book, I treat them differently. Matt Fellows has a great post that clarifies these terms: https://mng.bz/z8RQ.

In the next section, let's look at the first technique for using schema tests to ensure API conformance: code-based schema tests.

7.2 Code-based schema tests

Imagine your users have reported that the `numberOfReviews` and `reviewRating` fields are being returned by your live Product Catalog API but aren't in the reference documentation, even though your OpenAPI definition uses the `additional-Properties:false` entry to specify that there should be no additional properties in the response not specified in the definition. How can you write a schema test to check for this?

You can write an automated or code-based schema test that makes assertions against the response from the API server in two ways. The first way is to write individual assertions in code based on the schema. For example, assert that a given returned property is a string of maximum length x. With this approach, if the schema in the OpenAPI definition changes, you'll need to remember to update the test. The second way is to provide the API definition directly to the test and use a library that checks the response against it. Your test code can be a standalone test file using a unit testing framework (e.g., JUnit in Java) or test code embedded in a request collection using an API client tool such as Postman or Insomnia.

You can vary the scope of the provider API—the subject under test. It can be a fully deployed API, including the API gateway, so the schema test runs as an end-to-end test that exercises the entire stack. Or the scope of the schema test can be at a controller level, which exercises just the API service with dependent systems mocked out. Figure 7.2 shows a conceptual representation of this.

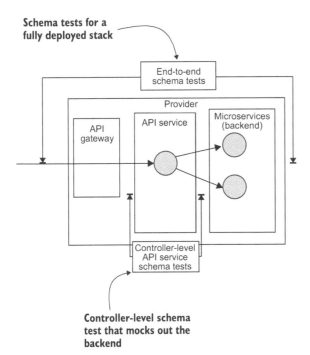

**Schema tests for a
fully deployed stack**

**Controller-level schema
test that mocks out the
backend**

Figure 7.2   A schema test can be
against the entire stack or just at the
controller level of an API service.

A controller-level test with mocked-out dependencies runs quickly, but an end-to-end test runs slowly and suffers from all the downsides of end-to-end tests: difficult to debug, maintain, and scale. Let's look at an example of writing an end-to-end schema test and a controller-level API schema test.

7.2.1   *Writing end-to-end schema tests*

Let's consider an example of writing a code-based schema test that runs against your Product Catalog API endpoint and verifies the response against the product-catalog-v1-0.oas.yaml API definition file.

You can write a Java test for this using the Rest Assured testing library (https://github.com/rest-assured/rest-assured). Rest Assured is a domain-specific language (DSL) for testing REST services in Java. It gives you a fluent interface for expressing your API tests using given/when/then syntax. To assert the response against the OpenAPI contract, use the open source Atlassian Swagger Request Validator library (https://mng.bz/0Gn6).

For this test, you need to start Kong. For users on Unix-like systems, start your Kong API gateway by navigating to your chapter7/kong directory, and start Kong by running the ./start_kong.sh script. In addition, start the API service by navigating to chapter7/product-catalog-api-service and running ./start_api_service.sh.

> **NOTE** For Windows users, first set the host value in the kong.yaml file to `host.docker.internal`. Then, run the `run_kong_docker.bat` script in the chapter7/kong folder to start Kong. In the chapter7/product-catalog-api-service folder, run `start_api_service.bat` to start the service.

With your API gateway and API service running, you can now write your end-to-end schema test. In the chapter7/product-catalog-api-service folder, navigate down the src/test/java folder to the EndToEndSchemaTest.java file. Use the Rest Assured DSL to make a GET request to the `http://localhost:8000/v1/catalog/products/{uuid}` endpoint (where {uuid} is any UUID value), and check that the returned status code is 200, as shown in the next listing. The `OpenApiValidationFilter` checks that the returned response matches the product-catalog-v1-0.oas.yaml API definition file.

Listing 7.1 End-to-end schema test

```
public class EndToEndSchemaTest {
    private final OpenApiValidationFilter validationFilter = new
    OpenApiValidationFilter("../product-catalog-v1-0.oas.yaml");
    @Test
    public void testGetProductEndToEnd() {        // Uses Rest Assured's fluent DSL
        given()
            .header("X-API-Key", "my_secret_api_key")     // Provides headers required by the API gateway
            .filter(validationFilter)      // Filter for validation against the OpenAPI definition.
            .when()
            .get("http://localhost:8000/v1/catalog/products
    /612b4280-b5c0-4ad5-bce7-ede7ab2b90fc")      // Makes a request to the API gateway on port 8000
            .then()
            .assertThat()
            .statusCode(200);      // Asserts a successful response
    }
}
```

Run this test by running the ./run_end_to_end_schema_test.sh (or ./run_end_to_end_schema_test.bat for Windows) in the chapter7/product-catalog-api-service folder. You should see an error like the following:

```
[ERROR] Tests run: 1, Failures: 0, Errors: 1, Skipped: 0, Time elapsed:
1.58 s <<< FAILURE! – in
com.acmepetsupplies.productcatalog.EndToEndSchemaTest
[ERROR] testGetProductEndToEnd  Time elapsed: 1.577 s  <<< ERROR!
com.atlassian.oai.validator.restassured
    .OpenApiValidationFilter$OpenApiValidationException:
{
  "messages" : [ {
    "key" : "validation.response.body.schema.additionalProperties",
```

```
    "level" : "ERROR",
    "message" : "Object instance has properties which are not allowed by
⇒  the schema: [\"numberOfReviews\",\"reviewRating\"]",
    "context" : {
      "requestPath" : "/v1/catalog/products
⇒  /612b4280-b5c0-4ad5-bce7-ede7ab2b90fc",
      "responseStatus" : 200,
      "location" : "RESPONSE",
      "pointers" : {
        "instance" : "/"
      },
      "requestMethod" : "GET"
    }
  } ]
}
    at com.acmepetsupplies.productcatalog.EndToEndSchemaTest
⇒  .testGetProductEndToEnd(EndToEndSchemaTest.java:19)
```

The test shows that the value of `additionalProperties` (set as `false`) in your API definition conflicts with the API that returns the undocumented `numberOfReviews` and `reviewRating` fields. Update the test by setting the `OpenApiValidationFilter` with the product-catalog-v1-1.oas.yaml file, which specifies the two properties. Rerun the test, and watch it pass.

> **TIP** From a security perspective, I recommend setting the `additional-Properties` field as `false`. This helps make it possible to have tests that detect when your API returns extra data you may not be aware of. Some gateways allow you to upload your API definition and use it to verify your API traffic at runtime. This helps you detect unusual behavior, for example, when an API attack causes your API to respond with unexpected extra data.

Because this test is validating the response from the API gateway from the point of view of an API consumer, it suffers from all the downsides of end-to-end tests. End-to-end tests are difficult to scale as the number of tests grows because they can be slow, difficult to debug if they fail (due to the many component services involved), and difficult to set up and maintain test data for. So think carefully about where you apply this approach.

7.2.2   *Writing controller schema tests*

You can write a similar test without having to test the entire stack. Spring Boot allows you to test your application controllers without having to start a server for the application by using Spring's MockMvc package. The package handles your incoming HTTP requests and hands them off to the controller. Rest Assured has a module, spring-mock-mvc, that allows you to unit test your controllers using MockMvc. Add the Rest Assured spring-mock-mvc module to the pom.xml file. In addition, add the Atlassian swagger-request-validator-mockmvc module (https://mng.bz/QZ6G), which enables you to not only validate request and responses against OpenAPI files but also integrate with Spring's MockMvc:

```
<dependency>
    <groupId>io.rest-assured</groupId>
    <artifactId>spring-mock-mvc</artifactId>
    <version>5.3.0</version>
    <scope>test</scope>
</dependency>
<dependency>
    <groupId>com.atlassian.oai</groupId>
    <artifactId>swagger-request-validator-mockmvc</artifactId>
    <version>${swagger-request-validator.version}</version>
</dependency>
```

Now write a test, `ControllerSchemaTest`, in the folder src/test/java/com/acmesup-plies/productcatalog that checks the `ProductsApiController` response, as shown in the next listing. The test validates the response with a ResultMatcher created from the OpenAPI definition.

Listing 7.2 Product controller schema test

```
package com.acmepetsupplies.productcatalog;

import com.acmepetsupplies.productcatalog.controller.ProductsApiController;
import org.junit.Test;
import org.springframework.boot.test.context.SpringBootTest;

import static com.atlassian.oai.validator.mockmvc
   .OpenApiValidationMatchers.openApi;
import static io.restassured.module.mockmvc.RestAssuredMockMvc.given;

@SpringBootTest
public class ControllerSchemaTest {
    @Test
    public void testGetProductController() {
        given()
                .standaloneSetup(          Registers and configures
 new ProductsApiController())            controller with Spring MVC
                .when()                    infrastructure
                .get
 ("/v1/catalog/products/612b4280-b5c0-4ad5-bce7-ede7ab2b90fc")
                .then()
                .assertThat()              Set up a matcher to
                .expect(openApi()          validate against the
 .isValid("../product-catalog-v1-0.oas.yaml"))   OpenAPI definition.
                .statusCode(200);
    }
}
```

In the chapter7/product-catalog-api-service directory, run the test with ./run_controller_schema_test.sh (or ./run_controller_schema_test.bat for Windows) on your command line. You should get a similar message as before notifying you of the missing two fields in the OpenAPI definition.

Notice that this test runs quite fast, as it's a unit test for your controller. In this example, the `ProductApiController` has no dependencies, but if it did, you could easily mock them out. Because it's a fast-running unit test, you could test not only the happy paths (usually 2xx responses) but also the sad paths (usually 4xx and 5xx responses). However, the downside of this test is that it doesn't capture any behavior from the API gateway—for example, sending a wrong API key header value and getting the API key authentication 401 error response.

7.3   Things to consider with code-based schema tests

You've seen that code-based schema tests can be written as end-to-end tests or as controller tests. One thing to consider with this approach is the effort required to maintain these tests. Every time you add a new endpoint to the API, you need to add tests for the different happy and sad path response messages for that endpoint. This can mean a growing suite of test code for developers to maintain.

This approach is useful when you want to combine multiple API calls into a single test scenario that exercises deeper parts of your application logic required to return objects in some complex state. You can programmatically create the sequence of API calls and test the response.

In the Java-based example you worked through, you used the Atlassian Swagger Request Validator library to write schema tests. Some other open source libraries that provide similar features include the Hikaku Java library (https://github.com/codecentric/hikaku) and the JavaScript-based jest-openapi library (https://mng.bz/X1yv). As mentioned previously, you can also write end-to-end API tests in JavaScript in API platform tools such as Postman and Insomnia. For an example of validating responses in Postman, see https://mng.bz/y8RB.

7.4   Generating schema tests

Rather than writing schema tests for each endpoint and each response type on an endpoint, what if you could generate the tests from the OpenAPI definition? With this approach, you can have a tool that generates and executes happy and sad path schema tests from the API definition against the API gateway or API service. Figure 7.3 illustrates how this would work. You have the option of storing the generated tests in version control or any location of your choice for future reference.

This is the approach taken by tools such as Schemathesis and Portman. First, let's take a look at Schemathesis.

7.4.1   Using Schemathesis for schema testing

Schemathesis (https://schemathesis.readthedocs.io) is a property-based testing tool for APIs that generates and runs tests based on a provided API definition file. It's used for fuzz testing and, as part of that, also verifies the API schema. It's written in Python and builds on the Hypothesis property-based testing library, but you can use it to test any API defined in an OpenAPI document and for testing GraphQL APIs.

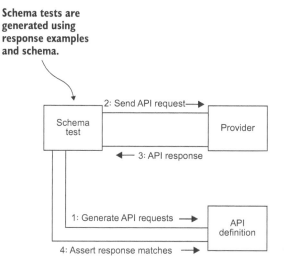

Figure 7.3   **Generating schema tests from an OpenAPI definition**

Suppose again that you're asked to write a schema test to validate the Product Catalog API against the product-catalog-v1-0.oas.yaml API definition file. To do this with Schemathesis, you need to run the Schemathesis CLI against the API and provide it with the API definition file.

Now run the Schemathesis CLI, and provide this strategy as a pre-run script for the Schemathesis CLI to execute before executing the tests, as shown in listing 7.3. (Remember that you should have the API gateway running, which you can start by switching to the chapter7/kong directory and running the `./start_kong.sh` script. You should also have the API service running, which you can start by switching to the chapter7/product-catalog-api-service directory and running the `./start_api_service.sh` script.) This specifies that the CLI should run all Schemathesis checks and record the test requests to a cassette.yaml file.

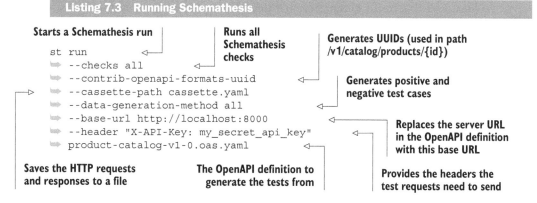

TIP   An alternative way to do this is by running the convenience script `./run_schemathesis_for_v1_0_api.sh` in the root of the chapter7 folder.

The test run should fail with an error message that includes the following:

```
- Response violates schema
    Additional properties are not allowed
⇒ ('numberOfReviews', 'reviewRating' were unexpected)
```

You've used Schemathesis to find the schema problem! Schemathesis has used the examples you provided in the OpenAPI definition file when sending API requests. Look in the product-catalog-v1-0.oas.yaml file. You can see that the example UUID specified for `productId`—that is, `c05aed25-97cd-4cbc-b299-3796538eee9c`—is used to send a request in the cassette.yaml file. So it's a good idea to provide example values in your API definition file, first for your users who will read your API reference and also for automated tools such as Schemathesis.

> **TIP** If you want Schemathesis to disregard the explicit examples in the OpenAPI document and generate new values instead, give it the command line argument `--hypothesis-no-phases explicit`.

Now instead of product-catalog-v1-0.oas.yaml, rerun the test against the product-catalog-v1-1.oas.yaml file, which contains the schema fixes. You can do this by executing the `chapter7/run_schemathesis_for_v1_1_api.sh` script. You should see a result similar to the following output:

```
==============SUMMARY =================
Performed checks:
    not_a_server_error              101 / 101 passed        PASSED
    status_code_conformance         101 / 101 passed        PASSED
    content_type_conformance        101 / 101 passed        PASSED
    response_headers_conformance    101 / 101 passed        PASSED
    response_schema_conformance     101 / 101 passed        PASSED
Network log: cassette.yaml
```

What does this result mean? Schemathesis has generated and run tests (in this case 101, but you may get a different number in your run) against the API. In each of these tests, it performed five kinds of checks:

- If the server responds with a 5xx HTTP status code, Schemathesis marks the test as a `not_a_server_error` failure.
- If the server responds with a status code that isn't defined in the API definition file, it marks the test as a `status_code_conformance` check failure.
- If the server responds with a content type that isn't defined in the API definition file, it marks the test as a `content_type_conformance` check failure.
- If the server response contains a header not defined in the API definition file, it marks the test as a `response_headers_conformance` check failure.
- If the server response body doesn't conform to the schema defined in the API definition file, it marks the test as a `response_schema_conformance` check failure.

Take a look at the generated chapter7/cassette.yaml file to see each test request run by Schemathesis and the response that came back from the server. The cassette.yaml file is in the VCR format (https://github.com/vcr/vcr). It consists of an array of `http_interactions`. Each `http_interaction` has fields showing its unique ID, the time the test was run, the status of the Schemathesis checks for that test, and details of the request and response. In my run of Schemathesis for this example, I found the following in my cassette.yaml file:

```
{"id": "791e653b-32c4-4602-a2db-99a95cb5e78f", "status": 400,
➥ "code":"validation.client_error", "title": "Bad Request",
➥ "detail": "Illegal character CNTL=0x1b"}
```

Notice that for this error, the detail field mentions the reason for the failure as an illegal character sent in the request. As a fuzz testing tool, Schemathesis has sent a request with an illegal character. An API fuzz testing tool finds defects in your API by generating and sending random API requests, and some of the requests include malformed or semi-malformed data. Normally, Jetty (the application server in your example Spring Boot application) will return a 400 error HTML page for this kind of error, which doesn't conform to the response defined in the OpenAPI definition. But I've defined a `CustomErrorHandler` in the `JettyCustomizer.java` class to override this behavior and return an `application/json` message matching the API definition file. A fuzz testing tool such as Schemathesis is great for finding edge cases like this that you would otherwise miss.

> **TIP** You can configure Schemathesis to disallow the generation of illegal characters using the command-line flag `--generation-allow-x00 false`.

Schemathesis works great for verifying that your API validates input because it makes independent API requests with random input data and validates that the response complies with your API definition. However, there are cases where to make a successful API request and test the schema response, the application has to be in a certain state resulting from previous API calls. That is, you want to test API calls in combination. For example, to retrieve a user profile, you may have to first make an API call to create a user and then use the returned user ID to make an API call to retrieve the user profile. To run such stateful tests in Schemathesis, you provide the relationship between the operations by defining link objects in your OpenAPI 3.0 document. An OpenAPI link provides a defined relationship and traversal structure between responses and other API operations. (A discussion on links is outside the scope of this book, but to find out more about links, you can see Swagger's information on links at https://swagger.io/docs/specification/links/.) Where link relationships are present in an OpenAPI document, Schemathesis uses the data in the API response to make subsequent API calls rather than generating random data.

Schemathesis is written in Python, and you can write Python tests that use the Schemathesis interface rather than using the CLI. The Schemathesis library has a programmatic API that allows you to perform all the same operations you can do with the CLI.

In this section, I've used Schemathesis as an example tool to show how you can generate and run schema tests from OpenAPI definitions.

One other interesting tool that follows the approach is Portman. Let's look at that in the next section.

7.4.2   *Using Portman for schema testing*

Portman (https://github.com/apideck-libraries/portman) is a CLI tool that generates and executes Postman collections to test that your OpenAPI definition matches your API implementation. With Portman, you can import the generated collection into your Postman desktop client or upload it to your Postman workspace. You can also use it to execute a collection. This enables you to add it to your continuous integration/continuous delivery (CI/CD) pipeline.

Use Portman to test the happy path (200 success case) of the API against the product-catalog-v1-1.oas.yaml file by running the following command from your chapter7 directory:

```
portman --cliOptionsFile portman/portman-cli.json
```

You should see the test report from the test run, including output like the following:

```
Product Catalog API
❏ Products
↳ View a product's details
  GET http://localhost:8000/v1/catalog/
➥  products/c05aed25-97cd-4cbc-b299-3796538eee9c [200 OK, 443B, 46ms]
  ✓  [GET]::/v1/catalog/products/:id - Status code is 2xx
  ✓  [GET]::/v1/catalog/products/:id - Schema is valid
  ✓  [GET]::/v1/catalog/products/:id - Content-Type is application/json
  ✓  [GET]::/v1/catalog/products/:id - Response has JSON Body
Collection run completed.
```

Portman is using the first example value in the endpoint definition to run the test. The Portman-cli.json file contains command-line options for Portman. In this example, it provides Portman with the location of the OpenAPI definition file to test and the name it should give the created Postman file. It also provides the reference to an environment file to hold any Postman variables for the generated Postman collection. Other CLI options include runNewman for instructing Portman to execute the tests using its embedded Newman runner (https://github.com/postmanlabs/newman) for running Postman collections on the command line, includeTests to add the Portman conformance tests to the generated Postman collection, and baseUrl for overriding the server URL when running the Postman collection. The Portman-cli.json file is shown here:

```
{
  "local": "product-catalog-v1-1.oas.yaml",
  "output": "collection.postman.json",
  "envFile": "portman/.env-portman",
  "portmanConfigFile": "portman/portman-config.json",
  "includeTests": true,
  "syncPostman": false,
```

```
    "runNewman": true,
    "baseUrl": "http://localhost:8000"
}
```

The `portmanConfigFile` field references the Portman configuration file that contains information on the conformance tests to run. Portman uses the term *contract tests* to describe the tests that check that an API conforms to its OpenAPI definition. In this example, the portman/portman-config.json configuration file specifies that for all API operations defined in the API definition, Portman should check that the status code, schema, content-type, and headers are defined as in the definition. It should also check that the response from the API is JSON. You can see this here:

```
{
  "version": 1.0,
  "overwrites": [                         ◄──┤  Specifies custom modifications to
    {                                          make to the request data in the
      "openApiOperation": "*::/*",             generated Postman collection
      "overwriteRequestHeaders": [    ◄──────  Applies the following
        {                               ◄────  overwrite to all API
          "key": "Host",                       operations
          "value": "api.acme-pet-supplies.com",  ◄──
          "overwrite": true                    Overwrites the
        }                                      request header
      ]
    }                                          Overwrites the value
  ],                                           of the Host header
  "tests": {
    "contractTests": [
      {
        "openApiOperation": "*::/*",
        "statusSuccess": {          ◄──  Checks that the response
          "enabled": true                status matches the
        }                                documentation
      },
      {
        "openApiOperation": "*::/*",
        "schemaValidation": {       ◄──  Checks that the response
          "enabled": true                schema matches the
        }                                documentation
      },
      {
        "openApiOperation": "*::/*",
        "contentType": {            ◄──  Checks that the returned
          "enabled": true                content type matches
        }                                the documentation
      },
      {
        "openApiOperation": "*::/*",
        "jsonBody": {               ◄──  Checks that returned
          "enabled": true                content is JSON
        }
      },
```

```
    {
      "openApiOperation": "*::/*",
      "headersPresent": {          ◁─┐  Checks that the
        "enabled": true               │  headers are present
      }
    }
  ]
},
"globals": {
  "securityOverwrites": {         ◁─┐  Sets the API key header
    "apiKey": {                      │  name and value
      "key": "X-API-Key",
      "value": "{{apiKey}}"       ◁─┐  Sets the API key header value to the value
    }                                │  of the PORTMAN_API_KEY environment
  }                                  │  variable defined in .env-portman
}
}
```

TIP   The Portman CLI has an initialization command to get started with creating its configuration. Try this out. Run `portman --init`, and walk through the steps to re-create the configuration.

Portman's ability to generate schema tests as Postman collections benefits teams that use collections. Portman can be set up to sync the generated collections to a Postman workspace to enable the sharing of collections.

7.5   *Using a validating proxy for consistency*

Another approach to API conformance testing is to use the validating proxy pattern. We'll look at the pattern and a concrete example in this section.

One way to validate that a schema matches the API behavior is to channel the requests and responses to the API through an intermediary server so that the intermediary server validates the response from the API server against the expected API definition. The intermediary or proxy server can report an error if the API server response doesn't match the expected schema. To do this, the proxy server needs a reference to the OpenAPI definition containing the response schema. Figure 7.4 illustrates this.

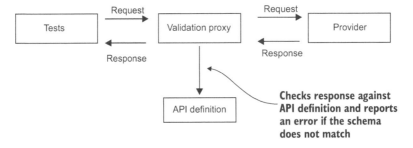

Figure 7.4   Using a validating proxy for API conformance testing

One advantage of this approach is that it's easy to get started by plugging in the validating proxy to an existing suite of API tests, especially end-to-end tests. But schema testing coverage will only be as comprehensive as the scenarios exercised by the end-to-end tests, which, for example, may not include every possible sad path scenario for every endpoint. And, of course, if you intend to apply this to end-to-end tests, you must consider all the inherent drawbacks (brittleness, difficulty to debug, hard to scale, etc.).

Let's look at an example of this in action. Consider the previous scenario where the `numberOfReviews` and `reviewRating` fields were documented on the Product Catalog API definition file. How can a test using a validating proxy reveal this? First, start by creating an end-to-end test, `ProductsApiEndToEndTest`, that makes a request to the API gateway and checks for a 200 OK success response, as shown in the next listing.

Listing 7.4 Java end-to-end test

```
package com.acmepetsupplies.productcatalog;
import org.junit.Test;
import static io.restassured.RestAssured.given;
public class ProductsApiEndToEndTest {
    @Test
    public void testGetProductEndToEnd() {
        given()
                .header("X-API-Key", "my_secret_api_key")
                .when()
                .baseUri("http://127.0.0.1:8000")
                .get("/v1/catalog
    /products/612b4280-b5c0-4ad5-bce7-ede7ab2b90fc")
                .then()
                .log()
                .body()
                .assertThat()
                .statusCode(200);
    }
}
```

Base URI points to the API gateway. (→ `.baseUri`)

Logs the body of the response (→ `.log()` `.body()`)

Run the test, and verify you have a successful response by navigating to chapter7/product-catalog-api-service and executing the `./run_products_api_end_to_end_test.sh` script (or `./run_products_api_end_to_end_test.bat` for Windows). In the output, note that the body of the response is logged.

Next, you need to change the endpoint of the end-to-end test to point to the validating proxy. Prism (https://github.com/stoplightio/prism) is a validating proxy and mock server for OpenAPI definitions and Postman collections. If you followed the instructions in appendix D, you have Prism installed. In the chapter7 folder, start up Prism, and give it a reference to your OpenAPI definition and API gateway. In addition, provide the `--errors` flag so response violations provide an error response:

```
prism proxy
    product-catalog-v1-0.oas.yaml
    http://127.0.0.1:8000
    --errors
```

By default, Prism runs on port 4010. Now that you have the Prism server running, update the `baseUri` in your `ProductsApiEndToEndTest` from `http://127.0.0.1:8000` to `http://127.0.0.1:4010` so that your test request goes to Prism rather than your API gateway. Again, run your test with `./run_products_api_end_to_end_test.sh`, and you should see the test fail. The response body logged has the following message:

```
{
    "type": "https://stoplight.io/prism/errors#VIOLATIONS",
    "title": "Request/Response not valid",
    "status": 500,
    "detail": "Your request/response is not valid and the
➡ --errors flag is set, so Prism is generating this error for you.",
    "validation": [
        {
            "location": [
                "response",
                "body"
            ],
            "severity": "Error",
            "code": "additionalProperties",
            "message": "must NOT have additional properties;
➡ found 'reviewRating'"
        },
        {
            "location": [
                "response",
                "body"
            ],
            "severity": "Error",
            "code": "additionalProperties",
            "message": "must NOT have additional properties;
➡ found 'numberOfReviews'"
        }
    ]
}
java.lang.AssertionError: 1 expectation failed.
Expected status code <200> but was <500>.
```

Prism errors follow the RFC7807 Problem Details format and has properties `type` (URI that identifies the problem type), `title` (short summary of the problem type), `status` (HTTP status code), and `detail` (explanation of this occurrence of the problem). Prism is returning a 500 error of type VIOLATION because the response from the API gateway doesn't match the API definition, and Prism is running with the `--errors` flag. The `validation.location` and `validation.message` properties provide details of the location in the API definition that triggered the error and a detailed message of why the error occurred.

In addition, note that the Prism error logs provide details of the request and response interactions with the upstream API gateway server:

```
[07:42:50] › [HTTP SERVER] get /v1/catalog/products/9764d95c-7757-4a4d-
➡ a800-660b8fe9392b ?  info      Request received
```

```
[07:42:50] >    [PROXY] ? info     Forwarding "get" request to
http://localhost:8000/v1/catalog/products/9764d95c-7757-4a4d-a800-
660b8fe9392b...
[07:42:50] >    [PROXY] ? info     The upstream call to
/v1/catalog/products/9764d95c-7757-4a4d-a800-660b8fe9392b
has returned 200
[07:42:50] > [HTTP SERVER] get /v1/catalog/products/9764d95c-7757-4a4d-
a800-660b8fe9392b ? error     Request terminated with error:
https://stoplight.io/prism/errors#VIOLATIONS:
Request/Response not valid
```

You can test what happens when you run Prism against an API definition file that matches the upstream server. Kill the running prism instance, and restart it with the product-catalog-v1-1.oas.yaml instead, as shown here:

```
prism proxy
product-catalog-v1-1.oas.yaml
http://127.0.0.1:8000
--errors
```

Now, rerun your test with `./run_products_api_end_to_end_test.sh`, and you see your test pass.

7.6 Comparing API conformance approaches

In this chapter, we've looked at various techniques for writing schema tests. Table 7.1 summarizes some tradeoffs between these approaches.

Table 7.1 Comparing API schema approaches

	Code-based end-to-end schema test	Code-based controller schema test	Auto-generated end-to-end schema test with a fuzzer	End-to-end schema testing with validating proxy
Fits into existing end-to-end test suite without writing new code	N/A	N/A	N/A	Y
Guarantees schema conformance for responses across the whole stack	Y	N	Y	Y
Can identify unexpected responses based on fuzzy testing	N	N	Y	If run as part of fuzzy testing
Fast feedback from testing service in isolation	N	Y	N	N
Doesn't require code change for new responses or endpoints	N	N	Y. Tests can be generated from API reference only, but may require some custom setup configuration.	Prism doesn't require change, but end-to-end tests themselves require a change to test the new endpoints or response.

Both schema testing and generating an API definition from code (discussed in chapter 6) address the problem of API conformance. Table 7.2 summarizes the tradeoffs between these approaches. In practice, you may want to combine both approaches to ensure good API conformance.

Table 7.2   Comparing the generation and schema testing approaches to API conformance

	Generating the OpenAPI definition from code	Schema testing of the OpenAPI definition
Speed of execution	Generated quickly as part of build process	Can be quick if done at a controller level, but slower if done as part of end-to-end test
Comprehensiveness	Only covers schema from API service controllers it's generated from and won't cover API gateway behavior or other intermediary components such as firewalls or intermediate proxies	Makes comprehensive assertions on response the consumer receives, which covers the entire stack
Cost of maintenance	Low. If done as part of CI/CD pipeline, it can regenerate the schema as a pipeline step any time a change is introduced.	If done as part of an end-to-end test, cost of maintenance will be tied to the cost of maintaining the end-to-end test, which can be high.
Ease of getting started	Where a single conceptual API is served by multiple API services, generating an OpenAPI definition for the API would involve combining the generated definitions for the multiple services. Generating the schema may involve annotating the API service controller and response model code.	Can get started quickly, for example, by using a validation proxy with existing end-to-end tests and can have a dedicated test suite that does schema testing across the whole API

7.7   How schema tests differ from consumer-driven contract tests

At the beginning of this chapter, I mentioned that schema testing is different from consumer-driven contract testing. Before explaining how schema testing is different, let me explain what contract testing is.

Consider a system where you have several evolving services interacting with each other. How do you verify that a new version of a service can still interact with other services? One way is to deploy all the services and run an integration test. But as the number of interacting services increases, the integration tests become more complex. To run an integration test, you first need to deploy and configure all the services ("deploy the world") in a production-like environment. The integration tests themselves can take a long time to run, become brittle, be difficult to maintain, and be difficult to scale.

Consumer-driven contract testing is a different approach to integration testing. It involves testing a service in isolation against a consumer contract—a document that defines the message conversations it expects the provider to support. That is, it's a way of ensuring that two services have a shared understanding of how to communicate with each other. It does this by checking each of them in isolation using concrete messages (specification examples). The document containing these messages serves as the contract that defines the expected message interactions, as shown in figure 7.5.

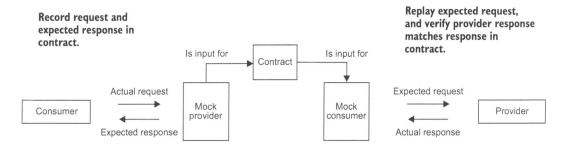

Figure 7.5 Consumer-driven contract testing

In consumer-driven contract tests, the consumer communicates its expectations on how the provider's API should behave with a consumer contract. The consumer contract documents the message conversations—the sequence or history of exchanged messages required to get the provider service to a certain state. In the message exchange, only the capabilities of the provider used by consumers get tested. This means that the capabilities of the provider not used can be evolved without breaking tests. Consumer contracts help initiate discussion and collaboration between teams on service evolution. Two examples of contract testing tools are Pact (https://pact.io) and Spring Cloud Contracts (https://spring.io/projects/spring-cloud-contract). Consumer contracts that describe message interactions (for request A, you get response B) are different from API definition files that just describe the structure and format of an API. Schema testing of API definition files checks that a provider's behavior matches its published schema.

> **TIP** For more on consumer-driven contract testing, see Mark Winteringham's *Testing Web APIs* (Manning, 2022; www.manning.com/books/testing-web-apis).

Consumer-driven contract testing is good for testing integrations between services in an organization. It can replace many end-to-end tests that test service integrations within an organization (e.g., testing microservice integrations). In this scenario, the provider team can manage the relationship with the small set of known API consumer applications.

Schema testing of API definitions to check for API conformance is more suitable for external APIs where it's impractical to use consumer contracts. For external APIs, there can be a large number of consuming services, and it can be impractical for the consuming teams to drive their individual requirements via consumer contracts—the consumer teams may not even be using the same consumer-driven contact testing tool as the provider team. In the absence of consumer contracts for external APIs, publishing an accurate API definition file that describes the provider's interface, capabilities, and message schema is important. Schema testing of the provider helps guarantee that the API definition is accurate.

Summary

- Schema tests are for checking that APIs conform to their API definition in situations where you can't apply consumer-driven contract tests, for example, for external or public APIs.
- With code-based schema tests, you write test code that makes assertions which compare the data type of the message returned from the provider with the schema in its published API definition.
- Code-based schema tests can either be run end to end or at the controller level of an API service. Controller-level tests are faster and avoid the drawbacks of end-to-end tests.
- Generating schema tests from an OpenAPI definition avoids having developers write code when there is a change to the API. Tools such as Schemathesis and Portman can generate and run happy and sad path scenarios based on the API definition and run these against the API server.
- A schema validation proxy can sit between your automated test suite and your API server and validate that the response from the server matches the schema. It's a quick method to get started with schema testing because you can fit the proxy into your existing suite of end-to-end tests.
- Using a combination of both generating OpenAPI definitions and schema testing helps ensure API conformance for your external APIs.

CI/CD for API artifacts 1: Source-stage governance controls

Large software projects can involve multiple teams building many external RESTful APIs for an organization. Centralized manual governance is one way to ensure APIs meet the organization's API consistency and usability standards. But as discussed in chapter 1, centralized manual governance doesn't scale, leading to reduced agility, long lead times, and developer frustration. How can governance teams minimize the need for manual design reviews and move toward consistently applied, automated self-service reviews to support many development teams?

Automated governance isn't the only problem. During the software delivery process, several *API artifacts* are generated from the API definition files. API artifacts are API definition files and the by-products generated from them, provided for API consumers and other internal stakeholders to use. They include API reference documentation, client SDKs, alternative API definition formats, API score reports, and more. Consistency suffers when dev teams create these artifacts using

195

manual and ad hoc processes. So how can the organization provide a consistent way for teams to generate API artifacts?

In this chapter, I discuss how to incorporate the governance and management of API artifacts into your existing *deployment pipeline*. A deployment pipeline—also called a continuous integration and continuous delivery (CI/CD) pipeline or delivery pipeline—is a set of processes that takes software changes from version control commit to releasable software in a reliable and repeatable way. I discuss how a deployment pipeline provides a central, automated, and speedy way of giving feedback to API designers on API design consistency, conformance, and other API definition scoring metrics. I also discuss how the pipeline can be used to generate and store API artifacts ready for publishing.

Why manage API artifacts in your CI/CD pipeline? In chapter 1, I mentioned how APIOps enables teams to have a simpler API development workflow, faster feedback on API design reviews, and more consistent and compliant APIs. Including API artifacts in the CI/CD pipeline is the central implementation that helps teams realize these benefits. The pipeline allows organizations to publish APIs and related API artifacts quickly and efficiently and to the right consistency standards. It provides a central, standardized way of running automated checks on the design proposal, running conformance checks, and generating artifacts from the API definitions. When new design guidelines are introduced in the organization's API style guide, they can be automated in the pipeline, providing a standard way to ensure that every API definition file change goes through the same automated design-quality checks. This minimizes the manual execution of governance tasks, the possibility of human errors, and the risk of defects related to API definitions.

I've outlined the benefits of managing API artifacts in the pipeline. But how does this fit into the theme of APIOps and the whole API product life cycle? Central to managing artifacts in the deployment pipeline is the idea that API artifacts are important deliverables, so API definitions and API guide documentation should be treated as code. In particular, raw API definitions may be published so API consumers can download and use them directly, or they could be used to generate API reference documentation or client SDKs. To outline all their usages, API definitions are used for the following:

- *Product design*—Used for discussions during product planning and design
- *Implementation*—Used to generate the implementation code
- *Testing*—Used as a basis for testing, generating test code, and mocking APIs
- *Documentation*—Used to generate API reference documentation
- *Tooling*—Used to generate server stubs and client SDKs
- *API scoring*—Used to generate API consistency score metrics
- *API monitoring*—Used in observability and security tooling, as well as API gateways, to monitor API behavior in deployed environments

Because of this, it's important to treat API definitions as first-class outputs of the software build process and apply similar software engineering disciplines to them, just as a team would do to code.

Here is how I'll explain the API pipeline concepts in this chapter: organizations have complex requirements around how they build and deploy software and API artifacts, so there is no one-size-fits-all way of managing API artifacts in CI/CD pipelines. Rather than presenting a recommended pipeline, I'll present an API artifact delivery problem and how a hypothetical API team uses its CI/CD pipeline to govern and manage its artifacts. My goal is to show you *how* the team goes about evolving its pipeline, not present a set of recommended pipeline stages. Remember, you can use the A3 thinking approach discussed in chapter 2 to approach your particular pipeline problem, which should enable you to design a pipeline for your context. I also use a risk and controls table to show you how the pipeline manages API governance risks at each stage of the pipeline.

This chapter assumes that you have some familiarity with build servers (also called CI/CD servers). A *build server* is a platform that automates all the tasks in your deployment pipeline and brings all the components together. I present examples of how to do this with a popular build server—the GitHub Actions platform. Again, my goal with this isn't to teach about all the details of GitHub Actions, but to show an example of how teams can incorporate their API definitions and API guide docs into their pipelines.

> ## A glossary of terms
> Here are a few notes on some terms I use in this chapter:
>
> - *API governance team*—APIOps tackles problems at scale, where you have multiple teams doing API design and need a team to be responsible for API governance to enable dev teams to design and build APIs. Small organizations with a small number of dev teams don't have this problem, but large organizations definitely do. Some large organizations give this responsibility to the team maintaining the API gateway, but some have a dedicated cross-functional API platform team. Whichever way they are structured or named, in this book, I refer to the team responsible for overseeing API consistency as the API governance team.
> - *API design proposal*—Following the API design-first approach discussed in chapter 1, section 1.5.1, dev teams can submit an API design proposal as a pull request (PR) for review by the governance team. API design proposal refers to the proposed API design changes (for RESTful APIs, this would be OpenAPI definition files), API guide documentation, and any other information the governance team needs to know to make sense of and review the API design.
> - *API reference*—This refers to a rendered API definition file. For REST-based OpenAPI design, according to the OpenAPI Specification (OAS), an API definition is a raw OpenAPI YAML or JSON file. An API reference is a human-readable documentation generated from the API definition file using tools such as Swagger UI, Stoplight Elements, Redoc, or a developer portal's API reference rendering system.

> *(continued)*
>
> - *API guide documentation*—This refers to API documentation that is different from the API reference generated from the OpenAPI definition. API guide documentation includes documentation pages shown on the developer portal on introduction to the API, authentication, errors, pagination, version, deprecation policies, tutorials, and so on. In this chapter, I treat the API guide documentation as Markdown files in the project repository. Even though for the purpose of this book, I treat API documentation content as either API reference or guide documentation, technical writers class API documentation content in more detailed ways. In *Docs for Developers: An Engineer's Field Guide to Technical Writing* by Jared Bhatti et al. (Apress, 2021), the authors break down API documentation content into different content types—READMEs, getting started documentation, conceptual documentation, procedural documentation, tutorials, how-to guides, reference documentation, API reference documentation, and glossaries.
> - *Code hosting service*—A code hosting service is a file hosting facility for a project's source files, documentation, and other file assets. It's built on a version control system (VCS, e.g., Git) that maintains file revision history, but it also has other software project management features such as defect tracking systems, wiki-based project documentation, mailing lists, and release management features. Examples include GitHub, GitLab, Bitbucket, and Azure DevOps Server.

Finally, in the sample project, you can find the code for this chapter at https://mng .bz/ngo2 and https://mng.bz/v8a4.

8.1   *The problem with sharing API design proposals*

Suppose your organization, Acme, has 10 teams building various external APIs. Imagine that the development teams design their API definitions first, along with some guide documentation, and send these to the governance team for review. How exactly should they send the files?

One option would be to email the files. The Acme governance team can review their changes and reply to the email to tell them if they approve. Or their reply could be recommending changes to specific lines of the files. When the development team makes changes, they can send it to the governance team, who then compare the before and after versions of the files to check that the changes match their recommendations. Figure 8.1 shows an example of the conversations that can happen in this flow.

This email exchange can quickly become complex and difficult to follow. In this scenario, when combined with the fact that this communication can happen with 10 teams, it can be difficult to track and manage. The core problem the teams face here is how to track changes across files and the conversation around those changes.

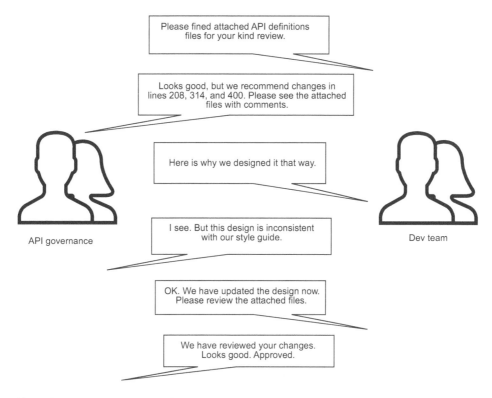

Please fined attached API definitions files for your kind review.

Looks good, but we recommend changes in lines 208, 314, and 400. Please see the attached files with comments.

Here is why we designed it that way.

I see. But this design is inconsistent with our style guide.

OK. We have updated the design now. Please review the attached files.

We have reviewed your changes. Looks good. Approved.

API governance

Dev team

Figure 8.1   An example flow of files and conversation between the governance team and a development team during the review of an API design change proposal

8.2   *Version control to the rescue*

The common solution to sharing and collaborating on file changes between teams is to store the API definition files in version control. In this case, the team should add their API definition files to their project's version control repository—just like they do all the other source files. And this applies not just to API definition files—any API-related source files, such as guide documentation and API conformance tests, can also be stored in version control. The dev team can submit their API design proposal as a PR for review by the governance team. Before the governance team reviews the PR, it must pass automated checks that signify that the PR meets its *minimum design review criteria* (MDRC). The MDRC is a quality checklist to verify that API design proposals meet the minimum requirements for the design review process to begin. In this scenario, imagine that the API governance team sets the following MDRC criteria:

1   The PR title has a reference to the work ticket. In this case, assume the team uses Atlassian Jira, and their work tickets follow the format DEV-*XXXX* where *X* is a digit. In addition, the PR description provides information on why the change

is required. I refer to these rules as the *PR description policy*—that is, a set of rules that PR titles and descriptions must meet before they can be merged.

2 The PR must pass all API linting checks.

3 The PR must pass all breaking change checks.

4 The PR should pass all automated *prose linting* checks on the API guide documentation. This checks for punctuation errors, spelling, grammar, and language style.

5 After passing the MDRC and before the PR is merged into the mainline branch of the source control repository, a fifth criterion needs to be met—the PR should be reviewed and approved by a governance team member. I refer to these five criteria as *merge criteria.*

8.3   Auto-validating the MDRC

In this scenario, for the first criterion, the Acme team can use a script to validate the PR title as in the PR build run. The team can also use a *PR template* to prompt PR creators to provide a description of why the change is being done for the benefit of the PR reviewer. For the second and third criteria, the team can use Spectral (discussed in chapter 3) to run linting checks and Tufin/oasdiff (discussed in chapter 4) to run breaking change checks in the build. The build server job that runs these checks on the PR is the *PR build.* And for the fourth criterion—that a member of the Acme governance team member reviews the PR—the team can use the code owners feature of their code hosting service to ensure that approval is received from a member of the governance team before the PR is merged. *Code owners* is a feature of code hosting platforms that allows teams to assign a domain expert or team of domain experts (usually outside the owning team) as a code owner to specific files, file types, or directories in a version control repository so that the code owner must approve PRs that touch the affected files before they can be merged. Figure 8.2 illustrates what a process that auto-validates this MDRC and meets the merge criteria can look like.

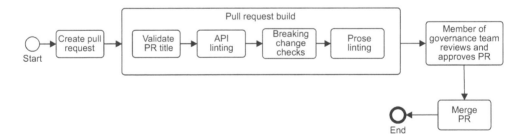

Figure 8.2   The process the Acme team uses to check that PRs satisfy the minimum design review criteria and get approval from the governance team

One contextual point to note in this scenario is that the Acme team has already adopted CI/CD and has a deployment pipeline for building and deploying their software services to different environments. The team is just not managing its artifacts in that pipeline.

The deployment pipeline

A deployment pipeline consists of two main phases—*continuous integration* and *continuous delivery* (or CI/CD, as mentioned earlier). Continuous integration (CI) is a practice where teams integrate their changes regularly (at least once a day) to the main line branch of their source code repository. A build server is a platform that runs tasks to convert code into software artifacts. It also tests the software to verify that the whole software system works after each change. In the CI phase, these tests are developer-focused technical tests to enable developers to quickly verify that they haven't broken anything. The output of the CI phase is a packaged release candidate that can be deployed to higher environments for further testing.

In the continuous delivery (CD) phase, the release candidate is deployed and tested in increasingly production-like environments (also called higher environments) to verify that they meet all acceptance, performance, security, and other criteria. Deployments to higher environments are automated and can be triggered automatically or on demand. Teams practicing CD use techniques such as feature flags and keystone interfaces to hide partially built features from users.

Continuous deployment is a further enhancement to CD, where every commit that passes all the stages of the pipeline gets automatically deployed to production without any human intervention. Continuous deployment means users can see a continuous stream of improvements in production, and deployments are less risky, but feature flags are used to hide partially built features.

I use the following terminology to refer to the stages and components of the deployment pipeline:

- *Source code repository*—A version control tool used to hold code, test, configuration, and infrastructure source files for the project.
- *Build*—An automated process to compile and package code and run developer-focused tests (e.g., unit and component tests). A PR build runs on a PR to give the PR creator quick feedback that the changes introduced by the PR work at a technical level. A *mainline build* is run when the PR is merged to the mainline branch of the repository, and the build publishes a passing release candidate to the artifact repository.
- *Dependency management system*—A system that holds external libraries and container images for internal consumption.
- *Artifact repository*—The release candidates are published to an artifact repository. An artifact (or binary) repository is a versioned store of binary artifacts and their associated metadata in a defined directory structure. Build artifacts are stored in an artifact repository and can be deployed to different environments in later stages of the pipeline.

(continued)

- *API registry*—An API registry is a runtime system that allows users to upload and share their API definition files so that API consumers can browse, search, and view details of an API.
- *Non-prod testing*—The pipeline deploys the release candidate to increasingly production-like environments and tests the software from the perspective of the user to improve the team's confidence that the software is ready for release. These tests include acceptance tests, performance tests, and other tests as the organization considers necessary.
- *Prod deployment*—Release candidates that pass all the non-prod testing checks are deployed to the production environment (or its equivalent, e.g., an app store).

A full discussion of implementing a deployment pipeline is out of the scope of this book. A foundation text on deployment pipelines is *Continuous Delivery: Reliable Software Releases through Build, Test, and Deployment Automation* by David Farley and Jez Humble (Addison-Wesley Professional, 2010). David Farley's *Continuous Delivery Pipelines: How to Build Better Software Faster* (Dave Farley, 2021) also provides a good introduction to pipelines. Henry van Merode's book *Continuous Integration (CI) and Continuous Delivery (CD): A Practical Guide to Designing and Developing Pipelines* (Apress, 2023) provides lots of practical advice on setting up pipelines.

Imagine that the dev team uses the deployment pipeline, as shown in figure 8.3. Adding their API definition files to the source repository means that they can run checks on it as part of their pipeline.

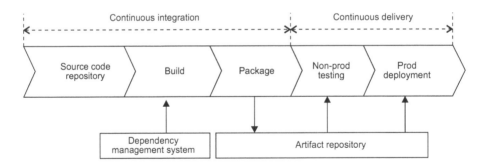

Figure 8.3   The Acme team's deployment pipeline

I've described what a high-level solution for automatically validating the MDRC in the pipeline looks like. But before I get you to open up the example project repository in your Visual Studio Code (VS Code) editor and work through the code example to set up the merge checks in this scenario, let me introduce you to the build server for this example—GitHub Actions.

NOTE If you're already familiar with GitHub Actions, feel free to skip the next section.

8.4 Introduction to GitHub Actions

GitHub Actions (https://github.com/features/actions) is GitHub's tool for automating workflows in the software development life cycle, and it provides full CI/CD capabilities. In GitHub Actions, workflows are triggered when specific events happen in a repository, for example, raising a PR or merging to a branch. Events can kick off workflows based on one or more triggers and can be set to run on specific code branches in the repository. The workflows themselves are configurable automated processes specified in YAML files placed in the .github/workflows directory in the repository. Apart from being triggered by events in the repository, workflows can also be triggered on schedule or manually. Workflows are executed on a server called a *runner*. GitHub provides cloud-based runners for Ubuntu Linux, Microsoft Windows, and macOS. You can also host your own runner, for example, on your local computer, to which the GitHub Actions can connect to execute a task.

Workflow files also contain jobs. A *job* is a collection of steps that execute on the same runner. A step is either a shell script executed in the runner or an action. An *action* is a custom application for GitHub's Actions platform for performing repetitive tasks. For example, checking out code is a common task in a CI/CD pipeline, and there is an action for this: `actions/checkout@v3`. By default, jobs in a workflow have no dependencies with other jobs and run in parallel. But you can configure and change this behavior. Steps in a job always execute sequentially and are dependent on each other.

NOTE For more information on the GitHub Actions platform, see the documentation at https://docs.github.com/en/actions.

To see these concepts in action, consider the following workflow example. Imagine that the Acme dev team has an API service, Products API, as contained in the chapter8 folder of your sample project. It's a Java project and already has a GitHub Actions workflow file defined. The workflow file can be found by looking in the .github directory in the project root, following the path .github/workflows/pr-build.yaml file. The PR build workflow defined in pr-build.yaml runs when a PR is raised against the main branch. It has five steps in the `pr-code-build` job:

- Check out the source code using the checkout/v3 action.
- Set up the JDK17 Java Virtual Machine (JVM) used to execute the code via the `setup-java@v3` action.
- Compile the code using Maven, a Java build automation tool.
- Run the unit tests in the project using Maven.

Figure 8.4 illustrates how these steps can be represented using the GitHub Actions model.

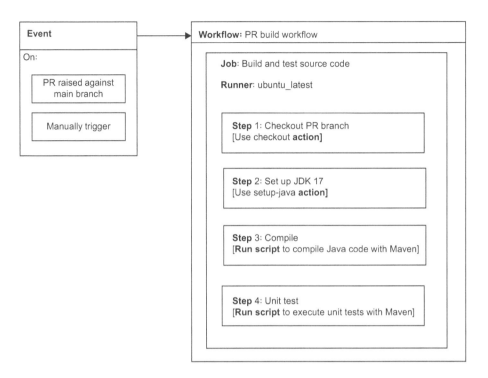

Figure 8.4   GitHub Actions concepts applied to the PR build workflow. On the GitHub Actions platform, events trigger workflows that are executed on runners.

The resulting code for the PR build workflow is shown in the following listing.

Listing 8.1   The PR build workflow

```
name: PR build workflow
on:
  pull_request:
    branches: [main]
  workflow_dispatch:
jobs:
  pr-code-build:
    name: Build and test source code
    runs-on: ubuntu-latest
    steps:
      - name: Checkout out pr branch
        uses: actions/checkout@v3
      - name: Set up JDK 17
        uses: actions/setup-java@v3
        with:
          java-version: '17'
          distribution: 'temurin'
          cache: maven
```

Triggers this workflow when there is a PR on the main branch

Enables this workflow to be triggered manually

The job to build the code

The GitHub-hosted runner image used to run the workflow

Checks out the code using the actions/checkout@v3 action

```
- name: Compile
  run: |
    cd chapter8
    mvn --batch-mode clean compile        ◁─── Runs the Maven clean
- name: Unit test                              and compile commands
  run: |                                       in silent batch mode
    cd chapter8
    mvn --batch-mode test
```

Start by running this workflow. If you haven't done so already, clone the sample project, and set it up as a private GitHub repository as described in appendix D. Now create a PR to trigger the workflow. This can be a minor change on any file, for example, adding a new line at the end of the README.md file. Create a PR for this change to merge your change to the main branch. Once you've created the PR, you should see the PR checks run. With this brief introduction to GitHub Actions, you're ready to create a workflow to execute the MDRC.

8.5 Setting up the MDRC

You've seen the existing `pr-code-build` job for compiling and running unit tests in the .github/workflows/pr-build.yaml workflow file. Suppose you wanted to add a new job that runs the MDRC checks in the workflow. How would you do that?

The job should execute these four checks, as discussed in section 8.2:

- Check that the PR title has a work ticket reference.
- Run API linting on the API definition.
- Run breaking change checks on the API definition.
- Run prose linting on the guide documentation.

Figure 8.5 shows these checks modeled in the GitHub Actions workflow.

Now implement the GitHub Action steps in the job using the following guide.

> **NOTE** If you don't want to work through this example but want to see the completed code, take a look at the .github/workflows/pr-build.completed file.

8.5.1 Check the work ticket reference

First, write a script to validate the first criterion—that every PR has a work ticket reference in its title, so PR reviewers can look up the related work ticket. The script should accept the PR title as input and validate that it contains a ticket reference matching the format [DEV-*XXXX*] where *X* is a digit. In addition, create a new job—`pr-api-minimum-review-criteria`—in the workflow file that calls your script in a new step with the name `Check PR title`.

Here is how to do this. In your copy of the sample project, navigate to the chapter8 directory. In there, create a file called pr-title.sh, and make it executable (in Linux/Unix based systems, do this by running `chmod +x ./pr-title.sh`). Add listing 8.2 to the file.

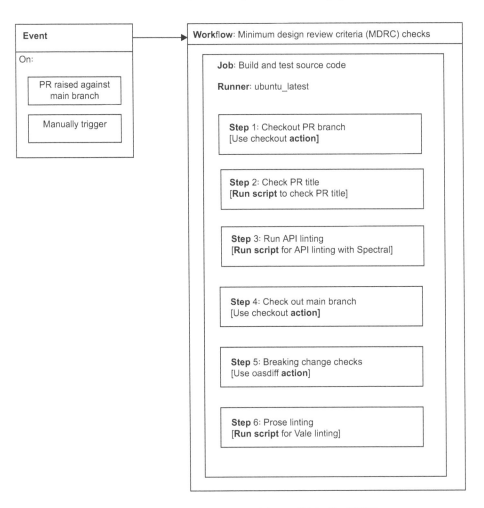

Figure 8.5   Extending the workflow file with a new job to validate the MDRC

Listing 8.2   Checking the PR title has a work ticket reference

```
#!/usr/bin/env bash

pr_title=$1
pattern="DEV-[0-9]{4}"

if [[ ! $pr_title =~ $pattern ]]; then
    echo "PR title: $pr_title"
    echo "Error: pull request title does not contain a
    valid Jira issue reference in the format DEV-XXXX."
    echo "Please include a Jira issue reference in the title of your PR."
    exit 1
fi
```

Regex pattern for the work ticket to match PR title against

If the PR title doesn't match, print a message, and return a nonzero exit code.

TIP To avoid typing in the listing code, you can find a `pr-title.completed` script in the chapter8 folder, which you can rename to `pr-title.sh`.

Next, create the new job `pr-api-minimum-review-criteria` in the .github/workflows/pr-build.yaml. Add the new job as a child node of the `job` node. First, the job should check out the project code into a `pr-branch` folder in the working directory (I'll explain why later when you write the code for breaking change checks). The GitHub Actions context object `'${{ github }}'` has a subproperty `${{ github.event .pull_request.title }}` that holds the title of the PR, and you can pass this to your script. Now create a step to run the script and pass in that property. The next listing shows the code for the job that you can append (not replace) to the existing pr-build.yaml file.

Listing 8.3 Workflow job for minimum API review criteria

```
...
  pr-api-minimum-review-criteria:
    name: Minimum API design review criteria
    runs-on: ubuntu-latest
    steps:
      - name: Checkout out pr branch
        uses: actions/checkout@v3
        with:
          path: pr-branch
      - name: Check PR title
        run: ./pr-branch/chapter8/pr-title.sh
  "'${{ github.event.pull_request.title }}'"
```

TIP You can find a completed GitHub Actions workflow file for this chapter in the .github/workflows/pr-build.completed file (follow the path from the project's root folder).

With this in place, create a PR. To test that this is working, add a PR title that doesn't have a work ticket reference so you can see the job fail. To make it pass, edit the PR title in GitHub, and start the title with a sample ticket reference, for example, `[DEV-1234]`. Update the PR with a minor change (say, a whitespace change on any file) to see the job retrigger and run. It should now complete successfully. Merge your PR.

NOTE This is a simple scenario. Of course, the script can be extended to validate the ticket reference against the Jira server using Jira's REST API.

8.5.2 *Create a PR template*

While you're on this, to meet the requirement of the first criteria of your MDRC—that the PR should have a useful description—create a PR template to guide PR creators on what information to provide.

In the .github/ folder, create a pull_request_template.md file with the following snippet:

```
## Why is this change needed?

## What is the scope of this change?

## Checklist
- [ ] Have you run tests locally?
```

> **TIP**   You can also copy from the pull_request_template.completed file in the same directory.

Commit your code, and create a PR. With subsequent PRs, you should now see the PR template appear when you create a new PR.

8.5.3   *Run API linting in the pipeline*

Now create an automated check for the second MDRC criteria—the PR must pass all API linting checks. To do this, add a step in the pr-api-minimum-review-criteria job to run API linting. The ubuntu-latest runner comes with Node installed, but not the Spectral CLI. Instead of installing Spectral, you can just execute it using the npx command. npx makes it easy to install and run a Node.js executable from an NPM registry. The following code snippet shows how to add the step, invoking Spectral linting on the API definition file using the json-api.ruleset.yaml ruleset file in the project. Add it just below the Check PR title step:

```
- name: Run API linting
  run: |
    npx @stoplight/spectral-cli lint
    "./pr-branch/chapter8/apis/product-catalog.oas.yaml"
    --ruleset "./pr-branch/chapter8/apis/rulesets/json-api.ruleset.yaml"
```

Commit your code, raise a PR (remember to add a dummy ticket reference in the PR title!), and watch the PR build run. You should see the output in the logs end with the following:

```
No results with a severity of 'error' found!
```

> **TIP**   In this example, you've run the linting step as a script from the runner's command line. An alternative way to do this is to use Spectral's GitHub action (https://github.com/stoplightio/spectral-action).

8.5.4   *Run breaking change checks in the pipeline*

For the third MDRC criteria—the PR must pass all breaking change checks—create another step in the pr-api-minimum-review-criteria job to check for breaking changes. This step should use the oasdiff/oasdiff-action/check-breaking@main action (documented on https://github.com/oasdiff/oasdiff-action) to do the check. But first, you need to check out the source code from the main branch into a main folder in the runners working directory so you can compare the API definition file in the main folder with that in the pr-branch folder. The following snippet shows how to do this:

```
- name: Check out main branch
  uses: actions/checkout@v3
  with:
    ref: main
    path: base
```

Check out the main branch into a base directory.

Then, add a step to run the breaking change check as follows:

```
- name: Breaking change checks
  uses: oasdiff/oasdiff-action/check-breaking@main
  with:
    base: './base/chapter8/apis/product-catalog.oas.yaml'
    revision: './pr-branch/chapter8/apis/product-catalog.oas.yaml'
    fail-on-diff: true
```

Commit this code, and raise a PR to validate it. Now test that this works. Make a breaking change to the chapter8/apis/product-catalog.oas.yaml file by changing the /v1/catalog/categories path to /vx/catalog/categories (essentially deleting one path and adding a new one). Commit this change, and raise a PR. You should see the PR build fail. You should see an error in the logs similar to the following:

```
error at original_source=./base/chapter8/apis/product-catalog.oas.yaml,
  in API GET /v1/catalog/categories api path removed without
  deprecation [api-path-removed-without-deprecation].
```

Create a new commit to undo your change.

8.5.5 Run prose linting

Add a step to check the fourth MDRC criteria—that the API guide documentation in the PR should pass all editorial checks on punctuation, spelling, and grammar. Vale (https://vale.sh) is an open source prose linting CLI tool for checking documentation against editorial style guides. Use Vale in your `pr-api-minimum-review-criteria` job as follows.

The chapter8 folder of your sample project has a .vale.ini file that contains default configurations for the Vale linter. The .vale.ini configuration in this sample project is set to download and use external style guide configuration files based on the Microsoft Writing Style Guide (available at https://learn.microsoft.com/en-us/style-guide). This is specified as a Vale package. A package is a shared Vale configuration, and you can find Vale packages at https://vale.sh/hub. The configuration in the vale file is shown here:

Where Vale's external style configuration files are stored

The minimum alert severity level that Vale will report. Vale's severity levels are suggestion, warning, and error.

```
StylesPath = ./../.github/styles
MinAlertLevel = suggestion
```

```
Packages = Microsoft          ◁──┐  Use the Microsoft package that
                                  │  implements the Microsoft style.
[*.md]                           ◁──────┐  Apply styles to
BasedOnStyles = Vale, Microsoft  ◁────┐ │  Markdown files only.
```
Styles that should have all their rules enabled

The API guide documentation for the project is contained in the chapter8/apis/docs folder. Add a step to download, install, and execute the Vale linter with this configuration, as shown here:

```
 - name: Prose Linting
   run: |
     wget -nv
➥ https://github.com/errata-ai/vale/releases/download/v2.15.4/
➥ vale_2.15.4_Linux_64-bit.tar.gz
     mkdir bin && tar -xvzf vale_2.15.4_Linux_64-bit.tar.gz -C bin
     export PATH=./bin:"$PATH"
     cd pr-branch/chapter8
     vale sync --config=
➥ 'pr-branch/chapter8/.vale.ini'                    ◁──────
     vale pr-branch/chapter8/apis/docs
➥ --config='pr-branch/chapter8/.vale.ini'           ◁──────
```

Downloads and installs external package configuration style files (as specified in .vale.ini) and stores them in the styles directory

Runs vale against all documents in the apis/docs directory using the .vale.ini configuration

Commit and create a PR with this. This should trigger the `pr-build` workflow run, and the step should print the message shown in figure 8.6 in the logs.

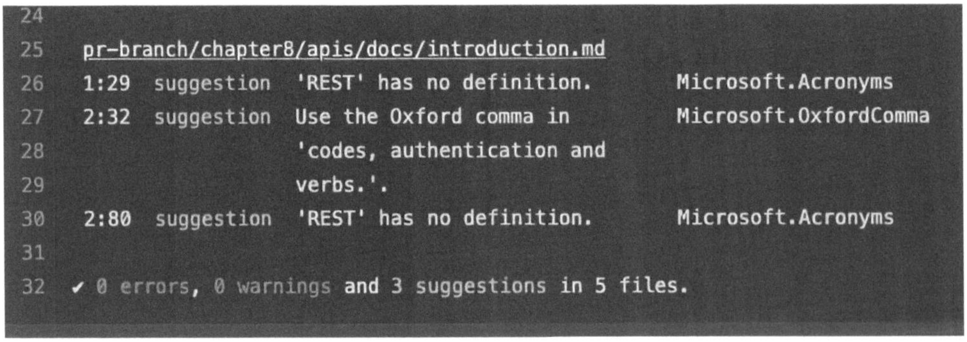

```
24
25   pr-branch/chapter8/apis/docs/introduction.md
26   1:29  suggestion  'REST' has no definition.        Microsoft.Acronyms
27   2:32  suggestion  Use the Oxford comma in          Microsoft.OxfordComma
28                     'codes, authentication and
29                     verbs.'.
30   2:80  suggestion  'REST' has no definition.        Microsoft.Acronyms
31
32   ✔ 0 errors, 0 warnings and 3 suggestions in 5 files.
```

Figure 8.6   Output from running Vale on the API guide documentation

> **TIP**   In this example, you've run the prose linting step by calling Vale from the runner's command line. An alternative way to do this is to use Vale's GitHub Actions, which you can find at https://github.com/errata-ai/vale-action.

8.5.6 *Requiring PR approvals from the governance team*

Let's imagine you want to enforce that all changes to API definition files or guide documentation require approval from a member of the API governance team. In this example, you need a colleague with a GitHub account to serve as your API governance team reviewer. Your colleague plays the role of a code owner—a domain expert who has to review a PR that changes specified files before they can be merged.

> **NOTE** If you have an additional GitHub account, you could use that as well for this example.

To do this, you need to enforce the following controls on the mainline branch:

- All changes must be done via PRs.
- All changes to files and folders in the chapter8/apis directory require approval from your colleague.
- All PRs must have the `pr-code-build` and `pr-api-minimum-review-criteria` jobs run and pass. That is, the status of these job runs has to be successful.

> **NOTE** For status checks, a CI build on the GitHub Actions platform uses GitHub REST API's commit statuses feature to mark commits with an `error`, `failure`, `pending`, or `success` state. The API also allows an optional description to be provided, which can give a high-level summary of the build. These states show up on the PRs that contain those commits on the GitHub UI. For more on GitHub statuses, see https://docs.github.com/en/rest/commits/statuses.

To enforce these controls, create a CODEOWNERS file in the root of the project directory with your colleague as the code owner for the chapter8/apis/directory. You can do this by renaming the _CODEOWNERS file to CODEOWNERS and adding your colleague's GitHub ID. Commit this file to the repository, raise a PR, and merge it to your main branch.

> **NOTE** In this example, you're using a single reviewer. But GitHub also supports assigning a team as a code owner. For more on this, see https://mng.bz/4JGj.

Next, add your colleague as a collaborator on your project. Go to the repository settings, and click Collaborators and Add People. Search for your colleague by their GitHub user ID, and add them.

Now set up GitHub branch protection rules to mandate that all changes are done via PRs, code owners must approve changes, and status checks on branch builds must pass before PRs can be merged to the Main branch. To do this, navigate to the Settings tab in your GitHub repository. Click Branches in the left-hand pane, and then click Add Branch Protection Rule. In the Branch Name Pattern field, enter your mainline branch name, `Main`. Then, select the Require Status Checks to Pass before Merging checkbox and Require Review from Code Owners checkbox. In the search field, look for and select Minimum API Design Review Criteria and Build and Test Source Code (figure 8.7).

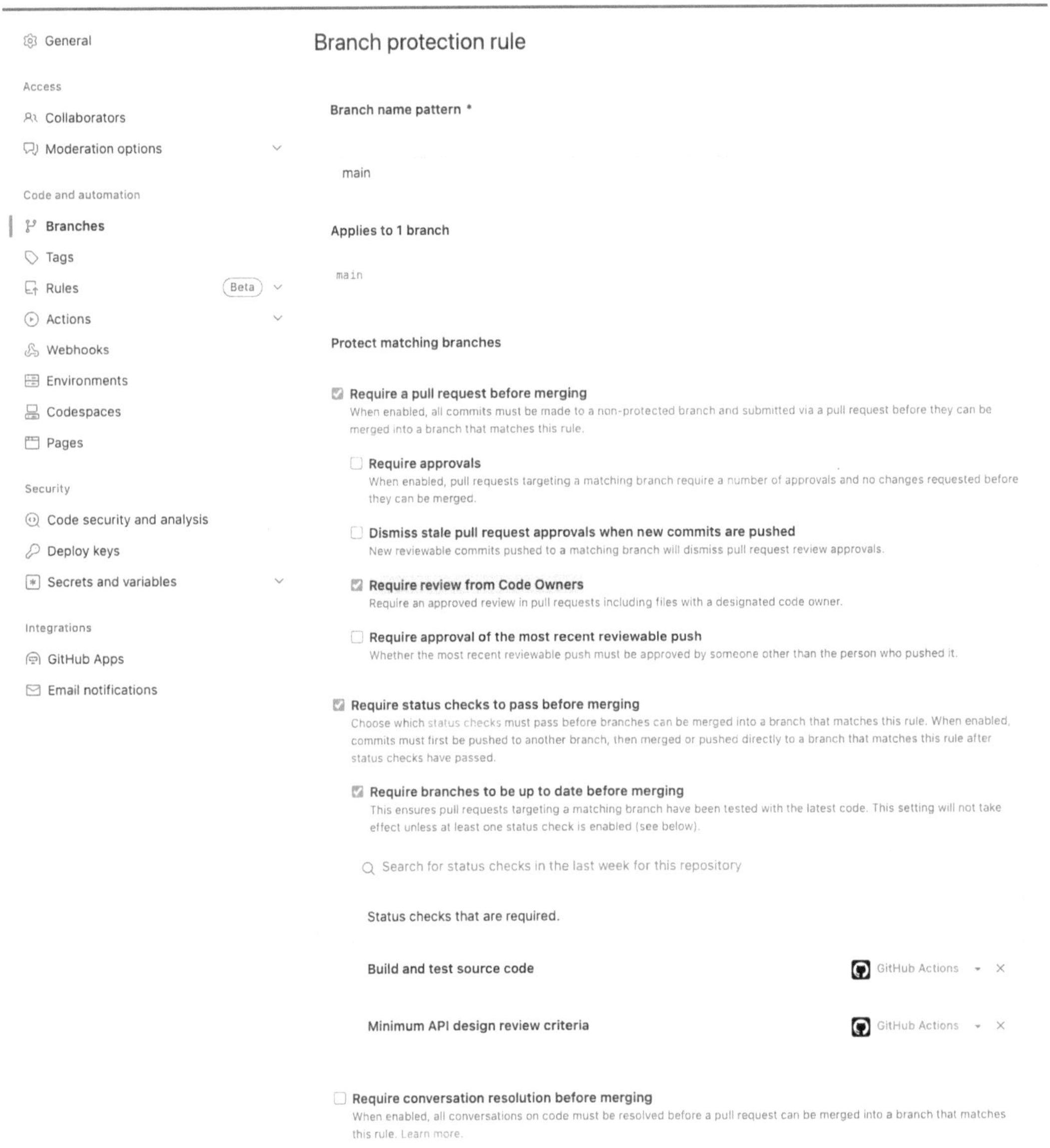

⚙ General

Branch protection rule

Access

👥 Collaborators

🗨 Moderation options   ⌄

Branch name pattern *

Code and automation

main

⌐ Branches

◇ Tags

Applies to 1 branch

⤷ Rules   (Beta) ⌄

main

⊙ Actions   ⌄

⅗ Webhooks

Protect matching branches

⊞ Environments

🖵 Codespaces

☑ **Require a pull request before merging**

📑 Pages

When enabled, all commits must be made to a non-protected branch and submitted via a pull request before they can be merged into a branch that matches this rule.

Security

☐ **Require approvals**

⊕ Code security and analysis

When enabled, pull requests targeting a matching branch require a number of approvals and no changes requested before they can be merged.

🔑 Deploy keys

☐ **Dismiss stale pull request approvals when new commits are pushed**

❋ Secrets and variables   ⌄

New reviewable commits pushed to a matching branch will dismiss pull request review approvals.

Integrations

☑ **Require review from Code Owners**

Require an approved review in pull requests including files with a designated code owner.

🐙 GitHub Apps

☐ **Require approval of the most recent reviewable push**

✉ Email notifications

Whether the most recent reviewable push must be approved by someone other than the person who pushed it.

☑ **Require status checks to pass before merging**

Choose which status checks must pass before branches can be merged into a branch that matches this rule. When enabled, commits must first be pushed to another branch, then merged or pushed directly to a branch that matches this rule after status checks have passed.

☑ **Require branches to be up to date before merging**

This ensures pull requests targeting a matching branch have been tested with the latest code. This setting will not take effect unless at least one status check is enabled (see below).

🔍 Search for status checks in the last week for this repository

Status checks that are required.

Build and test source code   🐙 GitHub Actions ▾ ✕

Minimum API design review criteria   🐙 GitHub Actions ▾ ✕

☐ **Require conversation resolution before merging**

When enabled, all conversations on code must be resolved before a pull request can be merged into a branch that matches this rule. Learn more.

Figure 8.7   Setting up GitHub branch protection rules

Now test that your code owner control is working. Update any guide documentation Markdown file in the chapter8/apis/directory. Commit your changes, and raise a PR.

You should see a notice on the PR that code owner reviews are required, as shown in figure 8.8.

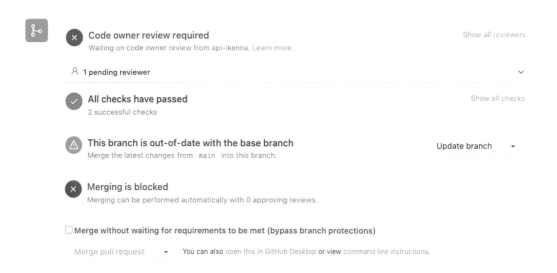

Figure 8.8   Code owner reviews are required on PRs that change files in the chapter8/apis directory.

You've implemented all the MDRCs. These serve as controls at this stage of your deployment pipeline. In the next section, I outline the risks these controls mitigate in this example.

8.6   Automated governance controls

The PR build executes a *quality gate* to ensure that the API governance team only reviews proposals that pass the required checks. A quality gate is a measure that ensures inputs to a stage in a deployment pipeline meet certain criteria before progressing to the next stage. At each stage of the deployment pipeline, there are inputs and outputs, but there are also *actors, actions, risks,* and *controls* to consider:

- *Risk*—The probability of damage or a negative occurrence caused by an avoidable vulnerability
- *Control*—An action taken to mitigate risk
- *Actor*—A role that performs tasks at the stage of the pipeline
- *Action*—A task performed by actors during the stage of the pipeline

These aspects serve as building blocks for a governance model to help governance teams define automated governance controls at each stage.

TIP   For more on this model of automated governance, see *DevOps Automated Governance Reference Architecture: Attestation of the Integrity of Assets In the Delivery Pipeline* by the DevOps Enterprise Forum (IT Revolution, 2019).

Consider table 8.1, which describes these aspects for the source control PR stage of an API design proposal in the example scenario you worked through. (Note that this model can be applied more generally to code changes in the repository, but here I'm limiting the scope to just the API design proposal.)

Table 8.1   Governance model for API design proposals at the source stage of a deployment pipeline

Aspect	Details		
Objective	Enables fast feedback for API designers on objective API style guide checks		
Inputs	API design proposal: • OpenAPI definition files • Draft API guide documentation Markdown files • Work ticket reference		
Outputs	An API design proposal that meets minimum design review criteria: • No error-level API linting problems • No breaking changes • No error-level API documentation problems		
Actors	• API designer • API governance team		
Trigger	PR raised		
Actions	• Raise a PR • Review, approve, and merge PRs		
Risks and Controls	**Risk**	**Mitigation**	**Control**
	API consistency	Check that OpenAPI definitions comply with the organization's API style guide.	• PR build API linting • Code owners approval
	Disruptive breaking changes	Check that API design changes don't introduce unplanned breaking changes.	PR build breaking change checks
	Difficult to read API documentation	Check API guide documentation for punctuation and grammatical errors.	PR build prose linting
	Lack of feature change traceability	Provide product features and release information metadata required for PR review context.	PR description policy checks

This shows the controls applied in this example project. In your project, some of these controls may not apply to you, or you may want other controls in your project. For example, some teams may want to check that submitted API definitions can successfully generate client SDKs. You can use this table to think about the controls you want to apply.

I've discussed API linting and breaking change checks in previous chapters, so I won't go over these again, but I will discuss the other code owners, PR description policies, and prose linting. But first, let's discuss the PR build in general.

8.7   PR builds

PRs make it easy for designers and reviewers to collaborate on changes. PRs notify reviewers of the need to review a change and also provide a user-friendly user interface (UI) for discussing proposed changes before they are integrated into a branch. This UI is a powerful way to track discussions and follow-up changes on the PR. The ability to refer to the PR where a change was introduced is helpful in tracing problems. But before PR reviewers review a PR, how do they ensure that all the required command line automated checks (e.g., API linting, breaking change checks, and other tests) have been executed and passed?

When a PR is raised, a build server can also be configured to kick off a job to validate it. Teams use these PR jobs to check that the code in the PR branch compiles, static analysis checks pass, and developer tests pass. On completion, the PR build displays the status of the build job on the PR UI, making it easy for PR submitters and reviewers to see. If the build fails, the PR submitter can click through from the PR to the build job results to see the build logs and investigate why the build failed.

PR builds can be applied to API design proposals as well. API linting can be run on the API definition files, and the build can be configured to fail on ERROR-level linting problems. Breaking change checks can run on new and old versions of the definition files, and the build should fail on breaking changes. For guide documentation in Markdown files, the build can fail depending on the configured level of linting problems raised. If the PR build passes all these checks, the API governance team can start reviewing the PR, being confident that its minimum design-review criteria have been met. But they still need to review the report from the build to find problems raised by the build (e.g., WARNING-level linting problems) that didn't cause a build failure. Apart from these, of course, you can also define scripts to do whatever custom checks you want.

For some code hosting services and build servers, PR builds may come pre-integrated, as you saw in the example with GitHub and GitHub Actions. But depending on the providers you chose, you may need to set up a webhook on the code hosting platform so it can make a call to the build server when a PR event occurs.

For many developers, using PRs and PR builds is their normal way of working, as they raise many PRs in a day. Using this same process for API design reviews fits into their natural way of working and requires little or no education.

8.8   PR description policies

PR description policies are the set of rules that determine what good PR titles and descriptions should contain to aid the PR reviewer in understanding what the content of the PR is and why it was raised. Because the PR submitter may not be on hand to provide the background of the PR, the PR should contain enough information to provide this context; otherwise, the reviewer is left to answer these questions on their own. For example, an API governance team can decide that an API design proposal PR should include a reference to the work ticket that explains the feature the API design is being made for. Providing a work ticket in the PR title or PR description message is helpful if the ticket provides useful information for the reviewer. If the referenced work ticket itself is empty or doesn't have the information the reviewer needs, this slows down PR reviewers, as they have to go hunting for the information or be left guessing.

A PR template can help remind submitters to provide this information. A PR template is a way to customize and standardize the information provided by PR submitters in the description of a PR. It's like a to-do list for the PR submitter to check and fill in when raising a PR. PR templates are usually configured as Markdown files in the code hosting system. For example, in GitHub, this involves creating a pull_request_template.md file in the repository. Some code hosting systems allow the creation of different PR templates for different branches. Some enforce checks on the contents of the template—for example, checking that a checkbox has been filled in.

While PR templates are a helpful prompt for PR submitters to provide the required context for reviewers, they don't validate any of the information entered. Because of this, it's possible for PR submitters to ignore them. In addition, to encourage PR submitters to fill them, it helps to keep the number of questions asked in a PR template short. GitHub provides a good reference for examples of PR templates at https://mng.bz/X1ma.

Commit policies

Obviously, PR description policies work at a PR level. But checking the title and description of a change can also occur at the commit level. I use the term *commit policy* to refer to the set of automated rules that can be verified against every new commit to a VCS. The commits are accepted if they pass the rules or are rejected otherwise, usually with a helpful message explaining why they were rejected. Commit policies can be used to provide traceability between a source code in individual commits to its related work tickets or user stories. When used in this way, commit policies can help speed up PR-based API design reviews, as the governance team can set up other light checks they feel are appropriate. Commit policies are important for GitOps and APIOps, where the VCS is both the source of truth and the central control mechanism for the project.

Depending on how it's set up, commit policies can work eagerly before the commit is created to prevent the creation of wrong commits. This supports a fail-fast mechanism, without waiting for the build server to validate the PR. This way, they don't slow the PR submitter down. Commit policies can also run on the server when commits are pushed. In Git, commit policies can be defined with client-side or server-side Git hooks. A *Git hook* is a customizable script that runs automatically when an event occurs in a Git repository. For example, to define a Git hook to verify that a commit starts with a JIRA issue ticket in the format *XXX-YYYY*, where *X* is a capital letter and *Y* is a digit, you can define the following in an executable file called pre-commit in your .git/hooks folder in the Git repository of your project:

```bash
#!/bin/bash

commit_msg_file=$1

# Read the commit message file
commit_msg=$(cat "$commit_msg_file")

# Pattern to match Jira issue reference (DEV-XXXX)
Pattern="DEV-[0-9]{4}"

# Check if the commit message contains the Jira issue reference
if [[ ! $commit_msg =~ $pattern ]]; then
    echo "Error: Commit message does not contain a valid
 Jira issue reference in the format DEV-XXXX."
    echo "Please include a Jira issue reference in your commit message."
    exit 1
fi
```

When setting up Git hooks, it's generally good practice to ensure that hooks are fast, reliable, and well-documented. They should not modify files without the committer's consent.

The challenge with client-side Git hooks is that they have to be set up on each developer's workstation—developers don't get them by simply cloning the repository. There are different techniques to get around this, one of which is to use a hook package manager such as the open source pre-commit (https://pre-commit.com), which manages the installation and execution of hooks.

Some code hosting services have sophisticated features or plugins that provide more easily configurable commit policies using a web UI. Examples of commit policy plugins for code hosting systems include Better Commit Policy for Bitbucket (https://mng.bz/y8pd) and Control Freak for Bitbucket (https://mng.bz/MZrB).

For checking the description of commit messages, open source CLI tools such as commitlint (https://github.com/conventional-changelog/commitlint) and Git Lint (https://github.com/bkuhlmann/git-lint) can also be used to validate commit messages.

8.9 Code owners

An OpenAPI definition file for an external API can reside in the same repository as an API service's source code (as in the example project), or it can be in a dedicated repository for API definition files. If the team responsible for updating the API design have write and PR approval permissions for the repository, there is nothing stopping them from approving the API design PR themselves without involving the API governance team in the review. This can be a problem because on a large project, the API governance team is responsible for overseeing API design consistency across the organization and are the domain experts on the API standards. If the team doesn't involve the API governance team in the review, the design may have inconsistencies that the API linting and breaking change checks don't cover. It can miss vital feedback that the API governance team could have provided. But how do you ensure each PR is reviewed by the governance team?

You can define the API governance team as code owners for the API definition files and documentation. Assigning a code owner to specific files, file types, or directories in a version control repository means that the individuals or teams listed as code owners have to approve any PRs that touch the affected files before the PR can be merged. And code owners get notified whenever a PR that needs their attention is raised.

In Git-based code hosting solutions that support code owner controls, you can set up code owners by adding a CODEOWNERS file in the root directory of the source repository. Note that for some code hosting systems, you may require a plugin or add-on to enable this feature.

CODEOWNERS is a useful way to involve the API governance team in the review, but do take care with how you implement it. Requiring too many code owner approvals outside the core team making the update to the source repository can introduce delays in PR approvals that slow down the pace of development. This would be counter to the goal of APIOps of minimizing development friction to enable faster design and delivery of your APIs, while maintaining compliance with standards. I recommend you only require the minimal number of code owners on the specific API definition that require that level of external governance. For most other changes, you want the team making the source changes to review the PRs within their team because communication within the team happens faster.

You can assign the API governance team as code owners for the API definition files. This ensures that they, as the API standards experts, have to review and approve changes to API definition files before they are merged to the main branch.

GitHub has a page explaining how you can set up code owners at https://mng .bz/4JGj, and so does GitLab at https://docs.gitlab.com/ee/user/project/codeowners/. Mibix Software provides a Bitbucket Code Owners plugin at https://mng.bz/aEpm.

NOTE In this book, I differentiate between internal APIs (e.g., microservice APIs owned by a team that need to be used by other microservices used by the same team) and external APIs (APIs that need to be exposed outside the organization or organizational unit and that need to be managed as a product with input from multiple stakeholders) product, technical writers, security teams, and so on. API governance teams are usually concerned with the latter, especially at the design stage. This is where a code owners file may come in handy because the API governance team will need to approve the design. This is a design stage of the software life cycle. The important question to ask is, Who is appropriate to review this change? For API governance teams, reviewing the external-facing API design changes is their primary area of responsibility.

8.10 Prose linting

Writing API guide documentation involves writing prose and complying with language usage guides and styles. Without guidance, writers can introduce punctuation, spelling, and grammar errors. They can also use redundant words, jargon, cliches, and unidiomatic vocabulary. This can make API guide documentation hard to read.

Prose linters can help with this problem. Prose linters scan and analyze documents to identify language syntax and style errors. They are based on expert style and usage guidelines. Unlike plain grammar checkers, they can provide custom rules and styles (just like an API linting tool). This allows writers to check their writing against organization-specific style, tone, and branding. Examples of Prose linting tools include Vale (https://vale.sh), textlint (https://textlint.github.io/), and proselint (https://github.com/amperser/proselint). They can run as command-line tools or can be used as an editor plugin (they all have VS Code plugins).

Vale is a popular fast prose linter. Its configuration file (by default, it expects to find a .vale.ini file in the folder in which it's invoked) holds the language style guide it's configured to use. It works with Markdown, AsciiDoc, and reStructuredText. Textlint is also a popular linter, written in JavaScript. It loads rules as plugins and can lint prose in Markdown, text, and HTML files. Finally, proselint is also a popular Python-based tool. It aims to precisely apply style guides from authoritative writers and editors.

> **TIP** For more on the motivation for prose linters, read "Linting Science Prose and the Science of Prose Linting" by the authors of proselint, Michael D. Pacer and Jordan W. Suchow (https://mng.bz/gvKv). And for more information on how Vale works, see Joseph Kato's post, "Introducing Vale, an NLP-Powered Linter for Prose" at https://mng.bz/eozV.

Following the APIOps principle of storing all project source files in version control where possible, I suggest writing your API guide documentation as Markdown files stored in your project's source repository. This enables you to use prose linters to check them in your delivery pipeline. As part of the deployment pipeline, you can have tools that upload the files to your developer portal. Developer portal CI tools such as the Readme CLI (https://github.com/readmeio/rdme) allow you to do this with the Readme dev portal. However, you can also create your own if you have a custom developer portal system.

Docs as Code

Running prose linting on API guide documentation is related to the idea of treating technical documentation as code—Docs as Code. In the book, *Docs Like Code: Collaborate and Automate to Improve Technical Documentation* (3rd ed., Just Write Click, 2022), Anne Gentle outlines the principles of the *Docs as Code* approach to API documentation:

- Store documentation source files in version control. Documentation should be in lightweight, plain text markup formats such as Markdown, reStructured-Text and AsciiDoc.
- Build the documentation artifacts from source files automatically.
- Run automated tests on the docs.
- Similar to code reviews, do reviews on documentation changes.
- Publish the documentation artifacts with little or no human intervention.

With a Docs as Code approach, the documentation workflow follows the same workflow as the development team. It enables teams to use the same tools for workflow automation, for example, by integrating the documentation tools into the deployment pipeline and using the same IDE the team uses for code for the documentation. And this can have a potential cost benefit, as many open source tools that can be used in this way (e.g., the prose linting tools I've just discussed) are free.

A major benefit of treating technical documentation as code is that it creates alignment in ways of working between development teams and technical writers, creating a culture of joint ownership of the documentation. Developers usually write a first draft of the documentation, which technical writers then enhance. Where possible, store the docs in the same repository as the application code (perhaps in a docs folder). This makes it easier for the team to update the documentation as they work on the code. It also means that the team can block merging new feature PRs until the documentation is ready. Because documentation is in plain text markup in the project source repository, it enables more people in the organization to contribute to the documentation.

Eric Holscher, a cofounder of the Write the Docs community, maintains an introductory page on the Docs as Code approach at www.writethedocs.org/guide/docs-as-code/.

8.11 Supporting API design proposals in the pipeline

In enhancing the source repository stage of a pipeline to handle API design proposals, here are a few suggestions to keep in mind. These practical tips can help you improve the pipeline for its users.

8.11.1 Understand the users and their requirements

From an API design review perspective, the two main users of the pipeline are the API designers and the API governance team. Observe how they use the pipeline and what problems they face. Use API design review meetings (as discussed in chapter 5) to identify design review problems that regularly occur but haven't been automated yet. Capture and include these as minimum design review criteria to be checked in the pipeline.

The MDRC build report should be optimized for API designers and the API governance team. That is, a run of the job should produce a build report that they can easily read. It should include the following:

- What MDRCs were run
- What linting rules were ignored
- Linting problems that were raised but didn't cause build failures

I think it's important to see the API governance team as a first-class user of the pipeline reports, so the reports should be optimized for their use.

8.11.2 Design the pipeline for fast feedback

In pipeline execution, speed is a feature. API designers and reviewers want the PR build to provide fast feedback, so optimize the automated checks at this stage to run quickly. As a rule of thumb, the PR build should take no more than 5 minutes. Consider using the different jobs that execute in parallel (as in the worked example you did with GitHub Actions) to speed up the build.

8.11.3 Make it easy to see why the build failed

When the build fails, API designers need to see a helpful report that points them to the cause of the failure. The UI of the CI/CD server should make it easy for them to see the cause of failure without hunting through logs. Linting problems should give enough context on the areas of the API definition file that have a problem and can provide links to sections in the API style guide that provide more information on the guideline that the linting rule is implementing. With this, a user can follow the link from the logs to the area in the API style guide that explains the problem.

In addition, when the pipeline fails, block the PR so it can't be merged. This prompts the API designer to fix the problem.

8.11.4 Linting failures can link to the API style guide

The minimum design review criteria should be defined by the API governance team, and the build should fail if this isn't met. Discuss with the team and consult with the API style guide to determine what level of linting problems or other problems detected by the pipeline should lead to a pipeline failure.

Linting checks should be based on the guidelines specified in the API style guide. Ideally, the style guide should make clear which guidelines are mandatory and which are optional, and this can be a good guide to setting the problem level in the linting rule (e.g., ERROR, WARN, or HINT).

Using RFC 2119 style keywords such as MUST, MUST NOT, and SHOULD in an API style guide helps in determining what problem level to apply to a linting rule. A good example of an API style guide that uses RFC 2119 is the *Zalando RESTful API and Event Guidelines*, available at https://opensource.zalando.com/restful-api-guidelines.

8.11.5 Collect design review time metrics

The time it takes from when a PR is raised and when the PR is merged is the *design-review lead time*. For organizations where too much time is wasted waiting for design reviews, this is an important metric to capture and track. Some code hosting services have plugins that can track and visualize this data. Alternatively, you may need to write some scripts to capture and present this information. As you do your process optimizations, you should see this metric decrease.

8.11.6 Include static security checks in the PR build

API security is about protecting the information transmitted by APIs and reducing the risk posed by API vulnerabilities. API security is a large topic and covers many parts of the API product life cycle, and I discuss it a bit more in chapter 10. One aspect of API security I want to cover here is the need to check for API security vulnerabilities at API design time. This is sometimes called static security testing of APIs. This ensures that security vulnerabilities in the design of APIs are found early and fixed. It usually involves running some kind of API linting with security-focused linting rules on your API definition files. You can incorporate these static security check tools in your PR build as part of your MDRC to help API designers think about API security early on.

Many API security vendors provide commercial API security platforms you can integrate into different parts of your API product life cycle to protect your APIs. Examples of these vendors include 42Crunch (https://42crunch.com), Noname Security (https://nonamesecurity.com), Salt Security (https://salt.security), and Traceable (www.traceable.ai). You can integrate with their platforms to scan for vulnerabilities in your API definitions as part of your deployment pipeline. These tools also check that you follow best practices on authentication, authorization, transport, and data payloads. For example, 42Crunch has a GitHub action (https://mng.bz/670A) you can add to a GitHub Actions–based pipeline. It gives each API definition an audit score on a scale of 0 (for insecure APIs) to 100 (no problems detected). And you can set a minimum score that API definitions need to meet to pass the build. Each run of the action produces a link to a detailed security report you can view on the 42 Crunch platform. API security platforms like these provide a security quality gate in your pipeline.

8.12 Rendering the API definition for review

Let's go back to the example scenario you worked through. With the controls implemented, the Acme API governance team ensures that the API design proposals it's asked to review meet its minimum design review criteria. But the governance team faces a new problem. In the past, when the API definition files were sent to them over their Slack messaging system, the team downloaded and opened them up in the VS Code text editor and rendered them as an API reference (using the Swagger UI view layout of the VS Code OpenAPI plugin). With the API definition files in the PR, they must check out the PR branch and load up the files in their VS Code editor. That's OK, but is there an easier way for the API governance team to view and render the API definition files as an API reference during their review without having to check out the PR branch?

Rendering and API definition during the design and design review phase are necessary tasks. There are a few ways the Acme team can tackle this problem as defined here and discussed further in the following subsections:

- Integrate the version-controlled source repository containing the API definition files with an API design collaboration tool (ADC). This allows them to view the API reference in the ADC.
- Make the PR-build publish the OpenAPI definition file on a server, and view the API reference there.
- Use a source repository plugin that renders the OpenAPI definition file as a visual API reference.

8.12.1   Integrating the source repository with an ADC

Web-based ADC tools such as Stoplight Studio (https://stoplight.io), Apicurio Studio (www.apicur.io/studio), SwaggerHub (https://swagger.io/tools/swaggerhub), and Postman (www.postman.com) provide a UI for collaboratively defining and editing OpenAPI definition files. These tools provide lots of helpful features for working with API definition files. But they are particularly helpful for designing and reviewing API definition files because they allow designers to edit the API definition source, switch between the API definition source view and the API reference view, and add review comments to the files (an important task during API review).

> **NOTE**   Many developers traditionally use Postman for making API requests, and one question I sometimes get asked is whether Postman has API design features. It does—Postman supports creating, importing, and editing OpenAPI definitions. It allows you to connect to a Git VCS to sync and manage your API definition changes. You can find more on Postman's API design features at https://mng.bz/oenp.

One essential feature to consider in deciding on an ADC to use in the workflow I've described is that it should support using a version control system (VCS), mentioned previously, as the primary store of API definition files. That means it should read from and write to the VCS.

Using ADCs as the primary store of API definitions

I've seen situations where rather than using a VCS as the primary store of API definition files, teams have used the ADC as the primary store of API definition files. In this
scenario, all design editing and review of API definition files occur in the ADC. This
appears appealing because some ADCs have API registry features. That is, as well
as acting as a store of API definition files, they provide APIs to allow for the search,
retrieval, and update of API definitions. (I talk more about API registries in chapter 9.)
With this pattern, the ADC becomes the source repository for API definition files.
Using ADCs as the source repository for API definition files has the advantage of
being the simplest way to get started, especially with teams new to using an ADC.
But it does come with several downsides.

First, while some ADCs have limited version history, file diff, and concurrent editing
capabilities, they are nowhere near the capability of similar features provided by dedicated VCSs. VCSs are the ideal tool for providing the version history of source files,
and this is a very important auditability requirement for any software project. One
foundational practice of DevOps is that all project source and configuration files
should be stored in version control. In *Accelerate* by Nicole Forsgren, Jez Humble, and
Gene Kim (2018, IT Revolution Press), the authors found in their research that software delivery lead time is highly correlated with version control and automated testing. They also found that deployment frequency was highly correlated with the use of
CD and comprehensive version control. Using lightweight, PR-based API design review
processes backed by version-controlled API definition files is important in improving
the lead time of software design and delivery. This is the reason the second principle
of APIOps I discussed in chapter 1, section 1.5.2 is about storing your API definition
files in version control.

Secondly, using ADCs as the primary store of your API definition files can limit your
integration options. VCSs such as Git and code hosting services such as GitHub, Git-
Lab, and Bitbucket offer excellent integration options with build servers, ticketing systems, IDEs, code quality systems, and so on. This provides more integration options
for the API definition source files stored in your VCS.

And thirdly, using ADCs as the primary store of your API definition files can tie down
the data (the source files) with the tool for editing them (the ADC). This can be a problem for developers and others who may prefer another tool for editing the API definition files.

8.12.2 Publish the PR OpenAPI definition file on a server

The PR build can publish the OpenAPI definition files to a server that renders them.
The server can render the files using SwaggerUI, Redocly, Stoplight Elements, and
other rendering styles. A useful open source tool for this is Swagger UI Watcher
(https://github.com/moon0326/swagger-ui-watcher). To give developers a fluid workflow, it detects changes in an OpenAPI definition file on your filesystem and reloads it
in the Swagger UI in a browser.

8.12.3 *Use a source repository viewer plugin*

Some code hosting services support, or have plugins that support, rendering OpenAPI definition files right in the source repository. This means that when reviewing an API design PR, the reviewers can look at the PR and see the rendered API definition file. An example of this is the Bitbucket OpenAPI viewer (https://mng.bz/aEpm). There are also Chrome browser plugins that enable the rendering of OpenAPI definition files, and you can find these in the Chrome web store.

8.13 *Reusing API objects: Multifile API definitions*

Large-scale software projects involving multiple teams can end up with monolithic OpenAPI files, sometimes up to tens of thousands of lines long. If not properly managed, these files can contain duplicated OpenAPI objects, making updating them tedious and the reuse of objects difficult. When multiple teams have to edit these files, there is a greater chance of file conflicts in version control. Due to their large size, the files are also difficult for PR reviewers to review, and some OpenAPI tools (e.g., editors, API gateways, etc.) may struggle with their size. So how can teams manage these large API definition files?

From an API design perspective, teams can prevent API definition files from growing too large in the first place by ensuring that API boundaries are well-scoped and clearly defined (for more info on this, see James Higginbotham's work on how to define API boundaries at the right granularity in *Principles of Web API Design* [Addison-Wesley Professional, 2021]). But from an API definition file perspective, the definition should be created to have (or refactored to have) references to reusable objects. The reusable objects the references point to should be in the Components Object of the definition. Per OAS 3.1, the Components Object holds reusable objects such as schemas, responses, parameters, examples, request bodies, headers, securitySchemas, links, callbacks, and path items.

This reference is done using OpenAPI reference objects. A reference object has the field $ref, whose value is a URI that identifies the target object being referenced. For internal references, that is, *same-document* references, the URI of the reference can include only the pound sign (#) followed by a fragment identifier. An example of this is shown in the following snippet:

```
/v1/catalog/products/{id}/reviews:
  get:
    tags:
      - Reviews
    summary: List reviews
    description: List all reviews for a product.
    operationId: listProductReviews
    parameters:
      - $ref: '#/components/parameters/productId'
    responses:
      '200':
        description: OK
```

```
      headers:
        RateLimit-Limit:
          $ref: '#/components/headers/rateLimit'
        RateLimit-Remaining:
          $ref: '#/components/headers/rateLimitRemaining'
        RateLimit-Reset:
          $ref: '#/components/headers/rateLimitReset'
      content:
        application/vnd.api+json:
          schema:
            $ref: '#/components/schemas/ReviewsResponse'
```

Using reference objects to internal components helps, but the resulting API definition file may still be quite large. To further optimize the file size, objects can be moved out of the API definition file into external fragments or child documents. The resulting *multifile API definition document* consists of a parent document with references to the child documents. The URI in the reference indicates the absolute or relative path to the document, followed by a JSON pointer reference that locates the object in the document (figure 8.9).

Figure 8.9   The structure of an external OpenAPI reference

8.13.1 *Splitting an OpenAPI definition*

The chapter8/apis/product-catalog-api directory contains an example of an OpenAPI file that has been split based on the following rules:

- Each parent API definition should have its own folder. The folder should have two subfolders—paths and components. The components folder should have a subfolder for each type of component the API has, for example, headers, parameters, schemas, responses, and examples.
- Every path object in the parent API definition should reference a path object that lives in its own file in the path's directory. That file can contain multiple operations (e.g., GET, POST, PUT, etc.).
- Every header element should have its own file in the headers directory.
- Every success (2xx) response schema should have its own file in the response directory.

- Every error response object should have its own file response directory.
- Every file should be a valid OpenAPI document.
- All references should have both the file and the JSON pointer parts.

The resulting directory structure for this is shown in figure 8.10.

```
↪  product-catalog-api git:(workbranch) tree .
.
├── components
│   ├── headers
│   │   ├── rateLimit.yaml
│   │   ├── rateLimitRemaining.yaml
│   │   └── rateLimitReset.yaml
│   ├── parameters
│   │   ├── filterCategory.yaml
│   │   ├── include.yaml
│   │   └── productId.yaml
│   ├── responses
│   │   ├── 400Response.yaml
│   │   ├── 401Response.yaml
│   │   ├── 403Response.yaml
│   │   ├── 404Response.yaml
│   │   ├── 406Response.yaml
│   │   ├── 415Response.yaml
│   │   ├── 429Response.yaml
│   │   └── 500Response.yaml
│   ├── schemas
│   │   ├── CategoriesResponse.yaml
│   │   ├── Category.yaml
│   │   ├── Error.yaml
│   │   ├── Link.yaml
│   │   ├── Pagination.yaml
│   │   ├── Product.yaml
│   │   ├── ProductsResponse.yaml
│   │   ├── Review.yaml
│   │   └── ReviewsResponse.yaml
│   └── securitySchemes
│       └── OAuth2.yaml
├── openapi.yaml
└── paths
    ├── v1-catalog-categories.yaml
    ├── v1-catalog-products-id-reviews.yaml
    ├── v1-catalog-products-id.yaml
    └── v1-catalog-products.yaml
```

Figure 8.10   An example of the directory structure containing a multifile OpenAPI document

Using these rules, here's what the paths and components objects in the parent API definition file look like:

```
openapi: 3.0.3
info:
  title: Product Catalog API
        version: 0.0.1
...
tags:
  - name: Categories
    description: A category is a class of products
⇒ with common characteristics
```

```
...
paths:
  /v1/catalog/categories:
    $ref: 'paths/v1-catalog-categories.yaml#
   /paths/~1v1~1catalog~1categories'
  /v1/catalog/products:
    $ref: 'paths/v1-catalog-products.yaml#
   /paths/~1v1~1catalog~1products'
  /v1/catalog/products/{id}:
    $ref: 'paths/v1-catalog-products-id.yaml#
   /paths/~1v1~1catalog~1products~1{id}'
  /v1/catalog/products/{id}/reviews:
    $ref: 'paths/v1-catalog-products-id-reviews.yaml#
   /paths/~1v1~1catalog~1products~1{id}~1reviews'
components:
  securitySchemes:
    $ref: 'components/securitySchemes/OAuth2.yaml#
   /components/securitySchemes'
security:
  - OAuth2: []
```

> Reference includes file and JSON pointer to the target object

> Each path object lives in its own file.

The referenced `v1-catalog-categories.yaml` path object looks as follows:

```
openapi: 3.0.3              ⟵——— This is an OpenAPI file.
info:
  title: Acme Product Catalog API
  version: 0.0.1
paths:
  /v1/catalog/categories:
   get:
     tags:
       - Categories
     summary: List all categories
     description: List all categories.
     operationId: listCategories
     parameters: []
     responses:
       '200':
         description: OK
         headers:
           RateLimit-Limit:
             $ref: '../components/headers/rateLimit.yaml#
   /components/headers/rateLimit'
           RateLimit-Remaining:
             $ref: '../components/headers/rateLimitRemaining.yaml#
   /components/headers/rateLimitRemaining'
           RateLimit-Reset:
             $ref: '../components/headers/rateLimitReset.yaml#
   /components/headers/rateLimitReset'
         content:
           application/vnd.api+json:
             schema:
               $ref: '../components/schemas/CategoriesResponse.yaml#
   /components/schemas/CategoriesResponse'
       '401':
```

> A reference to a header object in a file in the headers directory

```
        $ref: '../components/responses/401Response.yaml#
⟹   /components/responses/401Response'
        '403':
        $ref: '../components/responses/403Response.yaml#
⟹   /components/responses/403Response'
        '406':
        $ref: '../components/responses/406Response.yaml#
⟹   /components/responses/406Response'
....
```

A reference to a response object in a file in the response directory

The OAS doesn't impose any rules on the structure of the JSON/YAML file child documents referenced by the root document. However, structuring the child documents as fully valid OAS documents means that they can be linted, transformed, and upgraded from one version of the OAS to another by using OAS-compliant tools. It also means you can work with them in editors that support OpenAPI and get all the code assistance they provide. And the `$.info.version` field in the child document allows you to version the fragment separately from the root document if you need to.

> **NOTE**   Mike Ralphson, an OAS editor, writes more about making child documents standard OpenAPI definitions on the Dev website at https://mng.bz/Y74z.

8.13.2   Combining your multifile document

To combine your multifile API definitions into a single file (e.g., for use in tools that don't support external references), you can *bundle* them. Bundling involves pulling external references from different files or URLs and adding those references to the components object of the OpenAPI definition. You can do this with the `bundle` command of the Redocly CLI or Swagger CLI https://github.com/APIDevTools/swagger-cli (their bundle features are similar). In your sample project, try this out by bundling the definition in the product-catalog-api folder:

```
cd apis/product-catalog-api
redocly bundle openapi.yaml --output bundled.yaml
```

Look in the bundled.yaml file created to see all the external references consolidated as internal references.

> **TIP**   I've mentioned command line tools for bundling API definition files. But if you want an embeddable JavaScript library you could use to bundle definitions, consider JSON Schema $Ref Parser https://github.com/APIDevTools/json-schema-ref-parser.

8.13.3   Things to consider with multifile API definitions

Multifile API definition documents help make API definitions more modular and easier to understand and maintain. They also promote reuse and encapsulation, as the reusable components in separate files can be shared by multiple parent API definitions. This reduces duplication and helps ensure consistency in API reference documentation. Multifile API definitions also make it easier for multiple teams to work on different parts of the document and reduce the chances of merge conflicts.

However, multifile API definitions do come with some complexity. To avoid confusion, multiple files need to be managed with clear naming conventions and guidelines. In addition, developers must invest time in understanding the file structure and relationships between different components. While the OAS supports multifile documents, not all tools and frameworks do. It's crucial to verify that the API tools you use are compatible with multifile documents to avoid any unexpected limitations.

8.13.4 *Tooling for multifile API definitions*

API designers can create reusable components in API definition files by hand. But working in API definition YAML or JSON files in a text editor can be tedious. API design collaboration tools such as Stoplight, Apicurio, and SwaggerHub support reusable OpenAPI components and can make the task easier. They enable you to have a library of reusable API components to refer to in your API definition files.

However, suppose you have a large OpenAPI definition file you want to split into a multifile OpenAPI definition. This may be a one-time task you want to perform or something you would like to do in your deployment pipeline. You can do this with the Redocly CLI split function. Try this out in the chapter8/apis directory as follows:

```
redocly split product-catalog.oas.yaml --outDir out
```

One advantage of using the Redocly CLI to split files is that it has a configurable convention for naming the resulting files. Note that the resulting child document fragments contain just the reference objects and are YAML or JSON files, not standard OpenAPI documents. They are useable as is, but you may also want to update them to be valid OpenAPI documents.

Summary

- API governance teams can define minimum design review criteria (MDRC)—a set of automated checks that API design change proposals must pass before they go through a PR review. These automated checks in the pipeline should include API linting, breaking change checks, and any other automated checks the governance team thinks are important.
- Using PR templates to prompt API designers to provide contextual information on why API design change PR is required helps PR reviewers understand the reason and scope of changes and helps them review it quicker.
- Assigning code owners to files is a technique for requiring domain experts to review and approve changes to files in a team's source repository. You can set members of the API governance team as code owners for API definition files to enforce that all design changes are reviewed by them.
- Prose linters such as Vale can run in your PR build to check API guide documentation files for punctuation, spelling, grammar, style, and readability.

- When using an API design collaboration tool, you can integrate with the source repository that contains your API definition files. Ensure the version-controlled source repository is the primary store of the API definition files.
- Splitting API definition files into multiple files helps you make them more manageable and enhances collaboration on them with multiple teams. It also promotes the reuse of shared API components.

CI/CD for API artifacts 2: Build-stage and API configuration deployment

This chapter covers

- Transforming API definitions in the pipeline
- Publishing generated API artifacts to an artifact store
- Creating SDKs and mock APIs
- Deploying API gateway configuration

In chapter 8, I discussed source-stage governance controls to help teams apply automated governance checks to API definitions at the API-design stage. After the definitions have been reviewed and approved, the API team may need to do the following:

- Generate artifacts from the API definition. These artifacts can include SDKs, alternative API definition formats, and human-readable API reference documentation for the developer portal.
- Deploy the API service to higher environments.
- Deploy the API gateway configuration.
- Test the implemented API for conformance.

This chapter details how to perform these tasks in the deployment pipeline, which lies in the Build stage and the Deploy and Test stage (figure 9.1).

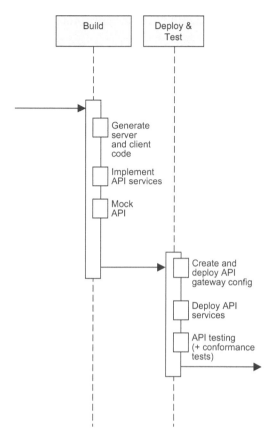

Figure 9.1 The APIOps practices discussed in this chapter

This hands-on chapter is aimed primarily at developers who need to set up a deployment pipeline to deploy and publish APIs. You'll walk through an example of setting up a pipeline to generate and publish API artifacts to internal API artifact stores using GitHub Actions. You'll implement deploying API configuration in two open source API gateways using an APIOps (i.e., GitOps-based) workflow.

While this chapter is aimed at developers, API product owners will also benefit from a high-level view of the main stages of the pipeline for API artifacts. They'll gain from understanding the different kinds of teams involved in the APIOps deployment workflow and how it fits into an organization's team topology. API product owners and product managers should consider points raised in the section on managing SDKs and the challenges with building them.

NOTE The code examples for this chapter reuse and extend the code for chapter 8, which you can find at https://mng.bz/ngo2, but also contain additional code in https://mng.bz/GZAD and https://mng.bz/z8O1. I invite you to work through the examples, but if you want to go straight to the completed solution, I've created the relevant files with a .completed suffix in the code repository, where possible. You must rename the files as appropriate for them to work.

Experience with Docker and Kubernetes is useful for this chapter but not essential. I provide a brief introduction to them in appendix E.

9.1   *Build stage: Transforming API definition files*

Imagine that before publishing your API definition files to your developer portal, you need to do the following:

1 Bundle your multifile definition into one file.
2 Filter the resulting definition file. Say you want to remove any OpenAPI objects marked with the `x-internal:true` OpenAPI extension.
3 Sort `operationId` fields in an OpenAPI definition file so they appear in a consistent order. For example, for all your API operation objects, you may want the `operationId` to appear first, the `summary` next, and then the `description`, `parameters`, `requestBody`, and `responses` fields, in that order.
4 Strip out any unused components in the definition file.
5 Create a Postman collection from your OpenAPI file.
6 Upload the processed OpenAPI definition file to an API artifact store so that later steps in the pipeline can retrieve, use, or publish it to the developer portal.

NOTE In chapter 4, I introduced OpenAPI extensions as a mechanism to extend OpenAPI to allow additional data to be added to API definition files. One use case for this is where an API definition file contains both internal-facing and external-facing endpoints. You can annotate the internal endpoint objects with an extension, for example, `x-internal:true`, to differentiate them from the external endpoints. Using an extension in the OpenAPI definition file means tools that understand the extension can process it as required, while other tools can ignore it.

I call these changes to the API definition file *transformations*. Regardless of the exact kind of transformation you make, you want to apply it in an automated way in your deployment pipeline to make the API definition suitable for external publishing or for a particular user of the API definition file. The external view can result from filtering, renaming, rewriting, bundling, merging multiple API definitions, or other transformations. Transformation is necessary where the organization maintains a different view of the API definition file than that published externally. Another typical example is where the server URL specified in the API definition needs to be changed from an internal server to an external sandbox server.

NOTE When I use the term *bundling*, I mean combining one multifile API definition into a single API definition file. And when I refer to *merging* or *joining* API definition files, I mean combining two or more standalone API definitions into one file.

You can store the transformed API definitions in an *API artifact store*, from where they can be retrieved by teams and applications that need to use them. The exact implementation of this API artifact store can be an *API registry*, a *Postman workspace*, or even a binary artifact repository such as JFRog Artifactory or GitHub Packages. An API registry stores API definition files and provides an API to allow users to upload, search, and retrieve them. A Postman workspace is like a directory on the Postman platform for working on and sharing API definitions, saved API request collections, and API request environment files. Regardless of what store you use, what matters is that after the generation of the artifacts in the continuous integration (CI) phase of your deployment pipeline, downstream steps in your pipeline can retrieve artifacts for their use.

Figure 9.2 shows how the CI phase retrieves a multifile API definition from a source repository, transforms it, and stores it in an artifact store.

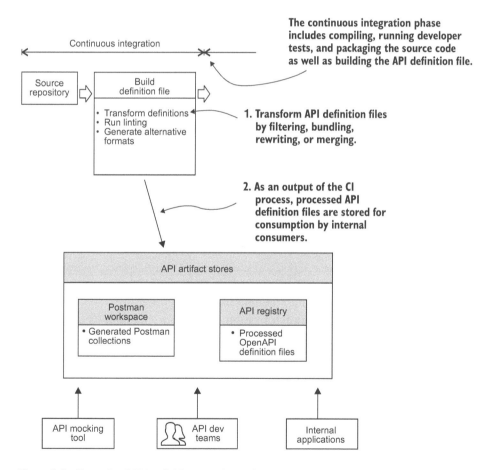

Figure 9.2   Example of API definition transformation in the pipeline

To give a clear picture of how your API artifact—in this case, your processed API definition file—will be used, you can summarize the users of the artifact and the tools used to generate the artifact in a table like table 9.1. Keeping a record of API artifacts generated by your pipeline in a table like this can be useful to keep track of what artifacts you're generating, who the users are, and what they need the artifacts for. This helps you keep focused on the needs of the users of the artifact.

Table 9.1 Summary of the generated API definition artifact

Type of artifact	Users of the artifact	What do they need the artifact for?	Source files the artifact is generated from	Tool to generate the artifact	Where artifact will be stored
Processed OpenAPI definition	■ External API consumers ■ Developer portal ■ Later stages of the continuous integration/continuous delivery (CI/CD) pipeline	■ Shared with external API consumers ■ Used for generating the API reference in the developer portal ■ Used to generate SDKs	Multifile API definitions	Redocly CLI, openapi-format, openapi-filter	Apicurio API registry

I've introduced you to transforming API definitions and storing them in an API artifact store as part of the CI phase of your pipeline. Now I'll guide you through writing the code to do this in the pipeline.

9.1.1 Updating the pipeline code

Typically, the CI phase of a deployment pipeline includes checking out the source code, compiling it, running fast developer tests (also called unit tests), packaging the compiled code into an executable, and storing the executable in a binary artifact store. In addition to these tasks, you want your pipeline to run the transformations on your API definition file and then store the definition file in your API artifact store. Here is how to do this in your example pipeline.

To start, create a new branch from main for your changes. Create a GitHub workflow file to build your application when a pull request (PR) is merged. In your example code repository, create a new workflow file .github/workflows/build.yaml, as shown in the following listing.

Listing 9.1 Creating a GitHub workflow file to run

```
name: Deployment pipeline


on:
  push:
```

```
    branches:
      - main
env:
  GITHUB_RUN_NUMBER: ${{ github.run_number }}
```

Add to this file by creating a job called `pipeline` to check out the application source code and compile it into an executable .jar file. The job should have permissions read the contents of the repository and write packages (to GitHub Packages https://github .com/features/packages, which is GitHub's binary artifact repository for publishing and consuming software packages). The following listing shows how to do this.

Listing 9.2 Creating the build job

```
jobs:
  pipeline:
    name: Pipeline
    runs-on: ubuntu-latest
    permissions:
      contents: read
      packages: write
    steps:
      - name: Build - Checkout
        uses: actions/checkout@v3
      - name: Build - Set up JDK 17
        uses: actions/setup-java@v3
        with:
          java-version: '17'
          distribution: 'temurin'
          cache: maven
      - name: Build - Check Java version
        run: |
          mvn -version
          echo $JAVA_HOME
      - name: Build - Create application jar
        run: |
          cd chapter8
          ./run_app_build.sh
```

When building microservices using CI/CD, typically applications are compiled into executables and packaged into containers (e.g., using Docker as I mentioned in appendix E). The containers have all the libraries and dependencies the applications need to run and are stored in a container registry. From there, they can be retrieved and run on different downstream environments in the pipeline.

> **NOTE** The application code for building the API service for this example isn't meant to show the best practices in building Spring Boot applications with Maven, as I take a few shortcuts with the code.

To build the application for this example, add a step to the job to package the created .jar executable as a Docker image, and push it to the GitHub Container Registry (GHCR), as shown in the next listing.

Listing 9.3   Pushing the application container image to GHCR

```
    - name: Build - Log in to the GitHub Container Registry
      uses: docker/login-action@65b78e6e13532edd9afa3aa52ac7964289d1a9c1
      with:
        registry: ghcr.io
        username: ${{ github.repository_owner }}
        password: ${{ secrets.GITHUB_TOKEN }}
    - name: Build - Build and push Docker image
      uses: docker/build-push-action
⇒ @f2a1d5e99d037542a71f64918e516c093c6f3fc4
      with:
        context: .
        push: true
        tags: ghcr.io/${{ github.repository_owner }}
⇒ /products-api-service:${{ github.run_number }}
        file: chapter8/Dockerfile
```

Now write the steps to transform your API definitions in your pipeline. You need to bundle the multifile API definition into one, and you can do this with Redocly CLI's bundle command. Add a step to bundle the API definition file and move the resulting file to a build-output directory, as shown in the following listing.

Listing 9.4   Bundling the API definition file

```
- name: Build - Create output directory for API artifacts
  run: mkdir build-output
- name: Build - Bundle API definition file
  run: |
    cd chapter8/apis/product-catalog-api
    npx @redocly/cli bundle openapi.yaml --output api.bundled.yaml
    mv api.bundled.yaml ../../../build-output/api.bundled.yaml
```

Next, filter to remove internal endpoints and unused components, and sort the OpenAPI object fields in the required order. Examples of tools that can help you filter an OpenAPI definition include Mike Ralphson's openapi-filter (https://github.com/ Mermade/openapi-filter), thim81/openapi-format (https://github.com/thim81/ openapi-format), or the filter and custom plugin features of the Redocly CLI (https:// github.com/Redocly/redocly-cli). You could even write custom code to parse your API definitions into an object in memory and filter it as you wish.

For this example, write a step to filter every OpenAPI object with the x-internal :true extension, which includes the GET /v1/catalog/products/{id}/reviews endpoint, using the Mermade/openapi-filter tool. Mermade/openapi-filter commands are run in the format openapi-filter <options> -- <input-file> <output-file>. After that, create a step to filter any unused components, and sort the OpenAPI fields using the thim81/openapi-format tool. To use thim81/openapi-format, provide it with the API definition to filter as well as the filter and sort configurations in the format openapi-format <openapi-definition> --filterFile <filterConfiguration> --sortFile <sortConfiguration>. The following listing shows show how to implement these steps.

```
- name: Build - Filter internal endpoints
  run: |
    npx openapi-filter --flags x-internal --verbose
 -- build-output/api.bundled.yaml build-output/api.yaml     ⬅ Use openapi-filter to filter the definition file.
- name: Build - Remove unused components
  run: |
    npx openapi-format build-output/api.yaml
 --filterFile chapter9/unused-components-filter.yaml     Remove unused components, and sort the definition file.
 --sortFile chapter9/sort.json
 --output build-output/api.yaml
- name: Build - Run API linting
  run: |
    npx @stoplight/spectral-cli lint build-output/api.yaml
 --ruleset chapter8/apis/rulesets/json-api.ruleset.yaml
```

The filter configuration file for thim81/openapi-format specifies the kind of filtering to be done, in this case, the kinds of unused components to be removed. Define the file in chapter9/unused-components-filter.yaml, as shown in the following listing.

```
unusedComponents:
 - schemas
 - parameters
 - examples
 - headers
 - requestBodies
 - responses
```

I've provided you a sort file configuration, chapter9/sort.json, to use for the sorting. The code is shown here and specifies the order in which the fields for each of the OpenAPI objects should be arranged hierarchically:

```
{
  "root": ["openapi", "info", "servers", "paths", "components",
 "tags", "x-tagGroups", "externalDocs"],
  "get": ["operationId", "summary", "description", "parameters",
 "requestBody", "responses"],
  "post": ["operationId", "summary", "description", "parameters",
 "requestBody", "responses"],
  "put": ["operationId", "summary", "description", "parameters",
 "requestBody", "responses"],
  "patch": ["operationId", "summary", "description", "parameters",
 "requestBody", "responses"],
  "delete": ["operationId", "summary", "description", "parameters",
 "requestBody", "responses"],
```

```
    "parameters": ["name", "in", "description", "required", "schema"],
    "requestBody": ["description", "required", "content"],
    "responses": ["description", "headers", "content", "links"],
    "content": [],
    "components": ["parameters", "schemas"],
    "schema": ["description", "type", "items", "properties", "format",
➥   "example", "default"],
    "schemas": ["description", "type", "items", "properties", "format",
➥   "example", "default"],
    "properties": ["description", "type", "items", "format", "example",
➥   "default", "enum"]
}
```

Commit your changes, and push them to your GitHub repository. You should see your GitHub Actions workflow run successfully.

Let's review what we've covered. You've seen that there are various ways you can process your OpenAPI definition file. In the pipeline, you can rename the title of an API definition file, translate the definition file from YAML to JSON or JSON to YAML, remove unused components, strip vendor extensions, and filter objects in the definition file. The resulting definition file needs to be stored somewhere, and you can store it in an API registry. API registries are the subject of the next section.

9.1.2   *Storing API definitions in an API registry*

An API registry serves as your organization's API catalog. An API registry is a runtime system that allows users to upload and share their API definition files and components with other users and software systems. API registries also have an API that allows for programmatic access to API artifacts by client applications. That is, they provide an API to your organization's API definitions. Examples of API registries include the Apicurio Registry (www.apicur.io/registry), SwaggerHub (https://mng.bz/0GeJ), and the Apigee Registry API (https://github.com/apigee/registry). Client applications can use the API definition or event schemas to validate messages at runtime. The ability to search for and discover API definitions also helps improve the consistency and reuse of schemas and components across the organization.

As I mentioned, one example of an open source API registry is the Apicurio Registry. It's part of the open source Apicurio project sponsored by Red Hat, and it supports creating, updating, and removing API definitions defined as OpenAPI, AsyncAPI, GraphQL, Apache Avro, Google Protocol Buffers, JSON Schema, Kafka Connect Schema, Web Service Description Language (WSDL), and XML Schema Definitions (XSD).

In the Apicurio Registry, items in the registry, such as OpenAPI definition files and Avro schemas, are called *artifacts*. A logically related collection of API artifacts is called an *artifact group*. Artifacts in a group are usually managed by a single entity, application, or organization. Apicurio Registry also supports the use of artifact references, where an API definition file or schema can reference another. This enables the use of reusable schemas and API components. You can manage artifacts programmatically from Apicurio's REST API. At the time of writing, the API reference for this is available at https://mng.bz/KZrX. Next, I'll show how to store and view items in the Apicurio API registry.

PUBLISHING TO AN API REGISTRY FROM YOUR COMPUTER

From the root of the project directory, run the following command to start Apicurio in a `docker` container (along with the Kong API gateway):

```
docker compose -f chapter9/compose.yaml up -d
```

You can see the Apicurio interface by navigating to http://localhost:9090/ui/artifacts in your browser. Now upload an API definition to Apicurio. Rather than use the UI, you can do this using Apicurio's REST API. Run the command `./chapter9/publish-to-apicurio.sh`, which executes the following `curl` request:

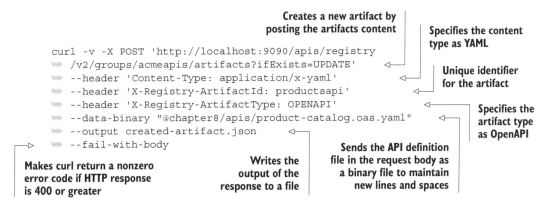

You can see your uploaded Products API definition file by going to http://local-host:9090/ui/artifacts/acmeapis/productsapi/versions/latest in your browser. Click the Version dropdown on the right side of the page to see the list of published versions. The Documentation tab shows you the rendered API definition (in ReDoc format; https://github.com/Redocly/redoc), and the Content tab shows you the raw API definition.

You can use the search functionality on the UI to search for your API artifact. Go to the home page, http://localhost:9090/ui/artifacts, and search for artifacts with "catalog" in the description. Be sure to switch the search selector from the default Name to Description. There is only one artifact in your registry—the Product Catalog API—but it should show up in your search results.

You've seen how to use the API registry locally. Now I'll discuss how to do this in your GitHub Actions pipeline.

PUBLISHING TO THE API REGISTRY FROM YOUR PIPELINE

Ideally, you should have a long-lived instance of the API registry to publish to so that other teams and applications can retrieve artifacts from it later. But to keep it simple for this example, you can start an instance of the API registry in the GitHub Action runner container (destroyed at the end of the pipeline run) and publish there. To do so, after the checkout step you previously created, add a step to the .github/work-flows/build.yaml file to start the API registry, as shown in the next listing. (Note that the step also starts the Kong gateway, which you'll use later in the pipeline.)

Listing 9.7   Starting the API registry as a background service

```
steps:
  - name: Build - Checkout
    uses: actions/checkout@v3
  - name: Build - Start background                    ◁── Adds the new step
services (Kong gateway and Apicurio API registry)         to start the API
    run: |                                                registry
      docker compose -f chapter9/compose.yaml up -d
  - name: Build - Set up JDK 17
```

Then, after your last step where you run the API linting, add steps in build.yaml to archive your transformed API definition file (so you can download it later and take a look if you want), publish to the API registry, and save the artifact version number from the registry, as shown in the following listing.

Listing 9.8   Publishing the API definition to the API registry

```
  - name: Build - Run API linting
    run: |
      npx @stoplight/spectral-cli lint build-output/api.yaml
--ruleset chapter8/apis/rulesets/json-api.ruleset.yaml
  - name: Build - Archive artifacts           ◁──┐ Adds new step to
    uses: actions/upload-artifact@v3                │ archive artifacts
    with:
      name: dist-after-linting
      path: |
        build-output
  - name: Build - Publish updated API         ┌─ Adds new step to
definition to registry                         │ publish API definition
    run: |                                   ◁──┘ to the API registry
      curl -v -X POST
'http://localhost:9090/apis/registry/v2/groups/acmeapis
/artifacts?ifExists=UPDATE'       \
        --header 'Content-Type: application/x-yaml'       \
        --header 'X-Registry-ArtifactId: productsapi'       \
        --header 'X-Registry-ArtifactType: OPENAPI'       \
        --data-binary "@build-output/api.yaml"       \
        --output created-artifact.json   \
        --fail-with-body
  - name: Build - Get created artifact version
    id: artifact-version
    run: |
      echo "ARTIFACT_VERSION=$(cat created-artifact.json
| jq -j '.version')"  >> $GITHUB_OUTPUT
```

Now commit your .github/workflows/build.yaml file, push your changes, and create a PR to merge to the main branch. When you merge the PR, you should see the work-flow run in the Actions tab of your GitHub repository.

NOTE In this example, I describe only how to upload your OpenAPI definitions to an API registry. You can add a further step to generate Postman collections from the OpenAPI definition and upload it to a Postman workspace using the Portman CLI (https://github.com/apideck-libraries/portman), which I first discussed in chapter 7. The Portman documentation provides an explanation of how to do this, and you can try that as an exercise after going through this section.

Your pipeline has transformed your API definition file and successfully published it to an API registry. Now I'll discuss how you can use it to simulate an API.

9.2 Build stage: Simulating APIs with mocks

While you're still writing the code for the API service, downstream applications that integrate with the API may want to start work on integrating with the API. How can you provide them an API they can work with when you haven't finished implementation yet? Or to rephrase the problem, how can you develop and test against an API dependency that may not be available or isn't within your control?

API simulations solve this problem. An API simulation mimics the real API by accepting the kind of requests and returning the kind of responses the API would to enable developers to work on and test applications that depend on the API. This is illustrated in figure 9.3. Without an API simulation, API consumers may need to pause development until the API dependency is available.

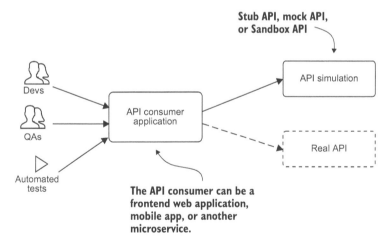

Figure 9.3 API simulations provide an alternative to the real API to support development and testing.

API simulations can be classified as follows:

- *Stub or dummy APIs*—A simple simulation of an API server with limited functionality. It's created to return predefined responses to client requests or return responses to all requests in the same way. This is useful at the early stage of testing an API integration where the focus is on creating a working integration for the client-side applications rather than on testing all the interactions and failure scenarios.

- *Mock APIs*—A more advanced simulation of the behavior of the actual API. It can be customized to return dynamic responses based on specified conditions, allowing developers to test a variety of success and error interaction scenarios while simulating real-world conditions more accurately.
- *Sandbox APIs*—An actual API implementation running in a controlled and isolated environment that developers can use to explore, test, and understand how the API works without affecting production data and systems. API providers usually provide sandbox APIs with a subset of the functionality of the full API and may provide access to it as part of the developer onboarding process and to improve the developer experience. Examples of sandbox APIs include the Uber API sandbox (https://mng.bz/9djj) and the eBay API sandbox (https://mng.bz/jXWa).

Stub and mock APIs can be created using an OpenAPI definition file (e.g., by retrieving the API definitions stored in your API registry). Or they can be provided with other static files (e.g., JSON or YAML) that specify what requests to expect and what response to provide. They can also support programmatic configuration and the ability to record and use responses from real APIs. Ideally, stub and mock APIs should behave in a way that is as similar to the real API as possible, but should not be onerous to create and maintain. With this introduction to API simulations, I'll outline their key benefits next.

> ### Mock-first API design
>
> Apart from supporting development and testing, one other area where mock APIs come in handy is prototyping at the API design stage. This approach, called *prototype-first* or *mock-first* API design, involves API designers starting their API design by creating a mock API rather than an OpenAPI definition. The API designers and API consumers collaborate in creating a mock using mocking tools that make it easy to create a prototype. In this way, they use the mock as a tool to sketch their intended design. The API designer can then generate an OpenAPI definition based on the prototype from the mocking tool.
>
> For more on the mock-first approach to API design, see the post "Mock-First API Prototyping" by Tom Akehurst (https://mng.bz/WEng).

9.2.1   Benefits of API simulations

API simulations provide several benefits for developers and testers:

- *Support parallel development*—Frontend teams can work on integrating with the API and testing their applications using an API simulation while backend teams work in parallel on coding the API.

- *Support availability*—API simulations can remove dependence on the need for the availability and stability of the real API service during the development and testing of consumer applications.
- *Help with test isolation*—Automated tests can run with mock APIs, decoupling the testing process from APIs that may be unreliable, expensive, or restrictive.
- *Support testing for real-world scenarios*—API mocks help simulate various test scenarios and conditions, for example, high network latency or random failures. This makes it possible to test the application in those scenarios.
- *Help reduce costs*—API simulations can help reduce the API request costs incurred during development and integration with expensive third-party APIs. Simulations can also reduce the need for the provisioning of additional hardware resources to run actual APIs.
- *Help improve test efficiency*—Using a mock or stub API for some tests can result in faster tests and lower network latency.

As you can see, API simulations provide several benefits. But when using mocking tools to create an API simulation, you need to know the different kinds of mock APIs it can create. I discuss this next.

9.2.2   *Types of mock APIs and mock tool modes*

Mock and stub APIs can be created with API mocking tools, of which there are many open source offerings, including Prism (https://github.com/stoplightio/prism), Microcks (https://github.com/microcks/microcks), WireMock (https://github.com/wiremock/wiremock), and Hoverfly (https://github.com/SpectoLabs/hoverfly).

Mock APIs can be classified based on where they run:

- *Local mocks*—These can be run from a developer's workstation. This is useful in scenarios where a developer needs the flexibility to run a local test or requires low latency or offline access.
- *Server-based mocks*—Also called public, hosted, or cloud mocks, these are deployed on public servers (e.g., as an external software-as-a-service [SaaS] platform) or on internal servers so that multiple people, teams, or applications can access them.

Mock APIs can also be classified based on the kind of API they are mocking:

- *Internal mock APIs*—These are mock APIs that you own.
- *External mock APIs*—These are mock third-party APIs that you don't control. External mock APIs are useful when third-party APIs you depend on only allow a fixed quota of requests you're likely to exceed, have an expensive usage plan, or are unavailable, unstable, or difficult to provision.

Depending on the type of API simulation they are trying to create, API mocking tools can work in different modes. They can run in *static* or *stub response* mode. In this mode, canned HTTP responses are returned for requests to each endpoint. This mode has the downside that the data can be repetitive and outdated. Try this out by starting a local static mock with Prism using the following command:

```
prism mock chapter8/apis/product-catalog.oas.yaml
```

Make a request to an endpoint in the API definition as follows, and notice that you always get the same response back:

```
curl --location 'http://localhost:4010/v1/catalog/categories'
  --header 'Accept: application/vnd.api+json'
  --header 'Authorization: Bearer my-secret-token'
```

They can also run in *dynamic response* mode. In this mode, you get dynamically generated responses. Try this out with Prism by running the following command, which starts Prism in dynamic mode:

```
prism mock --dynamic chapter8/apis/product-catalog.oas.yaml
```

Repeat the `curl` request, and notice that while the schema or shape of the response is the same, you get different values in the response each time.

Some mocking tools (e.g., WireMock and Hoverfly) also have other modes, such as record-replay (also called capture) and proxy mode. In the record-replay mode, the mocking tool runs as a proxy server, intercepting and transparently recording requests and responses between the client application and the API. During subsequent runs, the mocking tool can work in static mode and return the saved responses when matching requests are provided. In the proxy mode, the mocking tool serves stubbed responses for requests that are defined but passes on the requests that aren't defined to the actual API.

I mentioned earlier that one of the benefits of API mocks is that they help developers test for real-world conditions. Next, I'll show you an example of this.

9.2.3   *Using mock APIs to test for real-world scenarios*

Suppose you wanted to test how an API consumer behaves when the API has random delays in response times. Say you wanted to simulate a uniform distribution of latency between 50 and 800 milliseconds. It may be difficult to inject this behavior and produce it on demand in the real service, but you could do this with a mock API. Here is an example of this with WireMock, an open source API mocking tool that (along with several other methods) supports creating mock responses with a JSON file.

In the chapter9/mappings folder, provide WireMock with a JSON mapping file named test-response.json, which specifies requests WireMock should match against. It should also specify the delay you want to simulate, as shown in the next listing. This instructs WireMock to return a "Hello world" response for requests to `GET /some/endpoint`.

Listing 9.9   WireMock JSON mapping file

```
{
  "request": {
    "method": "GET",
    "url": "/some/endpoint"
  },

  "response": {
    "status": 200,
    "delayDistribution": {
      "type": "uniform",
      "lower": 50,
      "upper": 800
    },
    "body": "{ \"message\": \"Hello world!\" }",
    "headers": {
      "Content-Type": "application/json"
    }
  }
}
```

> Specifies a uniform latency distribution with upper and lower bounds

Now start WireMock by running the following commands, which start WireMock on port 8080 in a `docker` container and look for mapping files in the chapter9/mappings directory:

```
cd chapter9
./start-wiremock.sh
```

Now make multiple GET requests to http://localhost:8080/some/endpoint, and note the response time. You can use the provided `chapter9/request.sh` curl script, which returns the total response time in seconds, by running it as follows:

```
$>./chapter9/request.sh
{ "message": "Hello world!" }
[ Total time: 0.733438s ]
$>./chapter9/request.sh
{ "message": "Hello world!" }
[ Total time: 0.109310s ]
$>./chapter9/request.sh
{ "message": "Hello world!" }
[ Total time: 0.280190s ]
```

You can see how the response times form the API lines within the boundaries you specified. Consumers of this endpoint can now test how their applications will respond when the API has delays of this kind.

So far, I've discussed how you can transform your API definitions in the deployment pipeline, how you can store them in an API registry, and how you can create API mocks to enable development and testing. Now I'll discuss one other task you may want to do at the build stage—generate SDKs for your APIs.

9.3   *Build stage: Generating and storing SDKs*

What if you want to generate client SDKs from your OpenAPI definitions? Imagine that your API consumers need a Java SDK. This will help them quickly get started integrating with your API. How would you go about generating this in your pipeline?

There are a few ways you can generate a client SDK in the build stage of your pipeline. You can use an SDK generator (e.g., OpenAPI Generator CLI, discussed in chapter 6) to generate the SDKs from your bundled OpenAPI definition file. You can also use codegen-as-a-service providers (CGaaS) that hook into your deployment pipeline to generate multilanguage SDKs. Examples include Speakeasy (www.speakeasyapi.dev) and APIMatic (www.apimatic.io).

When you generate the SDK, you need to store the artifact in a location where it can be shared with teams and the applications that need it. In a deployment pipeline, it's usual to store generated artifacts in a *binary artifact repository*. A binary artifact repository is a store of both text and binary artifacts (e.g., software packages) along with their metadata.

It's valuable for API providers to provide multilanguage SDKs for API consumers. SDKs provide a better developer experience beyond just providing API documentation and helping API consumers integrate faster, leading to higher adoption and increased usage of the API product. The accelerated API consumption is made possible because the SDK provides utility classes and authentication helpers. The language bindings enable developers to directly use language objects and functions to interact with the API. I'll outline some benefits to API providers of offering an SDK.

9.3.1   *Benefits of providing an SDK*

SDKs offer a better developer experience for the following two reasons:

- Without an SDK, the burden is on the API consumer to create the functions for calling the API in their programming language, apply the right coding standards, and create a high-quality SDK. They must maintain and update the SDK when the API gets updated.
- SDKs offer a level of abstraction that makes them easier to use. Some operations require multiple API calls to complete, and well-built SDKs can abstract this away, giving the API consumer just one function to call. A good example is when an authentication token renewal is involved when making a request. Without a prebuilt SDK, API consumers need to detect the token expiration and initiate a token renewal call before continuing with the API call they want to make. An SDK can abstract away and hide this complexity from consumers. In some cases, the abstraction provided by SDKs can lead to fewer support queries as API consumers deal with the easier-to-use SDK interface that may require less guidance than raw REST calls.

Organizations building API-first products, that is, platforms where APIs are the main integration interface, should consider offering client SDKs. Organizations not building an API-first product should judge whether an investment in building SDKs makes sense for them.

When deciding if you should offer an SDK, consider whether providing an SDK in a given programming language will contribute to helping prospects make a buy decision for your API product. In addition, consider whether you want to own and maintain the enhanced developer experience that comes with the SDKs, rather than have developers rely on third-party or open source alternatives.

You've seen how SDKs help provide a better developer experience. Next, I'll discuss some problems you may encounter when creating SDKs.

9.3.2   Challenges with building an SDK

Creating and maintaining SDKs can present the following challenges for API providers:

- *Maintenance overhead*—There is the initial cost of creating an SDK for the API in a given programming language. This involves the cost of updating the deployment pipeline to support the generation, testing, and documentation of the new SDK. But there is also the maintenance overhead of addressing specific problems related to that programming language and applying bug fixes.
- *Resource allocation*—Each programming language has its coding standards and idiomatic practices. API providers need to have expertise in each language for which they provide SDKs to ensure they follow best practice. Thus, maintaining many SDKs in multiple languages requires a commitment of time and personnel resources, and smaller organizations may not have this capacity.
- *Release management*—A new version of the API can break compatibility with older versions of the SDK, so you need a new version of the SDK, which has to be thoroughly tested before release. Convincing API consumers using the old versions of the SDK to upgrade to the new version can be a challenge. Tracking the SDK version and language used by each client can be a problem at scale.

There are alternatives to providing an organization-supported SDK for clients. One is to delegate the creation of the SDK to the API consumer by just providing an API definition file and API documentation. Another is to create an open source SDK, releasing it with the disclaimer that the SDK is maintained by the open source community. The community can also provide alternative SDKs based on the API definition. The tradeoff with these approaches is that it may lead to the organization losing control of shaping and supporting the developer integration experience.

I've outlined the benefits and challenges of creating SDKs. Now I'll discuss how you can generate one in your example pipeline.

9.3.3   Updating the pipeline to generate the SDK

I'll show you how to plug in the OpenAPI Generator CLI to your GitHub Actions and store it in GitHub Packages, which is GitHub's binary artifact repository for hosting and managing software packages and containers. For this example, table 9.2 summarizes why you want to generate the SDK and other important points.

Table 9.2   Summary of generated Java SDK

Type of artifact	Artifact users	What do they need the artifact for?	Source files the artifact is generated from	Tool to generate the artifact	Where the artifact will be stored
Java client SDKs	• External API consumers • Internal applications consuming the API	Internal applications that integrate with the external API	OpenAPI definition files	OpenAPI Generator	GitHub Packages

---

An alternative API definition format for generating SDKs: Fern

In this example, you generated your SDK from an OpenAPI definition. But there are alternatives. Fern (https://buildwithfern.com) is an open source toolkit for building REST APIs, and the Fern API definition format is an alternative to the OpenAPI definition format. Fern comes with a compiler that can generate client SDKs, server-side code stubs, Postman collections, and even an OpenAPI definition file. Like OpenAPI, Fern definitions are in YAML. But Fern aims to be simpler to write than OpenAPI and avoids some of the ambiguities code generators face with OpenAPI's nondiscriminated unions and `anyOf` keyword. In addition, the compiler aims to generate idiomatic code. To learn more about how Fern compares with OpenAPI, see the Fern website (https://mng.bz/8w9K).

Before you begin, note that the chapter8/java-template directory contains an OpenAPI generator template for generating a Java client SDK based on the okhttp-gson client.

TIP   You may be wondering how the client template chapter8/java-template was created. As mentioned in chapter 6, one way to generate an OpenAPI template so you can modify it is to run the `openapi-generator-cli author template` command. The other way to do this is to copy the template from the OpenAPI Generator source folder. For this Java SDK, that means copying the https://mng.bz/EZrq folder. I've done this for you and provided the template file you need in the chapter8/java-template directory, but you can find more information about this at https://openapi-generator.tech/docs/templating.

Now add a step to generate the SDK by using the OpenAPI Generator CLI to generate it from the transformed API definition file, as shown in the next listing.

Listing 9.10   Adding a step to generate the Java SDK

```
- name: Build - Generate Java SDK
      run: |
        sed -i "s/OWNER/${{ github.repository_owner }}/g"
  chapter8/java-template/libraries/okhttp-gson/pom.mustache
        sed -i "s/REPO_NAME/${{ github.event.repository.name }}/g"
```

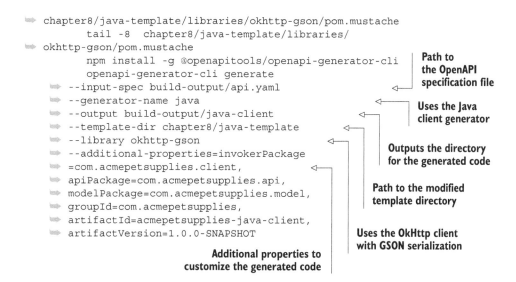

```
⇨ chapter8/java-template/libraries/okhttp-gson/pom.mustache
        tail -8  chapter8/java-template/libraries/
⇨ okhttp-gson/pom.mustache
        npm install -g @openapitools/openapi-generator-cli
        openapi-generator-cli generate
    ⇨ --input-spec build-output/api.yaml
    ⇨ --generator-name java
    ⇨ --output build-output/java-client
    ⇨ --template-dir chapter8/java-template
    ⇨ --library okhttp-gson
    ⇨ --additional-properties=invokerPackage
    ⇨ =com.acmepetsupplies.client,
    ⇨ apiPackage=com.acmepetsupplies.api,
    ⇨ modelPackage=com.acmepetsupplies.model,
    ⇨ groupId=com.acmepetsupplies,
    ⇨ artifactId=acmepetsupplies-java-client,
    ⇨ artifactVersion=1.0.0-SNAPSHOT
```

Path to the OpenAPI specification file

Uses the Java client generator

Outputs the directory for the generated code

Path to the modified template directory

Uses the OkHttp client with GSON serialization

Additional properties to customize the generated code

Specifying the GitHub Packages Maven repository

Notice that in the step you've just written, the first couple of lines begin with using Sed commands to replace OWNER with the name of your GitHub account and REPOSITORY with the name of your GitHub repository in the pom.mustache file. The pom.mustache file is a template used to create the pom.xml file by OpenAPI Generator. The OWNER and REPOSITORY values occur in the URL specified as https://maven.pkg.github.com/OWNER/REPOSITORY in the `<distributionManagement>` element. This element tells Maven where to publish the package to, which you're going to do in the next section.

Commit this change to your branch, create and merge the PR, and see the build run. With this step, you've generated the SDK. But where should you store the generated artifact? We'll discuss that next.

9.3.4 Storing SDKs in artifact repositories

The CI phase of a software deployment pipeline generates artifacts, and this can include compiled code, a deployable release candidate package, SDKs, and other artifacts. It's possible to store these in version control, but this is inefficient because source control systems are designed for managing text files, not binary files. A binary artifact repository serves as the central place to store the artifacts generated by the build stage in the CI phase of the pipeline so that downstream stages of the pipeline—the CD phase—don't need to regenerate the artifacts. They can fetch them from the artifact repository. This is illustrated in figure 9.4. Examples of artifact repository managers include Sonatype Nexus, JFrog Artifactory, and GitHub Packages.

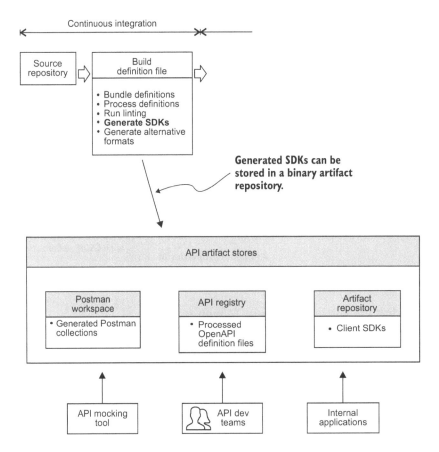

Figure 9.4   Updating the pipeline to generate an SDK

Artifact repositories provide the following benefits:

- *Collaboration and dependency management*—Artifact repositories provide a central place to share artifacts with other teams. Organizations may have multiple CI servers generating artifacts. The artifact repository can serve as the central place for them to publish those artifacts so that teams and later stages of the deployment pipeline can access them. Artifact repositories can store software packages and dependencies required in the build process.

- *Efficient builds*—Once the artifact has been built by the pipeline, you don't need to rerun the pipeline again for the same revision, as later stages of the pipeline that need the artifacts can fetch it from the repository.

- *Versioned artifacts and metadata*—For each artifact, the artifact repository can store it as a new artifact version. It can also store metadata such as the artifact hash, when it was built, and other information. In addition, when an artifact is published to the artifact repository, the artifact and its metadata don't change.

This is helpful for finding and debugging problems with past releases of software. You can simply download the artifact package that a defect was reported in and debug it.

- *Staged promotion*—You can promote artifacts (e.g., by moving the artifact to a different folder in the artifact repository) to represent the transition across various environments in your organization, such as Dev, QA, Staging, and Prod. And you don't need to keep all generated artifacts in the artifact repository. You can retain only artifacts that successfully pass all stages of the pipeline and purge ones that don't.
- *Access control*—Artifact repositories also have access control features to help you manage who has permission to publish to and retrieve artifacts from the repository.

You now know the benefits of storing your SDKs in your artifact repository. Next, I'll show you how to store the SDK you generated in your repository.

9.3.5   Updating the pipeline to store the SDK

In your .github/workflows/build.yaml file, add a step to publish the generated SDK to GitHub Packages, as shown in the next listing. The Maven `deploy` command publishes the .jar file for the SDK to the remote package repository, along with other metadata, MD5, and SHA1 hash files.

Listing 9.11   Step to publish the Java SDK

```
- name: Build - Publish SDK to GitHub Packages          Deploys the
  run: |                                                 generated code to
    cd build-output/java-client                          GitHub Packages
    mvn --batch-mode deploy          ◄
  env:
    GITHUB_TOKEN: ${{ secrets.GITHUB_TOKEN }}          ◄  GitHub token to
                                                           authenticate with
                                                           GitHub Packages
```

TIP To see what the completed workflow should look like, see .github/workflows/build-transform.yaml.completed.

Now raise a PR with your changes, commit, and merge your changes. You should see the build run and the generated SDK published to the artifact repository. On the right side of your GitHub repository's main page, you should see a Packages section with a link to the generated package: com.acmepetsupplies.acmepetsupplies-java-client 1.0. With your API artifacts generated, let's move to the CD portion of the pipeline—deploying the API to a gateway in higher environments.

9.4   Deploy and Test stage: Deploying API Gateway configuration

Imagine a scenario where you've built the backend API service and want to deploy it and expose its API externally through your API gateway in one of your environments.

Let's say you want to expose just one endpoint in your API—GET /v1/catalog/ products/<uuid>. Figure 9.5 shows at what stage in the pipeline you need to deploy the configuration.

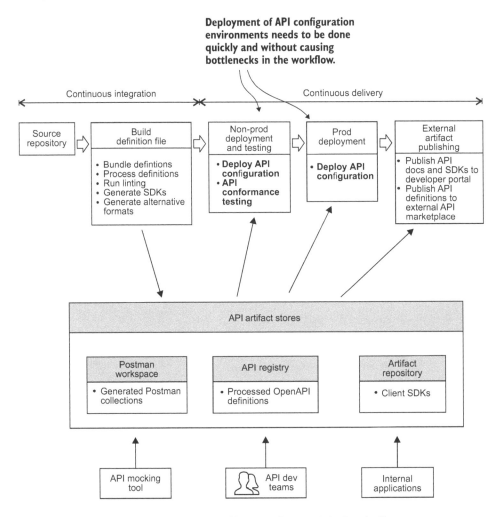

Figure 9.5   Deploying API configuration to different environments in the pipeline

Suppose your API is just one of many APIs that need to be exposed by your organization's central API gateway, which is managed by an API platform team. How can you create the configuration to expose the API in a way that doesn't involve raising a work ticket for the team that manages the API gateway? That is, how can you avoid the workflow bottleneck and reduced delivery lead time that results from handing off work to another team?

The answer to this is the heart of APIOps, which provides a way to automate the deployment of your API configuration to your API gateway using GitOps principles. You'll see how this works next.

9.4.1   APIOps deployments

In APIOps, all change to the configuration state is done by updating the configuration state file in the version control system (VCS). This is the GitOps workflow applied to API configuration. As mentioned in chapter 1, the basic principles of the GitOps model are as follows:

- *Declarative configuration*—The desired state of the managed system (i.e., all the configuration data required to re-create the instance of the system) is described declaratively. Declarative configurations describe the desired operating state without specifying how that state will be achieved. This approach separates the responsibilities of defining the configuration from its implementation. The implementation refers to the imperative commands, API calls, and scripts that are invoked to achieve the desired state.
- *Versioned and immutable configuration*—The desired state is stored in a way that holds immutable versions of it. The store used has the complete version history of the state declarations and provides access controls and auditing on changes to the desired state. Git is the canonical example of the state store. Mechanisms such as PRs and CODEOWNERS can be used to approve changes to the desired state configuration.
- *Automatically pulled configuration*—Automated processes, called software agents, pull the desired state declaration from the source where it's stored (usually, a Git source control system). The software agent can be a standalone process or a deployment pipeline.
- *Continuously reconciled configuration*—The software agents continuously reconcile the actual system state to the desired state. That is, they observe the actual system state to detect any divergence from the desired state (also called *drift*), and where this is detected, the agents attempt to update the actual state to match the desired state.

GitOps discourages manual changes—for example, via an API gateway user interface (UI)—because they can be error-prone, difficult to debug, and may not have the same audit history that the version-control log provides. Essentially, GitOps combines the approaches of infrastructure as code (IaC), PRs, and CI/CD pipelines. IaC is the practice of maintaining infrastructure configuration declaratively in VCSs. GitOps follows this pattern of maintaining state configuration in the VCS and using PRs to manage changes to them. The deployment pipeline picks and rolls out these changes to the systems running in different environments.

There are a few things to note about how teams work in this model:

- The dev team doesn't need to raise a work ticket for the API platform team to create API configuration. In other words, no handoff of configuration work is required. The dev team works in a self-service way by creating the configuration themselves and creating a PR that kicks off validation of the configuration, which the platform team can review. When merged into the mainline branch, the deployment process is kicked off automatically. This model allows faster deployments. Every feature developer team can ship updates many times a day, deploy API configuration, and see the results quickly.
- The dev team doesn't use the API gateway UI to update the API configuration. Everything is done with the VCS. In addition, the dev teams don't need direct access to the environment the API gateway is running on to make gateway configuration changes. They only need access to the environment configuration repository. This leads to more secure deployments.
- The team has access to the version history of all the API configuration changes in the VCS. The complete history of environment changes is in the version control repository. The configuration state file has a complete description of the API gateway state, and the commit log messages explain how it has evolved over time. This provides the team with clear documentation on the deployment state. Rolling back a change can just be a `git revert` and watching the process run to apply the change. The record in the VCS serves both as an audit history and a transaction log of changes to that environment, allowing roll back and roll forward to any point.

> **TIP**   For more on the advantages of GitOps, read the article "GitOps: A Path to More Self-Service IT" by Thomas A. Limoncelli (https://queue.acm.org/detail.cfm?id=3237207).

There are two ways to execute deployments in GitOps: push-based deployments and pull-based deployments. Both are explained in the following subsections.

PUSH-BASED DEPLOYMENTS

With this model, whenever a developer commits code to the application repository, the deployment pipeline is triggered, and it builds the application container. It also updates the configuration repository with deployment manifests for the application and other configuration files such as the API gateway. Usually, templates of the deployment manifests are stored in the application repository, and the deployment pipeline uses the templates to generate the actual manifest files, which are then stored in the configuration repository. When changes are merged to the mainline of the configuration repository, the deployment pipeline is triggered, and it applies the updated manifests to the running system in the specified environment, as illustrated in figure 9.6. The example scenarios you worked through use a push-based deployment approach.

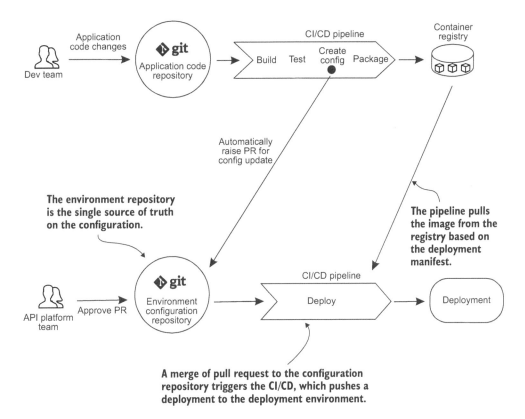

Figure 9.6 GitOps push-based deployments

There are two limitations to note about this approach. First, it requires that the credentials to the target environment be stored in the CI/CD system to enable it to get access to the target environment and update the configuration files there. While this may be acceptable in some cases, it can also be considered a security problem because if the CI/CD system is compromised, a bad actor can get access to the credentials for the target environments.

Second, deployment of the target state is only triggered by changes to the environment repository. If someone logs on to the API gateway UI and changes configuration manually, drift can occur between the target state as stored in the configuration repository and the actual state in the API gateway. This may not be immediately detected, except if a monitoring process has been set up to continually check that there is no drift. For example, the decK command-line tool, which I used in the first example, has a `diff` command that provides a diff of the current state of configuration in a running Kong instance against the specified target configuration state file. For gateways running in a Kubernetes cluster, `kubectl diff` can also be used to see the difference in configurations.

PULL-BASED DEPLOYMENTS

With the pull-based deployment approach, an *operator* continuously monitors the Git repository for changes. A GitOps operator is a software tool that continuously monitors a system and keeps it in sync with sources of desired configuration (usually a Git repository). When the operator detects a difference—whether caused by a change in the desired configuration repository or a change in the running system, for example, due to a manual configuration change using the system's UI—it pulls the updated configuration state from the Git repository and applies it to the target environment. The operator runs in the same environment or cluster as the deployed gateway. Because of this, it doesn't need credentials to access the environment. This provides improved security over the push-based model. Examples of such operators for Kubernetes include Argo CD and Flux. Figure 9.7 illustrates pull-based GitOps deployments.

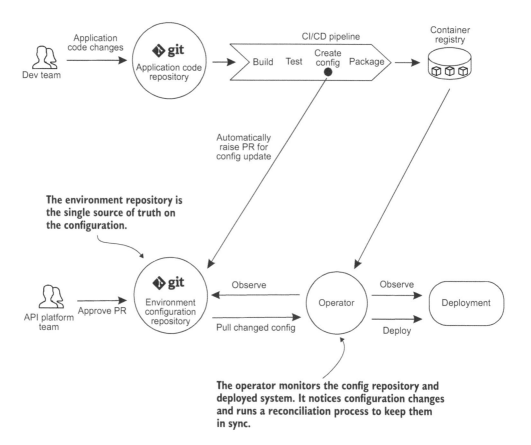

Figure 9.7   GitOps pull-based deployment model

We've now looked at how deployments to an environment work. Next, I'll discuss how APIs are promoted across environments.

9.4.2 *Updating application configuration*

In an enterprise, usually, there are many application services, each with its own repository. These services and their related API configurations need to be promoted across multiple environments—for example, Dev, QA, Staging, and Production. There are two things to consider when updating application configuration.

The first is how changes to the application's repository can trigger an update to the configuration repository (e.g., update application configuration, and in the case of Kubernetes, this can be updating the Kubernetes manifest file with the updated container version). To do this, application configuration templates in the application repository can be used to generate actual configuration and manifest files that are pushed to the shared environments repository using an automated PR. The configuration repository contains the application and infrastructure configuration for each environment. When the PRs are merged into the main branch, the deployment pipeline can then roll out the changes to the right environments.

The second is how to promote the configuration across environments. One approach is to keep different environment configurations on different Git branches, but this involves a lot of complexity in tracking changes across branches. A simpler approach is to maintain a folder of configurations for each environment. Promoting configuration involves copying the configuration from one environment folder to another (figure 9.8). Note that some teams may choose to maintain different configuration repositories instead of one central one, minimizing the chance of PR conflicts from the different pipelines trying to raise automated PRs.

> **TIP** For more details on this approach, see Kostis Kapelonis' article, "How to Model Your GitOps Environments and Promote Releases between Them" (https://mng.bz/NRrE).

I've talked about GitOps principles, deployment models, and approaches to updating configuration files. But as with everything that has advantages, the GitOps model can have its drawbacks too.

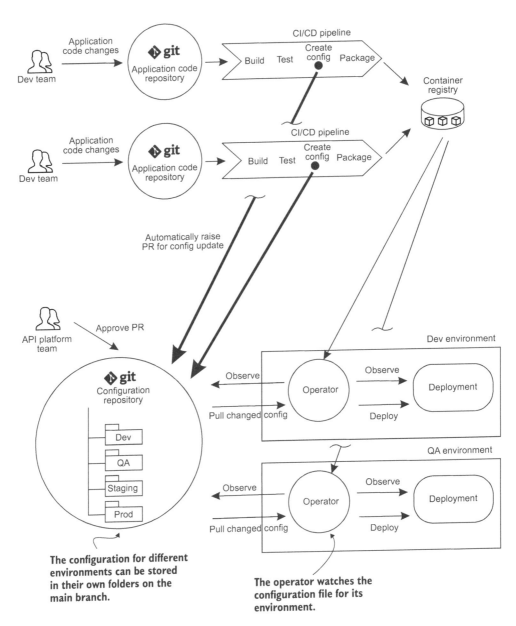

Figure 9.8   Managing multiple applications and environments using a pull-based GitOps model depicting the configuration for the different environments in one central configuration repository

9.4.3 Challenges with GitOps

Here are some challenges with adopting GitOps:

- *Automated PRs on configuration repositories can cause conflicts*—The CI part of the pipeline creates automated PRs on the configuration repository every time a new application version is built or some application configuration changes. This can occur frequently as code development proceeds. When there are multiple such application CI processes updating a configuration repository, conflicts can occur due to a lack of synchronization of different processes cloning the same repository (because their local copy is outdated, and they need to pull and retry pushing again). This can be mitigated by having a sophisticated retry mechanism for creating PRs or splitting the configuration repository (e.g., one for each namespace) to minimize conflicts.

- *The burden of managing many Git repositories*—Related to the first challenge, with more applications and configuration repositories, the repository management burden increases as the repositories need to be set up with the right access permissions and connected to the software sync agents (the software processes or build agents that sync the cluster state with the desired configuration state). Provisioning these repositories takes development time. You can mitigate this by having one configuration repository per API gateway cluster.

- *No support for centrally managed secrets*—Enterprise environments have a need to manage secrets such as private keys, passwords, and certificates outside the deployment pipeline, usually in a centralized secrets store where they can be audited. GitOps has no recommendations on how to manage secrets. Storing secrets in a source code VCS such as Git isn't recommended, as the Git log keeps a persistent history, and this gets distributed to any developers who clone the repository. Everyone who has access to the repository can have access to the secret.

Discussion on how to mitigate these problems is out of the scope of this book, but for an introduction to some tooling solutions, have a look at Ádám Sándor's article, "GitOps: The Bad and the Ugly" (https://mng.bz/Ddry).

In addition to looking at the challenges you can face with GitOps, it's also useful to consider how GitOps as a practice fits in with the types of teams you find in a typical enterprise. Let's do that next.

9.4.4 APIOps and team topologies

In *Team Topologies* (IT Revolution, 2019), Matthew Skelton and Manuel Pais describe four fundamental types of teams in an enterprise software organization: stream-aligned teams, platform teams, complicated-subsystem teams, and enabling teams. Each type is described here:

- *Stream-aligned teams*—These teams are focused on a single stream of work, building a product or service that delivers customer value. To enable them to deliver quickly, they need to work as independently as possible. That means with as little handoff of work to other teams as possible. Stream-aligned teams are the typical feature teams that have end-to-end delivery responsibility in the value stream, from gathering user requirements and feedback from customers to building the software product, testing it, supporting it in production, and fixing bugs.

- *Platform teams*—These teams build and maintain internal platforms—self-service APIs, internal tools, documentation, and support—that the stream-aligned teams use to deliver their product or service at a higher pace and with reduced coordination. The internal platform they work on is nondifferentiating for the organization's market offering but rather helps minimize the cognitive load on the stream-aligned teams, so they improve their workflow. Examples of platform teams are those that maintain the API gateway that stream-aligned teams use to expose APIs and teams that maintain the identity management systems used for authentication and authorization of an API product.

TIP   For a discussion about the definition of platforms, see Evan Botcher's excellent article, "What I Talk about When I Talk about Platforms" (https://martinfowler.com/articles/talk-about-platforms.html).

- *Enabling teams*—These teams of specialists in a given technical or product domain support the stream-aligned teams by performing research and experiments on new technologies and practices that can improve the steam-aligned team's workflow. They enable stream-aligned teams who are under pressure to deliver by helping them overcome obstacles and detect missing capabilities. They don't own any software components but act as a group of experts to help mentor and facilitate stream-aligned teams. An API governance team that helps evolve the organization's API standards, explores automated API governance tools, and helps teams with documentation and guidance on how to start developing APIs quickly is an example of an enabling team.
- *Complicated-subsystem teams*—These teams focus on building and maintaining complicated parts of the system that require heavy specialist knowledge, for example, algorithms or artificial intelligence. They are specialists who work on subsystems where heavy mathematics, calculations, or other deep technical expertise is required. Each member of the team is usually a specialist in the subsystem the team is working on. They also help reduce the cognitive load on stream-aligned teams.

Applied to the APIOps workflow, the stream-aligned teams (referred to previously as the *dev teams*) are responsible for updating the API configuration (using a PR) as required to expose their APIs. The platform team—in this case, the API platform team—reviews and approves the PR for their API configuration changes. The platform team is also responsible for setting up or providing guidance on setting up the APIOps workflow pipelines, configuration synchronization tools, and operators. They can also ensure that PRs don't stay open too long waiting for review so that they can optimize the workflow for the stream-aligned teams. The platform teams can ensure that as many checks on the API configuration as possible—for example, checks to ensure that the configuration files are valid or have specific settings—are automated and baked into the pipeline. Their goal is to help reduce the overall lead time for delivery by removing the waste of waiting for reviews. Many code hosting platforms provide analytics on PR statistics, such as PR frequency and review time. So this can be a useful indicator to track the flow of work in this part of the value stream. Now I'll walk you through deploying your gateway configuration in your example pipeline.

9.4.5 *Deploying in your example pipeline*

The API gateway's configuration defines how an API is routed externally, as well as security policies, transformations, and orchestration that can be applied to the request and response. APIOps advocates a GitOps model for deploying API configuration. The steps involved are as follows:

1 The dev team updates the API gateway's declarative configuration for the given environment in the configuration version control repository and raises a PR for their changes.
2 Automated checks run on the updated configuration files. The API platform team reviews the changes, and if they are happy with it, approves the PR.
3 On merge of the PR, a software agent runs to reconcile and apply the desired configuration with the actual instance of the gateway running in the environment.

The software agent that applies the configuration can be a deployment pipeline that pushes the configuration to the gateway environment or a Kubernetes operator in the environment that monitors the configuration Git repository for changes; when it detects a change, it pulls and applies it to the gateway. In the following sections, I present you with examples of how to do reconciliation using a deployment pipeline in the Kong API gateway and the Kusk API gateway. In both examples, the pipeline involves the following steps:

1 Deploy the backend API service.
2 Reconcile the gateway configuration.
3 Run API conformance tests to test that the routing configuration has been successfully applied to the API and to test for API conformance.
4 If the conformance test passes, label the API definition file in the API registry as passing conformance tests.

Two kinds of repositories
The GitOps model works with application code repositories and environment configuration repositories. The application code repository contains the source code for the deployed backend application. It also contains the files (e.g., the Dockerfile) required

(continued)

to build and package the application. The environment configuration repository contains configuration for the API gateway and other infrastructure and application configurations (for deployments to Kubernetes clusters, these are called *deployment manifests*). Because I have only one repository for this book, I use a combination of the chapter8 and chapter9 directories to hold both the application code and environment configuration.

In section 9.4, I presented you with the problem of deploying your Products API service to your API gateway in an APIOps way. Given the preceding conceptual steps, I'll show you how to do this in the Kong gateway.

DEPLOYING CONFIGURATION TO KONG

First, in the build.yaml file, add the step in listing 9.12 to install the Kong decK tool in the runner. decK (https://docs.konghq.com/deck) is a tool for managing Kong's configuration declaratively. decK can synchronize configuration to a Kong cluster and diff configuration to detect drift.

Listing 9.12   Installing decK in your runner

```
- name: Deploy-and-Test - Install Kong Deck
  run: |
    curl -sL https://github.com/kong/deck/releases/download/v1.18.0/
    deck_1.18.0_linux_amd64.tar.gz -o deck.tar.gz
    tar -xf deck.tar.gz -C /tmp
    sudo cp /tmp/deck /usr/local/bin/
    deck version
```

Next, add a step to deploy the Product API service with Docker Compose. The next listing shows the code you need to add to .github/workflows/build.yaml.

Listing 9.13   Deploying the Product API service

```
- name: Deploy-and-Test - Deploy Products API service
  run: |
    sed -i "s/OWNER/${{ github.repository_owner }}/g"
    chapter9/compose-api-service.yaml
    cat chapter9/compose-api-service.yaml
    docker compose -f chapter9/compose-api-service.yaml up -d
```

Now add a step to apply the Kong gateway routing configuration in chapter9/kong.yaml to the gateway instance. The step should first check that the configuration file is valid. Then it should run the synchronization process to apply the desired configuration state in chapter9/kong.yaml. Kong's Admin API is available on `http://localhost:8001`, and this is what the decK `sync` command interacts with. The code for this step is shown in the following listing.

Listing 9.14   Syncing the Kong configuration state

```
- name: Reconcile API gateway state
  run: |
    deck validate --state chapter9/kong.yml
    deck sync --state chapter9/kong.yml --kong-addr http://localhost:8001
```

Now add steps to run the integration tests using the chapter8/run_integrationtest.sh script. The integration tests verify that the routing has been set up correctly and also verify that the API conforms to the API definition file. The integration test script invokes the ProductCatalogueEndToEndSchemaTest.java test, which fetches the latest API definition file from the registry and tests it for conformance.

Next, add a step that uses the API registry's REST API to label the API definition file that passes the conformance test with `passed-conformance-test`. The code for this is shown in the following listing.

Listing 9.15   Running API conformance tests

```
- name: Deploy-and-Test - Run API conformance tests
  run: |
    cd chapter8
    ./run_integrationtest.sh
- name: Deploy-and-Test - Mark API definition as passing
  API conformance testing
  run: |
    curl -X PUT \
    http://localhost:9090/apis/registry/v2/groups/acmeapis
    /artifacts/productsapi/versions
    /${{ steps.artifact-version.outputs.ARTIFACT_VERSION }}/meta
    --header "Content-Type: application/json"
    --data '{"labels": ["passed-conformance-test"] }'
    --fail-with-body
```

Create a PR, and merge the changes. On merge, you should see the workflow run and fail when it tries to run the integration tests. This is because the API gateway routing for the endpoint hasn't been created yet.

> **TIP**   The completed workflow file is available at .github/workflows/build-kong.yaml.completed in the sample code repository.

Now you're ready to create the gateway configuration. Add the configuration for routing of the external endpoint to the backend API service in the Kong configuration file, chapter9/kong.yaml, as shown in the following listing.

Listing 9.16   Routing configuration for the Product Catalog API

```
_format_version: "2.1"
_transform: true

services:
  - name: Product_Catalog_API
```

```
protocol: http
host: product-api
port: 8080
path:  /
routes:
  - name: viewProduct
    methods:
      - GET
    paths:
      - "~/v1/catalog/products/(.+)$"
    strip_path: false
```

Routes request to base path http://product-api:8080/ of the upstream Product API service docker container

Match requests to this route and proxy them to the upstream API service, preserving the matched URL path in the upstream request URL.

Commit this change, and raise a PR. For this example, you can approve and merge your PR. You see the pipeline run and pass because the gateway routing now exists.

TIP   To see the completed example for this, see chapter9/build-kong.yaml .completed in the sample code repository.

At this point, you've updated the API gateway configuration to expose your API service endpoint externally, and the pipeline has run to apply the change to the API gateway using decK. Now I'll show you an example of how to do something similar with a Kusk API gateway running in Kubernetes.

DEPLOYING CONFIGURATION TO KUSK

Kusk is an open source API gateway that supports embedding API configuration in the OpenAPI definition file. It's built on top of a high-performance proxy called Envoy. Kusk is deployed in a Kubernetes cluster. For this example, you'll deploy Kusk in a Kubernetes cluster.

First, add the Kusk routing for the Product Catalog API. To do this, add the x-kusk vendor extension for the routing configuration to the API definition file, chapter8/apis/product-catalog-api/openapi.yaml, as shown in the next listing.

Listing 9.17   Adding the Kusk routing to the API definition

```
...
servers:
  - url: https://api.acme-pet-supplies.co.uk
x-kusk:
  upstream:
    service:
      name: productsapi-svc
      namespace: default
      port: 8080
tags:
  - name: Categories
...
```

Adds the x-kusk extension as a top-level object

Now you need to rewrite the build.yaml workflow file so that it deploys to Kusk, not Kong. In the build.yaml file, delete the steps you added for Kong in the previous section, and then after the `Build - Publish SDK to GitHub Packages` step, add a step to install Kusk CLI, as shown in the following listing.

Listing 9.18 Installing the Kusk CLI in the pipeline

```
- name: Deploy-and-Test - Install Kusk CLI
  run: |
     curl -sSLf https://raw.githubusercontent.com/kubeshop
➥ /kusk-gateway/main/cmd/kusk/scripts/install.sh | bash
```

The Kusk gateway needs to be installed in a Kubernetes cluster, so you'll need to set one up. Create a Kubernetes cluster in the runner using minikube (https://github .com/kubernetes/minikube), which is a simple way to get started with Kubernetes for local development and testing. It deploys a Kubernetes cluster containing only one node, and the GitHub Action at https://github.com/medyagh/setup-minikube lets you set it up in your pipeline.

Add steps to set up minikube and install and configure Kusk, as shown in listing 9.19. There are three things you need to note about this:

- When the Install Kusk Gateway step is run in the pipeline, you may get an error `resource mapping not found for name: "kusk-devportal-envoy-fleet"`. This isn't relevant for this example, and you can ignore it and move on with the entry `continue-on-error: true`.
- To send requests to the Kusk gateway in the cluster, you need to set up port-forwarding. This allows requests on the local machine (the GitHub runner) to reach resources running inside the cluster, such as the Kusk gateway. In this case, requests to the local machine on port 9000 are mapped to port 80 in the Kubernetes cluster, where the Kusk gateway is listening.
- To later deploy your Product Catalog API service container in the cluster, you need to provide Kubernetes with the credentials (secrets) to retrieve the service from the container registry. You do this by creating a Kubernetes secret object with your GitHub credentials, as shown in the following listing.

Listing 9.19 Installing the Kusk gateway in the pipeline

```
    - name: Deploy-and-Test - Start minikube
      uses: medyagh/setup-minikube@master
    - name: Deploy-and-Test - Install Kusk Gateway
      continue-on-error: true
      run: |
        kusk cluster install
    - name: Deploy-and-Test - Setup Kusk port forwarding to port 9000
      run: |
        nohup kubectl port-forward svc/kusk-gateway-envoy-fleet
➥ -n kusk-system 9000:80 &
    - name: Deploy-and-Test - Create GitHub Container Registry secret
      run: |
        kubectl create secret docker-registry ghcr-secret
```

```
--docker-server=https://ghcr.io
--docker-username=${{ github.repository_owner }}
--docker-password=${{ secrets.GITHUB_TOKEN }}
--docker-email=${{ github.event.pusher.email }}
```

Next, add a step to deploy your products-api service to the cluster. You'll need to replace some variables in the Kubernetes manifest file (product-api-deployment.yaml) so that Kubernetes can retrieve the image from the container registry. This is shown in the following listing.

Listing 9.20   Deploying the Products API service to Kubernetes

```
- name: Deploy-and-Test - Deploy products API service
  run: |
    sed -i "s/APP_VERSION/${{ github.run_number }}/g"     ◁──  Replaces the
  chapter9/product-api-deployment.yaml                           APP_VERSION variable
    sed -i "s/OWNER/${{ github.repository_owner }}/g"            in the deployment file
  chapter9/product-api-deployment.yaml      ◁──  Replaces the
        kubectl apply --filename                   OWNER variable in
  chapter9/product-api-deployment.yaml  ◁──       the deployment file
        kubectl apply --filename
  chapter9/product-api-service.yaml  ◁──  Applies the Kubernetes
                                          deployment object to
              Applies the Kubernetes      the cluster
             service object to the cluster
```

Next, use the kusk deploy command to deploy the API configuration in the OpenAPI definition to Kusk. In addition, check the status of the cluster to see that the pods are running, as shown in the following listing.

Listing 9.21   Deploying API configuration to Kusk

```
- name: Reconcile API gateway state
  env:
    LATEST_ARTIFACT_VERSION:
    ${{ needs.build.outputs.LATEST_ARTIFACT_VERSION }}    Deploys the OpenAPI
  run: |                                                   definition with the API
    kusk deploy -in        ◁──                             configuration into Kusk
  http://localhost:9090/apis/registry/v2/groups/acmeapis/artifacts
  /productsapi/versions/$LATEST_ARTIFACT_VERSION
- name: Deploy-and-Test - Check status of the cluster
  run: |
    ./chapter9/check_cluster_status.sh
```

In chapter 7, I introduced Portman and Newman as tools for conformance testing. For the conformance test step, you can use these (instead of the Java integration test as before). Generate a Postman collection with Portman, and run the collection with Newman. To generate a nice HTML report containing the details of the requests and responses, use newman-reporter-htmlextra (https://mng.bz/1M5j) as your Newman reporter. Code for this is shown in the next listing.

Listing 9.22 Adding Portman conformance testing for Kusk

```
- name: Deploy-and-Test - Run API conformance tests
  run: |
    cd chapter9
    npm install -g @apideck/portman
    npm install -g newman-reporter-htmlextra
    npm install -g newman
    portman --cliOptionsFile portman/portman-cli.json
    newman run collection.postman.json --verbose
➡ --reporters cli,htmlextra
➡ --reporter-htmlextra-export
➡ ../build-output/conformance-test-report.html
```

Finally, add a step to archive your test report (so you can view it after the pipeline run), and add a step to mark the API definition file as passing conformance testing if the run succeeds (see the next listing). This helps you record that API definition did pass conformance tests and gives you the assurance to distribute it or publish it to your dev portal.

Listing 9.23 Marking the API file as passing conformance tests in Kusk

```
- name: Deploy-and-Test - Archive conformance test report
  uses: actions/upload-artifact@v3
  with:
    name: conformance-test-report
    path: |
      build-output/conformance-test-report.html
- name: Deploy-and-Test - Mark API definition as
➡ passing API conformance testing
  run: |
    curl --request PUT
➡ http://localhost:9090/apis/registry/v2/groups
➡ /acmeapis/artifacts/productsapi
➡ /versions/${{ steps.artifact-version.outputs.ARTIFACT_VERSION }}/meta
➡     --header "Content-Type: application/json"
➡     --data '{"labels": ["passed-conformance-test-kusk"] }'
➡     --fail-with-body
- name: Mark API definition as passing API conformance testing
  env:
    LATEST_API_VERSION: ${{ needs.build.outputs.LATEST_ARTIFACT_VERSION }}
  run: |
    curl -X PUT http://localhost:9090/apis/registry/v2
➡ /groups/acmeapis/artifacts/productsapi
➡ /versions/$LATEST_API_VERSION/meta
➡ --header "Content-Type: application/json" \
➡ --data '{"labels": ["passed-conformance-test-kusk"] }' \
➡ --fail-with-body
```

And those are all the steps you need. Create a PR, merge your changes, and then watch your workflow run.

The pipeline run completes the Build and Deploy and Test stages of your example pipeline. You've transformed your API definition file, stored it in an API registry, generated SDKs with it, deployed the API configuration to a gateway, and tested the API.

Summary

- In the build phase of the deployment pipeline, the API definition files can be processed and transformed to prepare them for external publishing. This transformation can include filtering the OpenAPI API definition file, replacing values, sorting objects in the file, and so on.

- Processed API definition files can be stored in an API registry so that they can be accessed by teams, applications, and systems downstream of the deployment pipeline. An API registry serves as a catalog of the organization's APIs and should have an API to enable programmatic access to API definition artifacts.

- A variety of libraries and code-generation services exist for generating SDKs from API definition files. Client API SDKs help provide a better developer experience for teams integrating with an API. SDK packages can be stored in a binary artifact repository.

- An APIOps deployment workflow follows the GitOps practice of storing configuration declaratively in version control. Changes are made by PR, and a deployment pipeline or Kubernetes operator is used to sync the configuration with the API gateway instance.

More on API consistency: Custom linting and security checks

10

This chapter covers

- Writing custom linting functions
- Running OWASP API linting checks
- Validating API requests and responses in the gateway
- Generating OpenAPI from traffic

Having automated ways of keeping your APIs compliant with your API style guide is important in order to maintain an easy-to-use and secure developer experience for developers integrating with your APIs. API linting is a big part of maintaining that API consistency at design time. In chapter 3, I introduced API linting and discussed how to write custom linting rules in Spectral using its built-in functions. But using the core functions that come with a linting tool can only take you so far. To implement a linting rule based on your API style guide, you need to write a custom function because the built-in functions may not meet your requirements. In this chapter, I discuss creating custom functions.

Another aspect of API consistency that you need to keep in mind is API security. Your API style guide should have guidelines on how to design secure APIs. And if it doesn't, you need to update the style guide! In this chapter, I discuss some common security threats APIs face and how you can run linting checks to catch aspects of them at design time. I also touch on how you can ensure that you integrate security into every aspect of your application development life cycle.

This is a developer-focused chapter and will go a bit deeper into API linting. The source code for this chapter is in the chapter10 directory at https://mng.bz/MZMW. With that background, let's begin.

10.1 The need for custom functions

Suppose you need a linting rule to ensure automated compliance with a standard defined by your API style guide. For example, imagine that your company's API style guide specifies that the name of the `operationId` for all GET operations should begin with "retrieve" or "download." Imagine that none of your API linting tool's core functions provide the functionality you need to check for this. How can you extend the linting tool to cover your use case?

You can do so by writing custom rules and custom functions for the linting tool. API linting tools (e.g., Spectral, Redocly CLI, and Vacuum) provide a way to extend their capability using custom linting rules that specify where in the API definition document the linting validation should occur and custom functions that invoke custom code for performing the check. In chapter 3, you saw how to create custom rules. To apply them in this case, you should first check to make sure there isn't a built-in rule in your API linting tool you can turn on to provide you with this functionality or a publicly available one you can import. If there isn't, then you must write a custom rule. In doing so, it's good practice to start by writing a failing unit test that captures the behavior you want. Then you can write the custom rule and the custom function in code that has the validation check you require. We'll discuss these in turn.

10.1.1 Searching for reusable rules

Writing a custom function for a custom rule involves writing code that has to be maintained. So before writing a custom rule, you should check to see if your linting tool has a built-in rule you can use instead by simply turning it on and adjusting its severity setting. For example, `operation-operationId-unique` is a rule that comes with the built-in Spectral ruleset (i.e., `spectral:oas`) and by default has a severity level of warning. You can change this severity level to error as shown here:

```
extends: spectral:oas
rules:
  oas3-unused-component: error
```

It helps to become familiar with the built-in rules that come with your linting tool. Here are a few suggestions on where you can find the built-in rulesets of the popular linting tools:

- For Spectral, the list of rules in the built-in OpenAPI ruleset is available at https://mng.bz/Bdrv. As I mentioned in chapter 3, you can enable this ruleset by specifying `extends: spectral:oas` in your spectral.yaml file. This enables the minimal set of rules that comes with the ruleset (i.e., the ones marked as Recommended in its documentation). To turn on all the rules, you need to add `[[extends: spectral:oas, all]]`.

- The Redocly CLI provides a minimal ruleset with rules listed at https://redocly .com/docs/cli/rules/minimal and a larger recommended ruleset at https://redocly.com/docs/cli/rules/recommended.

- Vacuum also provides a minimal recommended ruleset (https://quobix.com/vacuum/rulesets/recommended) and a larger all ruleset (https://quobix.com/vacuum/rulesets/all).

If the built-in rulesets don't have a rule you can use, consider importing available open source rulesets that have what you need. In chapter 3, section 3.8, I mentioned publicly available rulesets you can import for Spectral. Another good place to start looking for Spectral rulesets is https://github.com/stoplightio/spectral-rulesets, which is a community-contributed list of publicly available rulesets.

If there are no open source rulesets that have a rule that meets your need, your next option is to write a custom rule that uses a core function from your API linting tool. If you can't find a core function that meets your needs, then you need to write a custom function. But this should be your last resort. For example, for the problem scenario I've presented, imagine that you use Spectral as your linting tool. You can avoid writing a custom function by reusing one of Spectral's core functions—the pattern function—which compares a target value against a regular expression to define a rule `operationId-get-should-follow-naming-convention` that does what you need, as shown here:

```
rules:
  operationId-get-should-follow-naming-convention:
    description: 'GET operations should have an operationId
    starting with retrieve or download'
    message: "GET operationId should follow naming convention. {{error}}"
    given: "$.paths[*]['get']['operationId']"
    severity: error
    then:                                      Uses the built-in Spectral
      function: pattern          ◁──────────   pattern function
      functionOptions:
        match: "(^retrieve\\w*)|(^download\\w*)"   ◁──────
                                    Provides a regular expression
                                    pattern to match against
```

For this problem scenario, though, I'll show you how to implement it as a custom function so you can see how it works.

10.1.2 *Writing a test for your linting rule*

As I mentioned, before writing a new custom rule, it's good practice to have a test suite around it. You can follow the test-driven approach here. The test suite helps protect you if you need to refactor the rule in the future.

All the usual rules of writing unit tests apply here. Your test should make clear what is the subject under test (SUT)—that is, the ruleset you're testing. It should invoke the operation you're testing (i.e., the name of your new rule) with the data it's testing against—an example API definition against which the rule should either pass or report problems on. The API definition file doesn't need to be a large OpenAPI file. It can be a snippet that contains the important parts; you just need to verify that the intention of the test is fulfilled. It's helpful if you make the unit test fixture turn off all the other rules, except the one you're testing. That way, the linting rule only returns problem messages you're interested in for that test. Finally, the test should assert on the returned problem messages returned from the linting tool, if any. Usually, the absence of any problem messages means that the API definition passes linting.

There are a couple of patterns used by various linting tools for testing linting rules. One way is to include both the API definition being tested and the problem messages asserted against it in the same test function. Another pattern is to have the API definition being tested and the expected linting message output in separate files from the actual test. If you use an open source linting tool, I recommend looking at its documentation or project repository to see the test patterns it uses for testing linting rules.

Let's revisit the problem scenario I started with. Start by writing a happy-path test and a sad-path test for the new rule. The structure for these tests is illustrated in figure 10.1.

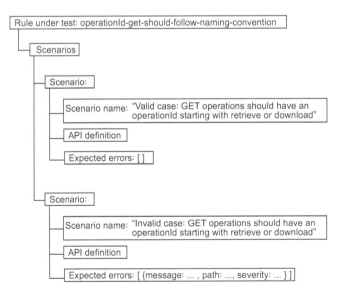

Figure 10.1   Structure of the API linting rule test to check the prefix of `operationIds`

The unit test structure is based on the pattern in the Spectral project. One advantage of this is that tests can be extended without requiring developers to have a deep knowledge of the underlying programming language (JavaScript or TypeScript), as the test only requires three fields—the scenario name, a sample API definition, and the expected problem messages. If you use a different open source linting tool, look in their codebase for patterns they use for testing their rules.

Now write the code to implement this test. Before beginning, navigate to the chapter10 directory, and run `npm install` to install all the required NPM packages. Then write the happy-path scenario that returns no error messages if an API definition doesn't fail the linting rule. The code for this is in the next listing, and you can write it into the file chapter10/__tests__/operation-id-pattern.test.ts using Visual Studio Code (VS Code) or your favorite IDE.

Listing 10.1 Unit tests for the custom linting rule

```
import { DiagnosticSeverity } from '@stoplight/types';
import testRule from '../__helpers__/helper';          ←───  Import helper
                                                              function
testRule( 'operationId-get-should-follow-naming-convention', [         containing the
  {                                                                     DSL functions
        scenarioName: 'Valid case: GET operations should have an
  operationId starting with retrieve or download',
        apiDefinition: {                              ←───  Defines a snippet
            openapi: '3.1.0',                                API definition as a
            info: { version: '1.0' },                        JavaScript object
            paths: {
                '/v1/users': {
                    get: {
                        operationId: 'retrieveUsers',    ←───  Follows expected
                    }                                           convention
                }
            }
        },                            ┌──  No errors are expected
        expectedErrors: [],    ←──────┘   in this scenario.
    },
```

The `testRule()` function initiates the embedded Spectral linter and turns off all rules except the one being tested. Next, extend the tests by adding a test scenario for the sad path. Assert that the right error message is returned when an API definition is provided with an `operationId` that doesn't follow the convention, as shown in the next listing.

Listing 10.2 Sad-path scenario in unit test for linting rule

```
...
{
        scenarioName: 'Invalid case: GET operations should have an
  operationId starting with retrieve or download',
        apiDefinition: {
            openapi: '3.1.0',
            info: { version: '1.0' },
            paths: {
```

```
            '/v1/users': {
                get: {
                    operationId: 'listUsers',      ◁─┤ OperationId name
                }                                       doesn't follow
            }                                           convention
        }                          ┌─ Array of expected
    },                             │  error message
    expectedErrors: [    ◁─────────┘  objects
        {
            message: "GET operationId should follow naming convention.
 ⇒  OperationId 'listUsers' should start with 'retrieve' or 'download'.",
            path: ['paths', '/v1/users', 'get', 'operationId'],
            severity: DiagnosticSeverity.Error,
        }
    ],
    }
}]);
```

Now run the test by running npm test on the command line. Your test should fail with an error containing the message ReferenceError: Cannot extend non-existing rule: "operationId-get-should-follow-naming-convention because you haven't written the custom rule yet. Good. Next, you have to write the custom rule for it.

10.1.3   *Writing the custom rule*

Next, define the custom rule by specifying its description, message, given expression, and function. I've discussed writing custom Spectral rules in chapter 3. Remember that the given expression specifies the part of the API definition file that the check should be applied to. This should be a JSONPath expression that, in this case, targets all the operationIds for GET operations in the OpenAPI file. The difference here is that the rule should invoke the custom function—which you haven't yet defined. Suppose you want your custom function to be named getOperationIdConvention. Figure 10.2 shows the structure of the custom linting rule.

And this time, write the rule in the ruleset.ts file, defining the new operationId-get-should-follow-naming-convention rule in TypeScript (rather than YAML as you did in chapter 2), as shown in the following listing.

Listing 10.3   Custom rule to check operationId prefix

```
export default {
    rules: {
        'operationId-get-should-follow-naming-convention': {
            description: 'GET operations should have an operationId
 ⇒ starting with retrieve or download',
            message: "GET operationId should follow              ┌ Locates the part of the API
 ⇒ naming convention. {{error}}",                                 │ definition file that is the target
            given: "$.paths[*].get.operationId",      ◁──────────┘ value of the custom function
            then: {
                function: getOperationIdConvention    ◁──┐ Calls the new
            },                                            └ custom function
            severity: DiagnosticSeverity.Error,
        },
```

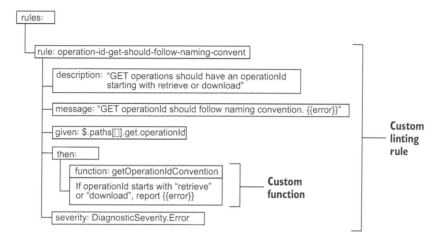

Figure 10.2   Structure of the custom Spectral linting rule for checking the `operationId` of `GET` operations

The next step is to define the `getOperationIdConvention` custom function.

10.1.4   *Defining the custom function*

In popular linting tools such as Spectral, Redocly, and Vacuum, custom linting functions take a target object (I'll also refer to this as the *target value*) from the API definition as input and return a message if the target fails a check implemented in the function. When writing custom functions, apply all the guidelines of keeping code readable. You can consider breaking a large function into smaller functions with single responsibility. Using code comments or a strongly typed language such as TypeScript can help improve readability. TypeScript is based on JavaScript but has the advantage of providing improved type safety.

So let me show you how to implement the `getOperationIdConvention` custom function. It should inspect the input target value, which is the `operationId` located by the given clause of the linting rule, and if it doesn't start with `retrieve` or `download`, it should report a problem with the definition file. This can be written as a TypeScript function that takes in the target value (based on the results of the `given` clause located by the custom rule), the expected schema of the target value, the value of the function options provided, and a context object giving more information about the API definition file and ruleset. It returns an array containing the linting problem error message, if any. To write this, define the new `getOperationIdConvention` custom function in the chapter10/functions/get-operation-id-naming.ts file, as shown in the next listing.

Listing 10.4   Defining the custom function in TypeScript

```
import {createRulesetFunction} from "@stoplight/spectral-core"
import type {IFunctionResult, RulesetFunctionContext}
```

```
⇒  from '@stoplight/spectral-core';
   type Input = string;
   type Options = null;
   export default createRulesetFunction<Input, Options>({
          input: {
              type: 'string'
          },
          errorOnInvalidInput: true,
          options: null,
      }, function operationIdConvention(targetValue,
   opts,
   context) {
          const results: IFunctionResult[] = [];
          if (!(targetValue.startsWith("retrieve")
   || targetValue.startsWith("download"))) {
              results.push({
                  message: `OperationId '${targetValue}' should start
   with 'retrieve' or 'download'.`,
                  path: ['paths', '/v1/users', 'get', 'operationId'],
              });
          }
          return results;
      }
   );
```

Defines the schema of the target value → (points to `input` block)

Flag to trigger failure if target value doesn't match schema → (points to `errorOnInvalidInput: true,`)

← (points to `options: null,`)

← (points to `function operationIdConvention(targetValue,`)

→ **opts,**

→ **context)** ←

→ **results.push({**

Context holds object information about the API definition

The target in the API definition where the function should be applied

If check fails, report an error

Defines the schema of the functionOptions part of this rule

Holds the value of the functionOptions defined in the rule, if any

Now run the test. You should see it pass as shown here:

```
$>: npm test

> apiopsbook@1.0.0 test
> jest

 PASS  __tests__/operation-id-pattern.test.ts
  Rule operationId-get-should-follow-naming-convention
    ✓ Valid case: GET operations should have an operationId
⇒ starting with retrieve or download (1 ms)
    ✓ Invalid case: GET operations should have an operationId
⇒ starting with retrieve or download

Test Suites: 1 passed, 1 total
Tests:       2 passed, 2 total
Snapshots:   0 total
Time:        2.942 s, estimated 3 s
Ran all test suites.
```

All your tests pass, and your implementation is complete. Note that you can also write the custom function as a simpler JavaScript function. You can create this in a file chapter10/functions/get-operation-id-naming-simple.js:

```
module.exports = function getOperationIdConvention(targetValue) {
    const results = [];
    if (typeof targetValue !== 'string'){
        results.push({message: `"operationId" must be a string`});
    }
    if (!(targetValue.startsWith("retrieve") ||
 targetValue.startsWith("download"))) {
        results.push({
            message: `OperationId '${targetValue}' should start with
 'retrieve' or 'download'.`,
            path: ['paths', '/v1/users', 'get', 'operationId'],
        });
    }
    return results;
}
```

Validates the type
to avoid TypeError

To use this, you'll need to import it into the ruleset.ts file using the following snippet:

```
import getOperationIdConvention from
 './functions/get-operation-id-naming-simple';
```

You've successfully implemented your function and run your tests. Now I'll discuss a few guidelines you should follow when writing custom functions.

10.1.5 *Notes on writing custom functions*

If you work in a large team, it's helpful to provide documentation on how to add new rules, modify existing rules, or ignore rules where required. Your documentation should also explain how to add unit tests for custom rules. This can help developers self-serve by adding new rules and raising them via your pull request (PR) process. Of course, care must be taken when ignoring rules, and a team member submitting such a change should explain why the rule should be ignored (e.g., in a PR message).

When introducing a new custom rule, remember that you don't need to turn it on for all APIs at once, which may lead to linting failure for existing APIs that aren't compliant. You can introduce it gradually to your inventory of APIs by choosing which rulesets to include and which rules to turn on.

Linting can run in various contexts, such as a code editor, a CLI, or a browser. Because of this, custom functions should be deterministic and should generally avoid side effects. For example, you should carefully consider whether to use side effects such as caching logic in your custom functions.

In addition, carefully consider the effect of using external libraries or APIs that may have cross-platform compatibility problems. For example, using the built-in Spell Checking API on a Windows operating system may limit the portability of your custom function. Another example is making HTTP requests—you have to consider any authentication requirements and other potential obstacles, such as Cross-Origin Resource Sharing (CORS) restrictions in a browser.

I've shown you how to define custom functions. Now, I'll discuss an important area where you may need to apply this knowledge.

10.2   *Automated security review of your API definitions*

Imagine that your company is building an API, and your manager has asked you to review an API design proposal to ensure it has been securely designed. The OpenAPI definition file your manager has provided for you to review can be found in the sample code repository, chapter10/crapi.api.yaml. How do you ensure the API is secure and doesn't expose well-known API vulnerabilities?

To detect the vulnerabilities in this API, you must first have a basic understanding of API security. The crapi.api.yaml file is a good API definition for learning about API security because it has been intentionally designed to be insecure. I copied it from the Open Worldwide Application Security Project (OWASP) Completely Ridiculous API (crAPI) project https://github.com/OWASP/crAPI. The crAPI application allows users to get their cars serviced. Users can create accounts, search for car mechanics, submit a servicing request, and purchase accessories. It also has a community forum where users can post comments and blog posts. The services exposed in the crAPI's API are shown in figure 10.3.

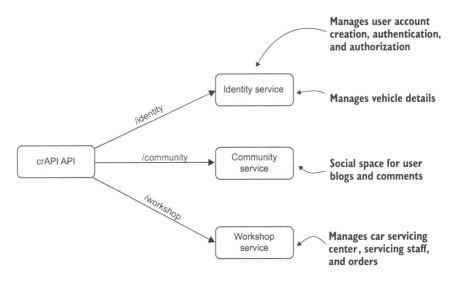

Figure 10.3   The backend microservices that make up crAPI

If you're interested, you can find the full implementation of the services that make up the crAPI in the project's GitHub repository. In this chapter, however, the focus for this exercise is analyzing the API design for security defects. To do this, let me give you a brief introduction to API security.

10.2.1 Introducing API Security

API security is about mitigating the risks to business assets posed by APIs. It involves protecting the APIs you provide to consumers using mechanisms such as encryption, authentication, authorization, audit logging, rate-limiting, and more. API security is a wide area that touches information security, network security, and application security. As your API goes through the design, development, test, and runtime operation stages of your software delivery life cycle, security checks need to be done at each stage to protect against *API vulnerabilities*. An API vulnerability is a weakness, flaw, or defect in an API that can be exploited by an attacker to weaken the security of a system.

Because APIs are the interfaces to software systems, it's important to consider the security threats they face. *Threat modeling* is about identifying and understanding the possible threats to a software system, their likelihood of occurrence, the impact an occurrence can have, key security controls, and countermeasures to adopt to protect the system. The likelihood and impact of the occurrence are both important in understanding the risk because a low-probability, high-impact problem can be worse than a high-probability, low-impact problem.

> ### Some common terms used in threat modeling
>
> - *Threat*—A potential occurrence that can damage or compromise a business asset or objective
> - *Vulnerability*—A weakness in implementing a system that makes an exploit possible
> - *Attack*—An execution of a threat; an attempt to steal, expose, modify, destroy, disable, or gain unauthorized access or use of a system or business asset
> - *Countermeasures*—An action taken to address vulnerabilities to reduce the probability of attacks and the impact of threats
> - *Attack vector*—The channel through which attacks are carried out, for example, a client browser or a network proxy
> - *Actor*—An individual or a group capable of performing functional use or abuse of a system
> - *Impact*—Value of damage due to an attack

As discussed in *Threat Modeling: A Practical Guide for Development Teams* by Izar Tarandach and Matthew Coles (O'Reilly, 2020), essentially, there are four questions involved in any kind of threat modeling approach:

- *What are you building?* Model the system you're building with data flow diagrams, use case models, and architecture diagrams so security analysis can be done effectively.

- *What can go wrong?* Use structured approaches and *attack trees* (diagrams that show the various ways a system can be compromised) to explore and identify what parts of the system can be attacked. An example of a structured approach used for looking for threats is STRIDE, which stands for spoofing, tampering, repudiation, information disclosure, denial of service, and elevation of privilege.
- *What should you do about it?* Propose security measures or controls to mitigate the identified threats, attacks, and risks. The identified risks and mitigations should be prioritized, and the proposed controls should be fed into the design and development process and the continuous integration/continuous delivery (CI/CD) pipeline that automates it so that the software produced is secure by design.
- *Did we do a good job?* Validate that the threats have been mitigated. Continuously improve the threat modeling process by reviewing it regularly and checking to see if anything has been missed or can be improved.

Figure 10.4 illustrates these steps. A larger discussion on the various tools and methodologies for threat modeling is beyond the scope of this book, but you can get an overview of it from OWASP's Threat Modeling Cheat Sheet at https://mng.bz/aEl7. For an in-depth look at API security, I recommend *API Security in Action* by Neil Madden (Manning, 2020; www.manning.com/books/api-security-in-action).

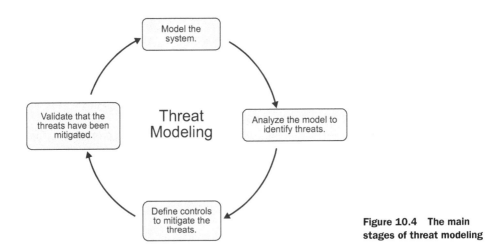

Figure 10.4   The main stages of threat modeling

The OWASP API Security Top 10 (https://mng.bz/gvlV) is a document that represents a general consensus from industry experts on the critical security threats that affect web APIs. The 2023 version lists the threats shown in figure 10.5.

In the following section, I give you a brief introduction to OWASP API Security Top 10. I won't give a detailed discussion on mitigating these vulnerabilities—you can find

Figure 10.5   The Top 10 API security risks identified by OWASP

more information on the OWASP website at https://mng.bz/gvlV. However, I do provide information on how to detect aspects of the following five of these vulnerabilities by linting an API's definition file:

- API1:2023 - Broken Object Level Authorization
- API2:2023 - Broken Authentication
- API3:2023 - Broken Object Property Level Authorization
- API4:2023 - Unrestricted Resource Consumption
- API8:2023 - Security Misconfiguration

Let me start by going down the list of the API Security Top 10.

10.2.2   *API1:2023 - Broken Object Level Authorization*

API endpoints can expose identifiers for resource objects, for example, the `accountId` object identifier in `GET /accounts/{accountId}`. The Broken Object Level Authorization (BOLA) vulnerability occurs when an attacker is able to modify the object identifier sent in a request, enabling the attacker to gain access to a resource they should have no access to. In this example, instead of providing their `accountId`, they send another user's `accountId`. This can result in unauthorized information access, modification, or destruction.

One way an attacker can obtain an object identifier is by sniffing API traffic from other users. But they can also try to guess object identifiers. Guessing an object identifier is facilitated by endpoints that use numeric, serial object identifiers, such as `GET /accounts/123` and `GET /accounts/124`. Therefore, it's bad practice to use guessable object identifiers. This is one aspect of this vulnerability that you can look for in API definition files. And, of course, API linting can help with this. Try this out with the crapi.api.yaml file in the following exercise.

In the chapter10 directory, I've created a linting ruleset (chapter10/.spectral .yaml) that combines Spectral's OWASP ruleset (https://mng.bz/eoAQ), which at the time of writing is based on the OWASP 2019 risks, with some other OWASP-related custom linting rules (discussed later).

> **NOTE**   There are some differences between the OWASP 2023 risks and the OWASP 2019 risks. Where these differences affect the Spectral OWASP 2019 ruleset you use in this linting exercise, I point them out.

Run this linting ruleset on the crapi.api.yaml file using the following commands:

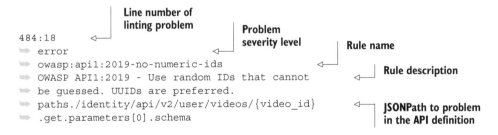

```
cd chapter10
npm install          ◁──── Installs the dependencies
                            defined in the package.json
spectral lint crapi.api.yaml  >  issues.log   ◁──── Lints and writes
                                                    results to file
```

Now search the file for linting problems beginning with `'owasp:api1'` by running the following:

```
grep -E 'owasp:api1' issues.log
```

You should see several problems like the following:

```
484:18   ◁──── Line number of linting problem
⇨ error   ◁──── Problem severity level
⇨ owasp:api1:2019-no-numeric-ids   ◁──── Rule name
⇨ OWASP API1:2019 - Use random IDs that cannot   ◁──── Rule description
⇨ be guessed. UUIDs are preferred.
⇨ paths./identity/api/v2/user/videos/{video_id}   ◁──── JSONPath to problem
⇨ .get.parameters[0].schema                              in the API definition
```

You can see from the results that several of the endpoints are using numeric identifiers, which can be guessable. To mitigate this, the design of the endpoints should be changed to use a Universally Unique Identifier (UUID) instead. Table 10.1 summarizes this vulnerability and how it can be detected with linting.

Table 10.1   Summary of detecting BOLA via linting

Vulnerability	Possible exploit	Detection via API linting
Your API operations expose guessable identifiers for resource objects.	An attacker can guess an object ID or detect an identifier by monitoring request traffic. They can use this to request an object they should not have access to.	Have linting rules that check to ensure the important object identifiers in URL paths, headers, and request and response bodies use random IDs that can't be guessed, such as UUIDs.

Let me reemphasize that a linting check like this can't catch all instances of a BOLA vulnerability. For example, an attacker can use the GET /community/api/v2/community/ posts/recent endpoint to get a list of posts, which includes the authors and their associated vehicle IDs (unguessable UUIDs), and then use those vehicle IDs to access a vehicle's location using GET /identity/api/v2/vehicle/{vehicleId}/location endpoint. If that endpoint doesn't have proper authorization checks (as in the case of the implementation of this intentionally vulnerable application), it will allow sensitive vehicle location information to be returned.

10.2.3   API2:2023 - Broken Authentication

The Broken Authentication vulnerability occurs with poorly implemented authentication flows. Most APIs have dedicated endpoints to authenticate and log users into the system. These endpoints establish the *security mechanism* for accessing the other endpoints in the API. Authentication flows are typically complex, and not every software engineer working on the system may understand how they work or how to implement them correctly. Because of this, authentication endpoints are usually the target of special attacks, as attackers can exploit poorly implemented authentication flows to assume the identity of other users, gain control of their accounts, and perform sensitive actions on their behalf.

OpenAPI security mechanisms

A security mechanism is a method or procedure for achieving a security requirement and enforcing a security policy. For APIs, this will be some defined method for authenticating and authorizing requests to the API, and the API definition is the place to communicate this to consumers. OpenAPI uses the term *security scheme* to refer to the authentication and authorization mechanisms available to the API.

The OpenAPI specification uses the *security scheme object* to allow API designers to define the authentication and authorization mechanisms they require to satisfy the security requirements for their API. OpenAPI 3.1 supports the following security schemes:

- *HTTP Authentication*—This uses the HTTP Authorization header defined in RFC 7235. HTTP Authentication supports different kinds of authentication schemes. These include Basic, Bearer, Digest, and more. (See the IANA HTTP

(continued)

Authentication Scheme Registry for the full list at https://mng.bz/5lEB.) For example, with basic authentication, the user sends credentials as user ID and password pairs encoded using Base64: `Authorization: Basic bXllc2VyaWQ6IG15cGGFzc3dvcmQ==`. By itself, this isn't considered a secure authentication method, except it's combined with a way to encrypt the transport protocol over which the credentials are communicated.

- *API keys*—An API key is a token (provided to the API consumer via some out-of-band process) sent to an API server. The user sends it to the API server (as an API header, cookie, or query parameter) to identify and authenticate the calling client application. Sending an API key as a query parameter isn't recommended, as it risks the API key being logged and accessed by attackers.
- *Mutual TLS (mTLS)*—In mTLS, the client and server authenticate each other using X.509 certificates. These are often used in business-to-business applications where the security requirements are higher. mTLS is different from the plain Transport Layer Security (TLS) protocol, which only requires that the server provide itself to the client using an X.509 certificate.
- *OAuth2*—OAuth2 is an authorization framework that allows a client application to access a protected resource on behalf of a resource owner. The resource owner grants access to the resource to the client application, and the client application exchanges the grant for an access token. The token contains information about the scope, duration, and other attributes of the grant, and the client application presents this to the resource server when making a request.
- *OpenID Connect (OIDC)*—OpenID Connect provides an identity layer built on top of the OAuth 2 protocol that allows client applications to verify the identity of end users and also obtain user profile information. It defines a flow in which a client application can obtain *claims* (a piece of information asserted about a user, e.g., a name or email address) about an authenticated user from an *authorization server* (the identity provider) as an ID token. This ID token is a JSON Web Token (JWT).

Now check for this vulnerability in the crapi.api.yaml file by running the following command:

```
grep -E 'owasp:api2' issues.log
```

This returns many problems:

The linting results show there are endpoints in the definition file that haven't been secured. The owasp:api2:2019-protection-global-rule raises a problem about endpoints that don't have a security scheme defined at the global or operation level. But public authentication endpoints having to do with signup and login should not have a security scheme defined, as users need them to be unsecured so they can use them to sign in. This is an example of where there should be an override in the linting rules to ignore the owasp:api2:2019-protection-global-unsafe rule for these authentication endpoints. But again, that doesn't mean this API is free from the Broken Authentication vulnerability. If an attacker knows a user's email address, they can use the change password functionality and brute force requests to the POST /identity/api/auth/v2/check-otp endpoint to find a valid one-time password (OTP) code and reset a user's password. However, discussion of how to do this is out of the scope of this book.

10.2.4 *API3:2023 - Broken Object Property Level Authorization*

Resource objects returned by an API can have multiple fields—that is, object properties. Some APIs tend to return all of an object's properties. The Broken Object Property Level Authorization vulnerability occurs when some of the properties returned contain sensitive information that the user should not have access to. Because proper authorization checks aren't being done on the returned fields, this can also lead to the user modifying these sensitive properties. Unauthorized data disclosure and data corruption from this vulnerability can lead to attackers taking over user accounts.

Now check for this risk in the crapi.api.yaml file by running a grep command that checks for Spectral issues with names beginning with `owasp:api3:` or `owasp:api6:`, as follows:

```
grep -E 'owasp:api3:|owasp:api6:' issues.log
```

Note that the reason why the `grep` expression in the command you just ran is searching for problems relating to rules beginning with `owasp:api3:` or `owasp:api6:` is because API risk 3 (Broken Object Property Level Authorization) in the 2023 version of the OWASP Top 10 is a combination of risk 3 (Excessive Data Exposure—where an endpoint exposes fields that are sensitive and should not be read by a user) and risk 6 (Mass Assignment—where an endpoint allows a user unauthorized access to modify or delete a sensitive field) of the 2019 version. Remember that the ruleset I provided here imports Spectral's OWASP 2019 ruleset.

The command returns errors such as the following:

```
862:20
⇒ warning
⇒ owasp:api3:2023-no-default-additionalProperties          Rule name
⇒ Objects should not allow additionalProperties.
⇒ Disable them with `additionalProperties: false` or        JSONPath to the
⇒ constrain them.                                            rule violation
⇒ paths./community/api/v2/community/
⇒ posts.post.requestBody.content.application/json.schema
```

The owasp:api3:2023-no-default-additionalProperties is a custom API linting rule I've added to the .spectral.yaml ruleset. It comes from Team Digitale (https://mng.bz/ 67ro), and it checks that all responses have `additionalProperties` set to `false`. This rule and setting `additionalProperties:false` helps ensure that every field returned by the response schema is documented. It helps catch instances where attackers try to make an API behave abnormally and return unexpected data.

> **NOTE** While setting `additionalProperties` to `false` is recommended from a security perspective, it does pose some challenges to API evolution. Setting `additionalProperties:false` places a limitation on what the schema accepts, but this can make the API schema rigid and hinder its evolution because it won't accept new fields from the server without updating the API definition. In addition, the `additionalProperties` keyword only recognizes properties declared in the same subschema as itself, and this restricts how you can use it along with combining keywords like `allOf` and `anyOf`. An alternative to `additionalProperties` is the `unevaluatedProperties` keyword, which addresses this combination problem. Discussion of this is out of scope for this book, but you can get more information on this at the JSON Schema website (https://mng.bz/oeDd). (JSON Schema is the underlying data schema specification used by OpenAPI.) Finally, note that by default, `additionalProperties` is set to `false` in OpenAPI 2.0 but is set to `true` in OpenAPI 3.0.

What about APIs that already return fields users should not have access to? These can be sensitive fields that have personally identifiable information (PII). The owasp:api3 :2023-no-default-additionalProperties rule won't catch that. Instead, you can mark such fields as sensitive and get the linting rule to notify you of where those sensitive fields are being returned in the response.

> **TIP** An important step is to consider what fields should be sensitive. They should be documented and shared with the teams involved in the API development so that there is a consistent view of this across teams.

I've provided rule owasp:api3:2023-sensitive-fields-in-response to do that. Now check the linting report for instances of this rule by running the following:

```
grep -E 'owasp:api3:2023-sensitive-fields-in-response' issues.log
```

This gives you a list of errors:

```
2176:15
⇨ warning
⇨ owasp:api3:2023-sensitive-fields-in-response
⇨ Possible sensitive fields in response. Field: email          Sensitive field on
⇨ components.schemas.Author.properties.email                    response schema

2178:19
⇨ Warning
⇨ owasp:api3:2023-sensitive-fields-in-response
⇨ Possible sensitive fields in response. Field: vehicleid       Sensitive field on
⇨ components.schemas.Author.properties.vehicleid                response schema
```

The `components.schemas.Author` schema object is included in the `components.schemas`
`.Post` object and returned by the `GET /community/api/v2/community/posts/recent`
endpoint. This means any user making a request to get the most recent posts on the
community forum is also retrieving the email address and `vehicleId` of all the
authors who have made posts recently. Those are fields that all users should not
have access to, thus manifesting the Broken Object Property Level Authorization
vulnerability. Table 10.2 summarizes how you can detect instances of this vulnerability by API linting.

Table 10.2   Detecting Broken Object Property Level Authorization vulnerabilities with API linting

Vulnerability	Possible exploit	Detection via API linting
Your API schema allows `additionalProperties`.	An attacker can aim to make your API behave in unexpected ways so that it responds with data that doesn't fit the defined schema and exposes sensitive information. If your API allows undocumented additional properties, then it may be returning fields you don't expect.	In your OpenAPI file, define all the properties of schema objects. Have a linting rule that checks that `additionalProperties` is set to `false` where possible. Have a linting rule that notifies you of sensitive fields in the response. This can be PII, such as email, phone number, credit card numbers, and so on.
Some of your API operations are missing 404 Not Found and 415 Unsupported Media Type errors and 500 Internal Server errors.	An attacker can aim to make your API behave in unexpected ways so they can learn more about your system. If common error cases aren't defined, it may not be clear how your API behaves in that scenario.	Have a linting rule that checks that a 404 Not Found status code is defined for all `GET`, `PUT`, `HEAD`, and `DELETE` operations. Have a linting rule that checks that a 415 Unsupported Media Type client status code is defined for `POST`, `PUT`, and `PATCH` operations. Have a linting rule that checks that a 500 Internal Server Error status code is defined for each of your API operations. Have a linting rule that checks that if an operation has an OpenAPI security requirement object defined, then a 401 Unauthorized and 403 Forbidden status code should be defined for it.

10.2.5   API4:2023 - Unrestricted Resource Consumption

Serving an API request involves resources on the API provider's side—for example,
memory, CPU, network bandwidth, and storage. Depending on the API operation, it
can also involve consuming resources such as sending an SMS, sending an email, or
initiating a phone call. This involves costs to the API provider.

The Unrestricted Resource Consumption vulnerability occurs when an API has no limits on what resources are consumed or has limits that are incorrectly set. In the absence of limits, an attacker can initiate requests that consume a large number of resources, leading to a denial of service due to resource starvation or a big increase in operational costs to the provider. Examples of resource limits include the maximum number of file descriptors and allocable memory a web application should have, maximum upload file size, number of records returned per page, and third-party provider spending limits.

Rate-limiting (sometimes called throttling) sets a limit on how often a client can make a request within a window of time. The goal of rate-limiting is to ensure that when one client increases its rate of requests, the service is still able to respond to other clients. A 429 Too Many Requests status code should be returned when the rate limit is exceeded. The 429 status code, defined in RFC 6585, should have a response body that includes details explaining that the client has sent too many requests and can include a Retry-After header indicating how long the client should wait before making additional requests.

> **NOTE**   The Unrestricted Resource Consumption risk is a reclassification of the OWASP 2019 risk, API4:2019 - Lack of Resources & Rate Limiting.

To mitigate this risk, you can put in measures to control resource consumption, such as rate-limiting policies on endpoints, defining CPU and memory limits for services, limiting payload size, and limiting the amount of data that can be retrieved by a query using pagination size or page counts.

Now check the linting report from the crapi.api.yaml file for this problem by running the following:

```
grep -E 'owasp:api4' issues.log
```

You get a list of errors:

```
2363:26
⇒ error
⇒ owasp:api4:2019-string-limit
⇒ Schema of type string must specify
⇒ maxLength, enum, or const.
⇒ components.schemas.ServiceRequests.
⇒ properties.service_requests.items.properties.created_on
```

The owasp:api4:2019-string-limit rule requires that you specify limits to string fields to prevent resource exhaustion from attackers trying to inject large string payloads into API requests. A similar rule exists for numeric fields. Table 10.3 shows a summary of how you can use linting rules to detect this.

Table 10.3   Detecting the Unrestricted Resource Consumption vulnerability with API linting

Vulnerability	Possible exploit	Detection via API linting
A string schema doesn't limit the values passed to an API by specifying a pattern for the string value or length limit.	An attacker can send large data payloads in API requests to make your API behave in unexpected ways.	Have linting rules to check that string schemas have a well-defined regular expression or enum values. For examples of validation regular expressions, see https://mng.bz/ngDa. String schemas should also specify a `maxLength`.
A numeric schema doesn't specify a minimum or maximum value.		Have linting rules to check that minimum and maximum values are defined for numeric schemas. Numeric values should specify a format such as int32 or int64.
Array schemas don't specify a maximum number of items.		Have linting rules to check that arrays specify `maxItems`.
Your API has operations missing 429 responses.	An attacker can initiate a brute force attack on an API.	Have linting rules to check that except for `HEAD` operations, all operations should have a 429 Too Many Requests response error defined. 429 responses should define a Retry-After header. Where `HEAD` operations do work in the background but just don't return a body in the response, the effect of the resource consumption for the `HEAD` operation should still be considered.

10.2.6   *API5:2023 - Broken Function Level Authorization*

This vulnerability allows attackers to perform unauthorized operations. An example of a Broken Function Level Authorization (BFLA) is a regular user being able to access admin endpoints and perform an admin action, for example, creating a user. Another example is an attacker whose user role is only authorized to read a resource (perform a GET operation) but is also able to update or delete the resource because the authorization module doesn't validate the HTTP request verb. Unlike the BOLA vulnerability, which is about unauthorized access to objects by manipulating object identifiers, BFLA is about access control at the function level.

Because this relates to user authorization for specific operations, this vulnerability can't be easily detected by API linting. Mitigation for this includes ensuring the authorization mechanisms in the code are properly designed and tested, allowing operations by users that have the right authorization group or role.

10.2.7   *API6:2023 - Unrestricted Access to Sensitive Business Flows*

It's usual for sensitive business flows that have a high effect on a business to be exposed via APIs. For example, the ticket booking process for an airline is a sensitive business flow that has a direct revenue effect. This flow can be exposed via a ticket booking API. A vulnerability can arise when there is no restriction on how this sensitive business flow is used. For example, if the ticket booking API allows users to purchase a ticket without a cancellation fee, an attacker can take advantage of this to purchase most of the tickets for a flight once the tickets are available. Close to the flight departure date, the attacker can cancel the tickets all at once, forcing the airline to resell the tickets at a discount. The attacker can then take advantage of this and buy a single ticket at a discounted fee. As you can see, exploiting vulnerabilities around sensitive business flows requires a good understanding of the business model, processes, and where usage restrictions are weak.

This vulnerability can't be detected by linting, though checking that endpoints have rate-limiting does help. However, this is an example of where adequate threat modeling can help make you aware of this risk beforehand. Mitigation starts with understanding business flows that can be sensitive to abuse and what controls can be added to protect them. APIs should be monitored, and suspicious behavior from clients using devices or risky IP addresses can be restricted. CAPTCHA and other human detection controls also help.

10.2.8   *API7:2023 - Server-Side Request Forgery*

Server-Side Request Forgery (SSRF) is a vulnerability that allows an attacker to make a server perform a request to an unintended internal or external location. This can be done to an otherwise unreachable internal system to extract secrets such as authorization credentials.

This vulnerability occurs in scenarios where a user is allowed to provide a URL that the server makes a request to. If the server doesn't properly validate the URL before making a request to it, attackers can craft URLs that result in unintended consequences. For example, social media applications can provide a feature for users to upload profile photos or a URL to where their profile photo can be fetched from. An attacker can exploit this by providing a location such as `http://localhost:8080` to perform a port scanning operation and enable them to launch further attacks if they discover a port open.

Mitigation measures include preventing HTTP redirects in the API server where possible, having an allowed list of permitted access and redirects, and restricting the range of URL schemes and ports allowed.

10.2.9   *API8:2023 - Security Misconfiguration*

This vulnerability occurs when misconfiguration of the API server exposes sensitive data and allows attackers to gain unauthorized access to the server or to compromise it. This can be due to any of the following in the API server: latest security updates missing, insecure default configurations, improperly configured permissions on cloud services, misconfigured HTTP headers, unnecessary HTTP verbs allowed, TLS missing, improperly set CORS policies, or error messages allowed to include stack traces and other sensitive information. Misconfiguration of the API server can occur during implementation, environment provisioning, or deployment.

> **NOTE** In the 2019 version of the API Security Top 10, this risk appeared as API7:2019 - Security Misconfiguration.

Mitigations include automating the hardening and patching of code, libraries, and containers; disabling unnecessary features; and automating tests of API endpoints for misconfiguration. One area of the Security Misconfiguration vulnerability that API linting can detect is the use of HTTP instead of HTTPS. You can see this in the linting problems by running the following:

```
grep -E 'owasp:api7' issues.log
```

This returns one linting problem as follows:

```
9:10
⇒ error
⇒ owasp:api7:2019-security-hosts-https-oas3
⇒ Server URLs MUST begin https://, and no other protocol is permitted.
⇒ servers[0].url
```

As you can see, the owasp:api7:2019-security-hosts-https-oas3 rule checks that servers use HTTPS and not HTTP. Table 10.4 summarizes how API linting can help with this risk.

Table 10.4 Detecting the Security Misconfiguration vulnerability with API linting

Vulnerability	Possible exploit	Detection via API linting
Your API accepts clear unencrypted HTTP communications.	Attackers can listen to network traffic and intercept all requests and responses.	Have a linting rule to check that server URLs should use HTTPS, not HTTP.

10.2.10 API9:2023 - Improper Inventory Management

This vulnerability occurs when the lack of API asset information results in an organization having unpatched or exposed APIs that can be the target of attackers. The lack of an inventory of API assets or outdated API documentation makes it difficult to find and fix vulnerabilities. There may be a lack of information on which environment the API is running on, what version of the API is running, the level of user access it should expose, or what the retirement plans for old versions should be. Security mechanisms and software patches in place on the most recent API versions may not be in place on older versions. Attackers may discover the old, unpatched API versions and gain access to sensitive data or take over the server. This vulnerability is related to an organization's API governance practice.

Keeping an up-to-date inventory of APIs combined with retiring old versions of APIs help mitigate this. The use of firewalls, strict authentication, and segregating access to production and nonproduction data also helps.

10.2.11 API10:2023 - Unsafe Consumption of APIs

APIs can interact with and depend on other third-party APIs. It's usual for developers to be cautious with, validate, and sanitize frontend user input thoroughly. But they can be quite trusting of data received from third-party APIs from well-known companies and be less strict with validating that. When APIs blindly trust the response from other APIs, they have the Unsafe Consumption of APIs vulnerability. This is manifested when APIs interact with other third-party APIs over unencrypted channels or blindly follow redirects from the third party. If the third-party API has been compromised by an attacker, then it can be used to attack other APIs that depend on it.

For example, if a third-party address API has been comprised such that an attacker has stored a Sequel injection (SQLi) payload as their business address, they can craft a request to a vulnerable API that depends on the address API and make it load the malicious address. The vulnerable API can execute the code on its database leading to data loss or exposing sensitive information.

Measures to mitigate this include using secure communication channels for third parties. Input from third-party APIs should be thoroughly validated at runtime, for example, in the application code or using an API gateway. That data should be filtered and sanitized to prevent injection attacks, just as with user input.

Let me round out this discussion on the OWASP API Top 10. As you can see, to use API linting to detect security vulnerabilities in OpenAPI definitions, it's important to have an OpenAPI definition with the schema of the request and response payload accurately and comprehensively documented. With this, you can have your API security linting rules run (along with your other linting rules) in your API design editor and most importantly, in you CI/CD pipeline.

> **TIP** I've talked about using the linting checks, such as the Spectral OWASP, to check your API definitions for vulnerabilities. If you use VS Code as your text editor of choice, remember that you can also use the 42Crunch OpenAPI (Swagger) Editor plugin (which you installed in appendix B) to scan your API definition files for vulnerabilities, which is also described in appendix B.

I've discussed five vulnerabilities you can detect aspects of by linting your OpenAPI definitions—Broken Object Level Authorization, Broken Authentication, Broken Object Property Level Authorization, Unrestricted Resource Consumption, and Security Misconfiguration. I've also discussed the other five vulnerabilities that you need other ways to detect and mitigate—Broken Function Level Authorization, Unrestricted Access to Sensitive Business Flows, Server-Side Request Forgery (SSRF), Improper Inventory Management, and the Unsafe Consumption of APIs. In the next section, I discuss a technique for using comprehensive OpenAPI definition files to provide protection using the API gateway.

10.2.12 Validating traffic in the gateway using OpenAPI

With an accurate OpenAPI definition document, you can consider providing your definition to your API gateway and using it to validate request traffic before the request reaches your backend microservices. Some API gateways (e.g., Amazon API Gateway, Kong using its OAS Validation plugin [https://mng.bz/v8D7], and Apigee using the OASValidation policy [https://mng.bz/4JEw]) allow you to do this. Requests that don't meet the schema specified get an HTTP 400 Bad Request response from the gateway. This reduces the load on the backend services and also gives you a consistent and central place to do request validation.

In addition, the gateway can also support response validation, enabling you to ensure that the microservice isn't returning any unexpected data property whose schema isn't specified in the OpenAPI definition. For the Kong OAS Validation plugin, if response validation fails, the gateway returns a HTTP 406 Not Acceptable status code. Apart from front-facing traffic, request and response validation through an API gateway can also be used to protect your system when interacting with third-party services—for example, from the Unsafe Consumption of APIs vulnerability discussed earlier. In this scenario, you can provide an API gateway (or a similar proxy or middleware that supports OpenAPI validation) between your platform and third party and validate traffic against the OpenAPI definition provided by the third party, as illustrated in figure 10.6. Optionally, you can configure your gateway to notify your monitoring systems on validation failure.

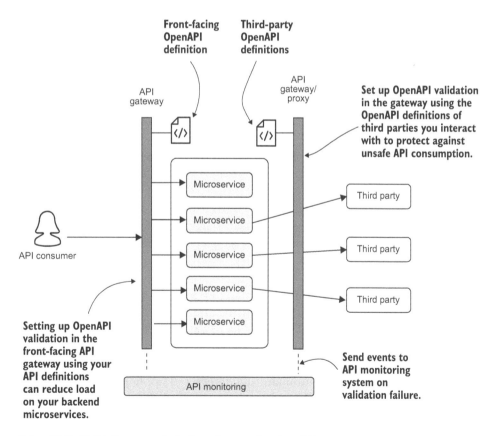

Figure 10.6 **Validating requests in the gateway using OpenAPI**

TIP   Apart from OpenAPI contract validation, a gateway or proxy for third-party APIs consumed by a server can also perform other functions, such as providing a central place to visualize and monitor volume, performance, and error rates of third-party APIs, including managing API request quotes to third parties. An example of a dedicated proxy that does this is Lunar.dev (https://github.com/TheLunarCompany/lunar).

Of course, for gateway validation to work, the gateway has to have an OpenAPI definition to work with. The organization may not always have this definition, which leads us to the next topic.

10.2.13 Generating API definitions from traffic

I've discussed API security linting checks in your API definition file to detect vulnerabilities, but what if your API doesn't have an OpenAPI definition available? Many organizations have APIs that haven't been properly documented. A good place to start then is to document the API—it's difficult to protect APIs you don't know about. You can do this by generating API definitions from application code where possible (as discussed in chapter 6). You can also do this by capturing API traffic and using that to generate an API definition. For this second approach, there are a number of ways you could do it.

You can use a tool that does this in one go, such as Optic (https://github.com/opticdev/optic). Optic can run as a proxy to capture API traffic (e.g., generated by your API tests or Postman collections) and then create an OpenAPI definition from this. You can find out more at www.useoptic.com/docs/generate-openapi-from-tests. Alternatively, you can use a dedicated proxy such as the Charles HTTP proxy (www.charlesproxy.com/) to capture traffic (again generated by your API tests or some other traffic source), and then export the traffic session as an HTTP archive (HAR) format file. Har2OpenAPI (https://github.com/dcarr178/har2openapi) is an open source tool you can use to convert the HAR file to an OpenAPI definition. Thirdly, you can consider using an API security platform that has the functionality built in. API security platforms are the subject of the next section.

10.2.14 API security platforms

API security is a complex and fast-changing area. Dedicated API security platforms (e.g., 42Crunch, NoName, Salt Security, and Traceable AI) exist to help organizations protect their APIs. They aim to integrate API security into the whole API development life cycle. Many of them also have machine learning capabilities that enable their platforms to learn about vulnerabilities and exploits across their network of customers and automatically detect and apply protection to others based on this. As an API provider, you should consider the benefits of integrating with API security platform vendors.

Broadly speaking, API security platforms tend to offer protection across three main stages of the API development life cycle: (1) At the API design stage, they offer a way to scan API definitions for vulnerabilities; (2) at the nonproduction testing stage, they provide ways to dynamically test application APIs for various vulnerabilities and business logic attacks; and (3) at runtime in production, they provide a way to monitor live traffic for threats, allowing API providers to identify attacks and take corrective action, such as blocking an attacker's IP or user account. They monitor the API traffic by adding some instrumentation agent to the API gateways and microservice applications, enabling distributed tracing and the ability to analyze the data in the request and response flows (usually with sensitive information anonymized). They also have the ability to discover *shadow APIs* (undocumented APIs that exist and operate outside officially monitored channels of an organization, sometimes created by developers to get work done quickly) and *zombie APIs* (deprecated, forgotten APIs that are still working in the background and are potentially exploitable by an attacker).

I've talked so far about checking API definitions for security vulnerabilities and the features offered by API security platforms. Zooming out from secure API design, let me show you the wider picture of securing applications by integrating security into how software is built.

10.3 DevSecOps

As I discussed earlier, threat modeling is a good place to start when designing applications for security, but teams need to keep the end-to-end development life cycle of the software in mind. To that end, DevSecOps (which stands for development, security, and operations) is a practice that extends DevOps to integrate security initiatives throughout the development life cycle to create secure applications. It promotes a culture of shared responsibility for security for everyone involved in building and running the software.

In addition to threat modeling, DevSecOps involves the following practices:

- *Static application security testing (SAST)*—Analyzing source code in a nonruntime environment early in the development process to check for vulnerabilities. Examples of SAST tools include Checkmarx and Snyk.
- *Software component analysis (SCA)*—Automating visibility into open source software used in building applications to ensure proper risk management, security, and license compliance.
- *Interactive application security testing (IAST)*—Interacting with and analyzing a running application (either by an automated test or human tester) to find potential vulnerabilities.
- *Dynamic application security testing (DAST)*—A black-box test to mimic attackers by testing application security from outside the network. DAST tools automatically crawl and test APIs for SQLi, cross-site scripting (XSS), cross-site request forgery (CSRF), and other vulnerabilities. Examples of DAST tools include InsightAppSec from Rapid7 and Burp Suite from PortSwigger.
- *Fuzz testing*—Injecting invalid, malformed, or unexpected inputs into a software system to reveal vulnerabilities and effects.

- *Container vulnerability scanning*—Scanning containers for instances of malware, outdated libraries, and incorrect configuration.
- *Image signing*—Adding digital signatures to a container image to ensure its authenticity and integrity.
- *Secrets management*—Using tools and methods for managing digital credentials such as passwords, API keys, access tokens, and so on in applications and privileged accounts. Examples of secrets management tools include HashiCorp's Vault and AWS Secrets Manager.
- *Infrastructure vulnerability scanning*—Scanning infrastructure (i.e., hardware and software, e.g., servers, switches, firewalls, routers, storage, and operating systems) and applications run for vulnerabilities.
- *Runtime Application Self-Protection (RASP)*—Security technology embedded in applications that uses runtime instrumentation and contextual information to monitor, detect, and block attacks automatically at runtime.

Figure 10.7 illustrates how these practices fit in a DevSecOps pipeline.

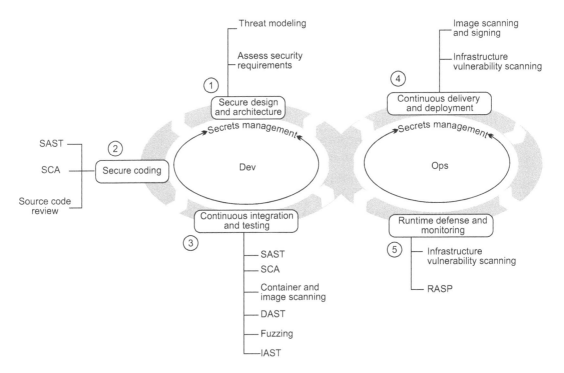

Figure 10.7   An example DevSecOps pipeline

You can see that securing your APIs involves carefully designing them with security in mind, but it also involves incorporating security controls throughout your deployment pipeline. With that, we come to the end of our discussion. Let me summarize the main points from this chapter.

Summary

- For some of your API style guidelines, you may need to define custom functions. A custom function takes in the target object you need to run checks on and gives you the full power of your linting tool's programming language to run the necessary checks.

- It's good practice to write unit tests for your custom functions. But before resorting to custom functions, first check to see if your API linting tool has a built-in function or rule that does what you need. In addition, check if there are publicly available linting rules you can import that do what you need.

- When designing APIs, you have to keep in mind the likely security threats your API will face. The OWASP API Security Top 10 provides an industry consensus on popular API threats. You should incorporate API security checks into your API linting rules to help you catch vulnerabilities at design time.

- Techniques such as runtime validation of API traffic against your OpenAPI definitions in your API gateway help reduce the load on your backend services, provide a common validation layer, and help improve your API security. This technique can also be used to validate traffic with third parties (using their API definitions) to protect against vulnerabilities relating to the unsafe consumption of third-party APIs.

- Beyond designing APIs for security, consider integrating with API security platform vendors to provide controls throughout your API development life cycle. You should also incorporate DevSecOps practices into your deployment pipeline to protect your applications.

Monitoring and analytics: Measuring API product metrics

11

This chapter covers

- Measuring API product analytics: API usage, time-to-first call, and active consumers
- Measuring API monitoring metrics: latency, traffic, and error rates

In chapter 1, you learned that APIOps is the end-to-end automation of the development life cycle using DevOps and GitOps principles. One of the DevOps principles, as presented by Gene Kim, is the principle of using continuous feedback to detect and fix problems in the software value stream. One way this is implemented is by the DevOps practice of continuous monitoring and measurement. This continuous monitoring and measurement is about collecting, analyzing, and sharing metrics from the production system with the development team to foster a cycle of improvements. It involves monitoring—using predefined metrics, dashboards, and alerting to understand, query, and analyze the behavior of running systems, as well as resolve problems.

Apart from the technical performance of the API, the development team and API product owners also need continuous feedback on the *API product metrics*. API product metrics measure the API product experience in relation to the overall product strategy. They help optimize product performance and align customer activity with business goals. With metrics, product managers can measure the exact success of individual product features. It also helps the API team make informed decisions on how to improve the product to meet business goals.

This chapter covers applying monitoring and product analytics to the operation stage of API. Figure 11.1 shows where this fits in the API development life cycle.

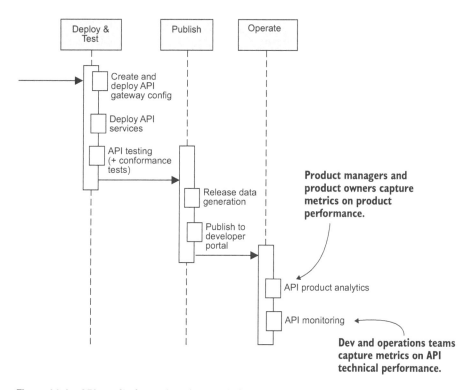

Figure 11.1   API monitoring and product analytics are in the operation stage of the API product delivery life cycle.

The monitoring and analytics tool used in the examples for this chapter is Moesif, and appendix D contains instructions on setting up a Moesif account.

11.1   API product analytics: The business challenge

Suppose your Product Catalog API has been deployed and running in production. It works well, but management has set an ambitious goal to increase the number of customers using the API by 10% in the next quarter. Your team has been asked to improve the overall product experience (whether improvements to the API itself or its documentation and marketing) to meet this goal. How would you go about this?

To approach this improvement objectively, you need data on the current product experience. This enables you to decide on and benchmark product improvement efforts. In this chapter, you'll learn how to gather metrics for this. But first, I'll explain how product analytics data is used to drive improvements using the plan-do-study-act (PDSA) cycle.

11.1.1   *API product development as a PDSA cycle*

Chapter 2 introduced the PDSA cycle as an iterative method for introducing change and making improvements. Remember from that discussion that the cycle has four stages—Plan, Do, Study, and Act. You can consider product development as following the PDSA cycle. Rather than product development being a linear journey with a defined start and end, organizations approach product development as a PDSA cycle of improvements and investments into the product. They use learnings, including product performance metrics from each completed iteration, to kick off the next iteration.

How does this work? At the Plan stage, the company management usually picks one high-level business metric (out of a handful it tracks) to improve in a given time period. These business metrics can be around some quantity (e.g., increasing the average order value of an e-commerce business by 20% or increasing the number of active subscribers by 10%), quality (e.g., improving customer satisfaction and retention), or reducing costs.

This focus metric (also called a north-star metric) should provide value for the customer and the business. Based on this, product managers identify and track lower-level metrics that should cause an improvement in this high-level metric or maintain the overall health of the product while the improvement is in progress.

Typically, for APIs, these lower-level metrics are API product metrics in the areas of API *discovery*, *engagement*, *activation*, *acquisition*, *retention*, and *experience*. I'll explain what these areas mean later, but you can think of them as metrics that track causal actions that can lead to the expected high-level outcome. The product manager's predictive theory, or cause and effect relationship, is that improving these lower-level metrics (e.g., the number of daily active users, an activation metric discussed later) should result in an improvement of the high-level outcome metric that the business wants to improve. Based on this hypothesis, the API team plans improvements—new APIs or API product features—to deliver these API product metric improvements.

Now that you know what the Plan stage of the PDSA looks like for product development, here's a bit about the other stages:

- The Do stage involves implementing, deploying, and publishing the API product improvements.
- The Study stage involves measuring the API product metrics over time to validate the hypothesis. You also identify learnings from the success or failure of this experiment.
- The Act stage involves sharing the learning widely. If the change is successful, identify action points for wider adoption and action points for further improvements in the next iteration. Or if it wasn't successful, you should investigate to find out why it didn't deliver the expected results and then outline actions for further improvement. Then, either way, you would go about repeating the whole loop again, as shown in figure 11.2.

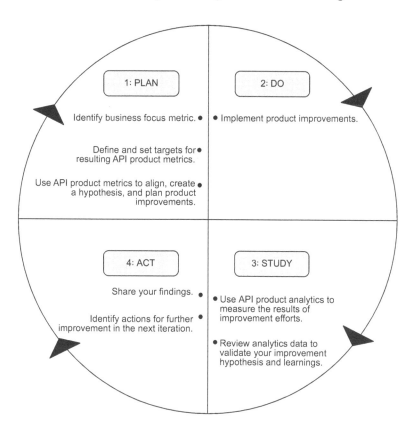

Figure 11.2
API product
improvements
as PDSA cycle

This iterative PDSA cycle highlights the importance of API product analytics. Being able to capture quantitative data to use to validate or disprove a product improvement hypothesis is key to building successful API products. But before discussing API product metrics in detail, let's discuss a concept that provides a guide on where exactly to track those metrics—the developer journey map.

11.1.2   *The developer journey map*

Chapter 5 introduced user journey maps as a visualization of the process a user goes through when interacting with a product to fulfill a job (using Jobs to Be Done [JTBD] terminology). When a user fulfills a job they set out to do, that's the point when they indicate that your product benefits them. This is sometimes called a *value moment.* Collecting events or actions at these points helps you measure value.

API product managers treat developers integrating with the API as their primary users, and a variation of the user journey map is the developer journey map. It visualizes the path a developer takes from discovering your API product to integrating with it and operating production systems that depend on it. This usually involves the stages of *discovery, evaluation, build, production usage,* and *scaling* of the API product, with the job the developer is trying to fulfill at each stage depicted in figure 11.3.

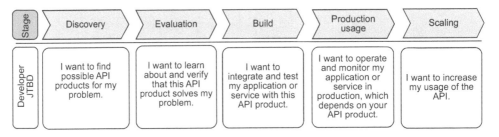

Figure 11.3   The beginning of a developer journey map, showing the job the developer seeks to fulfill at each stage

NOTE   These are the stages used for examples in this book, but for your organization, you can create stages that more closely reflect how your organization sees the developer journey.

The map also includes *developer touchpoints* for each stage. The touchpoints are interactions the developer has with your API product. These are the points at which you can implement API product metrics to measure the experience and performance of the API product from the customer's perspective.

The developer journey map helps API product managers and developer relations professionals gain insights into the API experience from the developer's perspective. Figure 11.4 shows an example developer journey map showing the developer touchpoints.

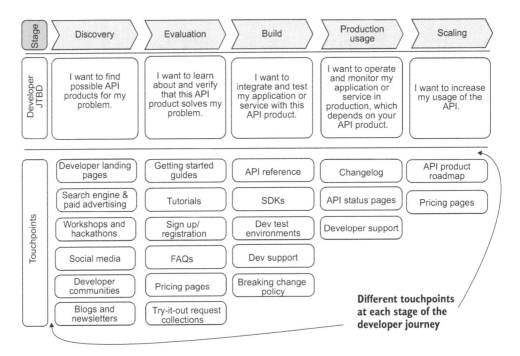

Figure 11.4   Extending the developer journey map with touchpoints

It's important to note that API product managers aim to get developers from the left to the right side of the map as quickly and with as little friction as possible. As a way to sell or increase the adoption of an API product, some API product managers aim to get developers to try the API so they can experience the value the API delivers and thus turn developers into enthusiastic advocates of the API product to their management and procurement teams. This approach to growing the usage of an API product is called developer-first adoption or a developer-first approach.

> ### Developer-first and developer-plus adoption
> Some organizations build products primarily targeted at developers and market the product using a developer-first approach—they get developers to adopt and use the product in a low-cost, low-friction way, then upsell later. Other organizations build products primarily targeted at businesses or consumers. But these products may have an aspect of the product (e.g., an API) made available to developers. They use a developer-plus approach and try to engage developers as partners, for example, by getting them to build an app for their API or engaging them through a marketplace. Some organizations are a hybrid of these. These different approaches mean API product managers may use different strategies for driving developer adoption. For more on this, see *Developer Relations: How to Build and Grow a Successful Developer Program* by Caroline Lewko and James Parton (Apress, 2021).

As mentioned, when the developer fulfills their intended job at each stage of the developer journey, that is the point in time when your product has brought value to them. At that point, you can capture API product metrics to measure the value delivered and also track how they contribute to the focus metric set by management. In the following section, we'll discuss API product metrics and how they are categorized.

11.1.3 API product metrics

In *API Analytics for Product Managers* (Pakt Publishing, 2021), Deepa Goyal outlines six API product metric categories that product managers track: *discovery metrics, engagement metrics, acquisition metrics, activation metrics, retention metrics,* and *experience metrics.* As mentioned in section 11.1.1, these API product metrics are action metrics that contribute to (and are thus leading indicators of) the focus metric set by management. In the following sections, I discuss some of the metrics under these categories, but note that this isn't meant to be an exhaustive list.

> **NOTE** In the following discussion, the term *prospects* or *users* refers to developers, and *end users* refers to consumers who use the applications built by developers that integrate with APIs. As I mentioned, API product managers treat developers as their primary users. Even though developers may build apps used by end users, for the purpose of API product metrics, we're classing all API calls made from the app they build (and its associated API key) as coming from that developer user, regardless of the number of end users using the app.

DISCOVERY METRICS

Discovery metrics track the performance of the marketing channels that API product managers use to make prospects aware of your API product. Examples of these channels include search engines, developer landing pages, social media, API marketplaces, and so on. Discovery metrics are usually implemented with web analytics tools (e.g., Google Analytics and Mixpanel) on developer landing pages in the developer portal. Examples of discovery metrics include the following:

- The number of *unique visitors* to the developer landing pages per day, week, or month
- The number *of page views* on developer landing pages.
- The number of *referrals from different traffic sources* (or developer account sign-ups by referral channel) as a measure of which marketing channels are most effective in getting developers to discover the API

TIP   Consider using web analytics tools (e.g., Google Analytics or Amplitude) on your developer portal to get continuous feedback on your user's experience. Some developer portals, such as Readme, have analytics features built in. (https://mng.bz/d6GD). If you publish collections to Postman public workspaces or to the Postman API network, this also has built-in analytics features to help you gather metrics on your API adoption. You can see the number of times users have viewed your collection, how many times your collection has been forked, and how many times API requests were made from your forked collection (see https://mng.bz/rVQg for more information).

One thing to mention here is vanity metrics. A *vanity metric* is one that doesn't help you understand the performance of the product in a way that informs future product improvements.

ENGAGEMENT METRICS

Engagement metrics measure how much interaction prospects have with your API documentation and developer portal tools as they learn about the API and find out if the API solves their problem. Again, these can be measured with web analytics tools. Examples include the following:

- The average time spent on the developer portal pages
- The *bounce rate* on the developer portal, that is, the fraction of visitors who see the landing pages or developer portal and then leave rather than continue to other pages on the site

ACQUISITION METRICS

The acquisitions metrics measure the number of developers signing up to use your API for the first time. After engaging with your API documentation, interested prospects would want to try out your API to better understand how it works. API providers have them sign up to indicate their interest and obtain an API key. This enables them to exercise the API in a sandbox environment. API providers can also provide web-based "try out" tools on the developer portal or a Postman collection to make this easy for the developer. Examples of acquisition metrics that API product managers track at this stage include the following:

- The number of new user sign-ups
- The time it takes a new user to make their first API call, which is called the *Time to First Call (TTFC)* or the *Time to First Hello World (TTFHW)*
- The number of users trying out your SDKs or a given version of your API (SDK and version adoption)

ACTIVATION METRICS

After evaluating or trying out your API, the developer may decide it solves their problem and want to use it in their application. Their next goal is to integrate their application with your API and deploy it to production. Activation metrics track this transition of evaluation users to active users:

- Every organization has a definition of what they consider to be an active user of their API. It can be as simple as the number of users using the API in production (as tracked by their use of a production API key or token) over a period of time. This is usually called the *daily active users (DAU), weekly active users (WAU),* or *monthly active users (MAU)* as the case may be. Note that because these developer users are represented by API keys, these metrics are also sometimes called daily active tokens (DAT), weekly active tokens (WAT), and monthly active tokens (MAT).
- Another important metric here is the time it takes for a user to make their first API call in a production environment. This is called the *Time to First Transaction (TTFT)* or *Time to First Production API Call.*
- For some organizations, simply making a production API call is insufficient. The user must use the API to complete a business transaction (or a number of transactions) representing significant value. This may involve multiple API calls. The time it takes to do this is the *Time to Value (TTV)*. For example, for an e-commerce API, this can be using the APIs to place orders exceeding a given average order size.

API RETENTION METRICS

Retention metrics show how much API consumers stay and use the product over a period of time. It's a measure of the loyalty or stickiness users have to a product. The opposite of retention is churn—the percentage of users who stop using the API:

- *Recurring usage*—This is a measure of the overall API call volume over a period of time. This can be daily, weekly, or monthly. Analyzing recurring usage for a user or a group of users (e.g., from the same company) helps identify trends in usage.

- *User retention*—This is a measure of how often users come back to use your API. This can be captured by tracking how often a user makes a repeat request to a given endpoint in the API in a 7-day or 30-day window. Users are placed in groups called cohorts according to the date of their first request. Then, the percentage of users in each cohort who make requests each day over the next 7 days or 30 days is tracked.

API EXPERIENCE METRICS

Experience metrics measure how satisfied customers are with the overall product experience of your API. Experience metrics include the following:

- *Total number of API consumers*—The consumers may be individual users or companies (where multiple users may belong to the same company). Your identity management system and authentication method should help you tie the authentication token used (e.g., an API key) back to the user. Knowing your API consumers can help you gain insights from their user profile, identify trends, and improve the user experience.
- *Top consumers by API usage*—These are your most successful users, and you can learn a lot from monitoring their usage patterns or interviewing them.
- *Conversion rate*—This is the fraction of the total users that "convert"—that is, reach some value goal set by the business.

After this whistle-stop tour of various API metrics, you can see that there are multiple metrics in each category. (And, as mentioned, this isn't an exhaustive list. You can even devise your own custom metrics.) To use these metrics, API product managers define which of these metrics to collect at different stages of the developer journey. This helps align improving the customer experience with achieving the business focus metric. Figure 11.5 shows an example of where these metrics can fall in a developer journey. The goal isn't to define every possible API metric—that can be overwhelming and should be avoided—but to use a small set of metrics in each category to help guide progress toward improving the business focus metric.

I've discussed how product analytics guide the product improvement cycle and how metrics can be captured at various stages of the developer journey. Now you'll experience a hands-on example of how to integrate an API product analytics tool into your API gateway and collect product metrics for a developer journey.

11.1.4 *Tracking metrics for the Product Catalog API*

Consider again the scenario presented in section 11.1. Management has set the goal to increase the number of users of the Product Catalog API by 10% in the next quarter, and you've been asked to set up API product metrics to track the current product performance and form the baseline for this improvement. For this scenario, imagine you've been asked to gather only metrics for the Evaluation, Build, and Production Usage stages of the developer journey. Walk through this example as follows.

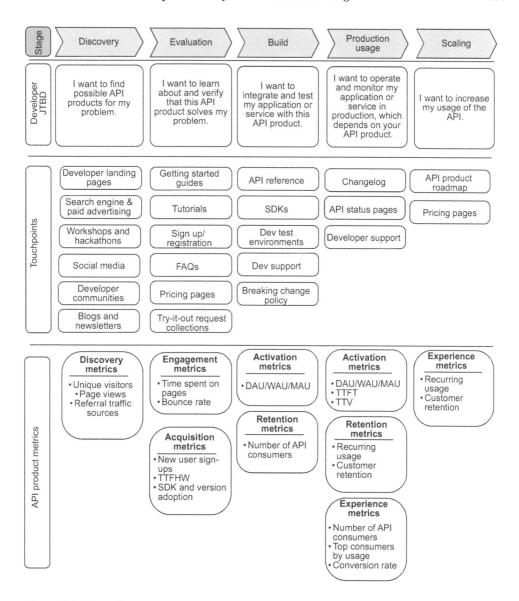

Figure 11.5 **Extending the developer journey map with API product metric categories**

First, define exactly what the metrics mean for the Product Catalog API. Imagine that the API team has discussed the business goal and come up with the product metrics to capture in the developer journey, as shown in figure 11.6.

The key metric that drives the business focus metric is the DAU—increasing the DAU should lead to an increase in the MAU. Note the definition of active users in the table—that is, one who makes an API call in production. But all the other six metrics contribute to help maintain the general health of the product. These metrics can be

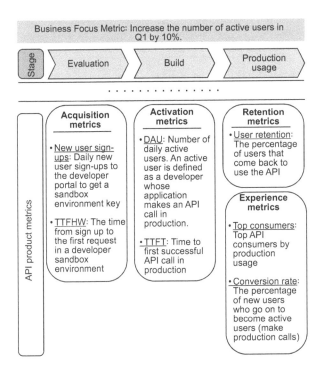

Figure 11.6   A section of the developer journey map showing how the API team has defined metrics they want to capture to drive improvements in the Product Catalog API

captured with API product analytic tools. These tools collect, analyze, and report on API experience and usage data. For this exercise, I'll show you how to use one such tool—Moesif.

Why Moesif?

Many observability and analytics tools are available in the market, including commercial and open source solutions. For example, Prometheus and Grafana are open source tools that are commonly used together to monitor and visualize metrics. Additionally, there are commercial solutions such as New Relic, Datadog, AppDynamics, and more.

In this chapter, I've used Moesif for the examples because it provides first-class support for API product analytics and comes with a set of predefined API analytics reports that are easy to use. Furthermore, it has excellent integration with the Kong API gateway that I've used in this book.

I'll begin by showing you how to capture the first acquisition metric—daily new user sign-ups.

NEW USER SIGN-UPS

With this metric, you want to see the trend of the total new sign-ups. Your improvement hypothesis can be that increasing new sign-ups should lead to an increase in active users. To set up this metric, you need to send an event to Moesif whenever a user signs up. You also need to set up a time series chart in Moesif to visualize and share the trend of daily sign-ups with your team.

One kind of event Moesif captures is a *user action*. A user action represents something a user has done using a user interface, for example, submitting a form or clicking a button. This is ideal for capturing when a developer signs up for a developer account on your developer portal and gets an API key. Moesif provides a collection of JavaScript client-side integration tools you can embed in your portal to help you with this.

To keep things simple for this example, however, I've provided a GitHub Action workflow file, .github/workflows/analytics.completed, to simulate the sign-up action. The workflow uses a script, `simulate-signups.js`, to simulate users signing up and getting an API key. It also sends a `Sign-Up` user action event to Moesif using Moesif's API (just like the client integration code would do). It then uses a `simulate-api-calls.js` script to simulate users making calls to the sandbox (with base path /sandbox) and production APIs (with base path /api) in the API gateway after they sign up (after a specified time period). Because of the Moesif integration with this instance of the Kong gateway, the gateway sends an API `Call` event to Moesif whenever it receives an API request. Figure 11.7 illustrates how this works.

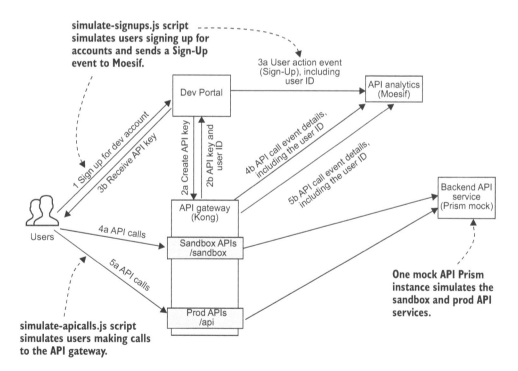

Figure 11.7   The workflow file simulates user sign-ups to a developer portal and API calls to the gateway. It sends the associated user action events and API call events to Moesif.

To use the workflow file, first disable any active workflows in your .github/workflows directory, for example, by renaming their file suffix from .yaml to .disabled. Then rename the .github/workflows/analytics.completed workflow file to .github/workflows/analytics.yaml, and commit your changes. GitHub Actions detects the workflow file and executes it.

> **NOTE** Your workflow file should run, but if you have any problems, check that the following scripts are executable: `chapter11/stop_kong.sh`, `chapter11/start_kong.sh`, `chapter11/simulate-signups.js`, `chapter11/configure-routes.sh`, `chapter11/restart_kong.sh`, and `chapter11/simulate-apicalls.js`. (On Unix-like systems, you can run `chmod +x <filename>`.) The simulation script for this example takes about 15 minutes to run in the pipeline and creates TTFHW and TTFT values in minutes. In a real-world scenario, these values would be in days, weeks, or months.

Now log in to Moesif to create a dashboard to see the signed-up users and the trend. First, create a dashboard in Moesif to save the reports you create. Go to New > Dashboard, and enter the name `ProductCatalogDashboard`. Then, click on the Add button to save it, as shown in figure 11.8.

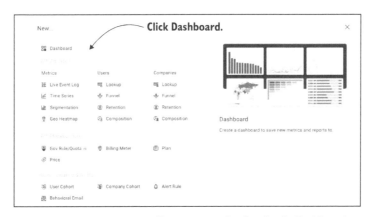

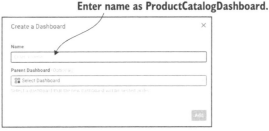

Figure 11.8   Creating a dashboard to save your analytics reports

Create a report that shows all events you send to Moesif. Click on New > Metrics > Live Event Log. The report you see shows a stream of events Moesif has received, including details of the user ID and event time, as shown in figure 11.9. Save the report with the name Event Log by clicking on the Save button on the top left of the page. If you don't see the report show up under ProductCatalogDashboard on the left menu, reload the page.

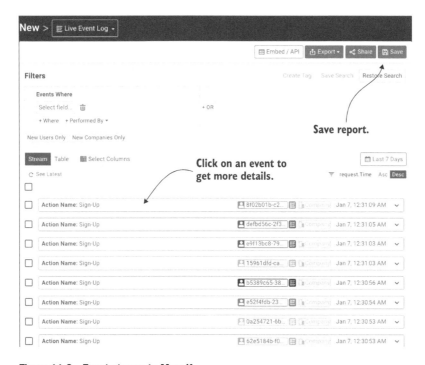

Figure 11.9   Event stream to Moesif

Create a report to display sign-ups by clicking on New > Metrics > Time Series. In the Filters section under Events Where, set up a filter where the Action Name is Sign-Up, as shown in figure 11.10.

Click the bar button to render the data as a bar chart, as shown in figure 11.11. The report shows the trend of sign-ups over the past few days, with eight users signing up on the day you ran the script.

Now save the report with the name Daily New User Sign-ups under the Product-CatalogDashboard.

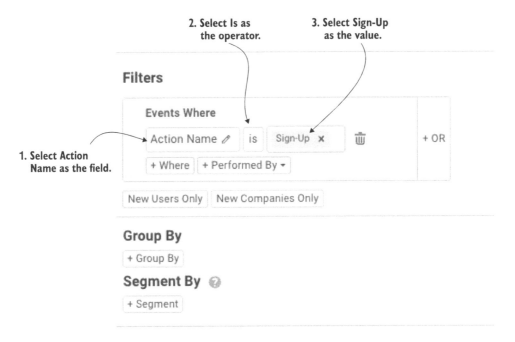

Figure 11.10   Creating a time series report to view new user sign-ups in Moesif

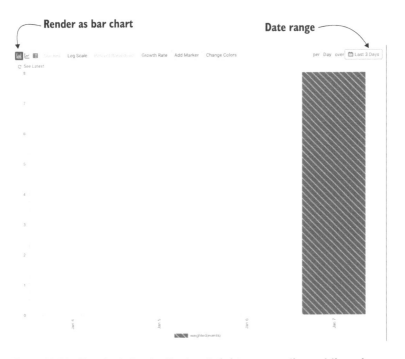

Figure 11.11   Bar chart showing the trend of sign-ups over the past three days

Create a report to show the details of the users who signed up. In Moesif, this is called a *Lookup* report. Go to New > Users > Lookup. In the Users Where filter, select Created Is After 1 Day Ago, as shown in figure 11.12.

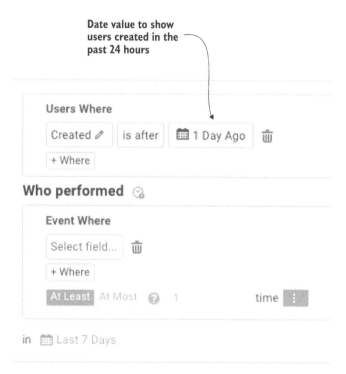

Date value to show users created in the past 24 hours

Users Where

Created 🖉   is after   📅 1 Day Ago   🗑

\+ Where

Who performed 🔍

Event Where

Select field... 🗑

\+ Where

At Least   At Most   ❓   1   time   ⋮

in 📅 Last 7 Days

Figure 11.12   Report criteria for the report on recently signed-up users

This generates a report showing the eight users who signed up, as shown in figure 11.13. Save this view under the ProductCatalogDashboard with the name New User Sign-ups in Last 24 hours by clicking the Save button at the top right.

You've now seen how to capture the trend of new user sign-ups. Next, you'll see how to capture the other acquisition metric—TTFHW.

TIME TO FIRST HELLO WORLD

Moesif works out the TTFHW as the difference between the time a user is created on the Moesif platform (in this case, when the user signs up) and when the user makes their first API call. As I mentioned earlier, the Kong instance you're running has the Moesif Kong plugin installed. The simulation workflow makes a small number of random API requests to the sandbox environment (with path /sandbox) for six of the eight users who signed up. That is, two users signed up but never made an API call. To view the TTFHW metric in Moesif, go to the New User Sign-ups in the Last 24 Hours dashboard you created. Look at the ttfhw_s column. You can see that it's populated

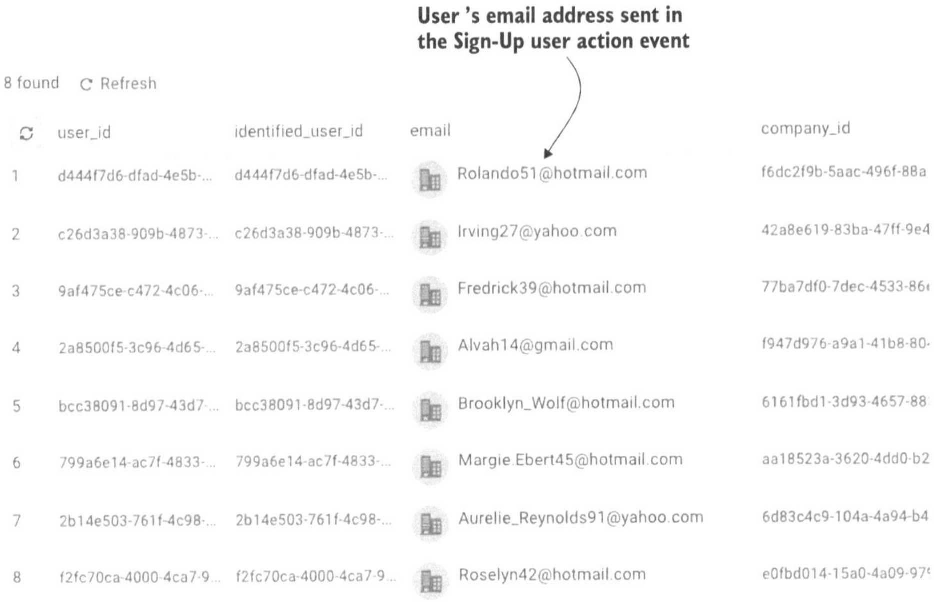

User's email address sent in
the Sign-Up user action event

	user_id	identified_user_id	email	company_id
1	d444f7d6-dfad-4e5b-...	d444f7d6-dfad-4e5b-...	Rolando51@hotmail.com	f6dc2f9b-5aac-496f-88a
2	c26d3a38-909b-4873-...	c26d3a38-909b-4873-...	Irving27@yahoo.com	42a8e619-83ba-47ff-9e4
3	9af475ce-c472-4c06-...	9af475ce-c472-4c06-...	Fredrick39@hotmail.com	77ba7df0-7dec-4533-86(
4	2a8500f5-3c96-4d65-...	2a8500f5-3c96-4d65-...	Alvah14@gmail.com	f947d976-a9a1-41b8-80-
5	bcc38091-8d97-43d7-...	bcc38091-8d97-43d7-...	Brooklyn_Wolf@hotmail.com	6161fbd1-3d93-4657-88
6	799a6e14-ac7f-4833-...	799a6e14-ac7f-4833-...	Margie.Ebert45@hotmail.com	aa18523a-3620-4dd0-b2
7	2b14e503-761f-4c98-...	2b14e503-761f-4c98-...	Aurelie_Reynolds91@yahoo.com	6d83c4c9-104a-4a94-b4
8	f2fc70ca-4000-4ca7-9...	f2fc70ca-4000-4ca7-9...	Roselyn42@hotmail.com	e0fbd014-15a0-4a09-97(

8 found   ↻ Refresh

Figure 11.13   Details of recently signed-up users

with the TTFHW value, as shown in figure 11.14. Because you didn't send API requests
for three of the users, they have no TTFHW value, so they show up as N/A.

Time to First
Hello World value

company_id	name	first_seen_time	last_seen_time	ttfhw_s
f6dc2f9b-5aac-496f-88a5-6898aa1185b1	Rolando Casper	12/30/2023, 4:49:05 PM	12/30/2023, 4:49:05 PM	N/A
42a8e619-83ba-47ff-9e45-92a3c52386b3	Irving Schumm	12/30/2023, 4:49:05 PM	12/30/2023, 4:49:05 PM	N/A
77ba7df0-7dec-4533-86e4-e50dd3666298	Fredrick Hermann	12/30/2023, 4:48:37 PM	12/30/2023, 4:57:07 PM	10 minutes
f947d976-a9a1-41b8-804d-2353b583187d	Alvah Conn	12/30/2023, 4:48:37 PM	12/30/2023, 4:57:07 PM	10 minutes
6161fbd1-3d93-4657-8837-f5b096199cee	Brooklyn Wolf	12/30/2023, 4:48:37 PM	12/30/2023, 4:57:07 PM	10 minutes
aa18523a-3620-4dd0-b207-ee817ab71790	Margie Ebert	12/30/2023, 4:48:29 PM	12/30/2023, 4:52:38 PM	4 minutes
6d83c4c9-104a-4a94-b4a0-2d074cd59fab	Aurelie Reynolds	12/30/2023, 4:48:28 PM	12/30/2023, 4:52:38 PM	4 minutes
e0fbd014-15a0-4a09-9799-d2a9da713975	Roselyn Sauer	12/30/2023, 4:48:28 PM	12/30/2023, 4:52:38 PM	4 minutes

Figure 11.14   TTFHW value on the lookup report for recently signed-up users

You've seen the TTFHW for individual users. But what if you wanted to see the average TTFHW metric across all users who signed up? You can see this by creating a *user funnel* that shows what percentage of users who signed up went on to make an API call and what their average TTFHW metric was. User funnel analysis is a way to visualize and understand the user behaviors and obstacles in the user journey.

Create a TTFHW user funnel as follows. Click on New > Users > Funnel. Set up a Stage 1 criteria called Signed Up, having events where Action Name Is Sign-Up. Set up a Stage 2 criteria called First API Request, having events where Event Type Is API Call and where request.segments.0 Is Sandbox. Figure 11.15 shows how this should look.

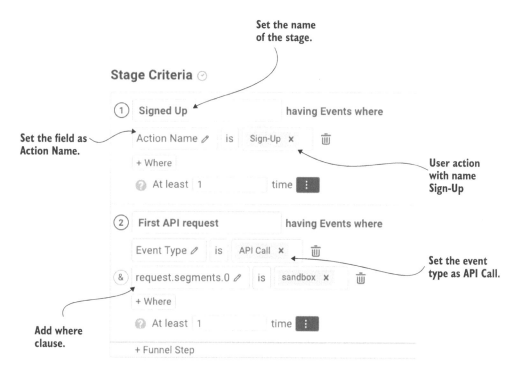

Figure 11.15   Setting the criteria for TTFHW funnel analysis

With these criteria set, a funnel analysis chart like figure 11.16 appears. (Note that new events may take up to 10 minutes to show up on the funnel chart.) For my example run in figure 11.16, it shows that only 75% of the users (six out of eight—remember that in the simulation, not all users sent requests after signing up) went on to make API calls after getting their API key. In addition, the average time it took for these requests is 6 minutes 19 seconds.

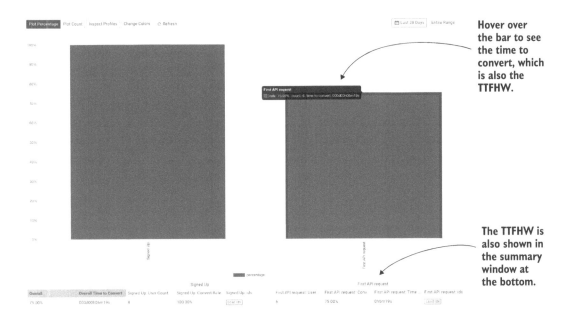

Hover over
the bar to see
the time to
convert, which
is also the
TTFHW.

The TTFHW is
also shown in
the summary
window at
the bottom.

Figure 11.16 In this example run, the TTFHW for the group of six users who went on to make API calls after signing up is 6 minutes 19 seconds.

Save your view with the name `User Funnel Analysis` under the ProductCatalogDash-board. Let's review. I've shown you how to build views for two Activation stage metrics—new user sign-ups and TTFHW. Now I'll show you how to create views for the next stage of the developer journey—Activation.

DAILY ACTIVE USERS (DAU)

Recall that the team defined an active user as one that makes an API call in the production environment. For this example, calls to the production environment have an `/api` base path. To measure the number of daily active users, you need to create a time series chart showing the unique users who make calls to production URIs. The simulation script sends production API requests for only three of the users.

Now head over to your Moesif account to create a view for DAU. Click on New > Metrics > Time Series. Create a filter where Event Type Is API Call, and Requests > URI Segment > 0 (i.e., request.segment.0 is Api). In the Metrics box, change the metric from Event Count to Uniques > Unique Users. Figure 11.17 shows how your criteria should look.

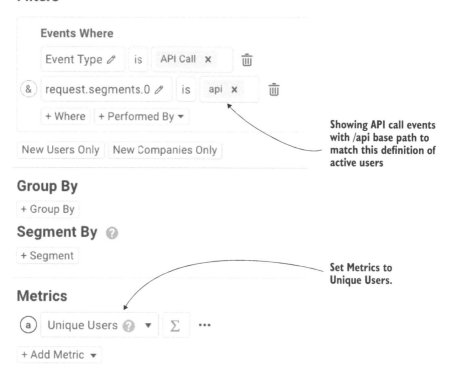

Figure 11.17 DAU criteria to show active users as those making API calls with an `/api`
base path

The resulting chart shows the number of unique users who have made requests to production. Click on the histogram icon to display the chart that way. As expected, you
should see three active users. Figure 11.18 shows how it looked for my run.

Now save the view with the name `Daily Active Users (DAU)` under the Product-
CatalogDashboard.

You've seen the trend of active production users. Next, you'll visualize the second
activation metric—the time to the first transaction in production.

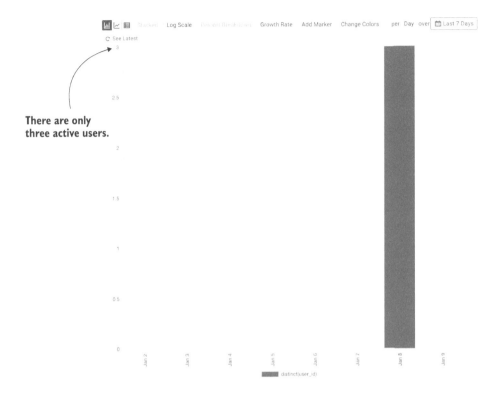

There are only
three active users.

Figure 11.18   Example DAU time series chart

TIME TO FIRST TRANSACTION (TTFT)

Recall that for this example, the team has defined TTFT as the time taken for the first API call in production. You can update your funnel analysis view to display this.

Go to the User Funnel Analysis report you created earlier. Add a new funnel step to show the production call stage by clicking on + Funnel Step. Give the new step the name First Production Call. Set the criteria for this as request.segment.0 Is Api, as shown in figure 11.19, and save your view.

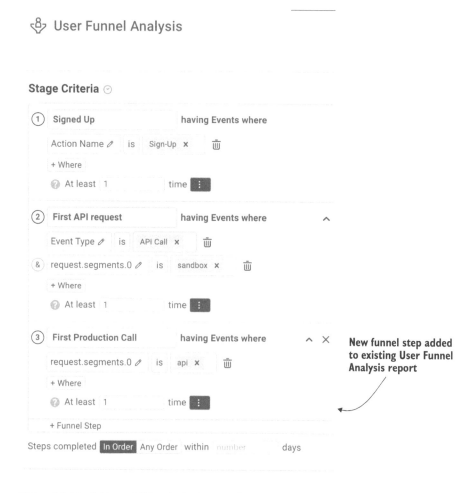

⚓ User Funnel Analysis

Figure 11.19   Add an additional criteria step, First Production Call, to the User Funnel Analysis report to update it to show the TTFT value.

For my run, this displays a chart, as shown in figure 11.20. By hovering over the First Production Call bar, you can see that the TTFT is 12 minutes.

Next, let's set up the user retention metrics for the Retention stage.

USER RETENTION

This metric tells you what percentage of your users come back to use your API over time. To set up a daily user retention report, click on New > Users > Retention. For the Event Criteria, set the First Event and the Returning Event to Event Type Is API Call. Figure 11.21 shows how these criteria should look.

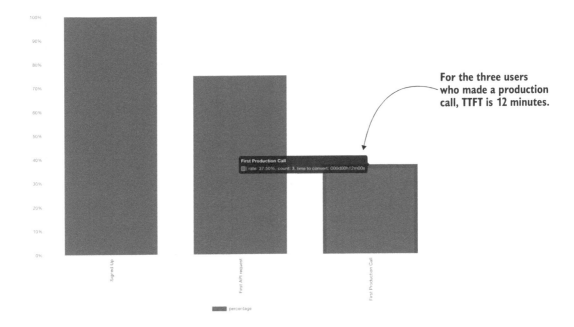

For the three users who made a production call, TTFT is 12 minutes.

Figure 11.20   Updating the User Funnel Analysis chart to show the TTFT

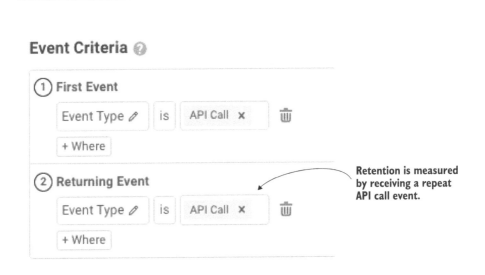

Retention is measured by receiving a repeat API call event.

Figure 11.21   Setting the user retention chart criteria

For my run, this displays a chart, as shown in figure 11.22. Because there have been no repeat calls after the first day, the retention rate drops to zero by day one (where day zero is the day the first request for a user was received).

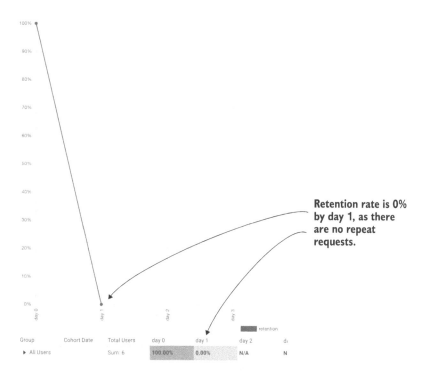

Figure 11.22   User retention chart

Save this view with the name Daily User Retention under ProductCatalogDashboard.

> **TIP**   To see an example user retention chart with data over several days, you can take a look at one of the demo applications. At the top left of your screen, switch from your account to Moesif Demos > SaaS. Then, on the displayed Product—E-sign API dashboard—click on the Daily User Retention report.

Next, let's move on to the Experience metrics—conversion rate and top API users by production usage.

CONVERSION RATE

The team has defined the conversion rate as the percentage of users who go on to become active, that is, make production API calls. You can see this value by going back to your User Funnel Analysis view shown in figure 11.23. As you can see from the table at the bottom of the figure, the conversion rate is 37.5%. That is, 37.5% of users who sign up go on to make an API call in production.

Figure 11.23   The User Funnel Analysis report shows the conversion rate of users who make a production API call.

NOTE   In practice, what the business considers as the conversion criteria depends on the business model and API monetization strategy. For a discussion on different monetization, billing, and packaging strategies for APIs, see *API Strategy for Decision Makers: Growing Your Product Through Customer Observability* by Mike Amundsen and Derric Grilling (2022, O'Reilly Media).

Next, I'll discuss the last metric—the top API users.

TOP API USERS BY PRODUCTION USAGE

You can see who the top users are for each environment by creating a Segmentation chart. Go to New > Metrics > Segmentation. To capture API calls in the production environment only, set the filter to Event Type Is API Call and request.segments.0 to Api. To group requests by users, update the Group By field to User.User Name, and set it to show the top five terms (in this case, usernames) only. Set the Metrics box to Event Count. Your criteria should look like figure 11.24.

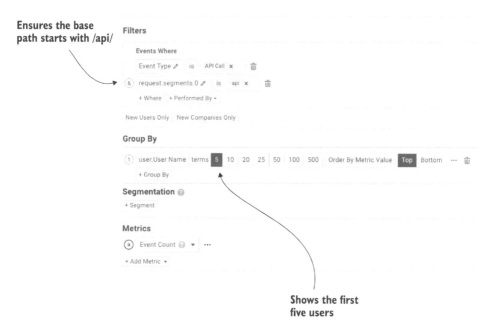

Figure 11.24   Criteria to show the top five API users in production criteria based on the number of API calls they make

Even though I've set the criteria to show the top five users, there are only API requests from three users in production. I can see my biggest users are Roselyn Sauer, with 18 API calls, and Margie Ebert, with 15 calls, as shown in figure 11.25.

Save this chart as Top Users in Production. You have now set up seven metrics to track the developer journey and provide your team and management with information to measure the performance of the product.

In this exercise, you've only used a small number of data points. To see more types of analytics charts, Moesif comes with a collection of demo apps. You can switch to them and view their preset dashboards by clicking on your username at the top left of the screen and selecting Moesif Demos from the drop-down.

So far, I've discussed product performance metrics. Next, we'll discuss technical performance metrics to detect and diagnose technical problems with the API.

11.2   API monitoring metrics

Your Product Catalog API is running in production. Imagine that it has a serious performance problem and is returning unexpected errors or has become very slow. How will your team get notified of this? What should they check first to determine what has gone wrong? For this, you need to set up API monitoring for technical performance metrics.

When discussing DevOps practices in chapter 1, you learned that monitoring is about having predefined metrics, dashboards, and alerting to enable teams to understand the

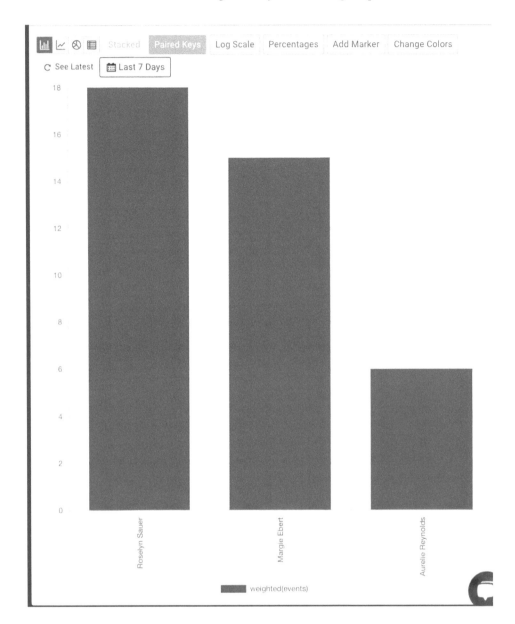

Figure 11.25   Top API users by usage

internal state of their systems. Monitoring gives teams visibility of their API's health using event data to help them diagnose and fix problems.

There are a lot of technical metrics around the performance, usage, and reliability that you can capture of applications and services. These fall into two categories—infrastructure metrics and service-level metrics.

Infrastructure metrics include hardware and software infrastructure components on which applications and services run. These include metrics on CPU utilization, memory, disk input/output (I/O), queues, network utilization and bandwidth usage, database connections, and so on. Service-level metrics relate to the health of individual applications or services. This includes latency, error rate, throughput, uptime, and so on.

However, without a clear strategy, the number of metrics can be overwhelming. To focus on the important metrics, you can depend on some popular site reliability engineering (SRE) monitoring formulas. These include the *Four Golden Signals*, the *RED method* (which measures request rate, error rate, and duration), and the *USE method*. In this book, I discuss the RED method, as it's particularly aimed at microservice architectures.

Other SRE monitoring formulas

While I discuss the RED method in the next section, it's useful to get an overview of other SRE monitoring formulas. One popular one for physical server components (e.g., CPUs and disks) is the USE method, which stands for the following:

- *Utilization*—The average time a resource is busy
- *Saturation*—The degree of queued work a resource can't service
- *Errors*—The number of errors the resource has

Brendan Gregg's article "The USE Method" (www.brendangregg.com/usemethod .html) discusses this method in more detail.

Another popular formula is the Four Golden Signals. Also called the LETS method, it measures the following metrics for user-facing systems:

- *Latency*—The time taken to serve a request.
- *Traffic*—The amount of demand on a system (e.g., HTTP requests per second).
- *Errors*—The rate of request failure (e.g., the number of failed HTTP requests per second).
- *Saturation*—How full or constrained a service is in relation to its current load. Saturation identifies what the key resource constraint is—that is, the resource you can't easily increase. For example, this could be CPU or network bandwidth.

The Four Golden Signals method originated at Google, and you can find more discussion on the method in *Site Reliability Engineering: How Google Runs Production Systems* (O'Reilly, 2021).

A variation of the Four Golden Signals method is STELA, which adds one more metric to the LETS formula—availability. Availability is the degree to which a service is operational and accessible for use. It's often measured in terms of "nines"—a system with "Three nines" availability (99.9%) means that it's down for no more than 8.76 hours in a year.

11.2.1 RED metrics

The RED method is a monitoring philosophy for microservices architectures. It originated at Weaveworks and focuses on three key metrics for every service, as discussed in the following subsections.

REQUEST RATE

Also called throughput, this is a utilization metric that measures the number of requests an API can process in a given time window. You can measure this for short time durations, such as per second or per minute, but you can also measure the volume of requests over longer durations, such as per week or per month. This helps you understand the usage trends and patterns being placed on the API.

ERROR RATES

Also called failure rates, this refers to the number of failed requests in a given time window (e.g., errors per second or errors per minute). Here, you want to track HTTP 4xx errors (user errors) and 5xx errors (server-side errors). Getting information on the context of the problem is important. For example, getting a large number of 401 Unauthorized errors for a particular geographic region (by displaying errors on a geographic heatmap) may indicate a malicious actor or bots in action. Information in your application logs can help you understand which infrastructure or application component is causing a 5xx error and why. You should also have alerts that fire to notify the API team when the error rate exceeds a given threshold.

DURATION/REQUEST LATENCY

This is the time it takes to complete an API request—that is, the time it takes from when a request is made by the user to when the user receives the response. Request latency is important because high latency means a slow response time for the user and a poor user experience.

Request latency is usually measured at the gateway level in a microservice architecture. But showing just the average latency of requests across all endpoints can hide poorly performing endpoints. Therefore, it's useful to show a breakdown of latencies per endpoint and also present data as percentiles, as shown in figure 11.26.

> **NOTE** A percentile is a way to separate a certain percentage of the values in a dataset from the others. For example, if the 90th percentile of just below 250 ms API latencies in a particular API latency dataset is 250 ms, it means that 90% of the API requests take 250 ms or less, and 10% of the requests take more than 250 ms.

When measuring API latency, it's useful to do it from the point of view of users in different geographic locations. This ensures that you capture all the components involved, including TCP connect time, SSL handshake, DNS lookup, and the backed server processing time. There are various API monitoring tools (e.g., APIMetrics [https://apimetrics.io]) that offer the ability to measure latency from multiple cloud data centers across the world.

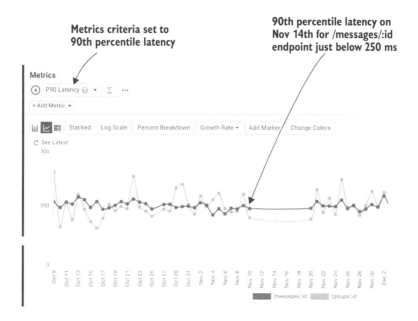

Figure 11.26   Example latency chart in Moesif, tracing the 90th percentile latency of two endpoints `/messages/:id` **and** `/groups/id`

I've discussed the RED method as a handy formula for measuring the performance of your API. But before rounding off the discussion on metrics, I want to mention one important constraint you should set on your APIs—rate limits.

11.2.2   Rate limits

Rate limiting is a way to restrict the number of requests that a consumer can make to an API. As discussed in chapter 9, rate limits help protect the API from excess traffic and certain types of attacks. Rate limits ensure that all users have fair access to the API and that users have a consistent and predictable experience. In *API Traffic Management* (O'Reilly Media, 2019), Mike Amundsen mentions that rate limits are sometimes called the *saturation point* to indicate that it's the rate at which the system can successfully process requests.

Based on the duration of the limit, rate limits can be classified into short-term limits and long-term API quotas. Short-term rate limits are set to protect API servers from being overloaded by traffic spikes. (Some gateways, e.g., Apigee, use the term *spike arrest* for this.) They are measured by counting the number of requests from a given IP address or API key in a short time window. This can be the number of requests per second or requests per minute. An example of a time series chart showing the number of requests per minute and a marker or the rate limit is shown in figure 11.27. This chart can help an API team quickly see when the rate limit is exceeded. If the API gateway has a rate limit feature enabled, requests after the rate limit has been exceeded receive a 429 Too Many Requests response status code.

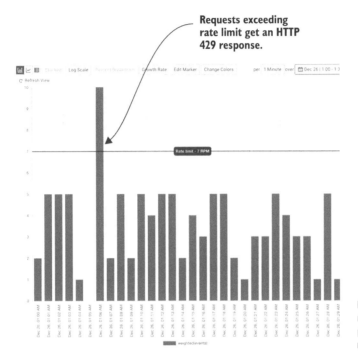

Figure 11.27   Time series report showing requests per minute and a rate limit marker

Long-term API quotas measure longer duration customer utilization of an API (e.g., in hours, days, or months) to check compliance with contract terms and monetization goals. For example, a customer can be allocated a quota of 10,000 requests per month based on the API product package they are subscribed to. Long-term API quotas are useful for usage-based billing. The customer success team can send the customer an email to notify them of their usage and the need to upgrade to the next API package. API quotas are also useful for blocking intentional misuse from automated processes that use excessive API requests, such as scrapers or spam messages.

11.2.3   Monitoring tools

You now know about the technical API metrics you can measure. Next, I want to touch on the tools you use to measure them.

Based on how they are deployed, monitoring tools fall into two categories—agent-basted monitoring tools and agentless monitoring tools. *Agent-based monitoring tools* require a lightweight software monitoring agent installed on the target system to read monitoring data, relay the data to the monitoring tool, and inject commands from the monitoring tool into the system being monitored. Moesif is an example of an agent-based monitoring tool. *Agentless monitoring tools* read monitoring data using network protocols such as SMTP, SSH, application-specific APIs, or built-in monitoring agents to track the health of the target system. That is, they don't require the installation of a third-party software agent on the target system. Some API gateways such as Apigee come with built-in API monitoring features, but you can also integrate them with third-party monitoring tools by installing the relevant agent.

As I mentioned earlier, there are a vast number of proprietary monitoring tools, including AWS CloudWatch, New Relic, Datadog, and Moesif, to name a few. Prometheus (https://prometheus.io) is a popular open source event monitoring and alerting tool that collects and stores time series data. It's often hooked up to Grafana (https://grafana.com), an open source analytics and data visualization tool for building dashboards.

11.2.4 Alerting and synthetic monitoring

API monitoring keeps you updated on any unusual activities or patterns occurring within your API. Examples of these events include sudden traffic spikes or increased API latency. As part of your API monitoring, you should create alerts that will be triggered when specific events occur. Your alerts will be based on preset rules, such as the occurrence of multiple 5xx error responses from your API. You can configure the alerts to notify you through various channels such as SMS, Slack, PagerDuty, and so on.

Another important aspect of monitoring is synthetic monitoring. This is about proactively monitoring the availability, performance, and functionality of your API by simulating user behavior in a controlled environment. Simulations can be set up with scripts or automated tests that mimic common user interactions with the API. For example, this can cover authenticating with the API and performing some common API requests. Synthetic monitoring should be performed at regular intervals in the day, ideally from various locations around the world (e.g., using cloud data centers in different geographic regions) to test the performance and availability of the API. Synthetic monitoring allows the organization to proactively detect problems with the user experience before real users are effected.

Many observability platforms (e.g., New Relic, AppDynamics, and Datadog) have synthetic monitoring features, but there are also specialized services such as Checkly (www.checklyhq.com) that do this.

11.2.5 Service level indicators, service level objectives, and service level agreements

Before finishing this discussion on API monitoring, I want to mention some important service measurement concepts that SREs use when discussing the performance of services: service level indicators (SLI), service level objectives (SLO), and service level agreements (SLAs). An SLI is a quantitative measure of some aspect of a service used to measure its health. Metrics such as latency, server error rate, and throughput can serve as SLIs. SLIs are important because they are the agreed measure of how well the service is performing.

SLIs are often used in conjunction with SLOs and SLAs. An SLO is the target value or goal that a service provider sets for an SLI. It's the threshold for that metric that a service should not break. An example of a latency SLO is achieving 500 ms latency or less for 99% of requests to an endpoint in a seven-day time period. SLAs, on the other hand, are formal contract agreements with customers for meeting the SLI targets.

> **TIP** Another related concept to the SLO is the *error budget*, which you can think of as the number of server errors your API is allowed to accumulate in a given period of time before your users start being unhappy. Discussion of this is out of the scope of this book, but you can find more information on this in *Establishing SRE Foundations: A Step-by-Step Guide to Introducing Site Reliability Engineering in Software Delivery Organizations* by Vladyslav Ukis (Addison-Wesley Professional, 2022). In addition, for more on SLAs for APIs, see the article "Pattern: Service Level Agreement" at https://mng.bz/x2e8.

The SLIs and SLOs for your API should be set from the customer's perspective and should be the basis of setting up your monitoring and alerts. But you should also evolve your SLIs and SLOs as your API product and its user experience evolves.

11.3 *Wrapping it up*

You've learned in this book that automating API product development is about the end-to-end automation of your API development workflow using GitOps and DevOps principles. You've looked at how to apply automation at various stages of your workflow, from design to development, deployment and testing, publishing, and operation. You've also seen conceptual tools such as the A3 that give you a framework for applying improvements, measuring the effects of improvements, and learning from them.

> **TIP** The field of API development workflow automation and automated governance is constantly evolving. If you would like to keep updated on the latest techniques, tools, and industry trends on automating your API development workflow, sign up for my newsletter at https://ikenna.co.uk/newsletter.

Using these techniques, you can continuously improve your API delivery workflow to improve your lead time and quality metrics. As I mentioned in chapter 2, start by mapping out your workflow and then look for areas of improvement. Then, use the techniques in this book to apply automation.

Summary

- API product metrics provide a basis for decision-making and benchmarking API product improvement goals.
- A developer journey map visualizes the process that developers go through to discover and use your API. Drawing a developer journey map helps you define the important product metrics to capture at each stage in order to paint a picture of the developer experience.

- Using an API product analytics tool helps you capture, visualize, and share important product metrics with your team. These product metrics include new user sign-ups, TTFHW, DAU, TTFT, user retention, conversion rate, and top API consumers.

- The RED method is a popular monitoring formula that can be applied to API technical performance monitoring. It captures the request rate, error rate, and duration.

- Rate limits indicate the saturation point of your API, and you should set them to protect your API from excessive usage that can lead to a poor user experience.

- To set monitoring and alerting, you need to define the SLOs for your API.

appendix A
Value stream
mapping icons

This appendix lists the value stream mapping (VSM) icons you can use for your process mapping. Feel free to complement these with any other icons you create to help you tell the story of how work and information flow in your stream, but make sure you define what they mean. Process mapping is an art, not a science, and it's important to present a shared understanding of the flow of work in the process along with data. Remember to keep it simple and unambiguous.

Table A.1   Value stream mapping icons

Icon	Represents	Description
Customer	Sources outside the process	External and internal customers and suppliers to the process
Design API / Dev team	Process step	A step in the process where a task is executed. The top part is a description of the process step, preferably in verb–noun format. The bottom is the name of the team or role that performs the task.
%CA= 85% / TT= 4 hours	Data box	Used to record significant data about the process
Jira	Information system	The IT systems used to support information flow in the value stream
(arrow)	Manual information flow	Flow of information between information systems and people. The arrow head shows the direction of flow.

Table A.1   Value stream mapping icons *(continued)*

Icon	Represents	Description
	Automated information flow	Automated flow of information between information systems. The arrow head shows the direction of flow.
6 work tickets	Inventory	Partially completed work queued between process steps awaiting processing. Typically shown by work tickets in a backlog. The inventory count is written below the icon.
	Push system	Cross-hatched arrow icon used to show work being moved from one step in the process to the next without checking if the downstream step has capacity to receive it
	Withdrawal	A circular arrow used to show a downstream step pulling work from an upstream process or, usually, a supermarket
	Go-see scheduling	Adjusting work prioritization based on human monitoring of inventory levels
	Release	Releasing finished software to production for the customer
	Supermarket	A controlled inventory of components that upstream process can pull from when they need it to do their work

appendix B
Installing API linting and OpenAPI diff tools

This appendix guides you through installing the tools you need to run the examples in this book. To test your setup of the tools, check out the book's code repository at https://github.com/apiopsbook/apiops.

You can follow the instructions in this appendix to set up the tools you need on your machine. But if you're familiar with Docker, I also provide a Docker image with all the command-line tools installed in it. (You still need to follow the instructions for setting up the non–command-line interface [CLI] tools such as Visual Studio Code [VS Code], GitHub Copilot, and Anthropic Claude.) You can create the Docker container and attach to its terminal by running the following scripts:

```
git clone https://github.com/apiopsbook/apiops
cd apiops
./2_create_apiops_container.sh
./3_attach_to_apiops_container.sh
```

This attaches you to the container terminal, and you can access the book source files on your host machine by switching to the books-source folder as follows:

```
root@apiops-host:/#
root@apiops-host:/# cd book-source/
root@apiops-host:/book-source# ls -l
```

You can detach from the container terminal by using the `exit` command. But if you want to install the command-line tools on your computer, proceed with the instructions given next.

B.1 Installing Node.js

Node.js is an open source JavaScript runtime environment that runs on the V8 JavaScript engine outside the browser. Node Package Manager (NPM) is the standard package manager for Node.js and is included with the Node.js installation. To install Node.js, download and run an installer package for your operating system from https://nodejs.dev/en/download. You can verify your Node.js installation by running the following commands in your terminal:

```
node -v
npm -v
```

B.2 Installing Spectral

Spectral (https://github.com/stoplightio/spectral) is a JSON and YAML linter for OpenAPI and AsyncAPI definition files. You can install Spectral using npm:

```
$ npm install -g @stoplight/spectral-cli
```

For other methods of installing Spectral using Yarn, Docker, or native binaries, see the Stoplight website (https://mng.bz/v8yM).

To test your Spectral installation, in the appendix directory, run Spectral linting on a minimal API definition file using the basic Spectral OpenAPI ruleset. The minimal API definition file provided for this is valid but doesn't comply with three rule recommendations in Spectral's built-in Open API specification ruleset; hence it will raise warning messages showing you an example of how Spectral reports problems:

```
spectral lint minimal.oas.yaml
```

This results in the following output:

```
1:1  warning  oas3-api-servers  OpenAPI "servers" must be present
➥ and non-empty array.
 2:6  warning  info-contact       Info object must have "contact"
➥ object.    info
 2:6  warning  info-description  Info "description" must be present
➥ and non-empty string.  info
✗ 3 problems (0 errors, 3 warnings, 0 infos, 0 hints)
```

B.3 Installing Visual Studio Code

VS Code is a popular free editor from Microsoft. You can download and install VS Code from https://code.visualstudio.com/download. VS Code has a CLI, run with the code command, that enables you to open files, install extensions, and print diagnostic information through the command line. VS Code installations for Windows and Linux have the code CLI enabled on the path by default. You may need to manually add VS Code to your path for macOS. For instructions on how to do this, see https://mng.bz/ZEQm.

B.4   *Installing Spectral Visual Studio Code plugins*

The Spectral VS Code extension from Stoplight enables you to run Spectral linting in your editor as you edit your API definitions. You can specify if you want to be notified of linting problems as you type or as you save your file. To install via the VS code CLI, run the following:

```
code --install-extension stoplight.spectral
```

Alternatively, you can install it via the Visual Studio Marketplace by clicking the Install button (https://mng.bz/RZ1j).

B.5   *Installing the 42Crunch OpenAPI (Swagger) Editor*

The VS Code OpenAPI (Swagger) Editor plugin from 42Crunch enables you to edit OpenAPI definition files with IntelliSense, linting, schema enforcement, code navigation, and preview support. 42Crunch (https://42crunch.com) is a commercial API security platform. Apart from editing API definition files, this plugin provides the important feature of enabling you to run an API Security Audit on the 42Crunch platform.

You can install the plugin via the VS code CLI by running the following command:

```
code --install-extension 42Crunch.vscode-openapi
```

Alternatively, you can install it via the Visual Studio Marketplace by clicking the Install button (https://mng.bz/2Km8), or by searching directly for OpenAPI (Swagger) Editor in the Extensions view in your VS Code Activity bar. The marketplace link provides guidance on how to use the plugin to create new OpenAPI files, navigate OpenAPI definitions, preview OpenAPI definitions, and use IntelliSense.

The plugin also allows you to render an OpenAPI file. Click on the OpenAPI: Show Preview Using the Default Renderer button to see a preview of an API definition in Swagger UI format in the right pane.

You should set up the plugin to run a Security Audit on your files. You do this by clicking the purple 42c button in the upper-right corner. The first time you do this, you'll be asked to provide your email address so that 42Crunch can send you an access token (figure B.1). After you receive the token, you can paste it into the provided prompt in VS Code.

You can now click the purple OpenAPI: Perform Security Audit button at the top-right corner. This will scan your definition for vulnerabilities and show you a report similar to figure B.2.

B.6   *Installing jq and yq*

jq (https://jqlang.github.io/jq) is a handy JSON processor for filtering and transforming JSON. It takes a stream of JSON data as input, applies filtering and transformation logic, and produces an output. To install jq, you can use the relevant package

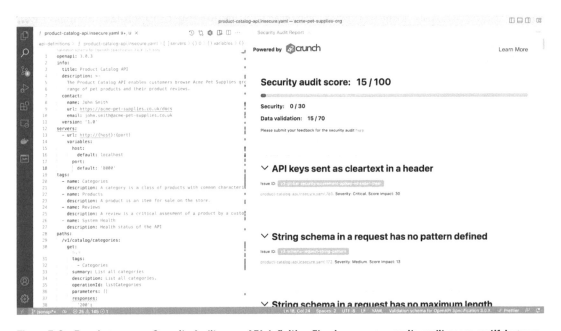

Figure B.1   Using the 42c button to run a Security Audit

Figure B.2   Running an open Security Audit on an API definition file gives you a security audit score, notifying you of possible vulnerabilities with your API definition file.

manager for your operating system. Mac users can run `brew install jq`. Windows users can install it with the Chocolatey package manager by running `choco install jq`. Finally, Ubuntu Linux users can run `sudo apt install -y jq`.

yq (https://github.com/mikefarah/yq) is a YAML, JSON, and XML processor, which can also be used for filtering and transforming structured data. You can also use it to convert YAML to JSON (and the other way around). It has a jq-like syntax. yq is written in Go.

You can install yq on macOS using brew with `brew install yq`; install it on Windows by running `choco install yq`, and install it on Linux via snap with `snap install yq`. For other installation options, see https://github.com/mikefarah/yq/#install.

You can test your yq installation by converting a test.yaml file to JSON with `yq -Poj test.yaml`. Convert a test.json file to YAML by running `yq -Poy test.json`.

B.7   Installing jpp

The jsonpath-cli (www.jsware.io/jsonpath-cli/) is a CLI for JSONPath Plus. You run it with the `jpp` command and can use it to transform and selectively extract data from JSON documents. You can install it with `npm`:

```
npm install -g @jsware/jsonpath-cli
```

Test your installation by running the `-h` flag to display usage options:

```
jpp -h
```

B.8   Installing Tufin/oasdiff

Tufin/oasdiff (https://github.com/Tufin/oasdiff) is a command-line OpenAPI 3.x diff tool. The examples in this book using Tufin/oasdiff are based on the 1.6.2 version of the tool. If you work on macOS, you can install Tufin/oasdiff with Homebrew:

```
brew tap tufin/homebrew-tufin
brew install oasdiff
```

Note that for this to work, you may first need Xcode Command Line Tools installed if you don't have it already. You can install this with `xcode-select -install`.

Tufin/oasdiff is written in Go, and if you have Go installed on your computer, you can also install it by running the following:

```
go install github.com/tufin/oasdiff@latest
```

It also has binaries available for Windows, Linux, and macOS. See https://github.com/Tufin/oasdiff for details on how to get this.

You can test your installation by running the following:

```
oasdiff -help
```

B.9   *Installing swagger-ui-cli*

Swagger-ui-cli (https://github.com/egomobile/swagger-ui-cli) is a handy tool for rendering OpenAPI definition files from the command line. You can install it by running the following command:

```
npm install -g swagger-ui-cli
```

Test this out on an API definition file by running the following:

```
swagger-ui products-api.json
```

It should open your browser to http://127.0.0.1:8080 and render your API definition file.

B.10   *GitHub Copilot*

GitHub Copilot is a coding AI assistant developed by GitHub in collaboration with OpenAI. It generates code snippets and autocomplete-style suggestions in a wide variety of programming languages.

To use Copilot with VS Code, you need an active Copilot subscription—either a personal subscription or as part of an organization subscription for GitHub Copilot Business. Before you start a paid subscription, you can use the one-time 30-day trial of Copilot. For details on how to sign up for the free trial and how to set up GitHub Copilot in VS Code via the Copilot extension, see https://mng.bz/1Gp1.

You should also install the GitHub Copilot Chat extension for VS Code. GitHub Copilot Chat is a chatbot companion to GitHub Copilot. With Copilot Chat, you can ask and receive answers to coding-related questions on topics such as programming language syntax, concepts, and more. It can be used for generating unit test cases, explaining code, or proposing fixes and improvements. For instructions on how to install the GitHub Copilot Chat extension for VS Code, see https://mng.bz/PZrY.

B.11   *Sign up for Anthropic Claude*

Claude is an AI chatbot from Anthropic. Like other chatbots (e.g., OpenAI's ChatGPT and Google's Bard), Claude has a messaging interface for receiving questions and gives detailed and relevant responses. Claude aims to be safe, helpful, and honest. The way it does this is by using AI feedback to evaluate its outputs. The AI feedback is based on a set of principles around themes called a "constitution," so Anthropic describes this approach as Constitutional AI.

To sign up, go to https://claude.ai, follow the sign-up instructions, and use its interface to chat with Claude in your browser. Note that at the time of writing, Claude isn't available in some parts of Europe. To see the regions Claude is available for, see www.anthropic.com/claude-ai-locations.

Introduction to JSON Pointer

This appendix introduces JSON Pointer, and you can work through the examples here using the project repository you cloned in appendix B. Navigate to the appendix folder in the project to find the products-api.json file you need for this.

Spectral uses the *JSON Pointer* syntax to specify the part of a JSON document to apply an override to. JSON Pointer is a syntax for locating a value within a JSON document, and the specification is defined in RFC6901. The syntax is a string of zero or more tokens prefixed by the "/" character. You can see this in action by evaluating JSON Pointer expressions on a JSON document. To do this, install json-joy (https://github.com/streamich/json-joy), which gives you a json-pointer command-line tool for testing JSON Pointer expressions:

```
npm install -g json-joy
```

Now you're given the following products-api.json document in the appendix folder:

```
{
  "openapi": "3.0.3",
  "info": {
    "title": "An example API",
    "version": "0.0.1"
  },
  "paths": {
    "/v1/products/{id}": {
      "delete": {
        "parameters": [
          {
            "in": "path",
```

```
        "name": "id",
        "required": true,
        "schema": {
          "type": "integer"
        }
      }
    ],
    "responses": {
      "204": {
        "description": "Product deleted."
      }
    }
  }
 }
 }
 }
}
```

To evaluate pointer /openapi, run the following command:

```
cat products-api.json | json-pointer /openapi
```

You get the following output:

```
"3.0.3"
```

To evaluate pointer /info, run the following command:

```
cat products-api.json | json-pointer /info
```

You get this output:

```
{
    "title": "An example API",
    "version": "0.0.1"
}
```

Pointer /info/title gives you the following:

```
"An example API"
```

The characters "~" and "/" have special meanings in JSON Pointer syntax and need to be encoded when they appear in a token. "~" is encoded as "~0" and "/" as "~1." Take note of this when specifying a JSON Pointer expression for an object inside an OpenAPI path object—the path item token will need to be encoded. Run the following on your command line to see this in action:

```
cat products-api.json |
?json-pointer /paths/~1v1~1products~1{id}/delete/responses
```

You get the following output:

```
{
    "204": {
        "description": "All products deleted."
    }
}
```

In addition, elements in an array can be referenced by digits specifying their index. Running the following command gives you the output `"path"`:

```
cat products-api.json |
?json-pointer /paths/~1v1~1products~1{id}/delete/parameters/0/in
```

A JSON Pointer expression can be a JSON string value as shown here. It can also be a URI fragment identifier (RFC3986). For example, if the JSON document is stored in a file named myapi.json, the following expression is a valid pointer reference for fetching an element in it:

```
myapi.json#/paths/~1v1~1products~1{id}/ /delete/responses/204/description.
```

Spectral uses this. You wouldn't be able to test this using the json-joy json-pointer CLI, though, as it expects the JSON value through standard input (STDIN).

> **NOTE** Apart from the command line, you can also evaluate JSON Pointer expressions on www.jsonquerytool.com.

appendix D
Tools for API
conformance and analytics

This appendix discusses a few more tools that you need to install. If you're using the provided Docker container I mentioned in appendix B, note that the tools mentioned here (apart from Moesif, which you need to sign up for) are already installed in it. But if you would like to install the tools on your computer, follow the instructions in this appendix.

D.1 Installing and running Kong

Kong (https://github.com/Kong/kong) is a popular open source API gateway known for its high performance. Kong has two configuration files: kong.yaml and kong.conf. The kong.yaml file is for configuring Kong entities. This is configuration information on how Kong routes requests, such as upstream services, routes, plugins, and API consumers. The kong.conf file is for configuring Kong server properties, such as working directory prefix, log file location, cluster, and database settings. Kong runs in two modes: with a database or without one (DB-less mode). In this book, you use Kong in DB-less mode.

You can install Kong directly on your computer if you run macOS or Linux. Kong has no support for direct installation on Windows. So if you run Windows, you need to run Kong via Docker. Following are instructions for running Kong on macOS and Docker. For other installation options, see https://docs.konghq.com/gateway/latest/install.

D.1.1 Installing Kong for macOS

Install Kong using the Homebrew package manager by running the following:

```
brew tap kong/kong
brew install kong
```

In the example project appendix directory, test your Kong installation by starting it with the following command:

```
kong start --conf kong.conf
```

The kong.conf file in the appendix directory is set up to create a working directory named kong_dir where Kong places temporary files and logs. By default, Kong listens for public traffic on port 8000 and for administration requests on its internal RESTful Admin API on port 8001. Test your installation by making the following request, which routes to the http://httpbin.org/get upstream service:

```
curl http://localhost:8000/mock
```

You should see a response like the following:

```
{
  "args": {},
  "headers": {
    "Accept": "*/*",
    "Host": "httpbin.org",
    "User-Agent": "curl/7.79.1",
    "X-Amzn-Trace-Id": "Root=1-63ba204c-33af0b84781054ba6d144785",
    "X-Forwarded-Host": "localhost",
    "X-Forwarded-Path": "/mock",
    "X-Forwarded-Prefix": "/mock"
  },
  "origin": "127.0.0.1, 2.124.41.27",
  "url": "http://localhost/get"
}
```

Stop Kong by running the following command:

```
kong stop -p kong_dir
```

D.1.2 Running Kong via Docker

This section assumes you have Docker running on your computer. Docker is a software platform that uses OS-level virtualization to allow you to develop, ship, and run software in packages called containers. See https://docs.docker.com/get-docker for how to install the Docker Desktop application for your operating system.

Create and start a Kong Docker container named `kong-dbless` by executing the `run_docker_container.sh` script:

```
./run_kong_docker.sh
```

If you run Windows, run the `run_kong_docker.bat` script instead:

```
C:\Users\dev\appendix>run_kong_docker.bat
```

In your browser, go to `http://localhost:8000/mock`, and you should see the same response as in the macOS example given previously.

To stop the running Kong container, run the following:

```
docker stop kong-dbless
```

To restart the container, you don't need to run the `run_docker_container.sh` script again. Just run the docker start command for the `kong-dbless` container:

```
docker start kong-dbless
```

D.2   *Install the Java Development Kit and Maven*

To run the Java code in this book and the OpenAPI Generator tool, you need a Java Development Kit (JDK) 20 or above. To install JDK 20, go to the Oracle JDK page at https://docs.oracle.com/en/java/javase/20/index.html, and click on Installation Guide. Follow the instructions for installing the JDK for your operating system.

Maven is a build automation for Java projects. To install Maven, download a Maven distribution from https://maven.apache.org/install.html, and follow the instructions given on that page to unzip the package and add the bin directory to your PATH environment variable. Test that your Maven installation is successful by running the following command to check the version:

```
mvn --version
```

D.3   *Install the OpenAPI Generator CLI*

The OpenAPI Generator CLI (https://github.com/OpenAPITools/openapi-generator-cli) is a command-line application that downloads and runs the OpenAPI Generator tool. Note that OpenAPI Generator depends on Java, so you need Java installed on your system (as described in the previous section) before installing and running the OpenAPI Generator CLI. In addition, note that OpenAPI Generator CLI requires that the Java executable is on the PATH environment variable.

To install the OpenAPI Generator CLI, run the following:

```
npm install -g @openapitools/openapi-generator-cli
```

Test that your installation is successful by running the following, which shows you the version of the CLI:

```
openapi-generator-cli version
```

D.4   Install Redocly CLI

The Redocly CLI (https://github.com/Redocly/redocly-cli) is a tool for managing OpenAPI definitions. It has powerful linter, filtering, splitting, bundling, and statistic features. It can generate a three-panel, responsive layout API reference from OpenAPI definitions in the Redocly format (https://github.com/Redocly/redoc). In this book, I use Redocly CLI 1.8.2. Install the CLI by running the following command:

```
npm install -g @redocly/cli
```

In addition, install the Node HTTP server to serve up HTML files by running the following:

```
npm install -g http-server
```

D.5   Installing Schemathesis

Schemathesis (https://schemathesis.readthedocs.io/en/stable) is a specification-based and property-based testing tool for OpenAPI and GraphQL APIs. To install it, you first need Python installed on your computer, which you can download and install from www.python.org/downloads. Then, to install Schemathesis, run the following:

```
pip install schemathesis
```

In this book, I use Schemathesis 3.25.0. If you already have an older version of Schemathesis installed, you can upgrade it by running the following:

```
pip install schemathesis --upgrade
```

D.6   Installing Portman

Portman (https://github.com/apideck-libraries/portman) converts OpenAPI specs to Postman collections. In this book, I use Portman 1.22.0. Install Portman by running the following:

```
npm install -g @apideck/portman
```

D.7   Installing Prism

Prism is a mock server and validating proxy for OpenAPI definitions and Postman collections. At the time of writing, you need NodeJS 16 or above to run Prism (for NodeJS 18.x, you need version 18.16 or above). In this book, I use Prism version 5.5.4. Install Prism by running the following:

```
npm install -g @stoplight/prism-cli
```

D.8   Setting up a Moesif account

Moesif is an API product analytics tool, and I use this for the examples of API analytics and monitoring in chapter 11. You can do the setup I describe here when you get to that chapter.

To set up a Moesif account, go to www.moesif.com, and sign up for a free account. In the modal that asks for an application name, specify ProductCatalogAPI. On the Quick Install page that shows up, you get a list of installations for server integrations. Ignore these, and click on the Demo button on the No Events Collected Yet modal.

On the dashboard view you're presented with, switch from the Moesif Demos app to your ProductCatalogAPI app. Then, go to your account settings, and copy your Moesif Collector API ID, as shown in figure D.1. This is the API key the simulation workflow scripts need.

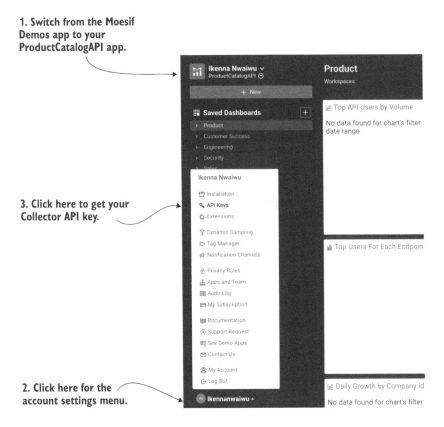

1. Switch from the Moesif Demos app to your ProductCatalogAPI app.

3. Click here to get your Collector API key.

2. Click here for the account settings menu.

Figure D.1   Click on your profile menu to get your Moesif API keys.

Moesif has two kinds of API keys: a Collector Application ID used for data collection and a Management API key used for accessing data in Moesif. To run the examples in chapter 11, you need to add the Moesif Collector Application ID as a repository secret to your GitHub repository. There are two kinds of Collector Application IDs—one for trusted apps and one for untrusted apps such as a browser. Get the one for trusted apps, and follow the instructions on the GitHub documentation page (https://mng .bz/pplz) to add it as a repository secret named `MOESIF_API_KEY`.

appendix E
Docker and Kubernetes

Kubernetes is the predominant open source cluster management and orchestration platform, and some examples in this chapter involve running API service and API gateway containers in Kubernetes using minikube. An in-depth explanation of Kubernetes is beyond the scope of this book, but I provide a brief introduction to it in this appendix. If you're familiar with Kubernetes, you can skip this.

E.1   Introducing Docker

Docker is an open platform that uses OS-level virtualization to deliver software in standardized units called *containers* that have everything the software needs to run. A *container image* is a static file that includes code, system tools, system libraries, and settings required to create a container on a computing system. The software that executes a container image and transforms it into a running container is the *container runtime*. The Docker Engine is a container runtime. Instead of virtualizing the underlying computer hardware like virtual machines do, containers virtualize the OS—CPU, memory, storage, and network resources—thus creating a view of the OS isolated from other applications, as shown in figure E.1. Containers are truly portable (unlike traditional software deployments) and help developers build, test, and deploy applications quickly.

E.2   Installing Docker

In appendix D, if you chose the option to run Kong via Docker (e.g., if you're a Windows user), you would have already gone through the process of installing Docker on your computer. If you don't yet have Docker installed, you can get instructions for installing Docker Desktop, an application containing a suite of Docker tools, at https://docs.docker.com/get-docker.

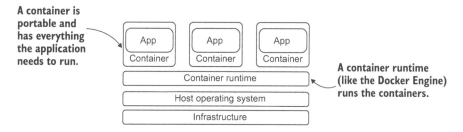

Figure E.1   Container runtimes like the Docker Engine provide OS-level virtualization and run containers that have access to isolated system resources.

E.3   Setting up services with Docker Compose

One of the tools that comes with Docker Desktop is Docker Compose. Docker Compose is a tool for managing multiple Docker containers at once. With Compose, you use a YAML file to configure the different containers for your application services, and you can start them all with a single command. You can start and stop services, view the status of services, get the log output of running services, and run a one-off command on a service. You get Docker Compose when you install Docker Desktop.

The chapter9/compose.yaml file is the Docker Compose file that sets up the different services you need for your deployment pipeline. It defines the services required to start the Kong API gateway and the Apicurio API registry. You'll be running these in your GitHub Actions pipeline. But to see how it works locally, you can start the services in the background by running the following:

```
docker compose --file chapter9/compose.yaml up --detach
```

To see the list of running services, run the following:

```
docker compose --file chapter9/compose.yaml ls
```

To stop the services and remove the containers, run the following:

```
docker compose --file chapter9/compose.yaml down
```

E.4   Introducing Kubernetes

Kubernetes (also known as K8s; https://kubernetes.io) is an open source platform for orchestrating the distribution, scheduling, and execution of applications in a computer cluster. It coordinates a cluster of computers, allowing users to deploy and manage containerized applications on it.

A Kubernetes cluster consists of the *control plane* for managing the cluster and the worker machines that run the containerized applications. These worker machines are called *nodes*. Each node has an agent, called a *kubelet*, that manages the node and communicates with the control plane. Each node also has a container runtime for running containers. An example of a container runtime is the Docker Engine. A *pod* is a group of application containers and the shared resources (e.g., storage volumes and IP addresses) for those containers. Multiple pods can run in a node. The Kubernetes control plane handles the scheduling of pods across nodes in the cluster. The control plane is the cluster orchestration layer and makes global decisions about the cluster. It exposes a REST API for defining, deploying, and managing the lifecycle of containers. The control plane is composed of several components, including the *API server, scheduler,* and *controller manager.* The API server provides the REST API. The scheduler assigns pods to nodes, and the controller manager is a daemon process that runs Kubernetes *controllers.* The Kubernetes command-line tool, kubectl, is used for managing Kubernetes. It interacts with the API server and can be used to run commands to deploy applications, view logs, and inspect cluster resources. The Kubernetes architecture is illustrated in figure E.2.

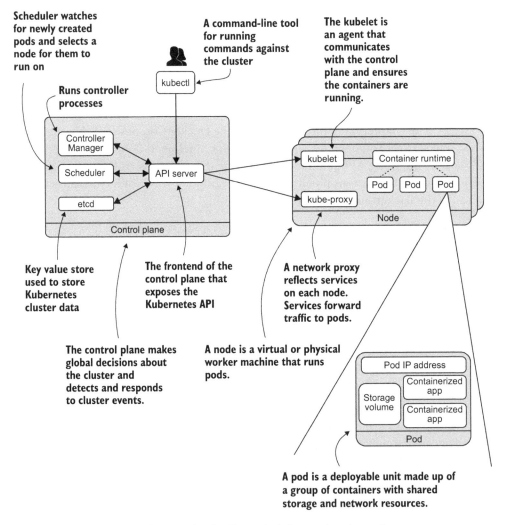

Figure E.2   Kubernetes architecture showing the control plane and worker nodes

A pod running in a Kubernetes cluster is running inside a private, isolated network. A pod is created and updated by a *deployment*. A deployment describes which container images to use for the application container in the pod, the number of running pods there should be at any time (i.e., the number of *replicas*), and how the pods should be updated. A pod is only accessible by its internal IP address within the Kubernetes cluster. To route requests to the group of pods running an application, you need a *service*. A service resource is a named abstraction of a software service consisting of a logical set of pods and policies for accessing them. A service has an IP address internal to the cluster.

An *ingress object* describes the collection of rules that allows inbound HTTP/HTTPS connections to services via externally reachable URLs. Ingress objects define *north/ south traffic*, that is, traffic from outside a cluster to service objects inside the cluster. They provide SSL termination, traffic load balancing, and content-based routing. An *ingress controller* runs the process that implements the ingress object. Figure E.3 shows how external traffic is routed to pods using an ingress and service. Examples of ingress controllers include the Kong Ingress Controller (https://github.com/Kong/kubernetes-ingress-controller), Traefik Kubernetes Ingress Controller (https://mng.bz/OZgE), and the Tyk Operator (https://github.com/TykTechnologies/tyk-operator).

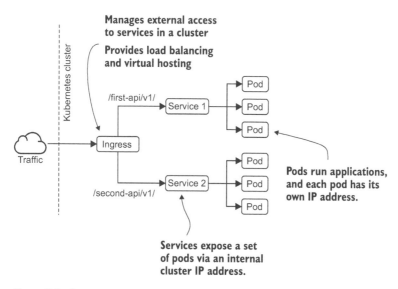

Figure E.3   Ingress and service objects route traffic to pods.

I mentioned that the control manager runs controllers. A controller executes a non-terminating control loop that watches the shared state of a cluster object and makes changes to move the object's current state to match the desired state, as illustrated in figure E.4. Each object has a *spec* field that defines its desired state and a *status* field that describes its current state.

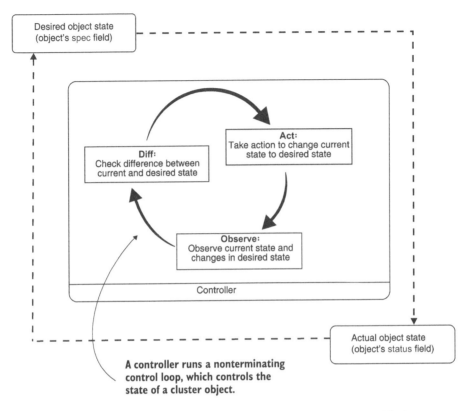

Figure E.4   **Controllers reconcile the desired and actual states of Kubernetes objects.**

Kubernetes objects, such as pods, deployments, services, and controllers, are persistent entities in the Kubernetes system and represent the state of the cluster. When you create a Kubernetes object, you're describing the desired state of the cluster. You can create objects in Kubernetes via kubectl or directly using the Kubernetes REST API. When using kubectl, you provide the object information in a file called a *manifest*. Manifest files are written in YAML (or JSON). Manifest files have four required fields:

- `apiVersion`—Specifies the version of the Kubernetes API
- `kind`—Describes the type of Kubernetes object the manifest creates
- `metadata`—Information that helps uniquely identify the object, such as its name or namespace
- `spec`—Describes the desired state of the object

An example of a manifest file is shown in the following snippet. Imagine that you have a set of pods that listen to port 8080 and are labeled `product-api`. The following manifest describes a service object, named `productsapi-svc`, that listens for traffic on port 7070 and forwards the traffic to port 8080 on any pod with the `product-api` label:

```
apiVersion: v1
kind: Service
metadata:
  name: productsapi-svc
spec:
  ports:
    - port: 7070
      protocol: TCP
      targetPort: 8080
  selector:
    app: product-api
```

Assuming this manifest is stored in a service.yaml file, it can be applied to the cluster by running the following kubectl command:

```
kubectl apply -f service.yaml
```

This concludes the short introduction to Kubernetes to prepare you for chapter 9 of this book. For a more in-depth exploration of Kubernetes, see *Kubernetes in Action* by Marko Lukša and Kevin Conner (2nd ed., Manning, 2020, https://mng.bz/Y7jA).

E.5 *Installing kubectl*

I mentioned that kubectl (https://kubernetes.io/docs/reference/kubectl) is the Kubernetes command-line tool for managing Kubernetes. kubectl commands are usually of the form `kubectl <action> <resource>`.

To install kubectl on macOS, use Homebrew by running the following:

```
brew install kubectl
```

To install kubectl on Windows, use Chocolatey by running the following:

```
choco install kubernetes-cli
```

To install kubectl for your flavor on Linux, see https://mng.bz/GZnO.

You can test your installed version is correct by running the following:

```
kubectl version –client
```

E.6 *Installing a local Kubernetes cluster with minikube*

minikube (https://github.com/kubernetes/minikube) is a simple way to get started with Kubernetes for local development. It deploys a simple Kubernetes cluster containing only one node on your local machine. minikube runs on macOS, Linux, and Windows. Make sure you've installed Docker before you install minikube.

For macOS, you can install minikube with Homebrew by running `brew install minikube`. For Windows, install it using the Chocolatey package manager by running `choco install minikube`. For Linux, see https://minikube.sigs.k8s.io/docs/start for instructions on how to install minikube for your flavor of Linux.

After installation, start minikube by running `minikube start`. Now you can check that minikube is running by opening the minikube dashboard, which is a web-based Kubernetes user interface that gives you an overview of applications running in your cluster. Do so by running the command `minikube dashboard`, and the dashboard should open up in your browser.

index